21 July 2011

1916 IN 1966

COMMEMORATING THE EASTER RISING

1916 IN 1966

COMMEMORATING THE

EASTER RISING

Edited by
Mary E. Daly and Margaret O'Callaghan

1916 in 1966: Commemorating the Easter Rising

First published 2007

by Royal Irish Academy
19 Dawson St
Dublin 2

www.ria.ie

This publication is the outcome of a research project funded by the Higher Education Authority's North-South Programme for Collaborative Research.

ISBN 978-1-904890-27-0

Printed in the UK by Athenaeum Press Ltd

10 9 8 7 6 5 4 3 2 1

CONTENTS

INTRODUCTION

IRISH MODERNITY AND 'THE PATRIOT DEAD' IN 1966

Mary E. Daly and Margaret O'Callaghan.

It is, I believe, almost impossible for any one of my generation to think about 1916 as an actual event in history, discrete and autonomous. The way in which 1916 had been presented to us was an important process in our understanding of the nature of our society, and of ourselves. For my generation, the events of Easter 1966 were crucial, so much so that I think it is almost possible to speak of a generation of '66.[1]

Every night during Easter week 1966 our family watched the drama documentary[2] about Easter 1916 on state television. A friend of the family who had been in the Rising and who had known the leaders came to watch it with us. The executions were drawn out, each moment dramatized—the grieving family, the grim prison, the lone leader in his cell writing his last poem or letter. Sometimes the emotion in our house was unbearable, and when it came to James Connolly's turn to be executed my mother ran out of the room crying. We had never seen her cry before. In less than ten years we moved from a time in which the state sponsored such emotions to a time when the songs we learned in school were banned on the state radio.[3]

This collection of essays looks at the golden jubilee in 1966 of the Easter Rising of 1916. That commemoration is indelibly imprinted on the minds of all who lived through it, but is virtually unknown to those born later in the last century. They, however, have heard it evoked to buttress one ideological position or another on 1916 itself, on the Irish nationalist tradition, on 'the North'; by historians, journalists, commentators. Much of the battle for control of the representation of the history of modern Ireland and its profound connection with debates about 'the North' is incomprehensible if the commemoration of 1966 is ignored. The struggle for control of the representation of the nature of the 1966 commemoration has accreted to the debate on 1916 itself in a way that has made it constitutive of it. Such a phenomenon is not unique to Ireland, but in the past three decades the debate about the meaning of commemoration in relation to the state or the nation may have been more immediate and more passionately contested in Ireland than elsewhere.[4]

The historian, and editor of a highly influential work on the politics of commemoration, John Gillis has written

> [c]ommemorative activity is by definition social and political, for it involves the coordination of individual and group memories, whose results may appear consensual when they are in fact the product of processes of intense contest, struggle, and in some instances, annihilation.[5]

Commemorations are ostensibly about memory and remembering, but neither remembering nor memory itself is unproblematic, as the work of the French historian Pierre Nora demonstrates. Nora tried to produce a new kind of French history in the years from 1984 to 1992. It was a collective venture involving over a hundred scholars that sought to tell the history of France through what he called 'lieux de mémoire', or sites or repositories of memory. In the introduction to the three-volume, American-English edition of the original seven volumes published in French as *Les lieux de mémoire*, he writes

> [t]he point of departure, the original idea was to study national feeling not in the traditional thematic or chronological manner but by analyzing the places in which the collective heritage of France was crystallized, the principal *lieux* in all senses of that word, in which collective memory was rooted, in order to create a vast topology of French symbolism.

He goes on to state that '…I took it (the phrase and concept *lieux de mémoire)* from ancient and medieval rhetoric as described by Frances Yates in her admirable book *The Art of Memory* (1966) which recounts an important tradition of mnemonic techniques'.[6] The classical art of memory was based on a systematic inventory of *loci memoriae* or 'memory places'. The Irish language already has a term for what Nora is talking about: *dinnseanchas* or lore of place, actual sites of memory through which pasts can be entered or reconstructed.

If adapting Nora for Irish purposes[7] it is immediately clear that the Easter Rising of 1916 has been the key site of memory in twentieth century Ireland, rivaled only perhaps by the border. The Rising has been embraced, repudiated, analysed, retold, contested, investigated, dismissed and lauded. There is endless fascination with its history, its ephemera, its traces and residues. But more importantly, and often regardless of its history in the narrow sense of what occurred, 1916 has been a ground of contestation and a battle site for representation. The representation of 1916 has been at the centre of debates about how Ireland's past was to be understood in the last three decades of the twentieth century. That debate frequently took place through a debate about what had actually happened in the commemoration of 1966. The subtext of the discussion was whether or not the commemoration of 1966 had in fact 'caused the Troubles'. The story of these debates and contestations has its own history that has yet to be told. We thought that one way of beginning that telling was through an attempt to trace the foundational anthropological moment in that debate—the commemoration of the Easter Rising by the Irish state in 1966.

On Easter Sunday (8 April) 2007, an estimated 7,000 spectators turned out to watch an hour-long official ceremony to mark the ninety-first anniversary of the Easter Rising. According to the *Irish Times*, the 'multicultural crowd' included 'Army veterans in wheelchairs, vast numbers of Poles and Chinese, and a generous smattering of English and American visitors'.[8] Presumably some Irish civilians were also present. The low-key ceremony contrasted with the more elaborate celebrations marking the ninetieth anniversary in 2006, when an estimated 100,000 spectators crowded Dublin's O'Connell Street to watch an elaborate military parade. The ninetieth anniversary sparked a widespread—though short-lived—debate on the appropriateness of commemorating the Easter Rising, because 2006 saw the revival of the official military parade on Easter Sunday, which had been abandoned in the early 1970s because of 'the Troubles' in Northern Ireland. For those who had experienced the golden jubilee, the 2006 ceremonies inevitably prompted memories of the last major commemoration of the Rising. For those who had not experienced 1966, the 2006 commemoration was something quite new.

Speeches by the respective Fianna Fáil taoisigh—Seán Lemass and Bertie Ahern—contained remarkably similar messages. While formally acknowledging the importance of remembering the past, the primary focus in both instances was on the present and the future: commemorating the past with a view to understanding the present and planning for a future that would build on the legacy of 1916 and of the founders of an independent, democratic Ireland. Both leaders emphasised the messages in the 1916 Proclamation and the continuity between the principles expressed in the Proclamation (religious and civil liberties; equal rights and opportunities) and the independent, democratic and successful Irish state, playing down rebellion and bloodshed. Both men paid at least lip service to a commemoration that would include wider strands of Irish opinion. Lemass went to considerable efforts to involve the Protestant churches, and he referred in sympathetic tones to the Irish nationalists who had supported Home Rule. Bertie Ahern recalled the Irishmen who had fought in the Great War, and the 2006 invitation list included Ulster Unionists, though they did not attend.[9] This reflected a shift as a result of the battles and accommodations about the past that had characterised the intervening forty years.[10] The presence of Sinn Féin at the 2006 event also reflected the transformation in the position of northern nationalists in relation to both states on the island of Ireland in the same period. In this sense the shadow of Northern Ireland was central to the Dublin commemoration of 2006, whilst it had lain silent, if present, in Dublin in 1966.

The upbeat, expansive commemorations of 1966 and 2006 in Dublin reflected the temper of the times: Ireland in the 1960s is now often seen as the forerunner of the twenty-first century Celtic Tiger—a simplification that glosses over a long interval marked by economic crises in the Republic and the Northern Troubles. The mid-1960s also brought a significant improvement in relations between Northern Ireland and independent Ireland, with the famous Lemass–O'Neill meetings of 1965, and examples of practical co-operation between both states.[11] Irish unity barely featured in the official speeches during the 1966 commemoration, and the Belfast and Dublin governments went to some efforts to prevent the commemoration from setting back this improving relationship. Nonetheless, the Rising was commemorated on a significant scale in 1966 by the very northern Catholics whose marginalisation from civil society in the North was about to give rise to the civil-rights movement. One of our aims in this volume has been to retrieve that northern nationalist commemoration, conducted without a state apparatus but nonetheless indicative of northern nationalist desire not to be excluded from the Irish nation, and not to acquiesce in a state-sponsored project that sought to make the Irish nation and the Irish state synonymous. The eruption of the Troubles in Northern Ireland in 1969, and the consequent aftershocks in the Republic, resulted in the 1966 commemoration being retrospectively interpreted as a factor in the resurgence of IRA military activity. This argument, most clearly enunciated by Conor Cruise O'Brien in his 1972 book, *States of Ireland,* and reprised and popularised by him and others in countless other publications, has dominated perceptions of the Golden Jubilee of the Rising.

Cruise O' Brien argued that Lemass–O'Neill's efforts at rapprochement were undermined by

> the great commemorative year [1966], a year in which ghosts were bound to walk, both North and South...The general calls for rededication to the ideals of 1916 were bound to suggest to some young men and women not only that these ideals were in practice being abandoned—through the Lemass–O'Neill meetings and in other ways—but that the way to return to them was through the method of 1916: violence, applied by a determined minority.[12]

Cruise O'Brien conceded that Lemass's government 'tried to discourage these last conclusions, but there is in fact no way of discouraging them effectively within the framework of a cult of 1916'.[13] Nineteen-sixty-six was also the Golden Jubilee of the Battle of the Somme, when thousands of men of the Ulster Division lost their lives. 'Just as the 1966 commemorations in Dublin favoured a recrudescence of the I.R.A., so the Northern commemorations, clashing with those in the South, favoured the recrudescence of armed Protestant extremism'.[14] What Cruise O'Brien's retrospective interpretation, written at the height of the violence of 1972 in Northern Ireland, shared with the intentions of the Irish government in 1966 was a failure to consider the position of nationalists in Northern Ireland.

From the 1970s the debate about the status of the commemoration became embroiled in a further, and connected, debate about the merits or demerits of the Easter Rising itself and, by extension, over time, reformulated itself into a debate about the status of the Irish Revolution. It can therefore be seen as lying at the centre of the so-called revisionist debate on modern Ireland.[15] The traditional nationalists of revisionist caricature, the revisionists themselves and so called-post nationalists and post-revisionists[16] can be said to have nailed their ideological colours to the mast by their approval or criticism of the kind of commemoration that allegedly took place in 1966. Roy Foster, writing in 1988, commented that 'the results of simplistic historical hero-cults had become obvious in the carnage of Northern Ireland', and he later went on to contrast the seventy-fifth anniversary of the Rising in 1991, which was 'treated by the Irish government as a sensitive issue, to be approached in the deliberately restrained way—very different from the unequivocal celebrations of 1966'.[17] What Foster saw as the 'sensitive' treatment of the seventy-fifth anniversary of the Rising, Seamus Deane viewed as 'official embarrassment'.[18] The contrast between the official commemorations in 1966 and 1991 appears to have served to accentuate the tendency to distort the images of the golden jubilee. In 1991 Declan Kiberd took issue with the memories of the golden jubilee articulated by Fintan O'Toole and Dermot Bolger, which appear to support Cruise O'Brien's interpretation. Kiberd points out that Bolger and O'Toole were schoolboys at the time. However, Kiberd's description of the 1966 jubilee as 'a last, over-the-top purgation of a debt to the past', his belief that 'the journalistic simplifications of history…reached their point of maximum publicity in the Republic, in 1966'[19] suggests that he may also be guilty of analysis based on untested memories. Colm Tóibín's memories, written as an intervention in the debates about the representation of modern Irish history, are more convincing, though he appears not to have been aware that the 'the songs we learned in school' which were 'banned on the state radio' ten years later, were also banned during the 1966 jubilee.[20]

One common feature of all the existing interpretations of the 1966 jubilee is the failure to buttress argument and opinion with evidence drawn from the contemporaneous record. This book tries to rectify this omission, while recognising that it is difficult, indeed impossible, to capture the actualities of the moment. For example, when we showed clips of *Insurrection*, a Telefís Éireann reconstruction of the story of

Easter Week, and the station's major offering for the 1966 jubilee, the audience was struck more by its amateurish quality than by the alleged 'militarist ethos'.[21] If a commemoration tells us more about the year when it is staged than about the actual event being commemorated, this book may well be more informative about Ireland in the twenty-first century, than about Ireland in 1966. Nevertheless, with these caveats we ask, and try to answer, Rebecca Graff-McRae's (chapter 6) central question: what is being commemorated and by whom?

Graff-McRae correctly notes that commemoration unites and divides. 'Commemorations—as events, as discourses and as theory—are inextricably linked to claims of legitimacy, power and truth which both invoke and elide their political basis'[22] The golden jubilee was an attempt by the Irish government to unite its citizens behind 1916 as the formative founding moment in the history of an independent Irish state. Nineteen-sixteen had the potential to bring together those who were divided by the Anglo-Irish Treaty and civil war. By focusing on the ideals of 1916, and on the subsequent history of the Irish state, Lemass hoped to bring those who had not supported the Rising or war of independence into the celebrations, and the record shows that he was largely successful in this. But this representation of 1916 as a moment that united Irish citizens was something of a novelty, because, as Diarmaid Ferriter shows (chapter 5), the commemoration of the Rising had been contentious and problematic since the 1920s, with various parties being excluded from the commemoration at different times, and the event being appropriated for specific ends. The history of official state 1916 commemorations prior to 1966, therefore, is largely one of neglect and low-key events. The golden jubilee was not simply a more elaborate form of the traditional 1916 commemoration: it was the first significant national commemoration of the Rising. Thus, the discontinuity is not between the commemoration of 1966 and the neglect of the 1970s and 1980s, but between the poorly-attended and frequently-divisive commemorations before and after 1966 and the large-scale state celebrations of that year.

Indeed, 1966 shares one key feature with the 2006 commemoration: both represent a determined effort by the Irish state to reclaim the memory/commemoration of the Rising from militant republicans and to establish the commemoration as an event that could unite all citizens and consolidate the state. Most men and women who marched to commemorate the Rising in other years marched in ceremonies organised by Republican groups who did not recognise the state, and they wore the Easter lily to highlight that point. This was a tradition of which northern nationalists were also a part, though having to contend with a more hostile government, as the events around the attempted commemoration of 1916 in West Belfast—which lead to the death of a Royal Ulster Constabulary policeman and the execution of Tom Williams in 1942—demonstrate. Commemorations in provincial Ireland were still overwhelmingly controlled by anti-treaty republicans, and these events undoubtedly attracted much larger numbers in total than the official ceremonies in Dublin. The clashes in many provincial towns during 1966 reflect the strength of the unofficial 1916 commemorative tradition. Yet, while disputes between the official commemoration and republican events were not unknown, they were contained during 1966, an indication of the relaxed attitude then being adopted towards the militant republican tradition.

Fifty years from the Somme and fifty years from the Rising, 1966 was a pivotal moment for the two partitioned entities on the island of Ireland. In hindsight what is striking are the features they had in common, and those that divided them. Both wished to project images of change. Both sought to project a prosperity that was more fragile than the images suggested. For Lemass's government the jubilee, which fortuitously coincided with the first sustained rise in population since independence, was seen as an opportunity to showcase a modern, prosperous state to a wider world, and to harness the idealism of 1916 with a view to building a prosperous, forward-looking state. Lemass's government was also determined that the commemoration would not damage improving relations with Britain and Northern Ireland. Catherine O'Donnell shows (chapter 7) that Terence O'Neill was equally concerned with image, but even more concerned with how the new Labour government in London would view any Stormont attempt to suppress northern nationalist commemoration in 1966; hence his reluctance to court the adverse publicity that a ban on commemorative parades would attract despite pressures from within his own party. Lemass's government undoubtedly played down any potential threat from the IRA, despite the fact that the IRA's latest military campaign—'Operation Harvest'—had formally ended only four years previously. By contrast, during the 1965 Stormont elections O'Neill initially played up the possibility of IRA violence associated with the jubilee, though he moved back from this in early 1966 as extremist Protestant groups attempted to use the threat of IRA violence to initiate their own. Ian Paisley, who had been casting around for a platform from which to challenge O'Neill as a quisling for some years, found it in the commemorations and used it relentlessly, culminating in his April 1966 counter-rally at the Ulster Hall in Belfast in celebration of the defeat of the rebels in 1916. This marked Paisley's highest point in over a decade of street politics, and that street politics continued throughout the summer of 1966 as he challenged O'Neill on the streets and through the columns of his newly-founded *Protestant Telegraph*. Though O'Neill played down the threat posed by Protestant paramilitary violence initially, a sequence of events culminating in Ulster Volunteer Force murders of Catholic men in June 1966 led to his banning of the UVF and to a political focus on a radically revitalised 'Paisleyite movement'.[23]

Yet despite the common features, the differences between the two states in 1966 are ultimately more significant. For a start, the parallel between commemorating 1916 and the Somme is an unequal one, since the Northern state did not stage official commemorative events on a similar scale around the Somme. Secondly, the official 1966 jubilee was an intensely partitionist affair: a celebration of (almost) fifty years of statehood that in its planning and execution within the state showed little longing to secure 'the fourth green field'. Most of the southern debate surrounding the jubilee related to the Irish state, and its future direction. Roisín Higgins suggests (chapter 3) that in Bryan MacMahon's pageant *Seachtar Fear, Seacht Lá*, commissioned by the GAA and staged in Croke Park and Belfast's Casement Park, the memory of the dead was used to navigate the country through the uncertainty of accelerated modernisation, because being modern was now seen—at least in government and business circles—as compatible with Irish nationalism. This emphasis on modernity and the future, and the uncertainties associated with change may help to explain why young people were targeted during the Jubilee. But Carole Holohan argues (chapter 4) that the message of 1916 and its relevance to contemporary Ireland remained obscure to young people because it was delivered in traditional terms.

The 1966 commemoration in Northern Ireland was more akin to the traditional commemorations held throughout the Republic and 'the North' in other years—a commemoration dominated by parades, mainly, though not exclusively, organised by militant republicans. The Belfast parade on 18 April and the associated ceremonies in Casement

Park were the key events in the northern commemorative programme, with West Belfast briefly becoming the republican capital of Ireland. These events were on a far grander and more dramatic scale than the traditional parade to Milltown cemetery in other years. This reflected the desire of sections of the republican movement, particularly those around Tomás MacGiolla, Seamus Costello and Seán Garland[24] to place Belfast at the centre of their push for a new left-wing republican politics in the mid 1960s. As a part of this, northern nationalists were keen to demonstrate that the Irish state could not just forget about them, or ignore the fact that they were part of the Irish nation. Lacking a state apparatus they organised through the communal institutions available—old networks of republican prisoners, the republican movement, the Gaelic Athletic Association, churches, bands and Irish dancing schools, ballad singing networks and Hibernians, Foresters, trades unions, the Communist Party and other fraternal associations.

The speeches made at the northern commemorative events, many given by southern republicans, or subversives as they were usually designated by the state, were much more direct; they focused more closely on what the speakers claimed to be the original spirit of 1916 and the failure to deliver northern nationalism, an Irish-speaking Ireland or economic prosperity. Irish unity and an end to British rule was the core message, rather than exhortations on building a prosperous (twenty-six county) Ireland as in the Republic. Though republicans did most of the organising, and though they brought tens of thousands onto the streets during Easter 1966, the Westminster election of March 1966 had not merely returned Gerry Fitt over and above the republican opposition, but it demonstrated throughout the North that nationalist voters were more interested in supporting candidates, like Fitt, who would go to Westminster and fight their case, than in supporting abstentionist republicans. This evidence of weariness with abstentionism strengthened the hand of those within the republican movement who wanted to break with this policy.

However paradoxical it might seem, the commemoration in Northern Ireland in 1966 was as partitionist as the commemoration in the Republic. This reflected the political actuality of partition. But in Northern Ireland the reiteration of traditional messages included a refrain that insisted on northern nationalists' place within the Irish nation, if not the Irish state. The tone of speeches was nostalgic and angry. Domestic events were one factor in this. Though the year

10

brought new stirrings in nationalist politics, with the election of Gerry Fitt as a Westminster MP, one of the underlying messages from the year is of nationalist divisions rather than unity. While the underlying message of the official Dublin commemoration—a celebration of the success of the southern state—implicitly excluded northern nationalists, their leaders were invited to attend the celebrations. The Nationalist Party and National Unity were reasonably happy with that, but their younger and more radical members made common cause with republicans and others in commemorating a Rising that was also theirs on their home ground. Supporters were urged to mark the event at home and not in Dublin. The strong emphasis placed on northern participation in the Rising was a source of pride.

But if, as Higgins and Holohan convincingly argue, the commemoration as conceived by the Irish state effectively functioned as a bridge into modernity for that state, northern nationalists' organisation of their own commemorations served to at least problematise that smooth journey. What the south wished to jettison by marching over the bridge of commemoration into 'normal modernity' was precisely what northern nationalism needed to hold on to and assert. Despite the shared cultural capital of Irish nationalism, the meanings of commemoration were radically different north and south. If the south could make this journey successfully, then that success implied that northern nationalists were but a residue that could be jettisoned. Roy Johnston complained after the northern commemorations that there had been too many decades of the rosary in Catholic churchyards, too many Catholic resonances to the commemoration. As a northern, Protestant republican, he wished that the non-sectarian nature of Irish republicanism could have been reflected more accurately.[25] But northern commemoration in 1966 shared more with the genre of nineteenth-century nationalist funereal memorialising than it did with southern state celebrations of achievement. It differed only in the degree that Catholicism and nationalism had become more synonymous through the entrenching of nationalism into Catholicism, given the ethos of the northern state. It was by definition the political action of a people who represented themselves as in bondage, as Davids to their unionist Goliath. The Nationalist Party in Northern Ireland was wary of commemoration because it had the capacity to highlight and open all of this. For the same reasons the republican movement supported it.

Easter Week saw the unveiling of memorials in Dublin to Robert Emmet and Thomas Davis; and the official openings of the Garden of Remembrance and Kilmainham Jail. Yet this apparent satiation of memorials in 1966 is rather deceptive: none was originally conceived to celebrate the Golden Jubilee—all had a much longer ancestry, and despite the almost 30 years' gestation of the Garden of Remembrance, Oisin Kelly's statue of the Children of Lir—the centerpiece of the Garden—was not yet complete, and was only unveiled in 1971. Roisín Higgins suggests (chapter 8) that these memorials have something else in common: a lack of finality or completion: Emmet's epitaph remains unwritten, while Kelly's statue captures the legend of the Children of Lir when they are being turned into swans, not at their final transformation back into humans. The delay in completing the central sculpture for the Garden of Remembrance was in large part due to disagreement over the form that the sculpture should take. While 1960s Ireland professed its modernity, and the old censorial attitudes were diminishing, they had not yet disappeared. Tony Roche shows (chapter 9) that *Aiséirí*, the pageant commissioned by the official commemoration committee and written by Tomás MacAnna, drew heavily for its major themes on two Irish writers of the 1916 era: W.B. Yeats and Seán O'Casey. Some of the international coverage of the Jubilee highlighted the links between the Rising and great Irish writers, and the Irish government was only too happy to foster such messages. Yet, the official orders issued to the Abbey Theatre were that there should be no O'Casey during Easter Week. Likewise, while Yeats's poem 'Easter 1916' is the best known poem about the Easter Rising, it did not find favour with de Valera or his peers. They preferred James Stephens's 'Spring 1916'.[26] This may have been because, as Roche suggests, Yeats's poem appears partially to question the merits of the Rising; or maybe it is simply evidence of the bad taste of some veteran politicians.

One of the predictable aspects of the 1966 commemoration is the relatively low prominence given to women. Cumann na mBan received, at best, marginal attention; the contribution made by women was largely ignored, except for the case of Constance Markievicz, despite the fact that women provided some of the most compelling eye witness accounts of the Rising on Telefís Éireann. Ecumenism, a strong reality in the post-Vatican II mid-1960s was honoured in the state commemoration. In Belfast, however, republicanism, ecumenism and the commemoration were seen as of a piece and were presented by Paisley and his fellow attackers of the Presbyterian General Assembly as a dire trio that would destroy Ulster. Though 1960s Ireland saw a crumbling of the strong denominational prejudices, in the North the attack upon ecumenism provided a platform for a new fundamentalist Unionism that would topple O'Neill.

We cannot summarise the legacy of the jubilee—we can merely attempt to revisit it. We can accurately probe the intentions of individuals like Lemass and O'Neill, but it is also clear that the outcomes did not necessarily meet these intentions. Michael Laffan shows (chapter 10) that, like most commemorative projects, it marked a major advance in historical writing and research on the period, including the first significant documentary material. Some of the historical works published also brought into question the more simplistic narrative of the Rising and its background, but few of these had readerships comparable with the audience for *Insurrection*, or even with the audiences for *Aiséirí* or *Seachtar Fear, Seacht Lá*. As for the impact on the unfolding of the Northern crisis, 1966 was a critical year, but the critical events were not the commemoration per se, but the uncertain response of the O'Neill government to the occasion, which served to strengthen his critics. Cruise O'Brien is correct in highlighting 1966 as the year when Rev. Ian Paisley first attracted international attention, and in noting the volatile mixture that went to fuel Paisleyite politics.

> For him the enemy was Rome, and matters apparently so diverse as the ecumenical movement, the I.R.A. and the Lemass–O'Neill rapprochement were simply different tactics for the fulfillment of Rome's strategy against Protestants, and in particular the exposed Protestant redoubt of Ulster.[27]

From the Dublin perspective, 1966 signalled a changing of the guard. Seán Lemass, a 1916 veteran, stepped down as taoiseach in the autumn, and was succeeded by a man who had no first- or second-hand connection with the Rising or the struggle for independence. Eamon de Valera, the last surviving leader of the Rising, was re-elected as president of Ireland, but with a majority of less than 10,000—which might indicate that the electorate was more focused on the future than on the past.

Roisín Higgins has argued that the state wanted a commemoration that celebrated the idea of 1916 but not the violence, and we would argue that that the state partly succeeded in this. But representations of the Irish historical experience put into the public sphere through language, television series, official pageants, information disseminated to schools were not amenable to state control. In a democracy people read them as they would. This is not to endorse Cruise O'Brien's notion of commemoration as responsible for the renewal of violence in Northern Ireland. In 1966 Irish historical memory was not owned by the state, nor was it owned by historians. Whatever about the ethos of Fine Gael or Labour, Fianna Fáil supporters who read the *Irish Press* had been presented for decades with a strong republican reunification message. The commemoration laid the discursive ground for years of discussion about Irish historical choices in the light of northern conflict; what Rebecca Graff-McRae has referred to as the haunting of the memory of the commemorations of 1966 by later events.

Northern commemorations as organised particularly in Belfast in 1966 may have prompted renewed interest in republicanism. But nationalist voting patterns and the diminished support for republican candidates; new movements within the nationalist community that spoke in a language of rights rather than a language of historical memory; the ending of nationalist if not republican parliamentary abstentionism; the decision to support Gerry Fitt for election to Westminster; to place northern nationalist concerns about discrimination on the floor at Westminster—these all suggest that the 1966 commemorations were not a catalyst for the northern nationalist community, except insofar as they gave testimony to the continuation of a powerful if disorientated sense of attachment to the Irish nation in changing times. Despite divisions within northern nationalism, a complex residue of attachment to the Irish nation and resentment at southern indifference commanded a unified effort in 1966. The networks that facilitated the parades and displays, marches and processions, speeches and songs in 1966 emanated from an organisational and iconographic range of those available to northern nationalists through the preceding decades. What was new in 1966 was the revised agenda of southern republicans in relation to their fellow-republicans in Belfast in particular;[28] new movements within northern nationalist politics and the conjunction of these developments with pre-existing fault-lines within the unionist bloc, made manifest in the street-politics of Ian Paisley.[29] It was the attempt to reform unionism and restructure Northern Ireland in the light of world change and of changes in the Republic and Britain that challenged unionism and strengthened Paisley. These changes also posed a challenge to northern nationalism.

The visibility of northern nationalist commemoration in 1966, confined though it was to 'nationalist areas', provided a focus for Paisley's objection to change.

Lemass succeeded where O'Neill failed in 'negotiating the bridge'. Southern commemoration paid lip service to the patriot dead, gestured to the nationalist past but sought to shape the future in the allegedly 'normal' modernity of the state. The Irish state sought to commemorate, while rendering residual and under control, the historical and cultural capital of Irish nationalist historical memory in 1966; that memory was to be deployed to advance the modern agenda of the state. Republicans outside the state, or 'subversives' as the Irish government called them, wished to activate that residue for alternative contemporary political purposes. A broader northern nationalist constituency simply wished to assert that the Irish state could not forget that they too were part of the Irish nation.

NOTES

[1] Michael O'Loughlin (born 1958) in Dermot Bolger (ed.), *Letters from the new island—16 on 16: Irish writers on the Easter Rising* (Dublin, 1988), 43–4: 43.

[2] *Insurrection* by Hugh Leonard.

[3] Colm Tóibín, 'New ways of killing your father', *London Review of Books,* 18 November 1993, 3, 5–6.

[4] Contestations about what, if anything, should be commemorated about the Revolution in France were conducted throughout the nineteenth century. Even after the establishment of Bastille Day as the 'official' French government commemoration, the Revolution was revisited over and over again—was it the key moment in the French nation and European modernity, or a saturnalia of slaughter and butchery? The commemoration after 1880 became a site through which contemporary political battles and battles for the ownership of French memory continued to take place. See Christian Amalvi, 'Bastille Day: from *Dies Irae* to holiday', in Pierre Nora (ed.), *Realms of memory*, vol. 3, (New York, 1998) 117–162.

[5] John R. Gillis (ed.) *Commemorations: the politics of national identity* (Princeton, 1994), 5.

[6] This was the first of a series of studies of the hermetic tradition in European thought published in the 1960s and 1970s by Yates, a Warburg Institute cultural historian. Pierre Nora, 'From *lieux de mémoire* to realms of memory', preface to the English-language edition, in Pierre Nora (ed.), *Realms of memory: rethinking the French past*, vol. 1, Conflicts and divisions. (New York, 1996), xv–xxiv: xv.

[7] There is an existing partial critique of such applicability; see Ian McBride, 'Introduction: memory and national identity in modern Ireland', in Ian McBride (ed.), *History and memory in modern Ireland*, (Cambridge, 2001), 1–42.

[8] *Irish Times*, 9 April 2007.

[9] See the Department of the Taoiseach website. 1916 commemorations.

[10] See Rebecca Lynn Graff-McRae, 'Forget politics! Theorising the political dynamics of commemoration and conflict', Chapter 6, this volume.

[11] Michael Kennedy, *Division and consensus: the politics of cross-border relations in Ireland, 1925–1969*, (Dublin, 2000), 175–300.

[12] Conor Cruise O'Brien, *States of Ireland*, (London, 1974), 143 (Originally published 1972).

[13] Cruise O'Brien, *States of Ireland*, 143.

[14] Cruise O Brien. *States of Ireland*, 144.

[15] For an introduction to this debate, see Ciaran Brady (ed.), *Interpreting Irish history: the debate on historical revisionism*, (Dublin, 1994).

[16] Luke Gibbons, 'Challenging the revisionist canon. Revisionism and cultural criticism', in Seamus Deane (ed.), *The Field Day anthology of Irish writing*, vol. III, (Derry, 1991), 561–8.

[17] Roy Foster, 'History and the Irish question' (first published 1988), as reprinted in Ciaran Brady (ed.), *Interpreting Irish history: the debate on historical revisionism*, (Dublin, 1994), 122–45: 141. Foster was writing about the decision by the editor of the Jesuit periodical *Studies*, not to publish an article by Francis Shaw on Pádraig Pearse in 1966, because he regarded it as unsuitable. The article was published in 1972, after Shaw's death.

[18] Seamus Deane, 'Wherever green is read', in Máirín Ní Dhonnchadha and Theo Dorgan (eds), *Revising the Rising*, (Derry, 1991), 91–105: 91.

[19] Declan Kiberd, 'The elephant of revolutionary forgetfulness', in Ní Dhonnchadha and Dorgan, *Revising the Rising*, 1–20: 2.

[20] Tóibín, 'New ways of killing your father'.

[21] Kiberd, 'Elephant of revolutionary forgetfulness', 2. The audience, at a conference in UCD's Humanities Institute of Ireland, consisted of graduate students and academics, including Professor Kevin B. Nowlan, who had been the historical advisor to Telefís Éireann in 1966.

[22] Rebecca Lynn Graff, 'Remembering and forgetting 1916: deconstructing discourses of commemoration and conflict in post-peace process Ireland', unpublished PhD thesis, School of Politics, International Studies and Philosophy, Queen's University Belfast, 2006, 2.

[23] Margaret O'Callaghan and Catherine O'Donnell, 'The Northern Ireland government, the 'Paisleyite movement' and Ulster unionism in 1966', *Irish Political Studies* 21 (2) (2006), 203–22.

[24] For opponents of this new emphasis at the time, see Robert W. White, *Ruairí Ó Brádaigh: the life and politics of an Irish revolutionary* (Bloomington, IN., 2006), 114–23.

[25] Roy Johnston, *Century of endeavour*, (Dublin, 2006).

[26] Be green upon their graves, O happy Spring!
For they are young and eager who are dead!
Of all things that are young and quivering
With eager life, they remembered!
They move not here! They have gone to clay!
They cannot die again for liberty!
Be they remembered of their land for aye!
Green be their graves, and greener their memory!

[27] Cruise O'Brien, *States of Ireland*, 144.

[28] See Margaret O'Callaghan, 'From Casement Park to Toomebridge: the commemoration of the Easter Rising in Northern Ireland in 1966', Chapter 2, this volume.

[29] Catherine O'Donnell, 'Pragmatism versus unity: the Stormont government and the 1966 Easter commemoration', Chapter 7, this volume.

1. 'LESS A COMMEMORATION OF THE ACTUAL ACHIEVEMENTS AND MORE A COMMEMORATION OF THE HOPES OF THE MEN OF 1916'[1]

By Mary E. Daly

INTRODUCTION

In 1966 Ireland celebrated the golden jubilee of the 1916 Easter Rising. The official programme of events was concentrated during Easter week, beginning on Easter Sunday, 10 April, and concluding on the following Sunday with a special children's day. Easter Sunday in Dublin began with a special Mass at the Pro-Cathedral, followed by a parade past the GPO, the official opening of Kilmainham Jail (where the 1916 leaders were held, tried and executed) as a museum, and a state reception. On Easter Monday—the day when the Rising began—all the major religious communities held special religious ceremonies, and President de Valera performed the official opening of the Garden of Remembrance, as a memorial to all who had died for Ireland. Other events in Dublin during Easter week included the presentation of a statue of Robert Emmet by an Irish-American group and the conferring by the National University of Ireland (Chancellor Eamon de Valera) of honorary degrees to surviving relatives of the seven 1916 signatories of the Proclamation. On Easter Saturday, de Valera unveiled a statue to Thomas Davis in Dame Street and presided at a parade past the GPO on Saturday evening. A state reception for veterans was held in Dublin Castle on Sunday, 17 April.[2]

Easter week in Dublin also saw the first performance of a specially-composed cantata, 'A Terrible Beauty is Born' by Brian Boydell; the premier of the Gael Linn film about 1916—*An Tine Bheo*; and *Aiséirí*—a pageant scripted by Tomás MacAnna, which was staged in Croke Park. The Abbey theatre presented three plays with a 1916-related theme: 'The Lost Light' by Robert Farren (Roibeard Ó Faracháin); P.H. Pearse's, 'The Singer' and 'Dervorgilla' by Lady Gregory. The official commemoration committee had advised that an O'Casey play 'would not be in keeping with the spirit of the occasion'.[3] At the Olympia theatre, Jack Cruise's show 'Easter Parade', described as 'a laugh-packed fast-moving revue', included a sequence depicting 'Ireland's struggle for freedom from the Williamite War and the siege of Limerick to the Rising of 1916'.[4] Special exhibitions relating to the 1916 Rising opened in the National Gallery, the National Museum and Dublin's Municipal Art Gallery; and the occasion was also marked by the issuing of special commemorative coins and stamps.

On Easter Sunday the government staged official ceremonies in twelve provincial centres: Cork, Cloughjordan, Dundalk, Enniscorthy, Galway, Kiltyclogher, Limerick, Monaghan, Sligo, Tralee, Waterford and Wesport. The venues were selected with a view to regional balance, and to mark the birth-place of 1916 leaders (for example, Cloughjordan—Thomas MacDonagh; Westport—John MacBride). Every community was encouraged to participate and an official list recorded a total of 230 commemorative events, with all 32 counties represented (see Appendix I). Most of these ceremonies followed a standard format: raising the national flag, reading the 1916 Proclamation—generally in Irish, though it was originally read in English—and a parade. Where an identifiable and suitable *lieu de mémoire* existed, such as a memorial to 1916 or to 1798 or the grave(s) of veterans of the struggle for independence, the ceremony might include a wreath-laying; a special Mass was also common.

A year of national commemoration

Easter week was merely the climax in a year of commemorative events that included historical lectures and publications; pageants; commemorative essay competitions; special scholarships, and the commissioning or unveiling of memorials. Every school received copies of the 1916 Proclamation in English and Irish, and each school child should have received a copy of *Oidreacht*—a commemorative booklet (however, I cannot recall any copy reaching our home, although there were five school-going children, and I have no recollection of any official unveiling of the 1916 Proclamation at school). The jubilee was marked by practically every organisation in Ireland. CIÉ, the state-owned transport system, renamed the major railway stations in honour of the 1916 leaders, and Dublin buses carried the official golden jubilee insignia—the flame of light.[5] Every national and local newspaper covered the commemoration at length, as did most periodicals; and it was almost de rigueur during the year for public speeches to include a 1916 theme. The official commemoration committee expected that approximately 5,000 people would march past the GPO on Easter Sunday 1966, including thirteen bands and representatives of sporting, cultural, community and political organisations: Conradh na Gaeilge; Gael-Linn; An Comhchaidreamh; Na Teaghlaigh Ghaelacha; Old Army and LDF comrades associations; Fianna Fáil; Fine Gael; the Bricklayers Trade Union; the GAA; the Camogie Association; the Football Association of Ireland (soccer); the Irish Rugby Football Union; Boy Scouts; Cómhaltas Cheoltóirí Éireann; the Language Freedom Movement; groups from Tullamore, Wexford, Limerick, Waterford and Banna Strand; the Walkinstown Residents' Association; and representatives of the Irish overseas, including Boston's Eire Society.[6]

The cast of *Seachtar Fear, Seacht Lá*, the pageant commissioned by the GAA, included 200 members from Dublin GAA clubs and 100 'girls' from the Camogie Association.[7] *Handing on the torch*, the historical pageant staged in Mallow, listed an impressive number of participating groups, including workers from the Borden factory, the White Star laundry, the Duhallow hunt, local farming groups and workers at the local sugar factory. The famine scene in the pageant was credited to 'the Mallow ladies'.[8] Mallow's emphasis on historical continuity was a common theme. *Handing on the Torch* opened with the 1798 rebellion in Wexford, and showed the defeated Wexford rebels handing on the torch to the next generation. *Aiséirí*, the official pageant to mark the golden jubilee, which was scripted by Tomás MacAnna, traced the story of the Irish Republic from the American War of Independence to the execution of Roger Casement in August 1916, with a brief coda that referred to Irish neutrality during World War II.[9] The pageant staged by St Louis Convent Monaghan (written by Seamus O Neill, a history lecturer at Carysfort teacher training college), portrayed 11 key episodes in Irish history, beginning with the formation of the United Irishmen and concluding with the Rising. Telefís Éireann's special programmes to mark the jubilee included a series of historical programmes covering the period from 1607 (Flight of the Earls) to 1916, with a concentration on the period after 1798. The Rising was therefore presented as the culmination of republican activity and rebellion, part of a continuous process in Irish history. This was reflected in other aspects of the commemoration: Tralee arranged for the Pikeman statue (a 1798 memorial) to be cleaned in honour of the 1916 jubilee.[10] In Castlebar, Co. Mayo the parade ended with a reading of the 1916 Proclamation at the 1798 memorial in the Mall.[11] Events associated with statutes of Robert Emmet and Thomas Davis figured prominently in Eamon de Valera's Easter week calendar, and 1966 saw renewed speculation about the burial place of Robert Emmet.[12]

The temptation to extend the commemoration beyond the actual Rising was almost inevitable. Most communities sought to identify with a local personality or event. But this proved rather difficult, because the Rising was concentrated in Dublin; however, Enniscorthy, (Wexford), Bawnard near Fermoy (Cork), Athenry (Galway), and Tralee and Banna Strand (Kerry) could commemorate local incidents. Birth-places of 1916 leaders provided a focus for commemorations in communities such as Athea (Limerick)—Con Colbert, and Kiltyclogher (Leitrim)—Seán MacDermott, but again the opportunities were limited. While both pageants staged at Croke Park stopped at 1916, as did the television and radio programmes, many ceremonies outside Dublin embraced the War of Independence, and sometimes the Civil War and more recent republican activities. The golden jubilee year saw the unveiling of memorials at Crossbarry and Kilmichael—sites of two major IRA ambushes in Cork during the Anglo-Irish war.[13] This slippage of the commemoration beyond 1916 is scarcely surprising; the old IRA featured in most parades, and Easter 1916 was commonly seen as the starting date for the final struggle to secure Irish independence.

Yet, for many Irish people, the 1916 jubilee was commemorated not by parades or pageants, but on television. Nineteen-sixty-six was the first year when a majority of Irish households had a television set, and it also marked a major landmark for Telefís Éireann—which had only begun broadcasting on New Year's Eve 1961. It is probably not a coincidence that a major investment in television transmitters, ensuring that 98% of households within the state could receive Telefís Éireann, was completed in April 1966, though at the time only 55% of households actually had a television set.[14] While the station went to considerable efforts to televise the parades, and other formal events, it was *Insurrection*—Hugh Leonard's docu-drama of Easter week 1916— that captured the imagination.

The only public ceremonies in the history of the Irish state to bear comparison with those of Easter 1966 were the centenary of Catholic Emancipation in 1929 and the 1932 Eucharistic Congress, and neither of those events was directly associated with Irish independence. The inauguration of the Irish Republic on Easter Monday 1949 was a rather low-key affair. Although the centenary of the death of Thomas Davis in 1945 was marked by a week of official events that in some respects anticipated the 1966 official calendar, [15] the Davis centenary was not celebrated throughout Ireland, and it did not turn into a year-long event. The new Irish state is often seen as being obsessed with its history—but this obsession (if correct) did not result in lavish memorials or commemorative events. The Cúchulainn statue, by Oliver Shephard, which was installed in the GPO in 1935, was not commissioned as a 1916 memorial; indeed the statue predates the Rising, it was sculpted in 1911–12.[16] Work on a formal memorial at Arbour Hill only began during the 1950s. The idea for a Garden of Remembrance to honour all who died for Ireland was first mooted in the 1930s; the site in the Rotunda Gardens (where the 1916 prisoners were held before being deported to Britain) was identified in 1935 and bought in 1939; the winning design for the garden by Dáithí Hanly was selected in August 1946, following a competition, but the work was halted in 1948 and did not resume until 1961.[17] It was something of a rush to have the garden ready for the official opening in Easter 1966, and the Children of Lir statue, which is the focal point within the garden, was not yet erected. The statue of Thomas Davis, unveiled at Easter 1966 was commissioned in 1945.[18] Proposals to turn Kilmainham jail into a memorial to those who participated in the 1916 Rising were drawn up in 1953; most of the restoration work was carried out by a committee of volunteers.[19]

Pressure for a major commemoration came from non-government ranks, notably the Fianna Fáil party and members of the Old IRA. The latter were increasingly feeling out of tune with contemporary Ireland. In 1962 the Honorary Secretaries of the Federation of IRA, 1916–21 informed Taoiseach Seán Lemass that 'there is no doubt that every year these parades are becoming less impressive and have ceased to command the respect to which they are entitled from the public'.[20] By November 1964 the Fianna Fáil National Executive had produced a draft programme for a week of events, beginning on Easter Sunday.[21] Elsewhere, there were calls to make the commemoration an all-party affair, as a result of fears that Fianna Fáil would try to seize control for political purposes. In 1964 the Cabinet determined that responsibility for the 1966 commemoration should be left to the Department of Defence, which was responsible for the annual Easter commemoration. But when the department presented proposals to government in January 1965 that were not markedly different from the standard Easter commemoration, Lemass sent them back to the drawing board, indicating that in 1966 the Rising 'should be celebrated on a grander scale than appears to be envisaged in the memorandum'. He indicated that 'the public will expect that the occasion will be marked by an extensive range of celebrations'. At this point 'An informal committee…of persons who were associated with the Easter Rising' was asked to come up with ideas.[22] The large turnout for the state funeral and reburial of Roger Casement in March 1965 confirmed that there was widespread public interest in such ceremonies.[23]

The international aspect of the commemorations

The golden jubilee was an unprecedented celebration of the Rising and of Irish independence at a time when many of those who had participated in those events were still alive. It was also an opportunity to promote Ireland's image abroad as a modern, successful democracy, and to extend the tourist season—an objective that also lay behind the 1950s launch of An Tóstal.[24] In January 1966 all Irish embassies were informed that the Minister for External Affairs was anxious

> that we avail ourselves to the greatest extent possible of the opportunity offered by the Commemoration of the 50th Anniversary of the Easter Rising for gaining favourable publicity for Ireland abroad and for encouraging persons of Irish birth and descent to visit Ireland during the Easter period or later in 1966.[25]

However, Bord Fáilte was of the opinion that visitors would only be attracted if there was 'greater audience participation' in the ceremonies; it suggested that some events geared to mass participation should be included in the programme, such as an open air mass in O'Connell Street or the Phoenix Park; but the only concession to Bord Fáilte's wishes was to permit groups representing overseas Irish organisations to march on Easter Sunday.[26]

A colourful brochure featuring the Rock of Cashel with a party of huntsmen (in hunting pink) and hounds at the base of the rock marketed 'The Easter Rebellion Anniversary Tour', under the special direction of Boston journalist Brendan Malin (a 15-day tour for $535 dollars). Described as 'A once in a lifetime opportunity to participate in the ceremonies honouring the valiant Irish struggle for freedom, and to see the Irish countryside in its Springtime Glory', the schedule included places associated with

> the glorious struggle for the freedom of Ireland in 1916...retracing the steps of Irish revolutionary history to Roger Casement's memorial at Banna Strand, to Cork City the home of Terence MacSwiney and Thomas MacCurtain. To Galway to see the glory of Connemara where Liam Mellowes assembled 1,000 volunteers...Cashel and Cloughjordan to visit the birthplace of the great Irish martyrs and to Dublin to take part in all the religious, military and civic pageants and ceremonies that will take place daily.[27]

In reality, the trip was very similar to a standard Irish coach tour, with visits to Killarney, the Blarney stone and Connemara (which had no association with Liam Mellowes), and a medieval banquet at Bunratty, with additional visits to Banna Strand and a short stop in Cloughjordan (probably because it was on the route to Dublin).[28] The jubilee did attract some additional visitors. The Ancient Order of Hibernians organised a special flight to Dublin in addition to its normal mid-summer charter.[29] The New York National Graves Association filled a plane, as did the Irish societies from Jersey City and San Francisco.[30]

Irish embassies were asked to arrange a special reception to mark the occasion—though some simply doubled up with the traditional St Patrick's Day reception. The foreign missions tried to give the Rising story a local colour. New Delhi hoped to arrange a lecture by V.V. Giri, the governor of Mysore, who had witnessed the Rising at first-hand as a student in Dublin in 1916. William Warnock, the ambassador in New Delhi, sent a short note to the major Indian newspapers, in which he referred to the interest and sympathy that Indian nationalists had shown in the Rising and the Irish struggle for independence. Warnock informed Iveagh House that he would include a reference to the mutiny of the Connaught Rangers in a talk on Indian radio.[31] The Irish embassy in Brussels reported that the Rising was still seen as having weakened the Allied war effort, and the staff there expressed relief that Professor Gorielli of the University of Brussels had defended Roger

Casement's action in the Congo and with regard to the Rising.[32] A number of foreign heads of state, including Lyndon Johnson, President Podgorny of the USSR, the president and prime minister of India and Prince Rainier of Monaco, sent formal messages to President de Valera to mark the jubilee. The governor of Massachusetts, John Volpe, proclaimed Monday, 11 April as 'Irish Republic Day'. Not to be outdone, Boston mayor John Collins proclaimed the week 10–17 April to be 'Irish Freedom Week'.[33] The most elaborate overseas ceremonies took place in London, where there was a week-long programme, beginning with Easter Sunday mass in Southwark Cathedral, a march to Trafalgar Square (this was an annual event), a concert, lectures and sporting events. Other English cities with large Irish populations, such as Birmingham, also organised events throughout Easter Week, with the GAA and the Irish Centres playing a major role in the commemoration. In Washington, D.C., the major formal occasion was the unveiling of a statue to Robert Emmet—created by Jerome Connor; another copy was presented to de Valera in Dublin some days later. However, the impact of this event in Washington was rather counteracted by the fact that the ceremony almost coincided with the unveiling of a statue to Winston Churchill a short distance away, outside the British embassy. The *New York Times* gave front page coverage to the Churchill statue, but it failed to report on the Emmet unveiling.[34]

Many of the overseas events had a strong cultural dimension, perhaps because of the links between the Rising and the works of major Irish writers such as W.B. Yeats and Seán O'Casey. US columnist Mary McGrory suggested that what distinguished the Irish revolution from other modern revolutions was 'the incomparable language in which it was recorded'. 'It was the only revolution which was fomented and fought by poets'; she went on to describe Pearse as 'near-saint and scholar'.[35] In Boston, the golden jubilee celebrations were run in conjunction with the Second Modern Arts Festival, at MIT. The festival, organised by Mary Manning, featured plays, films and lectures on historic and cultural themes, with a concentration on plays and poetry associated with the Rising. While it attracted wide support from Irish university graduates in the Boston area and from non-Irish people, it appears to have been largely ignored by the Boston-Irish community.[36] Boston Public Library issued a special 1916 reading list, and made additional copies of the books on the list available for borrowers.[37] Stanford University organised an exhibition of books and pamphlet material relating to Irish history.[38] The prize for the tackiest use of the jubilee must go to an Irish fashion show staged in New York's Waldorf Astoria hotel, where models, including one wearing 'the GPO trouser-suit', paraded to the background music from the execution scene in Mise Éire. Conor Cruise O'Brien and his wife Máire MacEntee (daughter of 1916 veteran and former minister Seán MacEntee) walked out in protest.[39]

This being the 1960s, considerable importance was attached to television coverage of the commemoration. On 31 January 1966 (little more than two months before the jubilee) the Department of External Affairs sent an urgent message from the minister, Frank Aiken, to all overseas missions, emphasising the importance of having a short documentary about the rising shown abroad. Aiken believed that such a film 'will not only help to correct erroneous views on the Irish struggle for independence but by including some material on the Dublin of today, will also assist in disseminating abroad a more accurate picture of modern Ireland'. All missions were requested to contact broadcasting bodies, including representatives of broadcasting companies from countries where there was no Irish mission, to arrange for an as yet unseen programme to be transmitted.[40] George Morrison was commissioned to make a 15-minute documentary, suitable for international transmission. A written commentary that could be translated into foreign languages would be supplied. This documentary, 'The Irish Rising, 1916', used newsreels from the 1916 period and ended with a short montage of present-day Dublin. Officials recommended that Morrison include shots of the ESB station, Ringsend; the Telefís Éireann Building, Donnybrook; and the ESB transformer station and Unidare factory, both in Finglas. However, when the film was shown a number of television stations omitted the scenes of contemporary Dublin; others gave such a confused commentary that diplomats feared that it made the story of the Rising unintelligible.[41] However, many television channels carried footage of the Easter Sunday ceremonies in Dublin.

In the remainder of this chapter, I propose to examine the official commemoration, as it was envisaged by the Irish government, and the interaction between that vision and various constituencies within Ireland and abroad. There are a number of underlying themes to explore:

- the degree to which the commemoration focused on the present and the future, rather than the past;
- efforts to present the jubilee as a celebration that included all Irish citizens; and

- two items of 'unfinished business' from 1916—reviving the Irish language, and partition.

PRESENT, FUTURE AND PAST

Ireland has passed through her period of revolution and the turbulent aftermath, and her long hard climb to economic prosperity is nearing success. She has reached a watershed in her development wherein the emphasis is no longer on political or constitutional transformation but on economic and social change.[42]

Ireland is a better place to live in than it was in 1916 for a greater number of its citizens, but not yet for all. Too much of the wealth of the people is still in the hands of too few. Too many of our children are still denied the opportunity to develop to the full their potential intellectual and artistic skills. We have not yet worked out in practice a truly Christian humanism. We have not after fifty years been able to make our society attractive to the Northern Protestant.[43]

Although Eamon de Valera emerges as the most prominent figure in the official commemorations in 1966—by virtue of his dual position as President of Ireland and the only surviving 1916 leader—the intellectual character of the official commemoration was determined by Taoiseach Seán Lemass. If de Valera represented the past, Lemass, despite being also a veteran of the Rising, interpreted 1966 in terms of the present and the future. The message of the commemoration was that what Ireland needed was not military action, or an anti-partition campaign, but a new and different form of patriotism designed to enhance the statehood won by the 1916 Rising. At the press conference setting out the official programme of commemoration, Lemass presented the golden jubilee as an opportunity to 'further enhance the status of our nation in the eyes of the world, emphasising both our pride in our past and confidence in our future'.[44] More specifically, he saw the 1916 anniversary as an opportunity to reinvigorate his drive to transform Ireland's economy and society.

The 1960s has commonly been seen as 'the best of decades', and by comparison with the grim 1950s this is an accurate picture.[45] Ireland enjoyed an unprecedented period of economic growth; emigration fell sharply from the record levels experienced during the 1950s, and the country belatedly enjoyed the post-war marriage boom, with a rising rate of marriage and a falling age of marriage. The 1966 census recorded the first sustained rise in the population of the state since independence. Lemass's term as taoiseach (1959–66) saw a decided improvement in relations between Britain and Ireland, and the first meeting since 1922 of an Irish head of government with the prime minister of Northern Ireland. The isolationism and anti-partition rhetoric that dominated Irish foreign policy in the early years following the ending of World War II, had given way to a more active engagement in foreign affairs through the United Nations and through diplomacy designed to promote Irish membership of the EEC. There is no doubt that Ireland in the 1960s was a more optimistic and confident country than it had been before, and Lemass and his colleagues saw the jubilee as an opportunity to present this new confident image at home and overseas. When asked by a journalist from the *Catholic Herald* about the major achievements of the past 50 years, Lemass replied that

> [i]n the past 50 years, we have developed as a vigorous forward-looking, self-respecting community, with growing experience in the management of our affairs, and confidence born of understanding of our potentialities…The slave spirit which afflicted so many people in Ireland, after centuries of foreign rule, has at long last virtually disappeared even if some residue is to be found. [46]

The previous 50 years had proved that the Irish were capable of self-government. But by 1966 the initial euphoria, which came with the reversal of the grim economic conditions of the late 1950s, was wearing off. There was no immediate prospect that Ireland would become a member of the EEC, and consequently the ambitious growth target set in the Second Programme for Economic Expansion —a 50% rise in GNP between 1964 and 1970—would not be met. The 1966 budget was introduced earlier than usual, ostensibly to get it out of the way before the golden jubilee events; in reality, the early date reflected an urgent need to raise taxes. [47] Expectations that economic growth would bring a steady rise in living standards had resulted in a succession of industrial relations disputes, which seemed beyond the government's capacity to resolve. A trade agreement signed in December 1965, and due to come into effect on 1 July 1966, opened the way for a free-trade area between Britain and Ireland. While the agreement appeared to offer more secure markets for Irish farmers, many Irish industrialists feared that it would put them out of business. The correspondent of the *Birmingham Post*, who covered the 1966 jubilee celebrations, noted that Irish complacency about economic growth had been 'sharply disturbed recently by a considerable recession'. He also claimed that 'The Irish economy is holding its breath, and praying among other things, that no die-hard political violence will alienate customers or damage the much-improved relations with Britain and Ulster'.[48] The spring 1966 issue of the Jesuit periodical *Studies* captured the mood of the moment when it suggested that

> it would be a tragedy if our present passing difficulties in the economic sphere and the growing industrial unrest were to undermine the new sense of confidence which the publication of Mr. T.K. Whitaker's *Grey Book* [*Economic Development*] sparked off. Preoccupation with 1916 and the tragedy of 1922 tend to make us too backward-looking and make us forget that we are living in a far different world in 1966.[49]

The 'far different world' that *Studies* had in mind was the Ireland of the 1950s, not 1916.

The 1966 jubilee was seen as an opportunity to take stock, to proclaim the achievements of the new state and to assist in the reformulation of Irish patriotism away from narrow nationalist objectives, such as the anti-partition campaign, towards social and economic transformation. Such a process had been underway since the late 1950s. The GAA's jubilee pageant *Seachtar Fear, Seacht Lá*—consisting of seven scenes, each focusing on a signatory to the Proclamation—embraced this modernising theme. In the scene commemorating James Connolly, the Irish working class was represented by men in 'new dungarees...white coats...welding visors'. Seán MacDermott, a member of the Irish Transport Workers' Union was accompanied by 'Irish sailors, Irish airmen and air hostesses, and Irish transport workers in uniform'.[50]

Looking to the future

While there was a tendency to use the jubilee as an opportunity to celebrate the achievements of the previous 50 years, Lemass preferred to reinterpret the spirit of 1916 to reinforce the messages that were central

to his vision for contemporary Ireland: economic and social development; fostering closer relations with Britain and with Northern Ireland;
promoting a more inclusive sense of Irishness; and presenting an image
to the world of Ireland as a modern and successful state. While it is
possible to disassemble these messages under a series of headings, it is
equally important to realise that they were all inextricably linked.

Once we move away from formal parades and commemorative
plaques to examine the rhetoric of 1966, it is evident that much of the
emphasis was on the future and the present, rather than the past. In an
article published in *New Spotlight* magazine—the first Irish magazine for
young people (it was established to promote Irish showbands, one of the
cultural phenomena of the early 1960s)—Lemass mused that

> [p]robably the historians of 2016, looking back at the Ireland
> of today, will be able to detect some at least of the influences,
> already operating, which will eventually decide the kind of
> country we will become, even if we today are not aware of
> them, or can only faintly detect their effects.

The next 50 years would result in the economic and political integration
of western Europe; he believed that one of the problems facing Ireland in
the future would be to preserve and develop national individuality within
a European community. And, reflecting on a much more immediate issue,
he suggested that industrial relations was one of the major problems facing
all democratic countries, and one that must be resolved if 'our hopes for
economic progress are not to dissolve in mounting industrial disorder'.[51]
At a dinner to mark the retirement of veteran Fianna Fáil TD P.J. Burke,
in October 1965, Lemass claimed that

> the celebration of the 50th anniversary of the 1916 Rising,
> while signifying primarily our understanding of its historical
> importance, will also be a time of national stocktaking, and
> for trying to look ahead into the mists of the future to see the
> right road leading to the high destiny we desire for our
> nation.[52]

As far as Lemass was concerned, attention should focus on the
opportunities for the future rather than the wrongs of the past, and he
expressed the hope that the commemoration of 1916 would 'lead to a
new birth of patriotism—a constructive patriotism which will be in tune
with the needs and circumstances of our times, and…the ever-changing

conditions that will face us in the future'. The immediate goal was economic and social development, because this was essential to sustain free political institutions and to eliminate any economic argument for partition. Economic growth would make it possible to achieve 'even more dramatic future accomplishments involving the realisation of all our national aims'. Recent economic development had fuelled materialism and the pursuit of sectional interests; the 1916 commemoration should be used 'to urge all people to learn to think and act again as Irishmen and Irishwomen first, and to keep their sectional and individual behaviour subordinate to the welfare of the nation as a whole'.[53] In the introduction to the *Easter Commemoration Digest*, which was targeted at a US readership, Lemass pointed out that

> [t]he deeds that are required of Irishmen today are of a different kind dictated by a different phase of history. But the need for every Irishmen and Irishwoman to accept his or her responsibility to the nation remains the same.[54]

While de Valera's official address to mark the jubilee also deprecated the modern emphasis on materialism, and he reiterated that political freedom was not the ultimate goal of the Rising, he went on to reprise his famous 1943 speech, suggesting that it was the objective of the Rising to make possible

> the enabling condition for the gradual building up of a community in which an ever increasing number of its members, relieved from the pressure of exacting economic demands, would be free to devote themselves more and more to the cultivation of the things of the mind and spirit.[55]

He expressed the hopes that

> [o]ur nation could then become again, as it was for centuries in the past, a great intellectual and missionary centre from which would go forth the satisfying saving truths of Divine Revelation, as well as the fruits of the ripest secular knowledge.[56]

This was not entirely in accord with Lemass's statement to the Irish Management Institute annual conference at Killarney that '[f]or the next fifty years the symbol of patriotism is not the Army, Irish Volunteers, but the student in the Technical College',[57] or with the views of Fianna Fáil TD Don Davern, who contrasted the true patriot of 50 years previously—'willing to give his blood for his country; with the true patriot of today—willing to give a little more of his capacity to work'.[58] Minister for Education George Colley regarded the wave of strikes and threatened strikes as evidence that the current generation lacked the spirit of sacrifice that was so evident in the 1916 generation.[59] However, popular sentiment was probably more in sympathy with the workers than with the government's point of view. Bernadine Truden, a member of Boston's Eire Society, who kept a diary of her experiences during Easter week in Dublin, reported that at the pageant *Aiséirí,*

> [t]o mark the trend of the times, the greatest cheers came, not for any of the marching men, but for the strikers of 1913, when they burst onto the field with their placards. And the loudest boos were not for the redcoats, with their muskets and their cannons, but for the baton charge by the police that helped to break the strike![60]

The spirit of 1916 and the name of Connolly were often invoked in support of workers' rights and more radical social agendas. Fr Edmund Kent, S.J., director of the College of Industrial Relations, suggested that a charter for industrial relations would be a fitting tribute to the spirit and dedication of the 1916 leaders.[61] Fintan Kennedy, president of the Irish Congress of Trade Unions, echoed a common theme when he suggested that

> [r]esolute tackling of industrial, economic and social problems would be a very good way to honour the men who died in 1916.[62]

The Ireland of the 1960s

The economic growth of the early 1960s did not bring any significant extension of social services. Indeed, a core tenet of *Economic Development*, the 1958 report by T.K. Whitaker, was to redirect public spending from social services to projects that would bring about a direct increase in national income.[63] By the mid 1960s the reversal of emigration and cuts in spending on housing had left the state with a full-blown housing crisis.[64] The seven tower blocks erected at Ballymun (which was then on the outskirts of Dublin city) to relieve the housing shortage in the capital, were named after the signatories of the 1916 Proclamation. On the eve of the 1965 general election, the main opposition party, Fine Gael, launched its 'Just Society' programme, which included commitments to providing comprehensive health and welfare services. Among the other social issues that were highlighted during the mid-1960s were the need to provide welfare assistance for Irish emigrants in Britain; demands for greater access to second- and third-level education, and continuing depopulation and economic depression in the west of Ireland—particularly among small farmers. The 1916 Proclamation and various 1916 leaders—specifically Pearse and Connolly—were commonly invoked to decry the shortcomings of contemporary Irish society, or as evidence that various programmes that were being proposed were consistent with the philosophy of 1916. 'Pearse summed it up in the word "Republic," but one has only to read the Declaration to realise what he meant was the "Just Society"'.[65] Fr O' Dea, OSB, writing in *Irish Spotlight*, an Irish Dominican magazine, referred to Pearse's concern for 'children with bare feet upon the sands of some ebbed sea, or playing on the streets of the little towns in Connacht'. Where, he asked,

> would he [Pearse] find them playing today? In Trafalgar Close, in Coventry, Birmingham, Bristol, in Camden town? Where is Pearse in all this? Is this the fruit of his mighty sowing? Were he to return what a spectre would he find in his well-loved west, lonesome roads, homesteads caving in, homes that had a continuity back, back; homes that weathered the Famine not the freedom; that had a built-in history of faith and tenacity…blight of an empty countryside.[66]

Garret FitzGerald was almost alone in refusing to interpret, or reinterpret the words of the 1916 leaders as a guide to contemporary Ireland: 'In the harsh light of to-day, seen with the hindsight of a much more sophisticated generation, what was written and said by them conveys few clear-cut ideas of political or social philosophy'. FitzGerald dismissed the political and social ideas of the leaders of the Rising as 'fairly limited and naïve, even by the standards of that time'; few of these ideas, even Connolly's 'could stand the test of fifty years'. He believed that 'their views on contemporary Ireland would probably be less valuable than those of many of our contemporaries'.[67]

But this did not stop others from invoking the dead leaders or the Proclamation in support of various causes. Pearse was generally cited in support of educational or Irish language matters. The 1960s saw a growing demand for increased access to second- and third-level education, for reasons of social equity and to promote economic growth. The 1965 OECD report *Investment in education*, with data showing the inequality in access to education in Ireland, by location and socio-economic background, intensified this demand. Providing a number of additional scholarship places, to secondary school or to university, was seen as a popular and practical way to mark the jubilee. The government announced seven new university scholarships—each named after one of the signatories. Kilkenny, Tipperary North, Leitrim and Dublin were some of the counties who expanded scholarship places to mark the occasion. Boland's bakery—site of the 1916 garrison led by Eamon de Valera—announced a scheme of secondary scholarships for girls.[68] The Educational Building Society funded 16 scholarships for vocational and secondary school students, valued at £50 a year for five years.[69] In September 1966, however, scholarships to second-level schools became almost redundant, with the announcement by Minister for Education Donogh O'Malley that free second-level schooling and a school transport system would be introduced in the following year; O'Malley did not link the announcement to the 1916 jubilee.[70]

It is significant that FitzGerald's quote given above referred to 'even Connolly', because Connolly was regarded as the 1916 leader of greatest relevance to contemporary Ireland, and his reputation undoubtedly gained from the commemoration. When Seán Lemass was interviewed by the religious publication the *Word* (much of the debate over the significance of the 1916 Rising was conducted via religious magazines), he began by stating that Pearse was the leader who most impressed him, but without saying anything more about Pearse, he went on to expound on his regard for Connolly,

> because he was attempting to do what others hadn't done— to translate this emotional desire for freedom into a practical social policy. Most of the others were inclined to discourage this…But at that time, even as a young fellow, I always had in my own mind that there was a great deal yet to be done. And in the various opportunities I had for studying, it was works which had a bearing on this problem that I found most interesting.[71]

Yet on another occasion, Lemass remarked that the material and social progress achieved since 1916, both in Ireland and throughout the world, meant that 'even many of the views of James Connolly, revolutionary although they were considered to be in his time, seem out-of-date in the circumstances of today'.[72]

Trade union and Labour leaders were more likely to assert Connolly's relevance for contemporary Ireland. Labour TD Patrick McAuliffe, unveiling a plaque to James Connolly in Mallow, claimed that

> if modern Ireland is to move forward it must move in the lines laid down by James Connolly...an Ireland in which there could be justice and prosperity for all sections of the community and in which freedom of thought and action would be preserved.[73]

But Connolly was a revolutionary socialist, who won the approval of Lenin; and revolutionary socialism was a political philosophy far removed from the Irish Labour party, as Conor Cruise O'Brien pointed out in the special commemorative supplement to the *Irish Times*. Cruise O'Brien noted that

> Connolly is venerated as a martyr, and labour leaders sometimes pay homage to his ideals without specifying what these ideals were.[74]

On 15 May, the anniversary of Connolly's execution (he was the last to be executed), more than 6,000 trade unionists marched through Dublin in a commemorative parade. They included a party of 500 who travelled from Belfast; one member of this group was Gerry Fitt, the Republican Socialist MP.[75] Connolly was the only 1916 leader executed in Dublin to be singled out in this manner. The opening of a James Connolly hall in Belfast also served to establish Connolly's relevance in an all-Ireland context—as a trade unionist and the only leader with close personal experience of Ulster.[76]

Connolly was probably the 1916 leader of most interest to Sinn Féin/IRA at this time. A draft plan in the possession of Seán Garland, IRA Chief of Staff, when he was arrested in September 1966, indicated that the organisation was planning to devote greater attention to socio-economic issues, and to political and economic education, though not at the expense of its military objectives. The 'Movement' wished to bring together a group of trade unionists to examine trade union law and structures, with a view to making trade unions more revolutionary. Other committees, under the direction of the 'Army Department', would concentrate on housing, free-trade co-operatives and other topics, with a view to mobilising the mass membership of 'the Movement' in any agitation.[77] Addressing the Wolfe Tone society (an organisation closely associated with Sinn Féin), veteran republican socialist George Gilmore accused the Labour Party and trade unions of invoking Connolly's name but abandoning his political position, because they supported what he described as 'Griffith's State'.[78] Tomás MacGiolla, president of Sinn Féin, told the Tionól (a colloquium organised by An Comhchaidreamh, a body that represented Irish language organisations in Irish universities) that 'it would be better for the whole country now if the whole nation was under British rule. The national objective would then be much clearer and it would be easier today to obtain help from abroad in any agitation for freedom'. MacGiolla expressed the opinion that

> 'Pearse would be disillusioned by the Ireland of today and the big British take-over of business. The new Treaty which welcomed them here [a reference to the recently-signed Anglo-Irish Trade Agreement] could be described as an addendum to the 1921 Treaty'.[79]

Speaking at the Wolfe Tone commemoration at Bodenstown on 19 June 1966, Seamus Costello (described by the Department of Justice as IRA Headquarters officer), said that the target should be 'the ownership of our resources by the people, so that the resources will be developed in the interests of the people as a whole': setting a limit to the amount of land owned by an individual; compulsory acquisition of the estates of absentee landlords; and the nationalisation of key industries, including banks and insurance companies.[80]

UNITY AND DIVISION

(A) The Nationalist/Republican family,

Seán Lemass described the Rising as 'the birth pangs of modern Ireland', and this is how it was commonly represented during 1966.[81] The Rising was seen as an event that united people who would have disagreed over the 1921 Treaty and civil war. The assumption that everyone (at least within the state) could and should celebrate the

Rising as 'the birth pangs of modern Ireland' failed to take account of the Home Rule tradition within Irish nationalism or the unionist minority in what became the independent Irish state, not to mention Ulster unionism. Seán Lemass's speech to the inaugural meeting of the King's Inns' Debating Society was a carefully-crafted attempt to include a wider community of Irish nationalists within the jubilee celebrations. Lemass recalled how his father 'a stalwart of the Irish Parliamentary Party' was so deeply moved by the Rising that he converted to republicanism. He also paid tribute to the tens of thousands of Irishmen who had joined the British army and died in Flanders and Gallipoli,

> believing that they were giving their lives in the cause of human liberty everywhere, not excluding Ireland. After 1916 the whole situation changed.[82]

All the main political parties laid claim to the 1916 legacy. Fine Gael leader Liam Cosgrave was the son of a 1916 veteran; Labour leader Brendan Corish was the son of a veteran of the war of independence; and Labour was more than happy to claim affinity with James Connolly. In his speech launching the official commemoration in 1966, Lemass expressed the hope that all causes of disagreement would be set aside for the duration of the jubilee celebrations so that all Irish men and women would join together in celebrating the Rising. He also denied that the events had any political significance 'in the party sense'.[83] For this reason he initially determined that persons who were active in party politics should not seek to play a prominent role in official ceremonies, lest this might be misinterpreted. Ministers were not to take the salute at the official parades, all orations were banned. In March Lemass informed Foreign Affairs minister Frank Aiken that he was 'somewhat perturbed' by arrangements being made by some ministers—including Aiken himself—to use the commemoration for party political purposes. By then it was apparently too late to ban ministers from taking the salute at official parades, so Lemass gave instructions that Aiken should take the salute in Cork, and not in Dundalk, which was in his constituency. Cork deputy and minister for finance Jack Lynch would preside over the Dundalk parade. Lemass also reminded Aiken that he wished him to host the premier of the Gael Linn film in Dublin on Sunday night, which would presumably rule out Aiken's attendance at any later events in Dundalk.[84] But Lemass's hopes that the jubilee should be a non-party political occasion did not extend to including representatives of opposition parties on the official commemoration committee, despite being pressed by Cosgrave to concede this on several occasions.[85] And his public statements about the non-party nature of the commemoration are not entirely consistent with a letter to Jim Gibbons (Minister for Defence), who was co-ordinating the programme of events, in which Lemass suggested that Gibbons should supply Senator Tommy Mullins, the general secretary of Fianna Fáil, with details of all the official ceremonies. He informed Gibbons that in areas where no government ceremonies were planned, the Fianna Fáil organisation should take the lead in organising events.[86]

The image of the commemoration as a non-party event was brought further into question when the Department of Defence neglected to send invitations to a number of prominent people to sit on the viewing stand outside the GPO on Easter Sunday, including leaders of the Opposition. The fact that the golden jubilee was followed shortly after-wards by a presidential election, and that Eamon de Valera undoubtedly used visits to 1916 commemorative events, such as the Mallow pageant, as campaign visits, also accentuated a sense of political divisiveness. In the event, de Valera was re-elected by a margin of only 10,000 votes, which might suggest that the party political dividends from the jubilee were rather limited.

Fine Gael was very concerned that the Rising should not be presented in a manner that would unduly favour Fianna Fáil. It requested (and was denied) advance sight of official commemorative material (presumably *Cuimhneachán*), and of the official history of the Rising that had been commissioned.[87] Cosgrave's suspicions reflect an earlier spat over the Department of External Affairs booklet *Facts about Ireland*, which failed to acknowledge the significance of Michael Collins, and the continuing refusal to permit the army to participate in the annual Collins commemoration at Beal na mBláth.[88] However, under the leadership of Cosgrave, the son of a 1916 veteran, Fine Gael went to considerable efforts to establish the party's close links with 1916, the war of independence and the foun-dation of the state: launching a Michael Collins Educational Foundation,[89] and holding a special dinner to honour veteran party members Richard Mulcahy, Richard Hayes, Seán MacEoin and Patrick McGilligan.[90] It would have been more difficult to establish such a pedigree under the former leader James Dillon, who was the son of an Irish Parliamentary Party MP. Divisions and tensions over the apostolic succession in Irish republicanism still rankled within the mainstream Irish political parties, but they were a very minor feature in the 1966 commemorations.

The claim by Sinn Féin and the IRA to be the true heirs to the spirit of 1916 was a trickier matter. That the Rising was carried out by a minority, and was seen at the time as unpopular, but then went on to secure retrospective approval, was a message that was dear to the hearts of all who were engaged in waging a long, unsuccessful and unpopular war to end partition. Many of the publications about the Rising that appeared during 1966 drew attention to this fact, though this aspect of the Rising did not figure prominently in speeches by government ministers or mainstream political leaders. By the early 1960s it would appear that ownership/control of the commemoration of the Rising had largely passed by default into the hands of groups that were closely associated with Sinn Féin/IRA. When the national committee or various local committees began to plan for the golden jubilee, these groups were unwilling to cede control. The National Graves Association, which was responsible for the republican plot at Glasnevin cemetery, rejected the view of the official 1966 commemorative committee that the design that the National Graves Association had drawn up for the plot was 'unsuitable and unworthy', and the association refused to permit the Board of Works to redesign the plot in time for Easter 1966.[91] This was not, however, an insurmountable problem, because Arbour Hill, the burial place of the executed leaders, was owned by the Department of Defence; Glasnevin was a less important site.

The choice of an emblem to mark the 1916 jubilee was more problematical. The traditional 1916 memorial emblem was the Easter lily, first sold by Cumann na mBan in the 1920s, but over time the Easter lily came to be identified with hard-core republicans who refused to recognise the legitimacy of the state. By the 1960s prosecutions for selling Easter lilies had come to be an annual event, because the sellers refused to apply for Garda permits.[92] The official commemoration committee decided to commission a new emblem. The choice, following a competition, was 'An Claidheamh Soluis' the 'sword of light'—the title of a Gaelic League periodical once edited by Pádraig Pearse. The committee claimed this emblem 'was taken up by scholars of the Gaelic revival, and was adopted by the revolutionary thinkers to indicate their dual objective: (1) an armed rebellion, (2) an Irish cultural renaissance'.[93] The decision to commission a new emblem was denounced by many 'republicans'.[94] Coiste Cuimhneacháin Seachtain na Cásca, the 1916 Golden Jubilee Commemoration Committee, placed a wreath of Easter lilies on the Republican plot at Glasnevin during Easter week.[95]

This committee, gave its address as the Sinn Féin offices in Gardiner Street. Sinn Féin president Tomás MacGiolla, claimed that it was a continuation of the committee formed in 1917 by members of the then Republican movement to commemorate those who died for Ireland; they had held a commemoration on every Easter Sunday since 1917. The Department of Justice reported that the committee of ten was composed of members of the IRA, Sinn Féin and Cumann na mBan; four were members of the IRA.[96] Asked why they had established a separate committee the chairman, Eamonn Mac Thomáis, said they felt that nobody who wanted association with Britain had the right to honour those men who had paid the supreme sacrifice, since the men who died in 1916 did not want any association with Britain.[97] The committee president was the veteran republican Joseph Clarke, who fought at Mount Street Bridge during Easter 1916. Having been invited to attend a state reception in Dublin Castle on 17 April 1966, he replied that he was rejecting the invitation 'in the same manner as I rejected the Treaty of Surrender in 1921 and the Second Compromise in 1932'. Clarke had been imprisoned by the government on three occasions: 'my only crime being that I still upheld the Principles and Ideals of Pearse and Connolly'. While others would be 'wining and dining in Dublin Castle', he would be in 'Belfast (British Occupied Ireland) with my comrades, old and new, who have never deviated one iota from the Republican Cause and the Separatist Tradition'.[98]

The 1916 Golden Jubilee Commemoration Committee announced its programme of events on 8 February 1966, three days before the taoiseach's press conference launching the official programme. The alternative commemoration started on Easter Sunday with a parade after 10am Mass in St John the Baptist Church, Blackrock to the Republican plot in Dean's Grange cemetery; with another parade at 3pm from the Custom House to the Republican plot in Glasnevin cemetery and a commemoration concert in the Gaiety theatre. On Easter Monday a religious service in St Patrick's Cathedral (it is uncertain whether this referred to the official commemorative service) would be followed by a bus tour to the sites of 1916 garrisons and outposts. On Easter Saturday evening the committee planned to parade from Parnell Square to areas of significance during the conflict, where there would be a series of open air lectures. On Sunday, 17

April, the group planned to travel to Belfast in the 'Freedom Train', and then to parade from the Falls Road to the republican plot at Milltown cemetery, where Cathal Goulding (described by the Department of Justice as a member of the IRA) would deliver an oration. The final event in the programme was the unveiling by the National Graves Association of a new memorial at the republican plot in Glasnevin cemetery.[99]

The only event on this programme that threatened to clash with the official ceremonies was a parade past the GPO on Saturday evening. In March the secretary of the government's commemoration committee met the chairman of the Golden Jubilee Committee Eamonn Mac Thomáis and the vice-chairman Jack Butler, and they had what the secretary of the government committee described 'as a long and very amicable discussion', which ended in an agreement that the Golden Jubilee Committee parade would not reach the GPO until 8.45pm or possibly 9pm, by which time the official ceremonies would have ended. Once this had been agreed, the Gardaí were prepared to permit MacThomáis and his group to go ahead with their programme of events within the state, though they were much less accommodating about the planned excursion to Belfast.[100]

The potential clash of parades in Dublin was settled without difficulty and the matter was not aired in public at any point. However, this was not the case in many provincial towns, where Sinn Féin councillors and other party representatives objected to involvement of the Irish army or the FCA in jubilee parades. In Waterford, Sinn Féin representatives threatened trouble if the army paraded.[101] In Drogheda, it was announced that members of the armed forces in uniform would not be allowed to take part, though they were welcome to parade in civilian attire.[102] Fianna Fáil and Fine Gael representatives responded by deciding to boycott the parade, and to opt to attend an official parade in Dundalk.[103] In Tralee, the North Kerry Easter Week Commemoration Committee—a republican group—claimed that it had no wish to 'enter into competition with political mercenaries', who were planning to hold what they described as a 'Party Political Parade'. Members of this committee had been parading to the republican plot at Rath cemetery (which contained the bodies of men executed by the Irish state) on Easter Sunday for more than 40 years, and would continue this tradition.[104] Tralee was by no means the only town where Easter Sunday parades had formerly been left to republicans; for many years the Drogheda parade had also been organised by a republican committee. In Monaghan town the official parade threatened to clash with a parade by republicans, to the grave of Ferghal O'Hanlon, who was killed in an IRA attack on Brookeborough army barracks in January 1957.[105] Limerick city held two rival parades on Easter Sunday for 25 years; the split ended in 1965 but re-emerged in 1966, despite efforts by the mayor to secure agreement on one parade that would include all sections of the community.[106] The Irish army took part in the official parade, from Sarsfield barracks to the 1916 memorial on Sarsfield bridge. This was followed by a second parade to the Republican plot in Mount St Lawrence cemetery, which was led by 'a colour party of young men'; other marchers included members of the Republican movement and the Old IRA. The mayor and members of Limerick Corporation in their robes attended both parades. Both ceremonies included a memorial Mass.[107] Waterford also held two parades. At 1pm on Easter Sunday, Minister for Education George Colley took the salute at the official parade. At 3pm a parade organised by the Waterford National Commemoration Committee marched to the Republican plot in Ballygunner cemetery.[108]

There were rival parades also in Kiltyclogher, Co. Leitrim, the birthplace of 1916 leader Seán MacDermott and the setting for one of the official parades organised by the government's commemoration committee. MacDermott's family had remained committed to Sinn Féin and his oldest sister, Margaret, refused to accept an honorary doctorate in his honour from the Chancellor of the National University of Ireland, Eamon de Valera; although a younger sister, Rose, did accept the award.[109] When informed of plans for an official ceremony on Easter Sunday at Kiltyclogher, his two sisters and niece replied that

> it is hypocritical for that Government to attempt to do honour to Seán Mac Diarmada while at the same time announcing a ban on the historic Easter Lily, the emblem of Easter week 1916...Seán died for a 32-County republic which has yet to be achieved. The forces of the 26-County state raided our homes in recent years while engaged in patrolling and maintaining the British made border...[110]

They had indicated to 'a Free State Army officer' who called on them

> that the Commemoration being held by the Breffni Branch of the National Graves Association in Kiltyclougher [sic] on

Easter Sunday afternoon is adequate and that it is against
our wishes that the Free State Army is coming there that
morning.

They refused to attend or be represented at what they termed 'the
26-County Army or F.C.A. parade'; and they pointed out that the
monument in Kiltyclogher included names of some killed 'by B
Specials etc after 1922'. The family reiterated that it remained 'true to
the 32-County Republic for which all these Leitrim men, including
Seán, died and we object to Commemoration ceremonies organised by
those who have accepted less'.[111]

While the MacDermott sisters were undoubtedly the most recalci-
trant relatives of the 1916 leaders to feature in the 1966
commemoration, others claimed the right to oversee the process.
Kathleen Clarke, widow of 1916 leader Tom Clarke, and a formidable
political activist in her own right (she resigned from Fianna Fáil in the
1940s because of de Valera's tough attitude towards republicans), asked
Lemass to nominate her to the official committee. In a diplomatically-
worded reply, he indicated that he had decided that it would be
inappropriate to appoint any relatives of executed leaders, because he
believed that associating them with the commemoration 'might be
thought to detract rather than add to the impressiveness of the national
tribute to them which is envisaged'.

Kathleen Clarke's campaign appears to have been prompted by a
wish to boost her claim that Tom Clarke, not P.H. Pearse, was the
president of the Republic that was declared in 1916.[112] This
determination to see Clarke as the most important figure of the 1916
Rising was supported by Clarke's nephew, Eamonn de hÓir, during the
course of various lectures and speeches given about the Rising.[113]
However, de hÓir was a member of the official committee, as was
Phyllis Bean Uí Cheallaigh, wife of former president Seán T. O'Kelly
and sister of GPO veteran and former Fianna Fáil minister James Ryan.
She was also a member of the Broadcasting Authority, and in that
capacity proved to be an energetic monitor of the series of programmes
made to mark the jubilee, as was Fianna Fáil senator Ruairí Brugha,
the son of Cathal Brugha. In July 1965 the latter suggested that the
authority was not confident that those who were planning the television
programmes fully appreciated the context of the Rising. When the
authority reviewed the proposed schedule in detail at its September
meeting, and discussed names of possible participants and compilers,

the minute initially recorded that the authority had expressed confidence in the proposals. When this was queried by Bean Uí Cheallaigh at the October meeting, it was noted that the minute 'was not intended to imply full Authority approval of all participants in 1916 programmes'. The record was amended to read that the authority had 'expressed its confidence in the capacity of the programme staff to implement them'.[114] By November Phyllis Uí Cheallaigh was inquiring about the amount of Irish to be used in the programmes. She also sought the appointment of a 'qualified advisory committee' to act as consultants to *Insurrection*. The station had recruited UCD historian Kevin B. Nowlan as official advisor, and it left him to consult 'specially appropriate advisors'. It is possible that Phyllis Uí Cheallaigh's request was prompted by the information that Professor Nowlan had already secured the cooperation of General Richard Mulcahy (Bean Ui Cheallaigh's brother-in-law, and a leading figure on the pro-Treaty side).[115] In March, when the authority appears to have viewed *Insurrection*, Ruairí Brugha suggested that the series might be criticised for failing to feature Eamon de Valera, whereas Michael Collins appeared in six episodes. Phyllis Uí Cheallaigh drew attention to some historical inaccuracies, which, she claimed, could have been corrected if her advice about consulting survivors had been followed; but she did not dissociate herself 'entirely' from the congratulations proffered by the authority.[116] Given the large number of survivors, such complaints were remarkably few; most veterans appear to have gloried in the commemoration.

(B) The Protestant and Jewish communities

The 1960s saw a growing ecumenical movement that was prompted by Vatican II and the papacy of John XXIII. At this distance, the expectations of the ecumenical movement of the 1960s appear rather naïve; however, this does not detract from its genuine idealism. In the run-up to golden jubilee the spiritual leaders of the Catholic, Church of Ireland, Methodist and Presbyterian communities in Monaghan (a border county with a significant protestant minority) issued a statement to their members regarding the 1916 commemoration.

> The historic events of Easter 1916 will be commemorated
> throughout Ireland this year in a special way. We trust and
> pray earnestly that such celebrations as are contemplated will

enhance the dignity and the image of our country in the eyes of the world. We are most anxious that all that takes place will be in accord with the universal message of the Holy Season of Easter which is above history and nationality.[117]

The government's efforts to encourage the Protestant churches and the Jewish community to participate in the commemoration, and their apparent willingness to be involved, reflected the more open and pluralist attitudes found during the 1960s. They also indicate a broad consensus that 1916 should be regarded as a landmark event in the creation of the Irish state. The 1916 leadership provides no obvious Protestant role-model (Casement and Markievicz both converted to Catholicism). However, the practice of tracing the roots of the Rising and the republican lineage back to Wolfe Tone and the United Irishmen, through Davis and the Young Irelanders—the historical narrative presented in *Aiséirí, Seachtar Fear, Seacht Lá* and the pageant scripted for St Louis Convent, Monaghan—reinforced the message that Irish republicanism had multi-denominational, all-Ireland roots.

Some civil servants were conscious that references to a multi-denom-inational republican tradition did not accord well with the prominent and exclusive public role given to senior Catholic clergy on some state occasions. When Nicholas Ó Nualláin of the Department of the Taoiseach became aware that the official opening ceremony at the Garden of Remembrance would include a religious blessing by the Catholic Archbishop of Dublin, he wrote a minute indicating that had he been aware of this at an earlier stage, he would have advised against it,

> on the grounds that it is invidious to single out one religious denomination for the honour of performing the ceremony, to the exclusion of the other denominations. The occasion is a nation's—not a denominational—one, and, after all, Tone, Emmet and Childers (to mention but a few) gave their lives in the cause of Irish freedom just as much as did any Catholic who made the supreme sacrifice in the national struggle.[118]

Ó Nualláin outlined two alternative courses of action: to dispense with the blessing and risk incurring the private displeasure of Archbishop McQuaid, or to continue with the proposed ceremony and 'run the risk of a public controversy over the exclusion of the other denominations'.

At his suggestion, officials met Dr McQuaid's secretary to explore the possibility of having a blessing concelebrated by different religious leaders, or a succession of blessings. They informed him that the garden would remember all who had died for Ireland, irrespective of their religious faith. Fr Mahon subsequently reported that Dr McQuaid 'would object, in principle, to a simultaneous blessing or to circumstances in which he would be present at a successive blessing by non-Catholic and Jewish clergymen'.[119] Another official protested on discovering that the three school choirs chosen to sing at the unveiling of the Thomas Davis statue were all Catholic schools. He felt that it would have been appropriate to include at least one non-Catholic school.[120]

It is unclear whether Dr McQuaid had prior notice of the 1916 commemoration in the Dublin suburb of Finglas, where the Catholic curate and the Church of Ireland rector together laid a wreath at the memorial to Comdt Dick McKee and led those present in saying the Lord's Prayer.[121] At the Garden of Remembrance ceremony, the Church of Ireland Archbishop and representatives of the General Assembly of the Presbyterian Church in Ireland found themselves locked out when McQuaid was blessing the garden. They allegedly arrived three minutes late, but found the gates locked, and the keyholder could not be located.[122]

The evident wish to involve the different religious traditions in the official ceremonies (however belated and hamfisted) mirrored a corresponding desire on their part to join in the commemoration. This was undoubtedly easier for the Jewish community than for the Protestant churches, because of the possible analogies between Israel and Ireland. When the Chief Rabbi, Dr Isaac Cohen, spoke at a thanksgiving service for the Rising he took his theme from a quotation from the 1916 Proclamation: 'In every generation the Irish people have asserted their right to national freedom and sovereignty; six times during the past 300 years they have asserted it in arms'. According to Dr Cohen,

> when a small band of citizens voluntarily took up their position 50 years ago for the freedom of this country, jeopardising their lives until death, they took upon themselves a task similar to that of the children of Israel when they parted the waters of the Red Sea.
>
> Humanly speaking there was no possibility of victory in such circumstances. The people of Israel marched on in the

hands of God to freedom but for the men of 1916 there was no miraculous parting of the waters of the sea, and the lives of many of them were engulfed in the ensuing destruction.[123]

The commemoration prompted some serious reflections on the place of the Protestant community (communities) in contemporary Ireland. This process was obviously influenced by Lemass's efforts to improve north–south relations, and by a growing dialogue between the Catholic and Protestant churches. The wider political significance of 1960s ecumenism for Irish cultural and political life is an unexpected theme that has emerged from this research project. A spokesman for the Church of Ireland, Rev. G.W. Ferguson, said that:

> Protestants this year were thinking about their position as a minority group in the country and were anxious to make the best contribution they could to the land…the Irish Republic is entitled to and thereby claims the allegiance of every Irishman and Irishwomen. The Republic guarantees the religious and civil liberty, equal rights and equal opportunities to all its citizens, and declares its resolve to pursue the happiness and prosperity of the whole nation and of all its parts, cherishing all the children of the nation equally…Thanksgiving for the integrity with which successive Irish Governments have honoured the declaration of religious liberty which the men of Easter Week wrote in their proclamation of the Republic of 1916 will be joined with prayers for our country and her future peace and prosperity at the Commemorative Service on Easter morning.[124]

At a special service in St Patrick's Cathedral to mark the Rising, the Protestant archbishop of Dublin, Dr George Otto Simms, expressed his church's gratitude

> across the expanse of the past 50 years for the goodwill, tolerance and freedom expressed and upheld among and between those of different outlooks and religious allegiances.[125]

He also gave thanks 'for the spirit of reconciliation and goodwill that has been evident in recent times'. Preaching at a commemorative service in St Flannan's Cathedral, Killaloe, the Bishop of Killaloe, Right Rev.

Dr Henry Stanistreet, said that members of the Church of Ireland must respect the ideals and courage of those who took part in the Rising and the noble and genuine sentiments set forth in the 1916 Proclamation.[126] Dr Perdue, the Church of Ireland bishop of Cork, suggested that

> the idealism, sincerity and determination of the 1916 leaders was a challenge to the people of Ireland, both as citizens and Christians...What stood out about 1916 was the courage of the little band of men who, for their ideals were prepared to risk and sacrifice all, even life itself...Men of such calibre must be held in the esteem of friend and foe like.[127]

This is the public record. Behind the scenes matters were more complex, and it is evident that the commemoration presented some difficulties for the Protestant churches. However, it is equally evident that these problems related to the position of the Protestant churches in Northern Ireland, not within the state. In December 1965 Lemass informed Minister for Defence Jim Gibbons that Dr Simms had called to discuss 'certain problems of the Church of Ireland regarding the Easter Commemoration Ceremonies. These arise from the reluctance of certain Six-County[128] Bishops to participate in the religious ceremonies which are contemplated'. Lemass told Gibbons that

> in any publicity regarding Church of Ireland religious functions there should be no reference to a decision by the Bench of Bishops. It will be correct to say that 'the Church of Ireland will arrange religious services' but not correct to say that 'the Bench of Bishops of the Church of Ireland' have decided on these services.[129]

Lemass indicated that it would be desirable to clear all relevant publicity statements with Dr Simms. The Presbyterian church was in a similar position: Right Rev. S.J. Park wrote to Lemass in October 1965 in response to a request that the Presbyterian church hold special services to commemorate the golden jubilee of the Rising. Having expressed his appreciation at the government's wish that Presbyterians should play a part 'on this major anniversary in the history of the Republic', he drew attention to 'the different political views and allegiances' within the church and their wish 'to keep the Church itself above these causes of bitterness and division'. For this reason, the

Presbyterian Church had decided to follow the policy that it adopted in 1963 at the time of the 50th anniversary of the Ulster Covenant, when it decided not to arrange any official ceremonies, but to leave it to individual ministers 'to arrange or share in services as seemed to them to be right and fitting'.[130] The concern shown by the Protestant churches was fully justified. The *Belfast Newsletter* reported that the attitude of the Church of Ireland towards the commemoration was arousing speculation in Northern Ireland. It quoted a columnist in the *Church of Ireland Gazette* who emphasised that

> the Church of Ireland must regard and treat her people, whatever their political difference, as an indissoluble whole...it is clear, therefore, that no action should be contemplated in connection with the forthcoming celebrations which would be interpreted, even by the most tenuous thread of reasoning, as an official alignment of the Church with one side or the other.[131]

When Rex Cathcart, then headmaster of Sandford Park school in Dublin, spoke on the theme of 'Protestants in the New Ireland' as part of a lecture series about the Protestant community in Ireland, organised at the Dublin Central Mission in Abbey Street to commemorate 1916, he suggested that 'the irresponsible celebration of 1916' posed 'a serious threat to the development of co-operation between North and South'. He asked whether it was possible

> to praise brave men and remember that they died for their conception of Ireland and what it ought to be without unnecessarily opening old sores and replenishing old fires?[132]

Cathcart indicated that Protestants in the Republic needed to cultivate a national civic pride in the two traditions, the Anglo-Irish and the Gaelic. To the extent, they did so they would be respected.

> There is a danger which has indeed manifested itself in some quarters, that the commemoration will be used to assert an exclusivist view of Irish nationality. If some of us cry Ireland one and Ireland Gaelic then we undermine the progress in North–South relations in recent years...Many Protestants of the older generation had a very hesitant allegiance to a state which at times had seemed to profess an affiliation to

the Gaelic tradition to the exclusion of the Anglo-Irish. Protestants of the generation born since independence, had given a more wholehearted allegiance to the state.[133]

CULTURAL IDENTITIES

Cathcart's concerns about an exclusivist view of Irish nationality, or exclusive claims to ownership of the tradition of 1916, were well-founded. A secondary complication in the plans for an Easter Sunday parade in Drogheda was the initial decision not to invite the local soccer and rugby clubs to take part. The Irish language newspaper *Inniu* condemned their exclusion, noting that the country was too small and the occasion too important to be putting the national commemoration in jeopardy.[134] Indeed, the decision to exclude the local soccer and rugby teams from the parade appears to have attracted more hostile comment than the refusal to permit the army or FCA to march. The FAI and the IRFU were invited to march in the official Dublin parade on Easter Sunday, and the FAI held a ceremony at Dalymount Park, before the cup final, to pay tribute to the many soccer players who participated in the Rising. Two-hundred survivors of the Rising were in attendance at the cup final, including Eamon de Valera.[135] Nevertheless, it is evident that the GAA tried to claim a special place, as the inspiration for the Rising and a major force in keeping the flame of republican idealism alive. This theme figured prominently in the pageant that the GAA commissioned: *Seachtar Fear, Seacht Lá*.

The GAA's response to the jubilee must be seen in the context of the growing criticism of the ban on its members playing 'foreign games', such as soccer, rugby, cricket and hockey, and fears within the organisation that television and economic prosperity were eroding Ireland's cultural identity and, specifically, the place of the Irish language. It would appear that the GAA felt that its future was threatened by the changing nature of Irish society. (The current strength of the GAA suggests that these fears were unfounded.) At the 1966 GAA Congress, one delegate, Donncha Ó Gallachóbhair, asserted that '[t]he spiritual conquest of Ireland, which Britain for so long failed to achieve, would appear to be almost complete'. For many GAA members, the refusal by Telefís Éireann to televise the pageant *Seachtar Fear, Seacht Lá* confirmed their belief that the core values of Irish nationalism were under threat.[136]

The golden jubilee of the 1916 Rising presented an opportunity to arrest, and perhaps reverse, this process, and to reiterate the paramount role of the GAA in preserving and promoting national culture. GAA president Alf Ó Muirí told delegates to the 1966 Congress that

> [t]o me its [the association's] greatest achievement has been that, in the years immediately before and immediately after '16 it gave to the separatist movement a part of that spiritual backing which made the fight for freedom something more than a mere attempt at changing the form of government and turned it into a people's struggle for National Identity.[137]

This role in fostering the spirit of 1916 was a reason for retaining the ban on 'foreign' games.

> It is very important that we should get across to our youth the reason why we should play Gaelic games, dance Irish dances and sing Irish songs. It is amazing that in 1966 we are more or less apologising to people because of our aims and ideals.[138]

An article by P. Ó Caoimh in the 1966 GAA annual, *Our Games*, set out to rally members to defend the GAA's traditional values.

> And yet by times, one wonders if the Association is sensible of its greatness and power, of its responsibilities and mission. It is essentially a national institution, without external alliances and existing alone for the preservation of race, consciousness and vigour. It has preserved its distinctiveness throughout varied phases of Irish modern history. Its members have never shirked a national issue…But there are circumstances which demand more positive proofs of Gaelicism in times like the present, when native ideals and customs are being derided and the glamour of an alien meretricious civilisation is seen at every turn and in every phase of existence…The recognition of individual duty is a personal privilege. The interpretation of collective loyalty must recognise that weakness, disgrace or treachery in any quarter is a menace to all.[139]

In a piece titled 'An ród seo romhain', Alf Ó Muirí emphasised that

> If the Jubilee of 1916 is to mean anything it must be more
> than a revival of memories. It must be a re-awakening of the
> spirit that inspired the men who were prepared to fight and
> suffer, who were prepared even to die, that the Nation might
> live on.[140]

He identified two 'idealistic crusades' that should be adopted to mark
the jubilee year: a commitment to making Irish the official language of
the GAA, and promoting hurling.[141] Speaking at Croke Park on 23 July
1966, Ó Muirí turned on its head the argument that promoting a more
inclusive cultural identity would bring about a united Ireland:

> the GAA and the Gaelic League and the Irish-Ireland
> Movement generally have preserved a unity, a communion
> of spirit, between the two parts of our nation, if as the Ulster
> Gaelic League has affirmed recently, the Irish distinctiveness
> is departed from; there is little reason for a Northern striving
> for unity.[142]

He attacked Fine Gael's proposal to end compulsory Irish in school
examinations, noting that the party's position 'approaches very near to
the position which prevails in the unrecovered part of our territory'—
where Irish was taught as an optional subject in second-level schools
and was not essential for public-service jobs. He urged GAA members
who had influence in Fine Gael to lobby for a change in the party's
language policy, and he ended his speech by urging

> in the Jubilee Year of 1916, that an all-Party conference…
> could lift the revival of our language from the realms of party
> politics and confirm our determination to make it the general
> means of communication in as short a time as possible.[143]

UNFINISHED BUSINESS

The Irish language

Within the state, the revival of the Irish language was commonly seen
as the most urgent piece of unfinished business that was necessary to
honour the spirit of 1916. This focus on Irish is not surprising, given
the close historic association between the Gaelic League and the

Rising, and specifically Pearse's status as a leading figure in the language movement and as the president of the Irish Republic of 1916.[144] Even more than the GAA, the Irish language movement claimed a paramount role as an inspiration to the 1916 leadership. At a special commemorative mass in Galway cathedral, Rev. P. Ó Laoi, president of Coláiste Einde (an Irish-speaking secondary school in the city) said that

> [i]t would never be known what was owed to the influence of the people of Rosmuc and Connemara in shaping the outlook of Pearse. It was in Rosmuc that he was resolved to liberate Ireland from the influence of an alien culture.[145]

The golden jubilee proved an opportune event for Irish language activists. There was a much more active debate during the 1960s over the future of the Irish language than at any time since the foundation of the state. This was prompted by several factors. During the 1961 general election, Fine Gael, the main opposition party, broke with the traditional cross-party consensus on the Irish language and gave a commitment to end compulsory Irish in the schools. Irish language enthusiasts sought to gain a significant toe-hold in Telefís Éireann with a view to using the station to promote the language aggressively; when this did not transpire they became increasingly fearful that the station would serve to further undermine the Irish language, bombarding the Authority, the director-general and the government with letters and resolutions.

The 'Report of the Commission on the Irish Language' (1964) was followed by a mass letter-writing campaign directed at Seán Lemass, urging the government to strengthen its commitment to reviving the language. With the 1965 White Paper on the Irish Language failing to meet their expectations, the golden jubilee emerged as the next opportunity for renewing the campaign.[146] The jubilee was marked by special Irish language essay competitions and a special jubilee competition of Glór na nGael—to identify the most active Irish-speaking communities.[147] The state's policy towards Irish also surfaced in the 1966 presidential election campaign. The 1 April issue of Irish language newspaper *Inniu* published several articles that were critical of the attitude of the Fine Gael candidate, Tom O'Higgins, towards Irish.[148] After the election, *Inniu* claimed that O'Higgins would have won if he had adopted a more positive attitude towards the Irish language.[149]

In 1966 Tim Pat Coogan stated that 'the Irish language movement is, after Partition, the most controversial subject in Ireland'.[150] On Easter Monday, the 1916 veteran Joseph Clarke laid a wreath at the Cúchulainn statue at the GPO, to inaugurate a hunger strike by 13 members of an organisation called Misneach. At a meeting in the Shelbourne Hotel on the eve of the hunger strike, Misneach explained that the hunger strike was to 'celebrate the death of the Gaeltacht, economic dependence on Britain, Partition and Emigration'. The organisation claimed that Connolly and Pearse did not die

> to have their death celebrated, but that their aims be achieved: neither intellectual, economic nor physical independence has been gained; nor is any conscious effort being made to move in the direction of the Republic; the opposite is the Truth as the White Paper in the Irish language and the recent Free Trade Agreement with England demonstrate.[151]

The Irish writer Máirtín Ó Caidhain said that the hunger strike was an effort to prove

> that there was something left in Ireland which those 'celebrating huxters' could not sell, some little spark that might someday light the road to the Republic which Tone, Pearse, Connolly and countless others died to obtain.[152]

Misneach picketed the GPO, the Garden of Remembrance and Leinster House to publicise its views. Six hunger strikers, all members of a Belfast branch of the Gaelic League, returned there in mid-week to complete the hunger strike.[153] While Misneach's protest was directed at a broad range of socio-economic and cultural issues—all seen as a betrayal of the spirit of 1916, most of the newspaper coverage presented the hunger strike as a protest about the Irish language. In advance publicity for the planned hunger strike, Misneach condemned those in power over the previous 50 years, who had failed to save the Irish language.

They specifically identified some key figures in contemporary Ireland: 'Taoiseach gan Gaeilge' (Lemass had a very limited knowledge of Irish); civil servants judges and students who lacked proficiency in Irish; 'An Gall McCourt' (a reference to the director-general of Telefís Éireann, Kevin McCourt); Dr 'Ireland of the Welcomes' O'Driscoll (Timothy O'Driscoll, director-general of Bord Fáilte, the Irish Tourist

Board); and Dr Electricity (presumably Dr. T Murray, the chairman of the Electricity Supply Board).[154] Misneach's campaign was in tune with language protest movements in Wales, Süd-Tirol, Belgium and elsewhere in Europe. The Department of External Affairs was apprehensive that Welsh, Breton or Flemish language enthusiasts might try to march in the Easter Sunday parade to promote their causes.[155] (Only Irish-based groups and representatives of the Irish overseas were permitted to take part.) The hunger strike received extensive coverage in national newspapers and in the foreign press coverage of the commemoration. Participants claimed that they succeeded in making people think about the language.[156]

Eamon de Valera may well have sympathised in private with this campaign. In his message to the people of Ireland on Easter Sunday, he said that Ireland could not adequately honour the men of 1916 if we did not strive to bring about the Ireland of their desire by reviving the language, because without it Ireland 'would sink into an amorphous cosmopolitanism—without a past or a distinguishable future'. Ensuring that the language would live 'would be the resolve of the men and women of 1916' and of the 'young men and women of 1966'.[157] At the closing ceremony of the commemorations on Easter Saturday he indicated that while much had been achieved since 1916, two major items of unfinished business remained in order to fulfil the aims of 1916: the restoration of the language and a united Ireland. The Irish language was the first priority, and he spoke about it at considerable length, linking love of language with love of country and service to the country.[158]

Partition

Northern Ireland was the second item of 'unfinished business' and de Valera alluded to it twice during Easter Week. Accepting a copy of a statue of Robert Emmet from a group of Irish-American congressmen, de Valera remarked that Emmet's epitaph could not yet be written because

> the Ireland that Emmet wished for, the Ireland that Tone wished for, the Ireland that Lord Edward Fitzgerald wished for and the Ireland in which differences between sections of our people would have been forgotten had not yet arrived.[159]

He went on to express the hope that

with prudence, patience, and time, all these sections that Tone wished to unite in a united Ireland will come together and we will ultimately have the great nation that he looked forward to. It will achieve the august destiny that the men who read the Proclamation in 1916 predicted for it.[160]

He revisited this theme in his speech at the closing ceremony on Saturday evening, when he refused to concede that

the land of the O'Neills, the O'Cathains the McDonnells, the Maguires the McGuinnesses...was going to remain permanently severed from the rest of our country.[161]

Unity would come, as Tone would have wished it to come: by uniting all the people and forgetting past differences and dissensions, and implicitly by consent. He looked forward to the people of the North 'wishing to be with us'. He suggested that the solution would be for Britain to transfer the powers held by Westminster to a representative all-Ireland parliament, with Stormont retaining its existing powers.[162]

It is possible to identify a number of themes in the limited references that were made to partition during the course of the 1916 jubilee. One approach was to celebrate the achievements of an independent Ireland since 1916 (and because of 1916)—and to reiterate that it was right to do so—while lamenting the reality of partition and reaffirming the goal of a united Ireland, but emphasising that it would be achieved by 'consent not coercion'.[163] Asked by a journalist from the *Guardian*, whether the Easter Rising 'and the subsequent struggle for the freedom and unity of Ireland was worth while', Minister for External Affairs Frank Aiken replied that it had been, 'although Ireland has not yet achieved the unity of her national territory'.[164]

At the press conference launching the official programme of commemoration, Seán Lemass was asked if he did not consider the celebrations to be premature in view of the fact that the country was not yet fully united. He replied that what was being commemorated was the 50th anniversary of a very decisive event and he would not like to attribute anything else to the ceremonies.[165] He was more expansive on the topic of partition in an interview for a special Irish supplement of *The Statist*. He began by expressing a wish

to abolish the memory of past dissensions, to strengthen contacts and promote co-operation between the two areas into which the country is divided.[166]

When asked whether political action would be needed to achieve Irish unity, and what role he envisaged for the British government, Lemass responded that partition was essentially 'a political arrangement'; any solution would require political action. Reunification was a matter for Irishmen in Ireland, but he expressed a wish

> to see a clear statement by British political leaders that there is no British interest in maintaining Partition.[167]

The aspect of Ulster unionism that featured most prominently during the 1966 jubilee was the role of Ulster's opposition to Home Rule and the formation of the Ulster Volunteers in the formation of the Irish Volunteers and ultimately the 1916 Rising. This was the story told in Tomás Mac Anna's pageant, *Aiséirí*, and the pageant staged in St Louis Convent, Monaghan, where students wore orange collars and sashes loaned by the local Orange Lodge, including one that had belonged to Edward Carson. When he addressed the UCD Law Society on the motion 'That this house would not celebrate 1916', Ernest Blythe, one of the few Ulster protestants who was a veteran of the struggle for independence, suggested that the Easter Sunday parade should be led by a detachment of former members of the Ulster Volunteers. He believed that

> the development of the agitation proved to be good thing for the country, because had it not been for Carson and the Ulster Volunteers, we would not have had the Rising.[168]

Former Fine Gael leader James Dillon (son of the Irish Parliamentary Party MP John Dillon) was very much in a minority when he suggested that the Rising might have resulted in partition. He told the Irish Club in London that

> whether the final act of the drama of the indomitable Irishry was served by the bloodshed of 1916, 1919 to 1921 and subsequent years—in civil war and all that flowed from it— only history can justly establish...One fact remains. When the Irish Party laid down its weapons, Ireland was known to history and to the world as an Ireland of 32 counties and a nation from the centre to the sea...Until it is that again, the story will remain unfinished, and whoever doubts this fact does so at his peril wherever the influence of the indomitable Irishry is felt throughout the world.[169]

On another occasion, he expressed the view that to hope that 'our people would accept the government of Northern Ireland as a permanent constitutional and fully legitimate government is illusory— de facto, "yes", de jure, "no"'.[170]

Lemass and his government were determined that the 1916 jubilee would not undermine the improved relations with the government of Northern Ireland, or with Britain. In reply to a Dáil question asking why there was no government participation in any commemorations in Northern Ireland, Lemass replied that Dublin was the scene of the principal official ceremonies, but all requests for a government presence at ceremonies outside Dublin had been met. This would suggest that no government representatives were invited to attend events in Northern Ireland.[171]

While the Irish government adopted a tolerant attitude towards the Golden Jubilee Commemoration Committee (chaired by Eamonn MacThomáis), this tolerance extended only within the state. When the committee tried to to hire a special train to travel to Belfast for a parade to the Republican Plot at Milltown cemetery on 17 April, CIÉ general manager Frank Lemass (brother of the taoiseach), sought advice as to the appropriate response.[172] The Gardaí and the RUC both advised against providing a train; the Minister for Justice suggested that the trip to Belfast was 'for IRA organisational purposes'; labelling the tickets 'Freedom Train 1966' would give rise to feelings of resentment in Belfast. The government advised CIÉ not to provide a train, but asked that the company did not make it known that it had sought the government's advice on the matter.[173]

In March, P.P. O'Reilly, head of news in Telefís Éireann, travelled to Belfast to collect some first-hand information from his contacts in the press on what they expected to happen at Easter. In his monthly report to the Broadcasting Authority, he noted that

> [t]o my considerable surprise I had a long conversation with the Prime Minister Capt. O'Neill, certain officials, the Inspector-General of the RUC and his two main deputies.[174]

O'Reilly had not sought any of these meeting; they were arranged when it became known that he was in Belfast. He reported that they 'produced for me a lot of extremely useful information and impressions', but unfortunately he did not go into detail.[175] This would suggest that O'Neill wished to keep one of the most influential Dublin media organisations on side for the commemoration. The Sinn Féin newspaper, the *United Irishman*, accused Leinster House of 'colluding in building up a sense of national crisis', fomenting an IRA 'scare'[176] around the commemoration; but the evidence suggests, rather, that the government's strategy was to keep cool and, if anything, to underplay possible threats.

The announcement by O'Neill's government of a ban on all northbound rail traffic from the evening of Saturday 16 April to the evening of Sunday 17 April, a possible ban on all traffic on the A1 (the main route from Dublin to Belfast) and the intention to subject all those travelling by road to police scrutiny, came as a surprise to the Dublin authorities and they were given no advance notice. Indeed on 13 April, what Peter Berry, secretary of the Department of Justice, described as 'confidential talks…at high police level' took place, and the RUC had requested that the Gardaí would inform them of the numbers travelling to Belfast by train on the morning of 17 April. Berry claimed that the meeting did not throw up any specific information that would have justified closing the border.[177] On the evening of 16 April, O'Neill's private secretary Jim Malley telephoned T.K. Whittaker, secretary of the Department of Finance, and explained that the Northern Ireland authorities had thought it better not to inform the Dublin government of this decision in advance, 'in order to save us embarrassment in the matter'.[178] In a similar spirit, the Irish authorities decided not to invoke the cross-border rail agreement, which gave CIÉ the right to run trains on the Northern Ireland lines, but to treat the cancellation as a political event. The official response was 'no comment', with the added statement that

> the Government were very pleased that the Nationalists in the North had already celebrated the Golden Jubilee of Easter Week in a fitting and appropriate manner on Easter Sunday last.[179]

The decision to seal the border, and the Northern Ireland government's fears of IRA violence, figured prominently in the coverage of the jubilee by the foreign press. The explosion (carried out by an IRA splinter group) that partly destroyed Dublin's Nelson Pillar in March 1966[180] attracted widespread international coverage. *Newsweek* reported that

> fanatic advocates of a united Ireland had already used the approaching 50th anniversary of the 1916 rising as an excuse to indulge in a rash of small bombings;[181]

however, according to the report, the Irish authorities were adopting a low-key approach to the explosion because there was no wish to have a lot of IRA men in prison for the commemoration.

The Irish embassy in London expressed some trepidation about an article in the *Daily Telegraph* magazine by Irish journalist Tim Pat Coogan, which appeared less than a week before the jubilee. Titled 'The I.R.A. fights on', it featured photographs of men undergoing arms training in the countryside and shots of arms caches. Coogan claimed that 'in the middle of a sane well-ordered democracy' there were up to 2,000 men 'who accept Clausewitz's dictum that war is just politics by other means'; the recent blowing up of Nelson's pillar had made it clear 'that the IRA time was here again'.[182] Coogan reported that the guard on Dáil Éireann had recently been issued with machine guns, and he referred to the 'fear, however remote' that a lapse in discipline by an IRA man might result in

> some desperate action—such as machine-gunning the Northern or Southern Irish cabinet.
>
> For republicans the significance of the Easter Rising is akin to that of the Resurrection for Christians, with the difference that politically some members of the movement may feel it incumbent on them as the true inheritors of 1916, to make the symbolism of the coming Easter redolent not of life but of death.[183]

AMERICAN AND BRITISH MEDIA COVERAGE OF THE COMMEMORATIONS

In *Ireland since the Rising*, Coogan reported that his IRA sources had informed him that the 50th anniversary of the Rising 'will be made memorable by a series of demonstrations'.[184] The threat of IRA action against Northern Ireland featured prominently in US coverage of Easter Week 1966, to the extent that it reads like a different event to the one described in the Irish newspapers. The *New York Times* headline on Friday, 8 April 1966, with a Belfast by-line was 'Northern Ireland is fearful of Easter disorders'. It reported that Northern Ireland security forces were on alert; there were fears of disorder along the Border. The follow-up story from Dublin, 'Fears that the commemoration might lead to violence' opened:

Religious and patriotic feelings, political tensions and the fear of violence intermingled here tonight on the eve of the 50th anniversary of the Easter Rising...for a minority, including the political organization, Sinn Fein, and its military wing, the Irish Republican Army, tomorrow is regarded as the funeral ceremony of the Republic proclaimed 50 years ago...They are embittered because this is a republic of only 26 counties, while six counties in the North remain under British control. They are also unhappy because the republic has not succeeded in reviving the Irish language.[185]

The final paragraph of the article wrote about Ireland's promising economic growth, the fall in emigration and the recently signed free-trade agreement with Britain. The *New York Times* also carried a long interview with Sinn Féin leader Tomás MacGiolla under the heading 'Irish leader backs violence'. Its opening paragraph read:

The President of the Sinn Féin party, Thomas [sic] MacGiolla, today endorsed violence as the only way to achieve his party's aims—the expulsion of the British from Northern Ireland and the unification of the North and South.[186]

The Irish embassy in Washington concluded that

[t]he *New York Times* correspondent Dana Adams Schmidt, when he was not merely factual, seems to have been most impressed by the sporadic acts of violence which the celebration of the Jubilee involved.[187]

The *Boston Globe* carried a Reuters' story under the headline 'Ireland jittery of observance of Easter Rebellion jubilee'. This story claimed that

Nelson's fate and some ominous rumblings from the dissident Republican underground threaten violent Easter protests against the partitioning of six counties of Irish territory.[188]

It went on to refer to 'the midget Irish Republic Army; the dynamiting of an arch near Skibbereen erected to commemorate Nelson; reinforcement of the border; a watch on suspect extremists and on memorials especially the Wellington monument in the Phoenix Park'.[189] Brendan Malin reported in the *Globe* on the rival parades in Tralee.[190] The *Boston Herald's* headline on 17 April was 'Belfast braces for violence'—the story was by Associated Press correspondent Godfrey Anderson. He reported that

> extremist activity continued in southern Ireland Saturday with explosions reported from Douglas a suburb of Cork. It appeared that an attempt had been made to blow up electricity poles. In County Kilkenny an explosion followed by five shots shook the village of Inistioge during a dance in a local hall which preceded a IRA parade. This is the area where Richard Behal, a 30-year old IRA leader who recently escaped from Limerick jail is believed to be hiding.[191]

The *Washington Post* reported on a bomb at Kilmacow, Co Waterford, with the headline 'Extremists use bombs in Ireland'.[192] The *Boston Herald* headline on the same story, by Donal O'Higgins, was 'Machine Gun rakes village. Irish extremists bomb Kilmacow'.[193] Most US newspapers also covered the Misneach hunger strike and Joe Clarke's wreath-laying at the GPO. Although the coverage in the *Washington Post* opened with the headline 'Ireland nervously celebrates 50th anniversary of uprising', and the story went on to state:

> [t]he Irish Republic today began the biggest celebration in its history with a perfusion of enthusiasm and just a slight trace of goose flesh...Rumours persist that the illegal Irish Republican Army may contribute an unwelcome noisy stunt to the commemorations,[194]

the Irish Embassy regarded *Post* journalist Karl Meyer's articles as the best US coverage of the jubilee. Meyer featured an interview with Seán MacEntee, in which the latter spoke positively about the improvements in housing and economic circumstances and his disappointment over partition. Although Meyer mentioned the threat of IRA violence in this piece, he ended on an upbeat note:

> Still, the surprising aspect of Ireland after 50 years is not the sporadic violence but the impressive stability of its republican government.[195]

An editorial in the *Washington Post* contrasted the Irish war of independence with modern anti-colonial guerilla wars, and ended

[t]he Republic of Ireland is prospering, and there is now hope that the animosity that separates the northern and southern parts of the island will eventually disappear.[196]

While Irish-American groups also welcomed the prosperity and stability of the Irish state, a number of them offered at least token support for a more traditional anti-partition policy, and for the IRA. In 1964 the Freedom for Ireland Committee of the Ancient Order of Hibernians reported that:

[s]ince the Republic of Ireland appears to have taken the position to discourage and play down the question of Partition as contended by the IRA and other patriotic groups and individuals, there has been since 1962[197] very little happening that we as American citizens could support, especially since the Irish Republic Government has taken no public stand on these matters.

The Committee's study of previous correspondence on Partition with the Republic of Ireland's Heads of State [sic] representing all major phases of Irish political thought seems to have been limited to a polite acknowledgement of our offer to support the government in any fight that they would make to regain the six northeast counties and the complete sovereignty of Ireland.[198]

When Lemass accepted an invitation in 1963 to address a dinner organised by the Irish Fellowship Club in Chicago (the most exclusive Irish Society in that city, which was controlled by Mayor Richard Daley), the consul-general, Seán Ó hÉideáin, advised that:

[p]artition and the need for territorial re-unification should be mentioned, at least briefly. Such a mention is important because as Taoiseach Mr. Lemass will represent the integral Irish tradition. Moreover, any old IRA men and Old Clan na Gael men present, on reading the speech afterwards will expect it and others will be interested to hear it as the *Time* Magazine article,[199] which so many read was a bit out of focus on the non-economic side, and on pre-1959 history. Moreover there is a numerically small so-called Clan na Gael group in Chicago who if the government policy on a peaceful solution of Partition is not publicized appropriately

may fill the vacuum with violent and non-violent words with possible grave results in deeds in perhaps a year or two'.[200]

The 1966 commemoration afforded Irish diplomats the opportunity to inform Irish-America about current government thinking on a range of issues, including Northern Ireland. All Irish missions overseas were instructed to contact Irish societies and to keep them informed about the commemoration;[201] but the gulf between the Irish state and some sections of Irish-America is indicated by the fact that the Irish consul-general in New York reported that he had attended the special Mass to commemorate 1916 at the Paulist Church of St John the Apostle, but had absented himself from the memorial parade organised by the Associated Irish Societies, where various IRA veterans were given a prominent role, and the dinner hosted by the Ancient Order of Hibernians.[202]

Shortly before the jubilee Brian Ua Ceallaigh, who had followed Ó hÉideáin as the Irish consul-general in Chicago, asked the Washington embassy 'whether there is anything in particular about which I should be warned or advised'. His question was undoubtedly prompted by the fact that he would be sharing the platform at a breakfast to commemorate the jubilee with Congressman Robert Sweeney from Ohio, who had recently proposed a motion in the US Congress welcoming the destruction of Nelson's Pillar. Congressman Sweeney believed that such monuments of an imperialist past should be forgotten, especially given the improving relations between Britain and Ireland. He went on to speak about reunification of Ireland, and the warnings from the Nelson's Pillar bomb that if freedom were not achieved by peaceful means men would turn to violence. The embassy described Sweeney as 'an amiable, if somewhat over-enthusiastic well-wisher of ours'.[203] Ua Ceallaigh also enclosed a copy of a recent speech that he had given to the Federation of Irish Clubs in Chicago—presumably as part of the commemoration of the Rising—asking whether there was any objection to it being published. The speech opened with a theme that echoed many official speeches: the primary task facing Ireland was economic development,

> so that continued progress can be made towards the restoration of national unity through peace and friendship and towards the restoration of our Gaelic culture. Much progress has been reported in these respects and this anniversary year of 1916 has given us a valuable fillip by reminding us of the past so that we can better plan the road

before us. Good planning ahead involves accurate information. That, in turn, means facing the facts.[204]

The facts that Ua Ceallaigh addressed concerned partition. He attacked the manner in which some Irish societies misrepresented these facts, highlighting one unnamed speaker who had said on radio the previous day, that there was

> no historical reason for the partition of Ireland. No one dissented. No one faced the facts. It is to be regretted that Irish radio program and newspaper columnists in America frequently let pass misinformation which will obviously not help us achieve the goals of our movement…
>
> That most vital recent statement of a British foreign [sic] Secretary to the effect that Britain now thinks the solution of partition is a matter for the Irish people themselves has hardly been noticed here, nor have the various statements of the present British Prime Minister in regard to Ireland. One hears nothing about the growing friendship between the different sections of the community in the Six Counties, paralleling the great Ecumenical movement. No one explains here why the three Nationalist seats out of twelve in the British Parliament of a decade ago have dwindled to none at all or to one, as in the election of last year. Recent petrol bomb outrages in Dublin and Belfast and extremist threats to the safety of your Military Attaché in Dublin have been ignored.[205]

The AOH used the jubilee to reiterate its opposition to partition. A report of the Foreign Relations Committee presented by Fr O'Callaghan at the 1966 AOH convention concluded,

> as we celebrate the Fiftieth Celebration of Ireland's heroic Easter we reaffirm our determination to drive England out of Ireland, whose purpose is to end the Partition of Ireland and again with Davis we say 'A Nation Once Again' (recited to standing applause). [206]

An editorial in the *National Hibernian Digest*, headed 'Easter 1916' told readers that

> Hibernians, everywhere, should remember that the task undertaken in Easter 1916 of winning full freedom for all 32 Counties of Ireland is still unfinished.[207]

An article outlining the official programme in Dublin ended,

> [t]his Ireland however has still the unfinished task…Until England gets its armed forces out of these Six Counties, the Irish Nation for which the Easter Week Patriots of 1916 fought and died for is still not a free nation.[208]

When the Dublin ceremonies failed to give the appropriate message, it would appear that some members of the AOH embellished the record. A report on the Easter Week ceremonies in Dublin by AOH president Judge Comerford—a 1916 veteran—told readers that Eamon de Valera spoke outside the GPO on Easter Sunday:

> His words dramatically reaffirmed the ideals of 1916 and purposefully proclaimed the necessity of having a unified Ireland of 32 Counties and of establishing one government for all the people of all of Ireland. As his speech ended, a soldier hoisted the flag.[209]

Comerford's report of the closing ceremony stated that

> [a]ll listened intently as President de Valera made a special appeal to all Irish men and women in North-East Ireland, which is the 6 Counties behind the wall of Partition, to join with their sisters and brothers living in the other 26 counties and remove partition and he urged them to form a unified Irish Nation and to elect one government for all the people of Ireland, to bring the six counties into a unified Ireland without bloodshed in 1966.[210]

But de Valera did not deliver a speech at the GPO on Easter Sunday; indeed there were no speeches on that occasion. While Comerford's account of de Valera's speech at the closing ceremony cannot be described as wholly inaccurate, he presented a more traditional anti-partition message than the transcript of the speech would suggest. (See page 56 above.)

While Irish officials expressed some concern at how the British media would present the commemoration of the Rising—this was one of the reasons for commissioning Morrison's film[211]—the overall coverage reflected a closer relationship between the British and Irish governments. Britain returned the green flag that flew over the GPO during Easter Week, which had been held by the Imperial War Museum; although, in deference to the wishes of the British ambassador—who had been criticised for walking behind Casement's coffin and attending the memorial Mass, the hand-over did not take place in a public ceremony.[212] The personalities and photographic images of the Rising provided good copy for the new weekend newspaper supplements. The cover of the *Sunday Times* magazine featured a framed photograph of Pearse and his revolver. It described Pearse as a poet, schoolmaster and martyr. The supplement reproduced the photographs and names of 16 leaders: the 14 who were executed in Dublin plus Eamon de Valera and Constance Markievicz (in formal evening dress with a tiara), and a copy of the proclamation. The Irish embassy in London described the photographs as 'interesting'. The embassy was more critical of an article in the supplement by Stephen Fay, headed 'Why the rebellion failed', which it dismissed as 'clumsy and lacking in sensitivity'. Officials were particularly exercised by the caption on a photograph, which referred to 'the murder of a fellow Irishman' (presumably by the rebels) at a barricade in St Stephen's Green.[213] They were much more favourable about coverage by Ian Hamilton, described as 'of Scottish nationalist background, which makes him particularly sensitive on the question of Irish nationality'.

Hamilton's piece in the *Telegraph*, titled 'The "heroes"—50 years later' combined a brief history of the Rising, and interviews with four survivors: de Valera, Lemass, former President Seán T. O'Kelly, and Professor Liam O Briain. Each was asked 'What do they think of their creation?' Hamilton emphasised that the Irish people were realists, not sentimental dreamers; Irish attitudes had shifted over the past 50 years. He dismissed suggestions that the Irish people were immersed in 'an orgy of nostalgic romanticism'; indeed, he reiterated that the veterans that he met were 'more alive to the Ireland of today than that of 50 years ago'. O'Kelly and O Briain stressed the importance of restoring the Irish language, and both were apprehensive about the factors that were contending against re-establishing an Irish Ireland. Hamilton described de Valera's vision as utopian but 'worthy of respect': a 'wish to see the nation guided by its native humanity and decency'; whereas Lemass aspired to membership of the EEC and building an understanding with the 'true-blue protestant rulers of the Six Counties'.[214] One official in the Irish embassy in London claimed that Hamilton wished

> to demonstrate as vividly as he can that the present reasonable state of Anglo-Irish relations stems directly from 'that self-sacrificial gesture' and so to indicate that the people

on this side of the Irish Sea have as much reason as those on
the other to honour the memory of the men killed during
the action or executed after it,[215]

a rather heroic task! The *Guardian* profiled Frank Aiken, again with a
focus on the present. Aiken concluded that the Rising had been
worthwhile, although Ireland had not yet achieved unity, 'our ancient
nation was saved from the brink of extinction'. He linked the sacrifice
of the men of 1916 with the 'sacrifice of all men who died believing
they fought for the freedom and dignity of man', and he expressed the
hope that such sacrifices would yet 'bear fruit for the children of every
colour, class or creed'.[216]

The *Daily Express*, a newspaper not normally regarded as favourable
to Ireland, featured a series of five articles on the Rising under the
heading, 'Six days that changed history' by Donald Seaman. The
coverage played up the colourful aspects of the story:

> One was tailor-made for the Hollywood films of today. Her
> name was Constance Georgina Countess Markievicz...She
> was a strapping redhead and won the nickname, Red
> Countess...a magnificent horsewomen: she rode point to
> point and she could handle a coach and four. She was a
> suffragette. She was also a crack shot with the heavy Mauser
> revolver that she strapped to her slim waist. What a cracker!
> She went to war in a gorgeous, high-necked, tight-fitting,
> bottle green uniform made to her own design. Over it she
> wore a matching green hat topped with a great green feather
> that clashed with her flowing auburn hair. At the time of the
> rising she was a sensational 42.[217]

> Joseph Plunkett died in a setting no film writer could better.[218]

The final article was highly critical of the British army: 'The British
Army command in Ireland won no laurels before, during, or after the
Easter Rebellion it crushed in six days...'. Seaman described the secret
trials of the leaders, and the executions, as 'the worst blunders ever made
by any Administration, civil or military, in Ireland since Cromwell's
day'. The article concluded:

> [w]e are friends again now. Principally because of that
> preposterous, foolish, bungled, costly, brave Easter Rebellion
> of 1916.[219]

Such coverage was very much in line with the wishes of both the London and Dublin governments; both were determined to focus on the present and the future, rather than the past. In October 1965 the British ambassador, Sir Geoffrey Tory, asked Hugh McCann, secretary of the Department of External Affairs, about 'the character' of the forthcoming commemoration of the 1916 Rising, 'in particular, whether it would be oriented towards the future or a re-enactment of the past'. McCann referred the ambassador to Lemass's speech at the dinner honouring P.J. Burke,[220] and reassured him that the commemoration would be 'a forward-looking occasion without any attempt to re-open old wounds'.[221] On 12 April the Irish ambassador in London, Paul Keating, reported that

> [t]he overall reaction in the foreign press to date is quite good and we stand to gain enormous publicity abroad through coverage of the celebrations. An exception of course, was Tim Pat Coogan's article and photographs on the IRA in this week's *Daily Telegraph Supplement*. He was contacted about his proposed article by an officer of the Department who knows him but he did not give much change and said that his article had already been sent in. Unless something particularly shocking is published we will not be likely to take any action.[222]

Irish diplomats were equally, if not more, sensitive about press stories that questioned official images of prosperity and modernity. 'Old shadows still walk Dublin', by Jimmy Breslin, was another article that prompted protests. Breslin described tenements in Sheriff Street, a short distance from the GPO, and suggested that not much had changed since Easter 1916 when tenement dwellers had looted the shops in O'Connell Street. He described children still living in tenement flats with overflowing garbage cans inside the front doors and no baths, and he drew analogies between the looting of O'Connell Street stores and recent riots in Watts in Los Angeles. Breslin's article was widely syndicated throughout North America, prompting several readers to protest to the Irish embassy in Ottawa, and even to Lemass. The Irish ambassador to Canada judged the piece to be 'hostile and misleading and...little more than a cheap attempt to hold the 1916 Commemoration ceremonies up to ridicule'.[223] William Stoneham of the *Chicago Daily News* complained that many places associated with the Rising were hard to locate; some had been torn down. He pointed out that Richmond Barracks, 'Dublin has been converted into a slum whose numerous kids and poorly dressed women-folk look miserably poverty-stricken, even by Dublin's notorious standards'.[224]

'Ireland fifty years after "The Troubles"', a feature in *Look* magazine, suggested that the story of the Rising began in 1171 when Henry II arrived in Waterford: 'This was the first attempt by the English to conquer Ireland, a task they never quite accomplished. But for nearly 800 years they tried'.[225] The writer of the feature, John Vachon, claimed that,

> [t]he twentieth century is seeping in slowly. There are smokestacks, cocktail lounges, great jet-busy airports, glass brick and even urban renewal. But it is easy to travel the country and never see them at all. More than most places in the world, Ireland has kept the look of 50 years ago, sometimes that of 800 years ago.[226]

The Irish journalist Lionel Fleming broadcast a piece on the fiftieth anniversary of the Rising, as part of the 'From our own correspondent' series on the BBC Home Service, where he told his audience, that 'for more than 700 years a section of it was in a state of almost constant revolt. Rebellion after rebellion was mounted and always suppressed'.[227]

In the *New Statesman* on 8 April, the Belfast writer W.R. Rogers claimed that the Irish were so attached to their tragic history and to the 1916 Rising and its heroes that they were unable to embrace the modern world.

> The more we try, the more memories of old Ireland return to us. We are like the Australian aborigine who, presented with a new boomerang, spent the rest of his life trying to throw his old boomerang away. The only thing to do is to drop it…[228]

Such articles indicate that the government's wish to use the jubilee to present an image of Ireland as a modern, prosperous state was at best partly successful.

CONCLUSION

It is not surprising that the jubilee did not live up to all the expectations. International interest in the Morrison film proved less than anticipated.

Irish exiles were slow to buy copies of *Cuimhneachán*, the souvenir publication produced later in 1966, perhaps because it did not cover jubilee events outside Ireland. Most embassies found themselves with large quantities of unwanted stock.[229] *Hibernia* claimed that

> a lot of what came out of the Jubilee fortnight was dull and uninteresting...there was an element of boredom and fatigue in the official celebrations.[230]

A strike by bank officials in the summer of 1966 and a lengthy protest by farmers in the autumn and winter suggest that Lemass's hope that the Irish people would reinterpret the spirit of 1916 as a call to sacrifice self-interest to the national interest in order to promote economic and social development was not fulfilled. The assertion made by the *Cork Examiner* that the jubilee had

> precipitated an open season for critics of all kinds. Some are home based, some are repatriates and others are temporary soujourners; but what they all have in common is a distaste of our institutions, lay and clerical, which impels them to disparage and condemn in most forthright terms[231]

is probably excessive; but it does suggest that the jubilee was not immune to the spirit of the 1960s—which was above all a decade of protest. An editorial in the *Wicklow People* in December 1966, which reflected on the jubilee, suggested that membership of the commemoration committee should have been restricted to those who were under 40 years of age. It expressed the hope that the 1967 centenary of the Fenian Rising would be

> commemorated in a more balanced way, and the younger generation may not come to feel that it is being over-played [sic]; at least we shall have no survivors this time.[232]

'Ireland in 1966 has come of age'. This is in many ways the most accurate summary of the official editorial line during the commemoration, and it is also an interpretation that was broadly accepted within Irish society. Tom Hennessy suggested that 'overall the Republic was at ease' with the 1966 jubilee.[233] Yet there were undoubtedly some discordances amid this sense of ease. Some elements of the 1916 story were not given adequate treatment—such as the thousands of Irishmen, many of them committed nationalists, who fought and died in Flanders, not in the GPO. Lemass did refer to them on at least one occasion, but when the *Evening Standard* published a piece by 'Arran', which claimed that

> [t]here is an Irish military cemetery at Thiepval in France for those who fell in the First World War. How much more glorious to lie there in that plot 'that is forever Ireland' than in the rebels' new burial ground in Arbourhill [sic],

it prompted complaints from some Irish residents in Britain, and demands that the embassy ask for a retraction. Officials in the Irish embassy dismissed the author as 'a notorious crank'.[234]

Both responses indicate an excess sensitivity on this issue. The story of Irishmen who fought in the Great War was largely a matter of history, and of giving recognition to the survivors, whereas the place of the IRA in the Ireland of 1966 had more contemporary relevance. There is a decided dichotomy between the official commemoration, with its emphasis on the future rather than the past; the playing down of violence and of partition; and some of the realities. The coverage of bombings and other acts of violence in the US papers was undoubtedly disproportionate—most of the events passed off without incident—indeed remarkably so. Most IRA-related incidents logged during Easter week involved the sale of Easter lilies without permits; several incidents reported in US newspapers do not figure on the Garda records.[235] However, it is equally evident that there were significant pockets of men and women in Kiltyclogher, Tralee, Waterford and elsewhere, who had not yet fully subscribed to the legitimacy of the Irish state and the right of its army and Gardaí to march in official parades. The policy of the government was to play down their existence. In May 1966 the Irish ambassador in London, Geoffrey Keating, wrote to a colleague in Dublin, and explained that

> we have on occasions been somewhat at a loss to reply to journalists' questions about 'I.R.A. activity', since they claim to be briefed by knowledgeable people in Ireland in a way that would appear at variance with the policy we in the Embassy normally would have about this group, that is to say we would tend, in normal circumstances, to play down their importance completely and to suggest that they

constitute no significant element of public opinion in Ireland and very little danger to the maintenance of good relations between Britain and Ireland. If we are mistaken in this view, we should be glad if the matter could be clarified.[236]

The decision to ban the playing of rebel songs about the 1916 period on sponsored programmes on Radio Éireann (I presume that they were also prohibited on other radio programmes) is further evidence of the government's wish to play down images of popular support for the physical force tradition, even of a retrospective variety. Irish record companies were very disgruntled at this restriction, since at least 14 records were cut specifically to tie in with the jubilee, including 'The Black and Tan gun', and a ballad by the popular group 'The Dubliners' to celebrate the destruction of Nelson's Pillar.[237] Bernadine Truden reported that during Easter Week everyone in Dublin was singing the no. 1 record—Dominic Behan's ballad 'The sea oh the sea...Long may it flow between England and me'.[238]

Did the 1966 jubilee revive the IRA? In December 1966 the Gardaí concluded that 'generally speaking, public interest and support for the IRA organisation's policy and activities appear to be of little consequence at the moment'; financial support from the USA was 'very small'. They estimated that in October 1966 the IRA had 1,039 members, compared with 923 in December 1965, but it would be simplistic to suggest that the growth was due to the jubilee. The only mention of 1966 as an aid to recruitment in the material captured in October 1966 relates to Cumann na mBan. A circular issued in March 1966 expressed the hope that tributes played to the role of Cumann na mBan during 1916 'will help to create a receptive atmosphere' for recruiting new members. Otherwise, the documents captured suggest that the IRA saw the greatest potential for recruitment in contemporary issues, such as the Anglo-Irish trade agreement and the closer economic links with Britain that it implied; housing shortages, agitation over ground rents; the decline of the West; the Irish language; trade union issues; and the farmers' protest. This would suggest that in 1966 the IRA shared one thing in common with Seán Lemass: both were more interested in the present and the future than in the past.[239]

APPENDIX I

Commemorative events by county

Antrim	4	Leitrim	4
Armagh	2	Limerick	8
Carlow	2	Longford	5
Cavan	4	Louth	4
Clare	8	Mayo	15
Cork	34	Meath	2
Derry	4	Monaghan	7
Donegal	5	Offaly	7
Down	2	Roscommon	2
Dublin County*	11	Sligo	4
Fermanagh	3	Tipperary	12
Galway	16	Tyrone	6
Kerry	11	Waterford	7
Kildare	14	Westmeath	4
Kilkenny	8	Wexford	4
Laois	4	Wicklow	7

* *Does not include the events in Dublin city.*

Appendix II

History Department, Boston Public Library
The Easter Rising, Dublin 1916
A selected reading list

General:

Conor Cruise O'Brien, *The shaping of modern Ireland*
Dorothy MacArdle, *The Irish Republic*
Chalres C. Tansill, *America and the fight for Irish freedom*

The Easter Rising:

Malachy F. Caulfield *Easter Rebellion*
Brian O'Neill, *Easter Week*
Desmond Ryan, *The Rising*

The War:

Tom Barry, *Guerrilla days in Ireland*
Richard Bennett, *The Black and Tans*
Dan Breen, *My fight for Irish freedom Dublin's fighting story 1913–1921*
Richard M. Fox, *The history of the Irish Citizen Army*
Frank Gallagher, *The four glorious years* (by David Hogan, pseudo)
John J. Horgan, *Parnell to Pearse*
Edgar Holt, *Protest in arms*
         Kerry's fighting story 1916–1921
         Limerick's fighting story 1916–1921
John McCann, *War by the Irish*
Desmond Ryan, *Seán Treacy and the third Tipperary brigade*

The participants:

Robert Briscoe, *For the life of me*
P. Colum, *Life of Arthur Griffith*
J. Devoy, *Devoy's post bag 1871–1928*, 2 vols
C. Desmond Greaves, *The life and times of James Connolly*

Emmet J. Larkin, *James Larkin*
M.J. MacManus, *Eamon de Valera*
Robt. Monteith, *Casement's last adventure*
M. O'Donovan, *An only child* (by Frank O'Connor)
P.H. Pearse, *Political writings and speeches*

Fiction:

M. Farrell, *Thy tears might cease*
W. Macken, *The scorching wind*
L. O'Flaherty, *The Informer*
L. O'Flaherty *Insurrection*
Michael Sandys, *Cruel Easter*

NOTES

[1] *Irish Times*, leader, 18 March 1966.

[2] Department of External Affairs, *Cuimhneachán: 1916–1966, Commemoration: a record of Ireland's commemoration of 1916* (Dublin, 1966).

[3] National Archives Ireland, Department of the Taoiseach (hereafter cited as NAI DT), 97/6/160, 'Rising Commemorations' (undated).

[4] *Irish Press*, 13 April 1966.

[5] NAI DT 97/6/160, 'Rising Commemorations'; report from Commemoration Committee.

[6] NAI DT 97/6/163, 'Rising Commemorations', arrangements for public parade; Boston College, Burns Library, Eire Society of Boston, Administrative Files, Box 14, 1916 Easter Rising Anniversary.

[7] UCD Archives (hereafter cited as UCDA), de Valera papers, P 150/3384, 'Croke Park' (undated). *Seachtar Fear, Seacht Lá*, programme notes.

[8] UCDA, de Valera papers, P 150/3400 'Mallow pageant' (undated).

[9] *Aiséirí*, unpublished script.

[10] *Kerryman*, 26 March 1966.

[11] *Irish Independent*, 12 April 1966.

[12] *Irish Press*, 5 March 1966.

[13] *Irish Press*, 2 February; 5, 8 and 12 July; 14 November 1966.

[14] K.C. McCourt, 'Broadcasting: a community service', in *Administration* 15 (3), (Autumn 1967), 173–81: 174; Alacoque Kealy, *Irish radio data: 1926–80* (Dublin, 1981), 1–16.

[15] Michael Quigley, *Pictorial record: centenary of Thomas Davis and Young Ireland 1845–1945* (Dublin, 1945).

[16] Yvonne Whelan, *Reinventing modern Dublin: streetscape, iconography and the politics of identity* (Dublin, 2003), 164.

[17] UCDA, de Valera papers, P 150 3376, 'Garden of Remembrance' (date unspecified).

[18] NAI DT S13610/D62, Thomas Davis memorial.

[19] NAI DT S6521D/63, 'Kilmainham Gaol report', Department of the Taoiseach, 5 April 1960.

[20] NAI DT S9815E/62, 'Easter Week Commemorations', 7 June 1962.

[21] UCDA, Fianna Fáil archives, P 176/348, 9 November 1964.

[22] NAI DT 97/6/157, 'Rising Commemorations', 28 January 1965.

[23] Casement was executed and buried in Pentonville Prison for his part in the Rising. The British government returned his remains to Ireland in February 1965. NAI DT, 96/6/190, 'Roger Casement's remains'.

[24] M.E. Daly, 'Nationalism, sentiment and economics; relations between Ireland and Irish America in the postwar years', *Éire-Ireland*, Special issue:

Irish America, xxxvii: I and II (Spring/Summer 2002), 74–92: 78–82. An Tóstal was an annual pageant of singing, dancing, recitations and staged scenes from Irish political history; it was inaugurated in 1953.
25 NAI, Department of External Affairs (hereafter cited as NAI DEA) 610/20/5, 'Embassies', Department of External Affairs to all Missions, January 1966, Madrid I.C. 3/9.
26 NAI DEA, 2000/14/72, Appeal to Irish abroad to come to Ireland for the ceremonies, 28 July 1965.
27 Boston College, Burns Library, Eire Society of Boston, Box 11.
28 Boston College, Burns Library, Eire Society of Boston, Box 11.
29 Boston College, Burns Library, *National Hibernian Digest*, November–December 1965, 'Ireland's Easter Week 1916 anniversary'.
30 NAI DEA, 2000/14/72, 'Appeal to Irish abroad'.
31 NAI DEA, 'Embassies', INF 8.2 New Delhi, 26 November 1965.
32 NAI DEA, 2000/14/77, 'Proposed television film to celebrate the Rising', Brendan Dillon, Brussels, to Department External Affairs, 21 June 1966. On Belgian views of Roger Casement, see Jules Marchal, 'Roger Casement in the Congo: Reactions in Belgium', in Mary E. Daly (ed.), *Roger Casement in Irish and world history* (Dublin, 2005), 34–5.
33 Boston College, Burns Library, Eire Society of Boston, Box 11, Correspondence and photos re. 1966 trip to Dublin.
34 *New York Times*, 10 April 1966.
35 *Sunday Star*, Washington, 10 April 1966.
36 *Irish Press*, 11 April 1966.
37 Boston College, Burns Library, Eire Society of Boston, Box 14. For list, see Appendix II.
38 NAI DEA, Washington files, 2001/37/781, P 153 II, '50th anniversary of the Easter Rising', 14 April 1966.
39 *Irish Press*, 14 April 1966.
40 NAI DEA, 610/20/5, 'Embassies', Department of External Affairs to all Missions, Urgent, 31 January 1966. Madrid I.C. 3/9.
41 NAI DFA, 2000/14/77, 'Proposed film to celebrate the Rising', 19 April 1966.
42 T.P. Coogan, *Ireland since the Rising* (London, 1966), xi.
43 *Hibernia*, April 1966.
44 *Irish Independent*, 12 February 1966.
45 Fergal Tobin, *The best of decades: Ireland in the 1960s* (Dublin, 1996).
46 *Catholic Herald*, Special Supplement, 28 January 1966.
47 *Dáil Debates* (hereafter cited as PDDE), vol. 221, col. 1284, 9 March 1966.
48 *Birmingham Post*, 11 April 1966.
49 *Studies*, Spring 1966, 1.
50 Bryan MacMahon, *Seachtar Fear, Seacht Lá*, unpublished script, 1966, 25–6, 31.
51 *New Spotlight*, May 1966.

[52] NAI DT, 97/6/159, 'Rising Commemorations', 9 October 1965.

[53] NAI DT, 97/6/159, 'Rising Commemorations', 9 October 1965.

[54] NAI DT, 97/6/160, 'Rising Commemorations', material for *Easter Commemoration Digest* (undated).

[55] UCDA, de Valera papers, '1916 Commemoration', P 150/3369, Message from the President of Ireland to the People of Ireland (undated).

[56] UCDA, de Valera papers, Message from the President of Ireland.

[57] *Kerryman*, 23 April 1966.

[58] PDDE, vol. 221, col. 2048, 22 March 1966.

[59] *Irish Press*, 10 January 1966.

[60] Boston College, Burns Library, Eire Society Box 14, Bernadine Truden, 'A compilation of notes for the stories that I subsequently wrote for the *Boston Globe*'.

[61] *Studies*, Spring 1966, 4.

[62] *Irish Independent*, 14 February 1966.

[63] Department of Finance, *Economic Development*, (Dublin, 1958, F.58), 2–3.

[64] Tony Fahey, 'Housing and local government', in M.E. Daly (ed.), *County and town: one hundred years of local government in Ireland* (Dublin, 2001), 120–129: 126.

[65] *Hibernia*, April 1966.

[66] *Irish Times*, 14 April 1966.

[67] *Studies*, Spring 1966, 31–2.

[68] *Irish Press*, 17 February, 1966.

[69] *Irish Press*, 24 May 1966.

[70] *Irish Times*, 12 September 1966.

[71] *The Word*, January 1966.

[72] NAI, Government Information Service (GIS), 1/221, Speech to King's Inns debating society, 19 February 1966.

[73] *Irish Press*, 13 June 1966.

[74] O.D. Edwards and Fergus Pyle (eds), *1916: the Easter Rising* (London, 1968), 235.

[75] *Irish Press* 16 May 1966.

[76] *Irish Press*, 30 May 1966.

[77] NAI DT, 98/6/495, 'IRA', Organisation *aide mémoire*, December 1966.

[78] *Irish Times*, 14 May 1966.

[79] *Irish Independent*, 1 January 1966.

[80] NAI DT, 98/6/495, 'IRA', Organisation *aide mémoire*, December 1966, 13.

[81] *The Statist*, Special Irish supplement, March 1966.

[82] NAI GIS, 1/221, Friday, 19 February 1966.

[83] *Irish Independent*, 12 February 1966.

[84] NAI DT, 97/6/162, 'Rising Commemorations', Lemass to Aiken, 7 March 1966.

[85] NAI DT, 97/6/158, 'Rising Commemorations', citing PDDE, vol. 215, 6 May 1965.

[86] NAI DT, 97/6/159, 'Rising Commemorations', 12 October 1965.
[87] NAI DT, 97/6/159, 'Rising Commemorations', Cosgrave to Lemass, 7 September 1965; James Gibbons (Minister for Defence) to Lemass, 29 September 1965. This was to be edited by Kevin B. Nowlan, see Kevin B. Nowlan (ed.), *The making of 1916: studies in the history of the Rising*, (Dublin, 1969).
[88] NAI DT, 96/6/641, 'Michael Collins anniversary', extract from PDDE, vol. 215, no. 15, cols 2178–9, 26 May 1965. The official reason given was that the government did not wish to see a proliferation of commemorative ceremonies.
[89] *Irish Independent*, 12 January 1966.
[90] *Irish Independent*, 3 January 1966.
[91] NAI DT, 97/6/159, 'Rising Commemorations', Lemass to Gibbons, 6 October 1965.
[92] *Irish Press*, 11 April 1966.
[93] NAI DT, 97/6/163, 'Rising Commemorations', 24 March 1966.
[94] *Irish Independent*, 11 February 1966.
[95] *Irish Press*, 11 April 1966.
[96] NAI DT, 97/6/161, 'Rising Commemorations', Office of the Minister for Justice to Lemass, 22 February 1966. The members of the committee, as given in a press-cutting on this file from the *Irish Press*, 9 February 1966, were Joseph Clarke, president; Eamonn Mac Thomáis, chairman; Máire Bean Mhic Giolla; Monica Bean Uí Riain; Fintan Smith; Eamonn Sammon; Jack Butler; Thomas McNeill; Joe Nolan and Larry Bateson.
[97] *Irish Press*, 9 February 1966.
[98] NAI DT, 96/7/490, 'State reception', 15 April 1966.
[99] *Irish Independent*, 9 February 1966.
[100] NAI DT, 97/6/162, 'Rising Commemorations', Piaras MacLochlainn to Department of the Taoiseach, 10 March 1966.
[101] *Irish Independent*, 10 February 1966.
[102] *Irish Independent*, 11 March 1966.
[103] *Irish Independent*, 18 March 1966.
[104] *Irish Independent*, 11 February 1966.
[105] *Northern Standard*, 14 January 1966.
[106] *Limerick Leader*, 5 February 1966.
[107] *Limerick Leader*, 16 April 1966.
[108] *Irish Independent*, 11 March 1966.
[109] *Irish Independent*, 15 April 1966.
[110] NAI, Department of Defence (DOD), 48151/3 (118), 'Ceremonies at provincial centres', Margaret MacDermott, Rose MacDermott and K.B. Keany to Minister of Defence, 2 April 1966.
[111] NAI DOD, 48151/3 (118), Margaret MacDermott, Rose MacDermott and K.B. Keany to Minister of Defence, 2 April 1966.
[112] NAI DT, 97/6/469, 'First president of the Republic', Lemass to Mrs. Clarke, 14 May 1965.

[113] *Irish Independent*, 1 January 1966.
[114] RTÉ Archive, 'Minutes of the Authority', 30 July 1965, 22 September 1965, 6 October 1965.
[115] RTÉ Archive, 'Minutes of the Authority', 24 November 1965.
[116] RTÉ Archive, 'Minutes of the Authority', 30 March 1966.
[117] *Northern Standard*, 1 April 1966.
[118] NAI DT, 96/6/193, 'Garden of Remembrance', January 1966.
[119] NAI DT, 96/6/193, 'Garden of Remembrance', January 1966.
[120] NAI DT, 97/6/164, H.L Mondow, Office of Public Works, 15 April 1966.
[121] *Irish Press*, 11 April 1966.
[122] *Sunday People*, 17 April 1966.
[123] *Irish Press*, 12 April 1966.
[124] *Irish Times*, 29 March 1966.
[125] *Irish Independent*, 12 April 1966.
[126] *Irish Press*, 12 April 1966.
[127] *Irish Press*, 12 April 1966.
[128] Gibbons's use of the term 'Six County' is interesting given that Lemass had tried to persuade Irish government officials, state agencies (including Radio and Telefís Éireann) and the *Irish Press* to use the term Northern Ireland rather than 'Six Counties'. See John Horgan, *Seán Lemass: the enigmatic patriot*, (Dublin, 1997), 260–62.
[129] NAI DT, 97/6/159, 'Rising Commemorations', Lemass to Gibbons, 18 December 1965.
[130] NAI DT, 97/6/159, 'Rising Commemorations', Park to Lemass, 15 October 1965.
[131] *Belfast Newsletter*, 5 February 1966.
[132] *Irish Independent*, 21 March 1966.
[133] *Irish Independent*, 21 March 1966.
[134] *Inniu*, 4 February, 1966.
[135] *Irish Times*, 25 April 1966.
[136] GAA, Annual Congress minutes, Croke Park,20 March 1966.
[137] Annual Congress minutes, 20 March 1966
[138] Annual Congress minutes, 18 April 1965.
[139] *Our Games*, 1966.
[140] *Our Games*, 1966.
[141] *Our Games*, 1966.
[142] GAA programmes 1966.
[143] GAA programmes 1966; 'Cumann Luthchleas Gael agus an teanga'.
[144] Yet Bean Mhadagáin, a columnist in the Irish language newspaper *Inniu*, acknowledged that some of the signatories to the 1916 Proclamation did not recognise the importance of the Irish language. *Inniu*, 18 Feabhra 1966 (18 February 1966).
[145] *Irish Press*, 12 April 1966.

[146] NAI DT, S13180D, 'Irish language policy'; S17627A/95; B/95; C/95; D/95; E/95; F/95. Commission on the Restoration of the Irish language; *Commission on the restoration of the Irish language: final report*, English language summary, July 1963. 'Athbheochán na Gaeilge. The restoration of the Irish language', White paper, January 1965, Pr. 8061.

[147] *Inniu*, 7 April, 13 May 1966.

[148] *Inniu*, 1 April 1966.

[149] *Inniu*, 10 May 1966.

[150] Coogan, *Ireland since the Rising*, 183.

[151] *Irish Press*, 11 April 1966.

[152] *Irish Press*, 11 April 1966.

[153] *Irish Press*, 13 April 1966.

[154] *Inniu* 'Iadsin Éire 1966', 1 April 1966.

[155] NAI DFA, 2000/14/78, 'Proposal to bring Breton groups to Ireland for the ceremony', December 1965.

[156] *Inniu*, 22 April 1966.

[157] UCDA, de Valera papers, '1916 Commemoration', P 150/3369, Message from the President of Ireland to the People of Ireland (undated).

[158] *Irish Press*, 18 April 1966.

[159] *Irish Press*, 14 April 1966.

[160] *Irish Press*, 14 April 1966.

[161] *Irish Press*, 18 April 1966.

[162] *Irish Press*, 18 April 1966.

[163] *Irish Press*, 14 January 1966.

[164] *Guardian*, 17 March 1966.

[165] *Irish Independent*, 12 February 1966.

[166] *The Statist*, February 1966.

[167] *The Statist*, February 1966.

[168] *Irish Independent*, 14 January 1966.

[169] *Irish Press*, 7 February 1966.

[170] *Irish Press*, 19 February 1966.

[171] NAI DT, 97/6/164, 'Rising Commemorations', Copy of PQ by Dr John O'Connell, 27 April 1966. The files do not record any communication between groups in Northern Ireland and the official commemoration committee.

[172] NAI DT, 97/6/161, 'Rising Commemorations', 18 February 1966.

[173] NAI DT, 97/6/161, 'Rising Commemorations', 22 and 23 February .

[174] RTÉ Archive, 'Telefís Éireann Authority minutes', and reports, March 1966.

[175] RTÉ Archive, 'Telefís Éireann Authority minutes', and reports, March 1966.

[176] *United Irishman*, March 1966.

[177] NAI DT, 97/6/164. On 15 April, Peter Berry, Secretary, Department of Justice, informed the Taoiseach's Department that the announcement had come as a surprise. The ban was not mentioned during confidential 'high level' police talks held in Dublin on 13 April between the RUC and the Gardaí.

[178] NAI DT, 98/6/495, 'IRA Organisation', hand-written minute by Nicholas Ó Nualláin, 16 April 1966.

[179] NAI DT, 97/6/164, 'Rising Commemorations'.

[180] NAI DT, 98/6/495, 'IRA Organisation', 51.

[181] *Newsweek*, 21 March 1966.

[182] *Weekend Telegraph* magazine, 6 April 1966.

[183] *Weekend Telegraph* magazine, 6 April 1966. The Garda estimated IRA strength in October 1966 as 1,039 members. NAI DT, 98/6/495, 'Review of unlawful and allied organisations: December 1 1964 to November 21 1966', 21 November 1966, 1.

[184] Coogan, *Ireland since the Rising*, 283.

[185] *New York Times*, 10 April 1966.

[186] *New York Times*, 9 April 1966.

[187] NAI DT, 96/6/96, Report of Irish ambassador to the USA to secretary, Department of External Affairs, 2 May 1966.

[188] *Boston Sunday Globe*, 10 April 1966.

[189] The Garda log of incidents involving the IRA during this time does not mention any incident in Skibbereen. NAI DT, 98/6/495, 'Review of unlawful and allied organisations', 21 November 1966, 46–52.

[190] *Boston Globe*, 12 April 1966.

[191] *Boston Herald*, 17 April 1966.

[192] *Washington Post*, 15 April 1966.

[193] *Boston Herald*, 15 April 1966.

[194] *Washington Post*, 9 April 1966. The columns of the *Washington Post* correspondent Karl Meyer also appeared in the *Boston Globe* and the *Los Angeles Times*. *Boston Globe* 8, 9 April 1966.

[195] *Washington Post*, 9 April 1966.

[196] *Washington Post*, 11 April 1966.

[197] In 1962 the IRA ended its border campaign, by declaring a unilateral ceasefire.

[198] Boston College, Burns Library, 'AOH Report of Congress in Albany', 4–6 August 1964, 84.

[199] Lemass featured on the cover of *Time* magazine on 12 July 1963.

[200] Daly, 'Nationalism, sentiment and economics', 85.

[201] NAI DFA, 'Embassies', 610/20/5, DFA to all Missions, 22 November 1965.

[202] NAI DFA, 'Embassies', Washington, 2201/37/781/ P 153 II, 50th anniversary of the Easter Rising, Dennis O'Sullivan, New York Consulate, 15 April 1966.

[203] NAI DFA, 'Embassies', Washington, 2201/37/781/ P 153 II, 50th anniversary of the Easter Rising, extract from Congressional Record, 8 March 1966.

[204] NAI DFA, 'Embassies', Washington, 2201/37/781/ P 153 II, 50th anniversary of the Easter Rising, 12 April 1966.

[205] NAI DFA, 'Embassies', Washington, 2001/37/781/ P 153 II, 50th anniversary of the Easter Rising, 12 April 1966. On the night of 1 March 1966 an

attempt was made to set fire to the residence of the British military attaché, Brigadier R.N. Thicknesse, by throwing a burning can of petrol into the kitchen. A note attached to the door threatened that Thicknesse would be shot if he did not leave the country by Easter Sunday. NAI DT, 98/6/495, 'Review of unlawful and allied organisations', 21 November 1966, 51.

206 Boston College, Burns Library, 'AOH 1966 convention, Chicago, 2–4 August', 219.

207 *National Hibernian Digest*, January–February 1965.

208 *National Hibernian Digest*, November–December 1965.

209 *National Hibernian Digest*, April–May 1966.

210 *National Hibernian Digest*, April–May 1966.

211 NAI DFA, 'Embassies', Madrid I.C. 3/9, 'Easter Rising commemoration', Department of External Affairs to all Missions, 31 January 1966.

212 NAI DT, 96/6/532, 'Return of the GPO flag', Note from Hugh McCann, 7 March 1966.

213 *Sunday Times* magazine, 8 February 1966.

214 NAI DFA, 2000/14/84, 'Proposed articles in coloured supplements to *Sunday Times* and *Daily Telegraph*', Keating to Coffey, 4 October 1965.

215 NAI DFA, 2000/14/84, 'Proposed articles in coloured supplements to *Sunday Times* and *Daily Telegraph*', 4 October 1965.

216 *The Guardian*, 17 March 1966.

217 *Daily Express*, 23 March 1966.

218 *Daily Express*, 23 March 1966.

219 *Daily Express*, 26 March 1966.

220 See note 52 above.

221 NAI DT, 98/6/495, Report of interview with British ambassador, 12 October 1965.

222 NAI DFA, 2000/14/90, Keating to Ronan, 12 April 1966.

223 NAI DFA, 98/3/10, Unfavourable article in the *Toronto Star*, 26 May 1966.

224 *Chicago Daily News*, 11 April 1966.

225 *Look* magazine, 19 April 1966.

226 *Look* magazine, 19 April 1966.

227 *The Listener*, 14 April 1966, 531.

228 *New Statesman*, 8 April 1966.

229 NAI DFA, 'Embassies', London L 114/89 Part II, 10 May 1967; New York, P. 153/I, 22 November 1967.

230 *Hibernia*, May 1966.

231 *Cork Examiner*, 4 April 1966.

232 *Wicklow People*, 20 December 1966.

233 Tom Hennessey, *Northern Ireland: the origins of the Troubles*, (Dublin, 2005), 50.

234 See NAI DFA, 2000/14/90, 'Foreign press comments', April 1966.

[235] NAI DT, 98/6/495, 'Review of unlawful and allied organisations', 21 November 1966, 49.
[236] NAI DFA, 2000/14/94, 'Foreign Press coverage', Keating to Charlie Whelan, 16 May 1966.
[237] *Irish Independent*, 23 March 1966.
[238] Boston College, Burns Library, Eire Society, Box 14.
[239] NAI DT, 98/6/495, 'Review of unlawful and allied organisations', 21 November 1966.

2. 'From Casement Park to Toomebridge'— The Commemoration of the Easter Rising in Northern Ireland in 1966

By Margaret O'Callaghan

It is right that triumphalism should have its place in the celebrations over the country, at this Eastertide, in honour of the brave men who died in the Easter Rising fifty years ago. But the story of their sacrifice does not need to be asserted stridently nor exaggerated rhetorically. English volleys hurled them into history; and there they remain given their rightful place; their names enshrined in our national litany with Emmet, Tone, Orr and Hope and McCracken...Those seven days of fifty years ago were the days of troubled ecstasy. At the end of it all, for many, was the firing squadron in the Square at grim Kilmainham Jail. By their deaths they exalted the cause of Ireland, indivisible and free. Our history has been forged by such men, struggling passionately to assert the national consciousness of freedom.

Irish News, 11 April 1966 [1]

The pockets of our great coats full of barley,
No kitchens on the run, no striking camp—
We moved quick and sudden in our own country.
The priest lay behind ditches with the tramp.
A people, hardly marching—on the hike—
We found new tactics happening each day:
We'd cut through reins and rider with the pike

And stampede cattle into infantry,
Then retreat through hedges where cavalry must be thrown.
Until, on Vinegar Hill, the fatal conclave.
Terraced thousands died, shaking scythes at cannon.
The hillside blushed, soaked in our broken wave.
They buried us without shroud or coffin
And in August the barley grew up out of the grave.
Seamus Heaney, 'Requiem for the Croppies[2]

CULTURES OF COMMEMORATION IN NORTHERN IRELAND AFTER PARTITION

Acts of unionist political and cultural commemoration were inscribed in the public and private spaces of Northern Ireland from its foundation. Those happenings or past events that were highlighted, revisited and represented through acts of celebration or commemoration were those aspects of an Irish unionist and Protestant past that had the plasticity and capacity to be re-imagined in a way that would serve twentieth-century political purposes, providing a genealogy for the newly constructed Northern Ireland.[3] The annual Orange Order walks or marches of 12 July, 'remembering' and giving thanks for the victory of William of Orange at the Boyne in 1690; the August celebrations of the Apprentice Boys' successful defence of Londonderry's walls; Armistice or Remembrance Day ceremonies, particularly those associated with the memory of the losses of the Ulster regiments at the Somme; and a litany of other local annual events and performances. All these provided a sequence that sought to testify to the rootedness and legitimacy of Northern Ireland in the United Kingdom. What was being constructed as public memory was enacted, as elsewhere, in rituals, monuments, language and anniversaries.

Nationalists in Northern Ireland, most of whom did not give allegiance to the Belfast government, and who were divided from their fellow Irish nationalists by the partition that had established Northern Ireland between 1920 and 1925, declined to join in, or were over time excluded from, these publicly sanctioned performances that sought to embody, represent and recreate that public, unionist memory. The most obvious examples of such exclusion were those northern Catholics who had served in the British army in both world wars, or whose fathers, brothers or sons had served in the British army.[4] As Catholics and nationalists, they were limited in how they could choose to celebrate that connection. Events commemorating the anniversaries of the First World War and the Somme had been appropriated by Ulster unionism within the public sphere of the state in Northern Ireland as a foundational myth of partition's origin, sanctified by the Protestant dead of the Somme.[5] Past a certain date, to acknowledge a British army connection through commemoration was to support partition and the state in Northern Ireland. The huge numbers of northern and southern Irish nationalist and Catholic men who had fought and died in the First World War in British army uniforms were inconvenient historical facts that served nobody's political agenda.

The nationalist minority in Northern Ireland had an alternative apparatus of practices that testified to their otherness from the state apparatus. Some of these practices were simply aspects of the discourse of Irish Catholicism itself—masses and confessions, novenas and sodalities that marked them out as 'other'. Catholics in Northern Ireland celebrated and commemorated saints' days, held Corpus Christi processions, engaged in church rituals, sodalities and confraternities that testified to their alternative symbolic worlds. Certain of them travelled south and participated in the public commemorations of the centenary of Catholic emancipation of 1829 and the 1932 Eucharistic Congress, through which the Free State was foregrounding its Catholic identity. Others looked to the Gaelic Athletic Association, conducting their social lives around it and through its local clubs and inter-county rivalries, which provided another all-Ireland context in which they could participate despite the confines of partition. Some participated in Ancient Order of Hibernian parades or Foresters marches, and some again lived in symbolic worlds framed by local pubs and betting shops, horse racing and 'the dogs'.

But for many it was the republican tradition as maintained through Irish nationalist rebellions and their leaders that provided the most potent means of asserting their identity. Wolfe Tone and Robert Emmet provided rhetorical and actual rallying points at specific times. However, as northern nationalists, it was the memory of the hanged 1916 leader Roger Casement, together with the annual commemoration of the 1916 Rising marked by the parade to Milltown Cemetery in Belfast and to other locations elsewhere, that most particularly gave expression to their public desire to express their identification with the Irish nation. Commemoration, then, was a mechanism through which contemporary political divisions could be represented and fought and communal allegiance and culture could be stabilised for both nationalists and unionists in Northern Ireland. [6]

Lacking a state apparatus in 'the North', nationalist celebrations and commemorations there stood apart from, if not against, the litany of official events and were generally represented as subversive, disloyal and challenging to the state's legitimacy. Such celebrations carried risks, in that to participate in them marked you out as a potential rebel, and risked incurring the weight of the state's law.[7]

Staging commemorations of the 1916 Rising in Northern Ireland in 1966 thus was a political act, and the key nationalist commemorative events in 1966 were located in places that had resonances, both historical and recent, for Irish nationalism in the north. First and most significant of these was the parade along the Falls Road in Belfast to Casement Park; among the significant secondary sites of commemoration was Toomebridge, Co. Antrim.[8] Nineteen sixty-six presented a unique point of potential conflict in Northern Ireland, in that it marked the fiftieth anniversary of both the Battle of the Somme and the Easter Rising. The Somme, over the decades, had come to be represented as a foundational moment for Northern Ireland, while Easter 1916 was seen as at least a crucial date in the history of the Irish nation.[9]

COMMEMORATING 1916 IN THE IRISH STATE IN 1966

The commemoration of the 1916 Rising in the Republic in 1966 was multiple, but it was above all official and state-sponsored.[10] It was promoted by the state and the state sought to control its meanings. Obviously, such an attempt could never be wholly successful. Historical enactments, invocations of the patriot dead could not be guaranteed to promote only those virtues that the state might have wished to promote. As the other chapters in this book show, the desire to eulogise successful Irish statehood—the notion that every generation had its task, and that the task of the 1966 generation was to make the economic effort to secure the future of the Irish state—lay at the core of the Irish government's commemorative project. The problem that this presented to what certain groupings saw as the 'unfinished narrative of the Irish *nation*' was not one that could easily be dealt with. Prior to 1966 the Irish state had not greatly concerned itself with commemorations. For 50 years the annual commemorations of 1916 had, throughout Ireland north and south, remained in many places the property of local groups; those who were, in their own eyes at least, republicans outside the state.[11]

This changed in 1966 as the state organised its own range of celebrations in the Republic, often through accommodation with pre-existing groups. Peculiarly, however, the 1966 celebrations in the north shared many of the features of the pre-1966 celebrations all over Ireland. The groupings—mainly Sinn Féin or the IRA—who had been the driving force behind most of the commemorative events before 1966 throughout all of Ireland retained primary ownership of the event only in 'the North' in 1966, and there only in certain places. Throughout 1966 Seán Lemass's Fianna Fáil government maintained the Republic's long-standing position of constitutional adherence to partition[12] and support for the new developments that had consolidated better relations with Northern Ireland through meetings with Prime Minister Terence O'Neill in the context of Anglo-Irish free trade. The tone of exchanges between Stormont and Merrion Street throughout this period is highly cordial. The Dublin government remained highly vigilant about what it saw as potential threats to stability from the IRA.[13]

But the commemorative process held within it at least the possibility of reopening debates about the meaning of Irish freedom, the status of the nation and the project of nationhood, partition and the Irish language, particularly in the north.[14] Representations of the Irish historical experience put into the public sphere in 1966 through television series, official pageants, information disseminated to schools could not be controlled. How individuals chose to read this material was equally indeterminable. In Northern Ireland there was the pressing question of how unionist groupings would control and read nationalist commemorations.

COMMEMORATING THE 1916 RISING IN 'THE NORTH' IN 1966

In Northern Ireland, commemorating 1916 was a simpler but in other ways a more complex act. The commemoration was not supported by the northern state, and was seen by its very existence to pose a challenge to that state. Unsupported and ignored by the official commemoration project of the Irish government,[15] in a highly segregated society the north's commemoration was enacted only in nationalist areas. Commemorative events were not hidden or secret, but they were nonetheless seen to be separate from the public sphere of the state.

Historically in the north, nationalist commemorative parades did not claim 'the Queen's highway', but happened by agreement within nationalist areas, often in consultation with the Royal Ulster Constabulary. Any overt nationalist commemorative or flag-waving action could lead to trouble, as had happened in Bovevagh and Dungiven in the 1950s and in West Belfast in 1964.[16] The troubles of the 1950s had resulted in the Stormont government passing the Flags and Emblems Act of 1954.[17]

Initially, no single central northern commemoration committee in 1966 had a view as to what commemorating 1916 was for or what it should be; but many nationalists in Northern Ireland felt it incumbent upon them to celebrate it, and in so doing to demonstrate their allegiance to the Irish nation. What was clear from preliminary meetings in 1965 to plan a commemoration was that the key sites of commemoration were to be linked with locations of past or present historical memory in the nationalist repertoire. Casement Park, the main GAA stadium in Belfast, was a centre of Irish nationalist culture in West Belfast.[18] The decision to call the main GAA grounds in Belfast after Roger Casement had been evidence of the Belfast GAA's desire to claim Casement as a northerner and an Antrim man, and to honour him in what was seen to be his own county. Cathal O'Byrne's invocation of Casement's love for the song 'The Castle of Dromore' in Casement Park promotional material also testified to the location of Irish nationalist culture in place, memory and song. Toomebridge was chosen as a key site associated in actuality and song with Roddy McCorley, 'who goes to die on the bridge of Toome today'. Only perhaps Thomas Russell held as powerful a hold on northern nationalist memory.[19] Dungannon resonated in the written nationalist tradition, as did Derry, Armagh, Newry and other key sites in the north.[20]

Tensions within northern nationalism

Moderate nationalists in the Nationalist Party were wary of staging a commemoration or commemorations in 1966. If Stormont did not take steps to 'normalise politics in the North' the Nationalist Party might have 'to take our troubles to Westminster again', Eddie McAteer, the leader of the Nationalist Party, announced before the Westminster election of March 1966.[21] The *Derry Journal* reported that he had said this at 'a delegates meeting in Belfast which adopted thirty-nine policy steps to reorganise the party'. According to McAteer, the decision by the Nationalist party to take up the role of official opposition party at Stormont had got little response from the O'Neill government...The Lemass–O'Neill meeting had created a new atmosphere and Nationalists were now prepared to play a full part in the political life of the North...He felt that this would make for a happier community here, and help to remove the sense of oppression which unfortunately hangs over it at the present time.[22]

One week later the *Journal* reported that 'the discord which has marked the plans for the commemoration of the 1916 Golden Jubilee was deplored yesterday by Mr Eddie McAteer, MP, Leader of the Nationalist Party'.[23] He said no decision had yet been taken by the party as to

> whether it would sponsor commemoration ceremonies but it was unlikely...There is unhappily already some discord from which we would wish to keep aloof...I consider it unseemly that anyone should try to make party capital out of this solemn occasion. We hope to set an example by participating quietly in local and national remembrances.[24]

Nonetheless, he said that the Nationalist Party realised that

> only as one natural entity can a true solution of its [Ireland's] economic problems be found...Equally it [the Nationalist party] realises...that what has to be hoped and striven for pending the eventual consummation of the ideal of national reunification by the arts of peace, is the best alleviation of the baneful effect of the border that can be achieved between both parts of Ireland. It stands too for the fostering of the best relationship that can be cultivated between both sides of the community in this part of Ireland.[25]

According to McAteer the primary focus in 1966 was to be the March Westminster election, not the 1916 commemoration:

> Our greatest incentive in this election must be the knowledge that Unionists are terrified lest the accusing voice of Ireland be found at Westminster...I urge all electors to pull the rug from underneath the Unionists feet.[26]

Newly emerging political figures like Austin Currie tried to link the commemoration of the 1916 Rising to a new agenda of protest on housing, the injustices of electoral divisions and gerrymandering.[27] Republicans of a traditional variety tried to use it to reiterate old lines. Ruairí Ó Brádaigh, or Rory Brady as he was frequently called in newspaper reports of the time, a Republican candidate in the 1966 election for Fermanagh–South Tyrone, is a classic example of this.[28] He told young men in Tyrone in April 1966 near Dungannon, a place associated with the 1916 leader and old Fenian Thomas Clarke, to fight for their freedom.[29]

After the disastrous 'Operation Harvest' or so-called 'Border Campaign' of the late fifties and early sixties, Sinn Féin had embarked on a new strategy that sought to move it from its failed military past to a left-wing Marxist, community-activist future.[30] In this new attempt at self-transformation, Sinn Féin sought to construct a network of alliances with left-wing groups, trades unions, communist activists and fringe protest movements. This reformulated Sinn Féin in Dublin sought to link its new left-wing agenda in the Republic with a revised northern policy. To this end, traditional Belfast republicans, many of whom had been in the Crumlin Road gaol during the 1940s and whose fathers and uncles had been interned in the 1920s,[31] were contacted in 1965 and exhorted by the Dublin Sinn Féin leadership to see 1966 as an opportunity to show that the national spirit was not dead in 'the North', that nationalism and republicanism were not the moribund forces that O'Neill proclaimed them to be.[32]

Simultaneously, however, Terence O'Neill and official cabinet unionism lent credence to the Rev. Ian Paisley's claims of imminent Armageddon should republican commemoration in Belfast go ahead, by announcing, from late 1965, that the commemoration of 1916 presented a serious danger to public order in Northern Ireland.[33] It was ostensibly in response to public announcements of the imminence of the Easter 1966 celebrations that Paisley set up his newspaper the *Protestant Telegraph* and that a key circle established the Ulster Volunteer Force (UVF) in imitation of the original force.[34]

The Irish government's official commemoration committee appears to have been wary of associating any aspect of the general celebration directly with 'the North' or partition. More peculiarly, there appears to be no evidence on the record that the commemoration committee or cabinet members ever considered the potential implications of the commemoration for Northern Ireland. Certainly they had no plans to mount any celebrations or commemorations there. If any cabinet or commemoration committee discussions of the implications or consequences of the state-planned commemorations for nationalists in a northern context took place no record of them has been found, apart from specific discussions of co-operating with Stormont in banning trains from Dublin to the northern events. Whereas cabinet members like Erskine Childers, Minister for Transport and Power, and Neil Blaney, Minister for Local Government, were present in 1966 for meetings at the Magee Presbyterian campus in Derry City and other locations on subjects such as the economic development of areas west of the Bann, or on plans to regenerate Derry City,[35] there appears to have been a complete official Dublin indifference to and ignorance of any such celebrations of the 1916 anniversary as northern nationalists might have planned. When, in the run-up to Easter, a northern committee calling itself the '1916 Jubilee Committee' requested that the Republic's transport authority CIÉ put on a special train for 17 April 1966, Minister for Agriculture Charles Haughey advised against it, suggesting that the train was to be used for 'for IRA organisational purposes'.[36]

The south in the north

Peculiarly, one of the few southern inputs into nationalist commemoration in Northern Ireland in this period was in the form of lectures given to various nationalist organisations in the north by prominent academic historians from University College, Dublin—Kevin B. Nowlan, Robin Dudley Edwards, F.X. Martin and others. F.X. Martin's work on Dennis McCullough and Bulmer Hobson[37] was particularly welcomed in certain northern circles, where there was a desire to remind people that Belfast was the crucible of Irish republicanism not just in the late eighteenth century, but also in the early twentieth. In the perhaps 50 or so orations given at public nationalist celebrations in Northern Ireland during 1966, there is a limited presentation of specific historical events, but there is a profoundly resonating common rhetoric of the part of northern nationalists in the Irish nation.

Commemoration enacted in Northern Ireland

Commemoration of 1916 took place in Northern Ireland outside of the arena of the state, if not blatantly in opposition to it. The commemorations celebrated in various different genres and discourses—visual, pictorial, verbal, through Masses, rosaries, ballads, Irish dancing displays, musical sessions—the separate identity, or rather identities, of the nationalist north. These productions sought to demonstrate the identity and role of northern nationalism within the Irish nation, while simultaneously enacting an expression of northern nationalist sense of place and community. They also reveal the particularities and interests of northern nationalist culture in the mid-1960s and the variations within it.

The commemoration of 1916 in 1966 in Northern Ireland provided for some the opportunity for advancing agendas of equality, reform, challenge or opposition to the state. The commemoration of the fiftieth anniversary of 1916 has been accused of provoking a Paisleyite reaction, but it can better be seen as part of a reaction to changes in Unionism, of which Paisleyiteism was already a highly visible and vocal part. The anniversary also served to provide Paisley with a concrete platform to launch his public career in a broad-based way. It commemorated a signifying mantra—1916—that was represented in the official southern celebrations as the prefiguration of a successfully achieved Irish state. This was scarcely a formulation that those nationalists commemorating in the north could fully share.

Seamus Heaney, who says that he composed 'Requiem for the Croppies' on the anniversary of 1916 in 1966, said of that poem, which is resonant with an identification with the foundational Irish republican moment at Vinegar Hill in 1798, 'I think the young nationalist in me was trying to give voice to things that the culture in Northern Ireland did not admit. There was no official space for anything of that kind'.[38]

It is precisely in the partitioned nature of the spaces within which nationalists had to perform their commemoration of the 1916 Easter Rising in Northern Ireland in 1966 that the commemoration carried the capacity to contest the political actuality of partition around issues that had begun to dominate northern nationalist politics from the early 1960s. For a divided northern nationalism, the commemoration provided at least one central moment around which they could unite and agree; something that had been beyond the agendas of a series of nationalist initiatives from the late 1950s, and arguably back to the 1920s. The fact of the commemorations reminded people that they were a part of the Irish nation, even if the Irish state did not have much to say to them; it confirmed them in a broader northern nationalist identity; it gave them courage as a community. As Edna Longley has written:

> [c]ommemoration is the process by which communities are
> bound together…'bound' hovers between bond and bind,
> between solidarity and suffocation…. And commemoration,
> communal *religio*, does not merely remember. It reinvents
> and reconstitutes according to present needs.[39]

There are a variety of political contexts within which the northern
nationalist fiftieth anniversary commemoration of 1916 can be placed.

PARTITION AND THE PECULIARITIES OF THE NATIONALIST NORTH

The key context is that of northern nationalist culture and politics after
partition. The peculiarities of the political nationalist north in the period
1886 to 1920—really the Home Rule era to its conclusion post-1918—
were transformed and exacerbated after partition in a political
jurisdiction where politics for northern nationalists was ineluctably and
permanently unconnected to any control of government or participation
in the new Irish state. For the nationalist north after 1925[40] the only
possibilities of political self-determination were in certain kinds of local
control in nationalist areas. There were, in fact, many Catholic norths
geographically.[41] Belfast was highly distinct, with areas of the city that
had formerly supplied men in huge numbers to the British army often
being highly politicised. West Belfast—the centre of Joe Devlin's fiefdom
for years[42]—also contained a republican core around the lower Falls and
the Springfield roads.[43] Belfast Catholics traditionally viewed themselves
as vulnerable and exposed, and likely to suffer disproportionately
through sectarian attacks for actions committed elsewhere.[44]

This sense was, however, inflected by precise geographic location.[45]
North Belfast, traditionally religiously mixed, particularly in the Docks
area and the areas around Corporation Street and York Street, was also
the main base of the Belfast Catholic middle classes, with the Antrim
Road as its core.[46] The small number of Belfast republicans who were
'active' in the IRA were wary of the border campaign of the late 1950s,
as Belfast nationalists under Joe Devlin had been wary of the Boundary
Commission in 1923–5. The varieties of northern nationalism—from
republicans through gradations of nationalist affiliations encompassing
Hibernians, Foresters and a range of other formations—can not be
geographically mapped with any precision. Distinct localised nationalist
political cultures reflecting local interreligious demographics, and

complicated genealogies of local relations, meant that nationalist political formation was both locally distinctive and fragmented. This is reflected in the different character of commemoration committees that existed in different areas in 1966. The so-called Lynch–McKenna re-partition line, as had been pressed for in the Boundary Commission submissions by northern nationalists of 1925, still had valency for nationalist political culture. As the memoirs of Maurice Hayes[47], Denis Donoghue[48] and Patrick Shea[49] make clear, differences were as important as similarities among nationalists in different areas and of different social classes. The writings of John Montague on Tyrone, Patrick Kavanagh on the Monaghan borderlands, Seamus Deane on Derry City, Seamus Heaney on Derry county and Paul Muldoon on Collegelands, Armagh, testify to other local class- and location-specific nationalist identities.[50]

THE BROADER CONTEXT OF THE 1960S—
THE NEW LEFT, ECUMENISM AND PAISLEY.

The election of a Labour government in Britain in 1964, the new international language of socialism and the post-Vatican II revision of Catholicism combined in Ireland to suggest new beginnings. In pursuit of the *zeitgeist* and after the failed Border campaign, a discredited and defeated Sinn Féin was in the process of change under Cathal Goulding and Tomás MacGiolla and a proclaimed new left agenda.[51] Despite this proclaimed new direction, Sinn Féin traditionalists like the Roscommon teacher Ruairí Ó Brádaigh more accurately reflected republicanism in the north. The Wolfe Tone Clubs, Labour's new agenda north and south, Labour student groups, a new Labour government in Britain, Labour backbenchers, the politics of the Council for Civil Liberties, analogies with Algeria—all of these were part of the new politics. Paisleyism, which can be seen as a reaction to O'Neillism and ecumenism, saw all of this as a threat. Communism and ecumenism figure as twin bogeys in the language of Paisley's key supporters at this time. The Divis Street riots of 1964 had been the most dramatic intrusion of Paisleyism into West Belfast. Flags and emblems defined territory in Belfast, but displaying the tricolour anywhere at any time was problematic. The riots surrounding the removal of the tricolour from Liam McMillan's election office in securely nationalist West Belfast in 1966 had produced the greatest unrest in Northern Ireland since the 1930s. Paisley had inserted himself in the consciousness of the inhabitants of West Belfast in particular through the pressure he placed on the RUC to remove the tricolour.

In speeches in the months preceding the April 1966 commemorations, Gerry Fitt, the newly elected Westminster MP for West Belfast, Austin Currie and other nationalist speakers referred to the range of new extremist Protestant organisations with which Paisley was associated.[52] There was widespread nationalist awareness of the refounding of the UVF. There was also awareness of the potential pressures on O'Neill from a British Labour government, and of the difficulty with which the 1964 riots had been put down. The new newspaper from Ian Paisley and his circle, the *Protestant Telegraph*, published since February 1966, was a lurid exercise in anti-ecumenism, anti-Catholicism and anti-nationalism, and most of its columns, as O'Neill was well aware, were incitements to hatred.

WILSON/O'NEILL/LEMASS

Another context for the 1966 commemoration is that of new policies at Stormont under Prime Minister Terence O'Neill and his meetings with Seán Lemass. Added to this apparent new departure were the anxieties that a new Labour government in Britain provoked in unionism generally, but particularly in O'Neill. Sympathetic noises made by Harold Wilson to the Dungannon-based Campaign for Social Justice some months before coming to office were not followed up.

> We work closely with our colleagues in the Northern Ireland Labour Party…Like them we deplore religious and other kinds of discrimination; and we agree with them that this should be tackled by introducing new and impartial procedures for the allocation of houses, by setting up joint tribunals to which particular cases of alleged discrimination in public appointments can be referred, and indeed, by any effective means that can be agreed.[53]

The most immediate context of the April 1966 commemoration in Northern Ireland was the general election campaign of March 1966, and its most startling outcome was the election of Gerry Fitt to Westminster as MP for West Belfast. A devastating blow to the unionist candidate James Kilfedder, and indirectly to O'Neill, Fitt's election represented a real political opportunity to bring the range of nationalist grievances that had been aired through the previous four or five years onto a coherent platform before the London government. In response to O'Neill, the political agendas of northern nationalist opposition had changed. The Nationalist Party had agreed to be the official opposition. A whole series of initiatives from the Garron Towers meeting onwards had tried to galvanise nationalism into some action and unity.[54] The election of Gerry Fitt for West Belfast marked a significant advance in this agenda.

Despite this breakthrough, however, contemporary Stormont government files suggest that Wilson's ministers in Westminster persistently referred complaints directed to them directly back to the relevant Stormont ministry.[55] Kenneth Bloomfield, O'Neill's private secretary, spent a lot of time internally dealing with these matters. Catherine O'Donnell's chapter in this present work (see Chapter 7) shows just how concerned O'Neill was about British opinion at this time. The context of a Labour government, even one dramatically less assiduous about tackling abuses than Wilson's pre-election statements would suggest he might have been, conditioned both what nationalist activists considered feasible and possible, and what O'Neill was prepared to tolerate. In other words, banning all commemorations was not a real political option for O'Neill in 1966. The 'beating them off the streets' approach pursued in the West Belfast of 1964 was not considered a desirable model. Harold Wilson and Roy Jenkins as Home Secretary were anything but proactive in relation to Stormont, but they did convey enough about the 'concerns of their backbenchers' to constrain Stormont options.

PLANNING THE NORTHERN COMMEMORATIONS

The organisation of a commemoration of 1916 in Belfast in 1966 was discussed and planned from at least August 1965. According to Eamon O'Cianáin,[56] who was on the Belfast organising committee, the arrival of the key Sinn Féin figure Tommy Gill, or Tomás MacGiolla, to speak to the Felon's Club[57] in West Belfast in the late summer of 1965 set the agenda for the Falls Road commemoration. The nationalist newspaper the *Irish News* reported on 30 August 1965 that a meeting of delegates from 'Republican, National, cultural and Labour organisations was convened in Belfast'. Initially three Belfast organising committees were set up but they converged into the West Belfast committee fairly early on. There was also a Central Committee, which overlapped with the West Belfast Committee.

Liam McMillan, who was in prison during the August meeting, was elected as overall organising secretary and promised a 'full programme of events'.[58] He had stood in the 1964 Westminster election.[59] Two northerners had been appointed to membership of the all-Ireland 1966 Casement Memorial Committee—Kevin McMahon, the Newry solicitor later prominent in the Civil Rights movement, and James Clarke of Ballycastle. This was significant because, despite attempts to turn Banna Strand in Kerry and Glasnevin cemetery in Dublin into prime memorialising sites for Casement, it was impossible to dislodge Murlough Bay, Ballycastle and the Glens of Antrim from local northern political memory and political agendas.

In January 1966 a body referred to as a directorate was appointed for the organisation of 1916 commemoration ceremonies throughout Northern Ireland. This happened at a meeting in Dungannon of 200 delegates representing the various local commemoration committees, and it seems to have represented a compromise between nationalist groupings with different agendas. Frank McGlade,[60] the veteran republican and close associate of Liam McMillan, was appointed chair.[61] Liam McDonagh of Armagh was vice-chairman and publicity officer; D. Moore of Newry was secretary; and K. Murphy from South Derry was treasurer. In February Jimmy Steele, another Belfast republican, was appointed president of the directorate.[62] At the Dungannon meeting Malachy McBurney, whose brother Billy McBurney was at the original Belfast meeting at the Felon's Club in 1965, spoke. He said:

> It was regrettable that the twenty six county governments, while creating a lot of ballyhoo about 1916 were themselves imprisoning men because they were fighting for the same cause, namely a free and independent republic.[63]

Frank McGlade asked that people in Northern Ireland who wanted to celebrate the Easter Rising do so in their own communities, rather than by going to functions south of the border. He also announced that Coalisland would be at the centre of the Tyrone celebration. Armagh announced its commemoration plans at a meeting presided over by Charles McGlennon, former Republican MP for south Armagh, on 16 January 1966. It proposed a public meeting in St Patrick's Hall, a special Mass in Irish, a parade to St Patrick's Cemetery with a wreath-laying ceremony at the Republican plot, a decade of the rosary in Irish and a reading of the proclamation. Liam McDonagh, secretary and press officer of the central organising committee, emphasised that 'the dead of 1916 would not be used as a political gimmick by any speaker on behalf of any organisational or sectional interest'.[64]

The Down county convention was presided over by George Tinnelly of Rostrevor, who was re-elected for his seventeenth term as chairman of the County Down Board of the GAA. Clearly, the organisers here were not primarily old republicans, as was the case in Belfast. He said:

> [t]his year could be the most historic one for the association. All the counties in the land are celebrating the memory of the men and women of 1916 who gave their all that we could have the life we have today. On the Sunday after Easter the Down part in these celebrations will be held in St Patrick's Park, Newcastle and I strongly urge all clubs to hold their own functions to honour those heroes of 1916…I believe that we today could best honour those heroes if we went away from this convention resolved to teach our members and the youth of the county to live up to the ideals of the Association. Encourage our youth to learn and speak our native language, dance our native dances, play and take part in the pastimes of out native land.[65]

L.T. O'Kane, the defeated Irish Labour candidate in the 1965 North Tyrone election for Stormont, was joint-organising secretary of the Strabane Commemoration Committee.

In early March one of the Belfast commemoration committee's key proposed events—a '1916 Concert' in the Ulster Hall in the heart of Belfast city, booked by the Commemoration Committee for 13 April—was banned by Belfast Corporation's Estates and Markets Committee on the grounds that 'a breach of the peace might occur'.[66] Gerry Fitt proclaimed this to be 'the first step taken to placate the extremist element in Northern Ireland'.[67] Significantly, this venue was later granted to Ian Paisley on the date of the key nationalist commemoration in Belfast to organise a counter rally celebrating 'the defeat of the rebels in 1916'.

In the same month, the Gaelic Athletic Association announced that, thanks to the efforts of four GAA county secretaries in the north,[68] the pageant *Seachtar Fear, Seacht Lá* or 'Seven Men, Seven Days', which was opening in Croke Park in Dublin on St Patrick's Day, would open under floodlights in Casement Park, Andersonstown, West Belfast on the evening of Sunday, 27 March. This was the core GAA golden jubilee pageant. Its performance in 'the North' was not organised by the National Commemoration Committee, 'which has its headquarters in Dublin', but by the initiative of the northern GAA. Northern Ireland was included in GAA plans for celebrating 1916 as a part of an all-Ireland organisation, in a way that it was not included in the state commemoration. 'Seven Men, Seven Days', it was proclaimed, would be 'the first of the Easter rising commemoration events in Northern Ireland'.[69] According to the *Irish News*, Sunday, 27 March 'will be unique and historic for Ulster Gaels when the GAA committees of Down, Derry, Armagh and Antrim present "Seachtar Fear, Seacht Lá"'. Bryan MacMahon,[70] the author of the pageant, was lauded by the *Irish News* and the rapt notices that the pageant had already received in Croke Park were mentioned.[71] The pageant was cancelled on the date it was due to be held in Belfast because of bad weather and eventually *Seachtar Fear* was staged in Casement Park on Sunday, 2 April.

In late March a dinner was given in the International Hotel in Belfast, then seen by Stormont government sources as a communist or republican haunt, by the Belfast pre-Truce Republican Army Association. The guest speaker was Dennis McCullough, former comrade of Roger Casement and of Bulmer Hobson, the former president of the Supreme Council of the IRB and officer in charge of the Volunteers in Belfast in 1916.[72] The public coverage of the dinner did not mention McCullough's close ties to Casement and Hobson's Belfast circle in the years before 1914.

West Belfast—the parade to Milltown cemetery on 10 April

The *Irish News* published a full timetable of the proposed Belfast commemoration events on 24 March. On Easter Sunday, 10 April 1966, the annual parade that always took place on Easter Sunday marched to Milltown cemetery from Beechmount at 3pm. This was not, however, the key Belfast event, nor was it the commemoration committee's priority. It appears to have been organised in the same manner as in other years. Over 5,000 marched in the parade with over

20,000 spectators lining the route, which was decorated with flags and bunting. It was one of the biggest Easter Rising commemoration ceremonies for years, but it was secondary to the main and special event that was to take place on the key date a week later.[73] The Easter Sunday parade was headed by the John F. Kennedy Memorial Band, 'survivors of the War of Independence' marched behind while the band played 'The Memory of the Dead'. The 1916 proclamation was read by Malachy McBurney and the oration was given by Niall Fagan from Leixlip, Co. Kildare. The old-guard republican Jimmy Steele presided, and speakers included Seamus O'Sullivan, chief marshal of the parade. In his oration Fagan, treasurer of Sinn Féin, proposed that in order to end the

> propagated confusion that existed in the minds of the present generation…a new constitution should be drawn up based on those freedoms so long sought and struggled for, and so clearly and unambiguously outlined in the 1916 proclamation.[74]

He suggested that, having sought United Nations approval, the constitution should be put to the electorate of all-Ireland for a national decision under UN supervision, and if it acquired a two-thirds majority its provisions should be carried out and a new 32-county state set up.

> It would be possible to make provision to allow United Nations or even British forces to remain in certain areas for a limited period of ten or fifteen years to allay whatever fears some might still hold. That is an honest and straightforward proposal which, if acted upon, will prevent Ireland becoming the scene of the next bloody upheaval in the world situation.[75]

The concert that had been banned from the Ulster Hall 'out of respect for the dead of the Somme' was rescheduled to take place in St Mary's Hall instead, securely within a nationalist area. Described as an Irish national ballad and folk-singing concert, it featured the McPeake family, Dominic Behan and the Brian McCollum folk group. On Saturday, 16 April, the night before the main Belfast commemoration, a film show featuring 'Mise Éire' and 'Saoirse' was to be shown in St Mary's Hall at 8 pm.

SPACE IN THE CITY: WEST BELFAST AS
ALTERNATIVE NATIONAL CAPITAL

The key event for Belfast was the parade along the Falls Road to the Casement Park GAA grounds on Sunday, 17 April. It was planned to be the biggest demonstration of its kind since 1953, when Belfast had celebrated the Robert Emmet anniversary.[76] All nationalist areas of Belfast were to be decorated with the 'national flag', and the Citizen Army flag was to be flown from thousands of homes. Contingents from all over Ireland were to form up in Hamill Street, Institution Place, John Street, and Barrack Street. In effect, 'nationalist areas' of Belfast always meant West Belfast, which was effectively partitioned within the city. There were, of course, nationalists in other areas—in the new housing estates of O'Neill's modernisation plan, the traditionally religiously mixed areas of the city or highly defensive enclaves like the Short Strand—but West Belfast was the heartland of Catholic and nationalist Belfast.

The Lower Falls, particularly the area around Leeson Street, was a key nationalist area in Belfast in the mid-1960s. It is now largely diminished below the Springfield and Grosvenor Roads—a major part of it, above the Pound Loney from where the Falls led down to the city centre near Kelly's cellars and St Mary's Hall, has had the Westlink driven through it. Other streets have been cut off as a result of the peace line and the building of the Westlink. Barrack Street and Durham Street and the area around St Mary's Chapel Lane, Smithfield Market and Castle Street, backing onto Hercules Street, now Royal Avenue—key parts of nineteenth-century Catholic Belfast—are now effectively part of the city centre. It is difficult now to have a sense of that area. It was later to become a stronghold of the Official IRA and was the world of the Falls curfew. This is also the seat of the construction and pulling down of the Divis Flats. It was a key hub of Catholic Belfast in 1966.

One of the main features of the 1966 parade was the range of schools of Irish dancers organised and brought together from all over by Eamon O'Cianáin, in what were described as 'their colourful national costumes'.[77] Speakers from Dublin, the GAA and the Belfast District Trades Council addressed the assembly at the end of the parade in the GAA grounds at Casement Park. Because the GAA owned the grounds it was in a position to veto certain speakers proposed by the parade's organising committee. Eamon O'Cianáin, a member of the organising committee, recalls that one of those so vetoed was Betty

Sinclair of the Communist Party. This was despite the objections of the organising committee, who held her in great affection 'because of her work with the families of Crumlin Road prisoners and detainees in the 1940s'.[78] The parade's proudest boast was that Joe Clarke, the 85-year-old veteran of the Rising, had declined an invitation to attend the reception to be held in Dublin Castle that Sunday, and had also apparently declined his place outside the General Post Office as a part of the official commemoration in Dublin, on the grounds that the Belfast parade was 'more in keeping with the spirit of 1916'.[79]

The parade, according to the *Irish News* was 'two miles long' and 70,000 were gathered to participate or to watch it. Described as a triumph for the organisers, the Belfast Golden Jubilee Committee, the parade was said to be the largest ever seen on the Falls. It was said to combine 'all sections of the community'.[80] The heaviest crowds lining the route were at the lower end of the Falls Road–Donegall Road intersection, the Glen Road junction and the approaches to Casement Park. The parade was lead by a colour party carrying the Tricolour;[81] others carried the Starry Plough, the Sun Burst banner of the ancient kings of Ireland and flags of the four provinces. Huge sheet-like banners with etchings of the faces of the executed leaders of 1916 were carried dramatically through the streets. They were followed by the John F. Kennedy Memorial Pipe Band, which headed members of the 1916–21 Old IRA and young girls wearing berets and military-style uniforms who were members of Cumann na mBan.[82] The Belfast Trades Council executive marched. It included the chairman E.J. Morrow, the vice-chairman Joseph Cooper and the secretary Betty Sinclair. Gerry Fitt, the newly elected Westminster MP for West Belfast, walked with the Transport and General Workers' Union.[83] Also in the parade were the Michael Dwyer, Jemmy Hope, Wolfe Tone '98 Gaelic football and camogie clubs, and 400 members of the GAA. Many carried banners and ensignia.

Tomás MacGiolla, president of Sinn Féin, Eamonn Mac Thomáis[84] of the Sinn Féin executive in Dublin, and Eamonn Ó Driscoill, described as being from the Sinn Féin executive in Cork, were present. The rally in Casement Park, at the end of the parade was addressed by Patrick (Leo) Martin, now described as chairman of the commemoration committee. He said

> there were those in the country who said that the country was free but they were forgetting about the six counties. The freedom they enjoyed in the twenty six counties was due to

the sacrifice of blood made by the brave men in 1916. But Pearse had envisioned Ireland as 'Not merely free but Gaelic as well'.[85]

He wondered what Pearse would say if he came back and saw the state of the country now. Referring to the ban imposed by the Stormont government on rail travel from Dublin or other locations south of the border on that weekend, Martin said that he deplored the fact that people had not been able to travel to participate in the commemoration as they pleased. The Proclamation of the Republic, the key text of the 1916 Rebellion in Dublin that proclaimed a republic for all-Ireland, was read by Malachy McBurney. The St Peter's Brass and Reed band played the 'Lament for the Dead'. When the parade moved in to the rally in Casement Park the main speaker was Seamus Costello of Bray, who was described as a member of the Dublin golden jubilee commemoration committee,[86] the Sinn Féin Dublin committee. According to Costello,

> [t]hey had come to Casement Park from the four corners of Ireland to commemorate the deeds of men and women who fifty years ago in Dublin fought and died for the principles of Liberty, Equality and Fraternity. Now in 1966, remembering the high-souled efforts of that gallant handful of men, remembering the volleys that followed the Rising, they wondered at what it was that went wrong. They wondered how it was that a revolution launched as this one was, could possibly have lowered its demands, could possibly have accepted less.[87]

Costello said that the Belfast commemoration was historic for many reasons. 'It was the first time in a long number of years that an All-Ireland Commemoration had taken place in Belfast'. He emphasised that Belfast was 'the cradle of Irish republicanism'. They had, he claimed, all branches of the republican movement present, side by side with representatives of the Belfast trade union movement. He said that for the past 45 years politicians in the south had been telling them that they were 'free'.

> What they really mean is that they have accepted the existence of partition, with its consequent evils of emigration, unemployment and sheer poverty. They would have us

believe that the selling of our national assets to the first foreigner who has the money is a hallmark of freedom. They would also like us to believe that the use of the infamous Offences Against the State Act against workers who are struggling for a just wage is a necessary and desirable thing.[88]

Here, Costello tried to pull together elements of the new Cathal Goulding-style social agenda of Sinn Féin with a revised northern strategy. Most of the tens of thousands who thronged the Falls on 17 April did not actually go into Casement Park. The parade itself, rather than the rally, was seen by the organisers as the significant event. It was huge street theatre, a massively colourful and dramatic enactment of the icons, images and verbal litanies of Belfast republicanism. It was, however, sufficiently broad to attract and draw in nationalists of different political persuasions. Austin Currie, for example, was said to be present, but there is no record of his presence in the newspaper accounts.

Clearly for Sinn Féin's commemoration of 1916, the Belfast march and rally was the key event in 1966. It was in fact their all-Ireland commemoration. Eamon O'Cianáin's recollection is that the original address from MacGiolla to those members of the Felon's Club who became the core committee in August of 1965 was intended as a means of galvanising Belfast republicanism. The scale and organisation of the West Belfast parade was to be the test of that, and an attempt to re-fire and re-politicise republicanism in Belfast. Belfast republicans' involvement in the border campaign of the late 1950s had been minimal, with few Belfast republicans subsequently being interned. There was a small, tight group of republicans like the Felon's Club and others who had shared prison experiences in the 1940s in Crumlin Road and the Curragh, but the intention in 1966 was to politicise a broader constituency in Belfast in particular.

The strategy of running people like Billy McMillan for election in West Belfast had not been a success, as the results of the 1964 election had shown. There had been some republican successes at the polls, but West Belfast was more eager to embrace Gerry Fitt, who promised an active, dynamic, proactive role at Westminster. If Sinn Féin wished to steer nationalist politics in Belfast it could do so only up to a point. The huge display and rally of Sunday, 17 April 1966 was to draw in a broader audience in Belfast, but it was not specifically billed as a republican celebration; although in Belfast, if not elsewhere, republicans of a traditional variety ran the commemoration in association with groups like the Connolly Clubs and fringe parties of the Left and the Communist Party. There is little or no evidence of Wolfe Tone Clubs, which figure so largely in the accounts of Roy Johnston and others, in Belfast at this time.[89] It seems too that the elevation of the socialist aspects of Connolly in particular was an outsiders' imposition, and the agenda of Dublin Sinn Féin rather than a local Belfast agenda.

FALLS ROAD REPUBLICANS AND THE ISOLATION OF NORTHERN NATIONALISM

The only people who placed Belfast at the centre of their commemorative agenda in 1966 were Sinn Féin. They approached West Belfast republicans and offered them help and direction in showing that the Irish nation was not dead in 'the North' and that the Irish government could not ignore them with impunity. West Belfast rose to the challenge. Anxious to forge a new identity and image for its republicanism in 'the South', trumped by the state for the ownership of 1916 there, Sinn Féin could construct Belfast as its capital for 1966. By locating their key commemoration in West Belfast, the only securely nationalist space in the city, Belfast republicans endeavoured to make their claim upon the nation from within their own territory. Ironically, the RUC and the Stormont government seem to have respected their ownership of West Belfast, at least for that day. The commemoration in West Belfast was a fantastic spectacle, a boost for northern nationalist morale and a feat of organisation by men and women no longer in their prime who wished to remind the young of their past. Apart from the day itself, this was to lead to a re-established Republican Clubs network in 1967.

Who were the Belfast organisers? They were mostly members of the Felon's Club. Billy and Malachy McBurney were brothers, one of whom owned a music shop near Smithfield Market. James (Jimmy) Sullivan was a young republican who was later to assume a brief role in the Leeson Street area of the Lower Falls in the early street disasters of 1968 and 1969. Kitty O'Kane, who was present at the original meeting in probably August 1965, was a very close friend of Billy McMillan's and subsequently became chair of the Republican Clubs' central committee. Another of the original organisers was Derek Peters, who was on the Communist Party executive with Betty Sinclair. Frank McGlade, Eamon O'Cianáin and Patrick (Leo) Martin were other significant figures in this circle.

Consequences

While the West Belfast commemorations proceeded, Rev. Ian Paisley conducted an alternative rally in the Ulster Hall—to celebrate the defeat of the rebels in 1916—that brought thousands of his supporters out on to the streets. The RUC was preoccupied by keeping both events separate. Four days after the commemoration, on 21 April 1966, the UVF declared war on 'the IRA and its splinter groups'. Some days later John Patrick Scullion was murdered. The real target had been Patrick (Leo) Martin, but he could not be found.[90] On 22 June three republicans who had been fined for organising the Falls Road parade without giving notice to the police refused to pay their fines. James (Jimmy) Sullivan (25) of Leeson Street said that neither he nor his colleagues would pay the fines, nor was anyone authorised to pay on their behalf. The others charged were Patrick (Leo) Martin of Baden Powell Street, who was 36, and Malachy McBurney of Kashmir Street, who was 45. According to Sullivan:

> [i]n view of the praise given to the organising committee for the orderly, dignified and peaceful manner in which the commemoration parade was conducted the action of the Government in prosecuting us can only be construed as a punitive measure against the organisers, and an attack on all those who participated...The Government action is in marked contrast to the attitude adopted to other parades organised then and since by Mr Paisley—the sole purpose of which is to stir up sectarian bitterness and strife, and to publicly attack members of the Government and the Moderator and members of the Presbyterian church...It would appear that there is one law for Republicans— however peacefully they strive to further their aims—which invariably leads to prison or the internment camp, and another for Mr Paisley and his followers who openly defy the powers-that-be and who claim immunity from the law which operates here under the guise of democracy.[91]

On 26 June Peter Ward, a barman at the International Hotel who had been drinking at the Malvern Arms in Malvern Street on the Shankill, the core street in what was Protestant West Belfast, was murdered, and his companions seriously wounded.[92] Terence O'Neill returned from a Somme commemorative event in the British Embassy in Paris and banned the UVF.[93] On 19 July Sullivan and McBurney were arrested and a warrant was issued for the arrest of Patrick (Leo) Martin.[94]

CASEMENT COMMEMORATION AT MURLOUGH BAY, ANTRIM, AUGUST 1966

The Belfast 1966 commemoration ceremonies were rounded off by a large contingent who went on the established date of the first Sunday in August to honour Roger Casement, who had been hanged on 3 August 1916. They went to Murlough Bay, near Ballycastle, where Casement had wished to be buried.[95] Wreaths were laid by the Casement Commemoration Committee, the Gaelic League, the Antrim GAA, the Feis na nGleann Committee, the Kerry Commemoration Committee, student associations from Queen's University Belfast, the National University of Ireland, Trinity College Dublin, the Irish Labour Association and the Wolfe Tone Association. The speakers were a rather motley collection of individuals with a range of agendas. They included James Connolly's son Roddy Connolly, Professor Seamus O'Neill, Gearóid O'Cuinneagháin, Seán Redmond of the Connolly Association in London and Alain Haisaff, described as a Breton, secretary-general of the Gaelic League, which, according to the *Irish News*, had rendered great assistance 'in bringing the Casement issue before the Celtic countries'.[96] Both O'Cuinneaghain and Haisaff had dubious past connections with fascism. Gerry Fitt was also present. Roddy Connolly told the gathering that 'they should not put their trust in the Stormont premier Mr O'Neill, Mr Brian Faulkner or even the British Prime Minister Harold Wilson against the forces of Paisleyism'. Rather, they should

> put their trust in consulting, conferring and concerting with all the forces of political social and cultural progress to take action, if action is needed, in the common interest.[97]

Casement, according to Connolly, had lifted his voice and worked his pen in Ireland's cause and aided the forming and equipping of the Volunteers.

> This is not a purely internal, local, provincial matter. It concerns all Ireland and all England; and all the United Nations as much as do the racial riots in the United States, a

crisis in Cyprus or the escalation—to use the word beloved of the Americans—of the threat to world peace in Vietnam…It is much more important to the cause of Ireland to support Gerry Fitt than to slap O'Neill on the back. Captain O'Neill deserves no commendation for weakly and belatedly carrying out duties incumbent on any chief executive. Those who rely upon him to bring law and order into respect among the irresponsible sectarian maddened supporters and to curb their growth and activity may find too late that they would have been better advised to rely upon themselves…Until the British government realise that, in this modern world, there is no place for this unnatural division of Ireland, until they take positive steps towards the reunification of Ireland there will remain the threat of a recurrence in the North East of Ireland, of sectarianism gone wild…[98]

After all of the Belfast events were over, a series of meetings were held of existing republicans and those who had been involved in organising the 1916 commemorations; a reformulated Republican Clubs seem to have been formed out of these meetings. The older guard—Jimmy Steele, Joe Cahill and Frank McGlade[99]—disliked the new strategy, dictated by Dublin Sinn Féin. The Dublin line was that military campaigns were futile, that the border campaign had been a disaster with no public support, and that the aim of Republican Clubs was to change tactics and join or influence trades unions, credit movements, anti-discrimination groups; any popular movement with popular support. When Michael Farrell, as part of a Housing Action Group a few years later, went with Cyril Toman to meet the Belfast Housing Action Group, he was surprised to meet Joe McCann and Gerry Adams.[100] The new republicans of Republican Clubs, reformed out of the planning of the 1966 commemoration in 1965–66, attempted to set the agenda for a new politics. They sought to infiltrate and shape the agendas of popular movements. They themselves saw Algeria as their model. Whether most of the republicans mentioned above were IRA members or not is unclear. Estimates for the numbers of IRA members in Belfast at this time are very low.[101] Late in 1967 Bill Craig, as Minister for Home Affairs, banned the recently reconstituted Republican Clubs. According to Eamon O'Cianáin, Craig had excellent sources. His statement as to the strategy and intentions of Republican Clubs was 'spot-on'.[102]

COMMEMORATION IN ANTRIM, TYRONE, DOWN AND ARMAGH

The only other significant Antrim commemorative event in 1966 was in Toomebridge on Easter Monday, 11 April, to the Roddy McCorley monument on the shore of Lough Neagh. Similar to the Belfast parade in its diverse composition, it consisted of members of the Old IRA; the commemoration committee of Toomebridge; standard-bearers of the flags of the four provinces; Seán Larkin's accordion band, Bragerailly; contingents from Toomebridge and district, from South Derry, from Belfast and from other parts of Northern Ireland; and St Ergnant's Pipe Band, Toomebridge; Gaelic football clubs from Moneyglass, Cargin, Portglenone, Cregan and Glenravel; together with St Patrick's Accordion Band.

The Tyrone commemorations were more diverse. In Dungannon, recent and unsuccessful Sinn Féin candidates Tom Mitchell and Ruairí Ó Brádaigh managed to dominate the speeches in an eclectic commemoration. Austin Currie, who was at the forefront of young nationalist movements in Queen's University, participated as a member of his local GAA team and called for a more active Nationalist Party. Preparations for the celebration of the 1916 golden jubilee in Tyrone had begun at a meeting in Pomeroy just before Christmas 1965. A provisional committee was elected with responsibility for making arrangements for the commemoration. The chairman was Jim O'Donnell from Coalisland, and Jim McQuaid from Donaghmore was the secretary. A number of sub-committees were operating in a number of areas throughout the county. Coalisland was the venue for the principal celebrations in Tyrone. The organisers declared

> [e]veryone who believes in the principal 'Ireland one, Ireland Free', is cordially invited to come along and join in this all-county tribute to the men who carried the cross for Ireland in that memorable Easter Week of 1916.[103]

Another meeting of the Tyrone County 1916 Jubilee Year Committee was held in Carrickmore, a mainly nationalist town, in January 1966.[104]

The overall Northern Directorate of the 1916 Jubilee Year Commemoration Committee was appointed by delegates representing various commemorative committees from across Northern Ireland. The directorate, at least nominally, co-ordinated the commemorations and was elected at a meeting in Dungannon in January;[105] and in February at a further meeting, Jimmy Steele, the 'well-known Belfast republican', was appointed president.[106] Dungannon celebrated the anniversary with a series of lectures on subjects relating to 1916, the first of which was delivered by de Valera's biographer, Tomas P. O'Neill, who spoke on the origins of the Rising. Other lectures in the series included one on James Connolly and the Citizen Army by Proinsias Mac an Bheatha, editor of the weekly Irish language magazine, *Inniu*.[107] The Tyrone County 1916 Jubilee Year Committee decided that celebration ceremonies would be held on Easter Monday and also that a republican memorial should be re-erected in Carrickmore.[108] At a meeting of the committee in February at Pomeroy it was announced that a plaque would be erected in Coalisland, to mark the spot where republicans had gathered in Easter Week 1916. It had been hoped that Nora Connolly O'Brien, daughter of James Connolly, would be present to unveil the plaque, but she was unavailable on Easter Sunday, the day decided upon for the unveiling.[109]

The commemorative parade in Coalisland was intended to be the main focus of the celebrations in Co. Tyrone. Around 20,000 people and 20 bands attended the Easter Sunday ceremonies there. The parade was led by the colour party, which consisted of some men in black berets, followed by a diverse gathering of groups from the area, including republicans, Hibernians, nationalists, Foresters, Gaelic footballers, Gaelic League members, dancing teams and boy scouts, and bands from Fintona, Ardboe, Dungannon and Loughmacorry, Moy and Killeshil, Kinturk and Pomeroy, Edendork and Coalisland. A large proportion of the participants wore the Easter lily. Dungannon was represented at this commemorative event by the Foresters Silver and Ancient Order of Hibernians Accordion Band. Members of the Coalisland Fianna were also present and some participated in the parade.[110]

The two local republican candidates in the then recent general election, Tom Mitchell and Ruairí Ó Brádaigh, marched to the front of the parade. Austin Currie, the Nationalist MP for East Tyrone, marched further back with the Edendork Gaelic Football Club. The 1916 Proclamation was read by a local 1916 veteran, Patrick Crawford. Ruairí Ó Brádaigh delivered the oration. In it he referred to Thomas Clarke, who had spent his early years in Dungannon and, according to Ó Brádaigh, had inspired several generations with his patriotism. Ó Brádaigh went on to urge Irish youth to join voluntary organisations and to be prepared to fight to free the Six Counties:

Ireland is not yet free. It is not yet free either politically or economically. So the aims of the men who fought and died in 1916 remain unfulfilled. There is still a job to be completed. Let us brace ourselves for the final push.[111]

He stressed the need for unity amongst republicans declaring that 'we must help each other. We must work together, for in unity there is strength'. He hoped that one day soon Pearse's ideal of an Ireland, politically and culturally independent of England, would be realised. When the parade returned to the town, a plaque to commemorate the congregation of volunteers in the town in 1916 was unveiled by another 1916 volunteer, Joseph O'Neill.[112]

The celebrations in Dungannon were also well attended. In keeping with the prominence given to honouring Thomas Clarke, the Thomas Clarke Gaelic Football Club organised a special programme of commemoration. The participants at the parade on Easter Monday included various other GAA clubs, NACA clubs, Irish Catholic Boys Scouts groups, youth clubs, Irish dancing schools and Gaelic League branches. The celebrations there concluded with a concert held in the town, which included the staging of a pageant called 'Eastertide', produced and directed by Frank O'Neill of Coalisland[113] and performed by a Coalisland group 'assisted musically by the voice of John McNally of Radio Éireann', who sang songs including 'Kelly, the Boy from Killane', 'She is far from the Land' and 'The Bard of Armagh'.[114] In Strabane, Mass was held in Melmont and wreaths were laid on the graves of locals Seán Sharkey and Charles McCafferty. On Easter Monday Senator John O'Kane of Bridge Street, Strabane, was forced by police to remove a tricolour that he had flown in his garden.[115] The main Strabane commemorations were postponed until the first week in August. A member of the commemoration committee explained:

> rather than go ahead with makeshift or incomplete plans we have decided to fix the celebrations for the 1st week in August when we are assured of the attendance of a large number of bands. The celebrations will include *ceilidhe*, concerts, plays, parade, open-air traditional dance and carnival festivities.[116]

Newry, Newcastle and Warrenpoint

In Newry, a committee of twenty was set up to organise the golden jubilee celebrations in County Down. It was chaired by Dr Pádraig Quinn, a member of the Northern Division Old IRA,[117] with James Rowntree as secretary.

In marked contrast to its attitude in other counties, the Nationalist Party in Down gave its full support to the Easter commemoration in the county and called for full participation by its members,[118] but it did not appear to play a full role in the organisation of the commemorative events in the same way that the GAA and republicans did. The celebrations in Down included a special Mass in Newry Cathedral on Easter Sunday, followed by a parade of local bands and national organisations to the local cemetery.[119] As in Dungannon, a lecture series had run through 1966 as part of the commemorative programme. The Literary and Historical Society, which was formed as part of the Newry Christian Brothers Past Pupil Union, sponsored the lecture series. This series included, in February, a lecture by Dr Kevin B. Nowlan, lecturer in History at UCD, on the subject 'The IRB and 1916'.[120] A separate lecture, 'From Parnell to Pearse', was delivered in Castlewellan by John Magee, Professor of History at St Joseph's Training College, Belfast. Magee's lecture covered the roles played by the GAA, the United Irishmen, Isaac Butt, the IRB, the Land League, Pearse, Carson and Clarke in the development of the ideals associated with the 1916 Rising.[121] Special Masses were organised by the Catholic Church hierarchy for the spiritual and temporal welfare of Ireland. Masses of this kind took place in Newry Cathedral, in St Catherine's Dominican Church in Newry and in St Peter's Church, Warrenpoint.[122]

Down GAA staged its own commemorative parade, with ceremonies being held in Newcastle on the Sunday after Easter.[123] This does not appear to have occurred in any other northern county. Every football, hurling and camogie club in the county was represented. Flags displayed included the county colours of red and black, the flags of the four provinces, the Plough and the Stars and the Sun Burst banner of the Fianna. About 4,000 people were reportedly present to witness the procession. An oration was delivered by the GAA's former president, Pádraig McNamee, when the procession reached St Patrick's Park. He declared:

> [w]e must keep the ideal of an Ireland, Gaelic and free constantly with us and while we may not see it fully realised

at least we can hand on the banner to generations to come and some day Emmet's epitaph will be written.[124]

The GAA was, he said, central to the separatist tradition:

All agree that the formation of the GAA in 1884 and of the Gaelic League in 1893 played an important part in the National revival that led to the 1916 Uprising. A large number of members took part in the Rising, many making the supreme sacrifice.[125]

The GAA parade was in fact the second commemorative parade in Newcastle. On Easter Sunday a procession organised by the special commemorative committee—made up of members of various national organisations in the area and chaired by Dr Pádraig Quinn—was held in the town.

The Easter Sunday parade in Newry in 1966 was the biggest parade held in the town since the local community had openly defied a government ban on the Easter 1916 commemoration parade in 1949. Several thousand representatives of various national organisations were involved in the procession, which passed through a two-mile route to St Mary's Cemetery.[126] Among them were the Irish National Foresters and the Ancient Order of Hibernians, who marched in 'colourful regalia'.[127] The *Frontier Sentinel* referred to a tradition whereby southern politicians delivered orations at northern commemorations solely for the purposes of political propaganda. The newspaper stated that it was pleased that this had not been the case with Dr Quinn's oration.[128] His speech was quoted in full. Having first honoured the men of 1916 who gave their lives and 'restored Ireland's self-respect and dignity as a nation', Quinn then called on his audience, in an invocation of a litany of United Irishmen, all but Tone from Ulster,

to declare your association with the aspirations and purposes of these noble patriots in the words of Tone, Russell, Neilson, Simms and McCracken…we declare never to desist in our efforts until we have subverted the authority of England over our country and asserted our independence.[129]

Later that evening at a commemorative cabaret dinner, Quinn spoke of the ideal of a 32-county Republic and said that 'it could be near to realisation'. He claimed that the six counties only existed through the support of England, and that those who had traditionally supported it were becoming tired with it. He said that the commemorative parade in Newry that day had instilled in him a belief that the Irish people could not fail in their quest for full nationhood.[130] At a GAA-organised wreath-laying ceremony at Newtownstewart, Charles McNamee said: '[l]et us hope that their example will help us to remain steadfast until our goal: The All-Ireland Republic is accomplished'.[131]

The Easter Sunday parade in Newry, which attracted people from various parts of south Armagh and south Down and Warrenpoint, had been preceded by a week of functions, which included lectures by Professor Robin Dudley Edwards from University College Dublin on '1916—A reappraisal'[132] and by Dr Art Cosgrove, also of UCD but originally from Newry, on 'The Easter Rising'. The local committee also staged a cabaret, a Gaelic League concert and Seán O'Casey's 'Juno and the Paycock' on Sunday 17 and Monday 18 April.[133] Some 5,000 people from the Newry area took part in the organisation or staging of the commemorations.[134] At Warrenpoint 'Seven Men, Seven Days', the commemorative pageant staged at both Croke Park and Casement Park and based on the script by Byran MacMahon, was staged on Easter Sunday night before a large audience.[135]

The local newspaper argued that the large demonstrations and large number of spectators illustrated that nationalism was still vibrant in the area:

> Sunday's Easter Commemoration parade in Newry must have come as quite a shock to those people who in latter years had been literally boasting that nationality was dead in the Newry area, and who also felt that they could, without fear of public disapprobation, sneer at those who sought to prove that Newry was, is and always will be a strongly nationalist town.[136]

The editorial in the same issue expressed particular satisfaction at the unity within nationalism that the commemorations demonstrated:

> [n]o one who witnessed Sunday's demonstration of national faith and the people's tribute to those heroic men of 1916 who sacrificed all in their love of country could fail to be deeply moved by the spectacle of men of varying political and social beliefs coming together in a community of common interest to show that in

whatever other way they differed they were one in the
fact that they were Irishmen.

Again, the editorial referred to the strength of nationalism and also
declared that the commemorations were illustrative of the level of
support that still existed for the ideal of a united Ireland.

So in times when the people's strong sense of nationalism
would appear to be dormant, let it not be taken as a sign
that the enemies of the ideal of an All-Ireland Republic may
come out and openly insult that ideal.[137]

COMMEMORATIONS IN OTHER AREAS OF THE NORTH

Commemorative celebrations followed a similar trend throughout
Northern Ireland. Commemorative parades, wreath-laying ceremonies,
GAA games, lectures, cabaret dinners were common-place. Wreath-
laying ceremonies were held at the republican plot in Carrickcruppin
and at St Michael's Cemetery in Killeen, where an oration referring to
local men who had been involved in the struggle for Irish independence
was delivered by the key republican activist Dr Roy Johnston, who was
rather disingenuously described as simply being 'from county Tyrone'.[138]

In Armagh two separate parades were held in the town. The first
was held in the morning at the republican cemetery and was headed by
a colour party of 12 men wearing black berets, dark suits and tricolour
armbands. The tricolour was carried at the front of the procession. It
was carried in a similar fashion at the second parade, which attracted a
large attendance. The second event was much more representative of
various national organisations, with the GAA, Sinn Féin, the Gaelic
League and Gael Linn taking part.[139]

There was some friction at the speeches in Armagh, with rival
speeches delivered by Seán Stephenson (MacStíofáin) and James G.
Lennon of the Ancient Order of Hibernians. Stephenson addressed the
crowd first and referred to the IRA, which he said had never ceased its
physical struggle against Britain and would continue to seek the opportunity to continue that struggle by the only means possible, through
physical force. Senator Lennon, repudiated this and claimed:

we have to learn that while the cause of unity and freedom
must now as in the past be the ideal of the Irish people the

methods of the past cannot be those of 1966 and onwards, but that in other spheres and in our time the same spirit and courage which imbued the man of 1916 and before must enlighten our effort to attain to that ideal.[140]

Importantly, he did not disagree that Irish unity and a break from Britain were desired, rather it was the appropriateness of the violent struggle that he disowned. Senator Lennon had previously referred to the possibility that the Easter commemorations might be used by some in their own interests. Earlier in the year, speaking at a St Patrick's Day Ancient Order of Hibernians rally at Bellaghy in Derry, Lennon had said that the people of Northern Ireland had the task of continuing the struggle for justice, but that the methods of 1966 could not be those of 1916.[141] The level of enmity between these nationalist formations was clearly expressed in Stephenson's response in Armagh:

> I did not know he was going to be present and did not know he was going to speak. If I had known this I would not have addressed the meeting, as I feel that the Senator and I represent two irreconcilable attitudes.[142]

Londonderry/Derry and Dungiven

Discussion as to the organisation and form of Easter commemorations for 1966 began in Derry months in advance. Initially the Nationalist Party appeared ambivalent, and any enthusiasm that its members may have had about the prospect of the celebrations was overshadowed by fears of unrest.[143] Eddie McAteer made this clear when he said that it was unlikely that the party would be organising its own Easter celebrations. He deplored the possibility of violence:

> [t]here is, unhappily, already some discord from which we would wish to keep aloof...I consider it unseemly that anyone should attempt to make party capital out of this solemn occasion. We hope to set an example by quietly participating in local and national remembrances...I have wondered sadly whether the most telling commemoration might not be simply a moment of silence, with James Connolly's great death prayer: 'For all good men who do their duty'.[144]

McAteer made a similar point when he announced that he and the other Nationalist MPs and senators were to go to Dublin to attend a special viewing of a documentary film 'An Tine Bheo' and to a separate reception to be hosted by the taoiseach. He contrasted the atmosphere north and south: 'The mood of the north seems to be one of quiet pride tinged with prayerful melancholy and perhaps a little fear lest the jubilee celebrations be marred by anything sectional or unseemly'.[145]

McAteer's lack of enthusiasm did not, however, deter the local commemorative committee's plans for the golden jubilee of 1916 in Derry. The committee proposed to hold ceremonies at 3pm on Easter Sunday, with a parade starting from and returning to Celtic Park by way of Elmwood Terrace, Westland Villas, Blucher Street, Eglinton Terrace, Bogside, Abbey Street, William Street, Rossville Street, Lecky Road, Anne Street and Lone Moor Road. Prayers and an oration would be delivered at Celtic Park. Those invited to attend the parade and ceremonies included Irish dancing groups, Gaelic Athletic Association clubs, the Gaelic League, St Columb's College, Magee College, Foyle College, the Christian Brothers and other schools, the Ancient Order of Hibernians, Irish National Foresters, Irish Transport and General Workers Union and the city rugby and soccer associations. Irish national flags were made available by the Jubilee Commemoration Committee to those who wished to display them at their houses.[146] The *Derry Journal* expressed its satisfaction at the inclusion of the schools of all denominations and the football and rugby clubs by the organisers of the Derry commemorations; this was in direct contrast to the announcement by the Football Association of Ireland that it would not partake in the national commemorations of 1916.[147]

Neil Gillespie, 66, a well-known republican from Derry, who according to the *Derry Journal* joined the Irish Volunteers in 1913 and subsequently became a member of the IRA, was selected as the Sinn Féin candidate in the constituency in the 1966 general election, in opposition to the Nationalist candidate P.J. Gormley. Gillespie was also the secretary of the local 1916 golden jubilee commemoration committee.[148] It was decided that the focal point for the commemoration would be the local GAA grounds, Celtic Park, where a parade with bands was planned. The Ancient Order of Hibernians informed the commemoration committee that it had decided not to be officially involved with the parade but that individual members were likely to take part in the celebrations.[149]

While controversy was generally avoided in relation to routes for the parade, a planned parade for the Loup area in Derry was banned by the Minister of Home Affairs, Brian McConnell, due to the belief that it might lead to public unrest. The organisers of the commemorations denied the possibility of such trouble. Dermot Devlin, secretary of the South Derry commemoration committee, maintained that the decision was unjustified because:

> [t]he route for our parade was carefully selected to make sure that it would cause no offence to anyone. There is only one Protestant house along the route and this house is not near the public road, it was absolutely ridiculous for the Minister to say that there would be public disorder if the parade took place.[150]

As in other areas, wreath-laying ceremonies took place in Dungiven, where wreaths were laid on the graves of two locals, Lieutenant Carolan and Volunteer Gilmartin. This event concluded with an oration by Neil Gillespie.[151]

At the main commemorative event in Derry on the Sunday, a crowd of 1,000 accompanied by two bands marched in a parade over a three-mile route. The parade went through the previously noted nationalist areas of the city and there were some police on duty. Participants included members of the Old IRA and children dressed in national costume. It was headed by a colour party bearing the Tricolour, the flag of the Fianna and the flag of the Citizen Army. When the parade ended at Celtic Park, the proclamation was read and an oration was delivered by another well-known republican, Seán Keenan.[152] The event at Celtic Park was presided over by the secretary of the Derry golden jubilee commemoration committee, Neil Gillespie. As well as the Old IRA, the GAA, Gaelic League, Irish schools of dancing, Derry and District FA and republican youth were among those represented.[153] In Derry City, where a ban had been imposed on the Loup parade, some 700 people accompanied the sister of Brigadier General Seán Larkin to the local cemetery where he was buried. He was one of four IRA officers executed at Drumboe Castle in Co. Donegal in 1923. His sister, Mrs Laverty, had been asked by police to postpone her visit to the grave, 'but declined as she had visited every Easter Sunday'. The crowd who accompanied Mrs Laverty were eventually allowed by police to visit the grave and trouble was averted.[154]

As a result of the commemorations in Derry, a number of the events' organisers were later summoned to appear in court, because of their failure to give 48–hours' notice of the parades at Celtic Park. Those charged were Gillespie, the secretary of the Commemoration Committee, Seán Keenan, the vice-chairman of the committee, as well as Seán Shields, Patrick Kirk, Michael Montgomery and George F. O'Doherty. In turn, a protest meeting was planned for the following Saturday evening, at the junction of Rossville Street and William Street. The meeting was to be addressed by speakers from Dublin and Donegal. Mr Gillespie protested that the parades in question had been held in a nationalist area of the city and that public meetings in commemoration of 1916 had taken place 'over the past 20 years either at Meenan Park or at the Bogside' and that this was the first time any police action had resulted.[155]

When those summoned appeared in court, a republican picket was held outside in protest. Six republicans carried placards that read 'Justice is Being Mocked Here Today', 'Summonses for Us, None for Others', 'End Unjust Laws' and 'We Demand the Right to Honour Patriot Dead'. The police report on the commemoration was provided by Sergeant Goldrick, who told the court that there were between 600 and 700 people taking part in the parade as it left from Celtic Park. Five of the defendants, Neil Gillespie, Patrick Kirk, Michael Montgomery, George Finbar O'Doherty and John (Seán) Shields, were fined £5. The other defendant was John Keenan, who claimed that parades in Derry were traditional and did not require notice, and that the fines would not be paid. The prominent activist Kevin Agnew from Maghera said that there had been no disorder associated with the Derry parades, and he intimated that police action was only taken because of the recent antagonism by Ian Paisley.[156] The defendants had one month to pay the fines, which remained unpaid when that month expired.[157]

Despite this police action against the organisers and the subsequent fines, the Easter commemoration events in Derry were seen by the organisers as successful. As had been the case in Newry, the local nationalist paper in Derry, the *Derry Journal*, proclaimed the national celebrations a huge success and a fitting demonstration of pride in the events of 1916. Unusually for a northern nationalist paper of the time, the *Journal* gave its approval to the display in Dublin. Referring to the celebrations in Northern Ireland, the *Derry Journal* was pleased that the commemorative events had not been affected by the Stormont government's suggestion of an 'atmosphere of tension and even crisis', or by the Belfast *Newsletter*'s implications that the north 'had even been placed on a war footing'. The *Journal*'s editorial approved of the Northern Ireland government's decision not to impose a blanket ban on the commemorative events, since 'bans, batons and the paraphernalia of force would only have left a legacy of bitterness and undone all the efforts for a new approach to the community problem in this part of Ireland'.[158]

LANGUAGE, IDENTITY, HISTORY, UNITY

The issue of the Irish language was raised on a number of occasions at commemorative events in counties Down and Tyrone. Rev. L. MacEntaggart, president of St Patrick's Boys' Academy, Dungannon, referred to the need, in the commemorative year, to invest in a movement to revive the language. Senator Dr P. McGill and individuals from across Tyrone who were involved with the language movement were present when the Fáinne Nua was unveiled by the movement, to be worn by those who supported Gaelic in an effort to popularise the language.[159] As part of the GAA's support in 1966 for a renewed interest in Irish culture, it encouraged the present and future generations to minimise the effects of the division of their land by retaining their own Irish identity and by making sure that their children were taught the history and language of their country.[160] Reverend Eamon Devlin, who delivered the oration at the Dungannon commemoration on Easter Monday, said that Irish was not taught as much as it should be and that no effort was being made at training colleges to foster the language, literature or history of Ireland.[161]

Coverage of the commemoration foregrounded stories relating to the contribution made by northern republicans to the Easter Rising in 1916. The *Dungannon Observer* relayed a story of a journey made by a Father Coyle and a Father Doyle accompanied by a Miss Owens to Dublin from Fintona, on Holy Saturday 1916, to meet with the Military Council in Liberty Hall, where they were informed that a Rising would indeed take place. Thus Co. Tyrone and the republican leader there at the time, Dr McCartan, were aware of the plans by Sunday morning when the priests returned. The driver of the car, Patsy Bradley from Omagh, who was still alive in 1966, verified the story. Similarly, portrayals of Denis McCullough and Dr Patrick McCartan were presented. The lack of enthusiasm for a Rising on both their parts was commented on.[162] Because of his connections with Co. Tyrone, Thomas Clarke got frequent mention in relation to the 1966 commemoration. The *Dungannon Observer* depicted the Dungannon commemorations as a tribute to Clarke. The reporter referred to the 'fundamental' part that Clarke played in the Rising and proudly described him as 'one of ourselves, a Northerner'.[163]

Father Eamon Devlin from Donaghmore, when speaking in Dungannon, situated the Easter Rising of 1916 within a historical tradition of opposition to England dating back to 1169. The 1916 Easter Rising was

> no mere violent eruption against an entrenched ascendancy, but a deliberately planned and executed sacrificial offering for the purpose of saving Ireland's soul. It is indeed in the strict tradition of Irish opposition to foreign tyranny and oppression.[164]

Referring specifically to Clarke, Father Devlin linked him to Dungannon and in turn claimed that:

> Dungannon has symbolised Irish resistance down the centuries to the despotism of the conquest. For 500 years, Irish resistance, guided from Dungannon, succeeded in containing that conquest, and in that long struggle produced many leaders whose names are enshrined for ever in the pages of Ireland's history.

He described Clarke as 'no mere average man. He was a brave man, and heroic man, and typical of our race, an unconquerable man'. While singling Clarke out he also honoured Pearse:

> Pearse…was the patriot *par excellence* [who] typified for his comrades of Easter Week, as he typifies for us today all that is best and noblest in Irish manhood. Steeped in the language and history of his country, he had established complete contact with his Gaelic past, and the closer an Irishman gets into contact with that Irish past through the language and the literature, and the history of Ireland, the clearer does he realise the necessity for the political freedom of Ireland.[165]

Father Devlin had already delivered a lecture, as part of a commemorative series presented in Dungannon, on the subject of Pearse. On that occasion he described the 1916 leader in religious terms and declared him to be beyond criticism:

> I do not know if Pearse was a Saint. I believe that he was: but I do know that if ever a Devil's Advocate searches his writings to find some word or phrase or thought or sentiment to use against him he shall not find it. Nothing bawdy or coarse or vulgar ever came from Pearse's pen.[166]

In his lecture, Father Devlin offered his interpretation of Pearse's relationship with bloodshed and the physical force tradition in Irish history:

> Pearse did not teach Irishmen to kill, but that Irishmen should die in open fight for freedom seemed to him a supreme object. He believed in the shedding of blood, not so much for the purpose of inflicting injury as for the purpose of consummating a sacrifice…'War' Pearse said 'is a terrible thing, but war is not an evil thing: it is the things that make war necessary that are evil'…they [1916 leaders] knew that by their sacrifice they would save Ireland's soul.[167]

Most speeches placed the Easter Rising within a wider nationalist, literary and language movement that was historically separatist. The participation of a number of northerners in the Easter Rising was frequently stressed as a source of pride. The thoughts of Professor F.X. Martin expressed in the Thomas Davis Lectures on Radio Éireann on the subject of 'McCullough, Hobson and the Republican movement in Ulster' were reported with interest. Martin detailed new documents that revealed that the Ulster leaders, including Dr Patrick McCartan in Tyrone, were not made adequately aware of the Dublin leaders' plans for Easter 1916, which meant that northern republicans could not play a full part in the Rising. Martin argued that Ulster, nonetheless, was a significant factor in understanding the origins of the Rising, since it was the loyalist reaction to Home Rule that had formed a crucial role in bringing the Rising about.[168]

Father Devlin also brought the attention of his audience at the Dungannon commemorative celebrations to a number of unfinished tasks:

[t]oday, 50 years after the Rebellion of 1916, it is surely necessary to make a new assessment of the national situation…There are still several unfinished tasks. The first great task is the reunion of our country.[169]

Bringing this about required the amalgamation of the two parliaments in Ireland:

Let us never underestimate the fact, however, that Ireland today is ruled by two native governments. The task of all true Irishmen must be to bring these two parts of Ireland together in a new Irish nation. The constitutional position of the Six-County state is not so sacrosanct that it cannot be changed by the people. In that new united nation that will inevitably come, there must be room for all men and for all opinions, for the new English who came in the 17th Century as for the Old Irish of Ulster. This state within a nation that had its origins in 17th and 18th Century colonisation must surely soon show itself to be an anachronism.

Devlin's more interesting assertions, in the context of 1966, were to follow. He lamented the lack of unity and leadership within northern nationalism since the foundation of Northern Ireland and pinpointed this as the reason for the growth of apathy within the community:

[i]t is not without significance that Nationalist Ulster has produced no leader during the past 40 years to whom all could give allegiance. During that time, in fact, there has been no truly Nationalist Party. There are, indeed, half a dozen splinter groups that manifest themselves only for about a month before each election but none of these has a policy or a programme…nothing but the innate anti-unionism that flows in our very blood stream.[170]

True nationalism, he said, did not manifest itself in

an occasional outburst about discrimination in the allocation of houses…A dismal sociology is no substitute for Irish Nationalism. An occasional taunt at a Unionist opponent in Stormont, a cheap jibe or a good stunt, seems to be the sum total of the Nationalist ambitions of our public representatives.[171]

During the March 1966 general election campaign, the leader of the Nationalist Party, Eddie McAteer, gave his view of what nationalism needed when he addressed a number of new party branches in Warrenpoint and Rostrevor. He outlined his belief that what was needed in that year of remembrance was a dedication to building an Ireland of good neighbours.[172] McAteer said:

> [c]ontinuance of partition has forced us over to a position where we must open our eyes and acknowledge that the Government here has through effluxion of time almost acquired a right to recognition as an Irish-based institution. The need of the times is towards peaceful negotiation and we shall have to adapt ourselves to the idea that the local Parliament will be a fairly long time surviving…to give security to these who fear incorporation in a wider national and indeed European community. This is not to suggest that nationalism has been watered down to acceptance of British over lordship of any part of Ireland. But we do recognise that we are now faced with nearly a half century of legislative and administrative growth which cannot be uprooted overnight.[173]

He stressed the need for progress and real improvements for the nationalist community:

> [w]e must step up our demand for real civic rights. The fair words of peace must be matched by some real remedy. Failing that, Westminster must be made to accept responsibility for the sins of Stormont.[174]

His speech appears to indicate a decisive movement on the part of the Nationalist Party in this time towards a concentration on civil rights and also an intimation that progress might have to be sought by bypassing Stormont and targeting Westminster.[175] Indeed, at the meeting in Warrenpoint, the chairman of the South Down Nationalist Executive, Barney Carr, reportedly said that there was a great movement afoot to establish a strong Nationalist Party to meet the ongoing challenges facing the nationalist community.[176] At a meeting of the Newry Branch of the South Down Nationalist Organisation, the chairman, Nationalist MP Joseph Connellan,[177] referred to the election campaign in South Down and argued that the only way to defeat the unionist candidate was through unity of all nationalists in the constituency, so that the community could give its full support to one nationalist candidate. He also referred to the hope that the Nationalist Party would soon be sufficiently organised to achieve this kind of support and success.[178]

That the ideal of national unity was still sacrosanct was made clear at Easter 1966. One writer in the *Dungannon Observer* who reported on the commemorative events in Dublin expressed hope. He described how, while attending the parade in Dublin his thoughts drifted to the Loup, the Falls, Newry, Armagh, Rosslea, Coalisland and Pomeroy. He lamented the fact that these places 'matter not until men from Derry, Antrim, Down, Armagh, Fermanagh, and Tyrone recognise Dáil Éireann, give allegiance to Dáil Éireann and, please God, one day control Dáil Éireann'.[179]

The desire for unity was also explicitly expressed in a number of orations delivered in the course of the commemorations. Neil Gillespie said: 'We are not here to celebrate the setting up of a statelet or two. We are here to appeal to the people of Derry to follow the teachings of these men'.[180] At Toomebridge in Co. Antrim, Kevin Agnew sent a message to the RUC and to the minister of home affairs that they would not succeed in dampening the spirit of republicanism that was evident throughout the north. Like Gillespie at Dungiven, he argued that Pearse and the other 1916 veterans had not died for two Irelands, and in a comment addressed 'to the leaders in the south', he said that if they believed the republicans in the north would be content to spend their lives under the Union Jack and in half-slavery, they were mistaken.[181] Similar points were made by Seán Keenan at the main commemoration event at Celtic Park in Derry. He claimed that the national spirit was at a low ebb, but he was consoled by the fact that it had also been low before Easter 1916. He put a number of questions to his audience:

> Is it too late to appeal to all Irish men and women to come together for the only cause worth pursuit? Can we recognise that spirit which existed during the war of independence when the people ratified by their votes that declaration of freedom which was signed in blood?[182]

In his subsequent appeal he said it was time for the Irish to break the link with England and that freedom would be delivered through a united stance:

[w]e appeal to you as Irishmen and women to break the connection with England. Ireland can only be prosperous when she controls her own destinies. We must stand together and say we want freedom. We must have freedom. Then we will have freedom and our duty will be fulfilled.[183]

Keenan spoke of the division of Ireland and declared that the current situation in Ireland did not live up to the ideals of 1916:

Ireland, North and South, is today ruled by Special Powers Acts and Offences Against the State Acts which deprive each of us of every single right that democracy confers. This is not the Ireland of which our patriot dead spoke. Ireland is one nation, anyone who tells you differently is lying. The two-nation idea must not be accepted by the Irish people.[184]

He offered a warning to those who sought to maintain partition in Ireland: 'I would tell them to be always on their guard for while this country remains divided there will always be need for security'.[185]

THE GAELIC ATHLETIC ASSOCIATION

The GAA played a prominent role in organising the jubilee celebrations and participated in various Easter Rising celebrations throughout Northern Ireland. Early in 1966 the Co. Down GAA chairman, George Tinnelly, called for an enthusiastic participation in the commemorations.[186] Not only did he express the association's pride at being 'associated in some small way with the heroic men and women of Ireland who, in face of extreme odds, challenged the might and power of the British empire to rule and govern our country',[187] he also stressed the importance of 1966 for the association.

This year could be the most historic one for the Association. All the counties in the land are celebrating the memory of the men and women of 1916 who gave their all that we could have the life we have today…I believe that we today could best honour those heroes if we went away from this convention resolved to teach our members and the youth of the country to live up to the ideals of the Association. Encourage our youth to learn and speak our native language, dance our native dances, play and take part in the pastimes of our native land. This is our duty and if we fail future generations will blame us. Let us not fail but go out and teach our children not to be ashamed of our pastimes and celebrate the memory of those of 1916.[188]

The GAA viewed the ideals of 1916 and of the association itself as coterminous. The golden jubilee of the 1916 Rising was a time for the association to revive its commitment to playing a more dynamic cultural role in Irish society. This was a prominent theme in GAA speeches. Alf Murray (Ó Muirí), president of the GAA, was also vocal in expressing his view as to the meaning of 1916 and the celebration of its anniversary. When opening the Dungannon Gaelic Drama Festival and addressing representatives from a number of GAA clubs in East Tyrone, he outlined the importance of such a festival in the commemorative year and called for a greater effort on the part of the language movement. He continued by referring to '[t]he obligation that rests on each and every one of us to spread the Gaelic ideal'.[189] He referred to 'the second phase of the work begun by Pearse and his associates in 1916. The Drama Festivals have played a very prominent part in the execution of that phase'. He called on a greater commitment to this Gaelic ideal in 1966.

> In our celebrations this year, let us not just attend a lecture or a concert or a pageant and leave it at that—rather let us experience a re-awakening of the Gaelic spirit that is in us and engage actively in the furtherance of the work which was initiated 50 years ago. [190]

Murray envisaged the GAA playing a much more diverse role in the community, that it would play a cultural role through its participation in activities such as the Drama Festival. The GAA president gave a similar address at a GAA convention in Dublin towards the end of March. He referred to the jubilee year:

> All of you, I would think, have seen 'Seachtar Fear, Seacht Lá', which has put into tangible form the pride that we feel in our heritage, the message that we hope to pass on, the determination that is ours to keep alive the tradition of Nationhood which inspired those Seven Men and all their comrades…To me its [the GAA's] greatest achievement has

been that, in the years immediately before and after 1916, it gave to the separatist movement a part of that spiritual backing which made the fight for freedom something more than a mere attempt at changing the form of government and turned it into a people's struggle for national identity.[191]

The GAA president clearly placed his association in the foreground of the Rising and its ideals and thus in the midst of the preparations to celebrate the fiftieth anniversary of that event. In his address to the GAA county convention in Omagh, the county chairman of the GAA there, Paddy Cullen, again discussed the role of the association in the nationalist revival and the separatist tradition inherent in the 1916 Rising.

> The GAA in 1884 brought the manhood of Ireland from its knees to a proud and purposeful erectness—through the unity of the playing field but more truly through the ideals of nationality it instilled in its members…the GAA was not the least of the great forces that brought about the events of 50 years ago.[192]

He stressed that the commemoration of the 1916 Rising posed questions that must be answered by the association:

> …today more than at any time, should we be aware of the national purposes of our own Association. But is realisation of the glories of the past of any good if it carries no message, no inspiration for the present and the future? We may well say, and truly say, the GAA was a force in the national awakening and 'remember the past for pride' but the fact that fifty years ago this Association was adhering to the ideals of its founders, is of little good if we can lay no claim to be doing the same. [193]

The GAA, in this view, must still strive for the ideal of 'Ireland Gaelic, Ireland free'. Nineteen sixty-six was the year in which the GAA could reassert itself in this role.

The Easter Rising was presented in 1966 as a radical turning point. A columnist in the *Dungannon Observer* endorsed William Butler Yeats's portrayal of the Rising as giving form to 'a terrible beauty'. The columnist believed that Yeats's poetry reflected the way in which the Rising had overturned a legacy of indifference that had been associated with the Irish Parliamentary Party and the Home Rule campaign after Parnell's death. The columnist also evoked the work of George Russell in illustrating the impact of the Rising:

These dreams had left me dumb and cold.
But yet my spirit rose in pride.
Refashioning in burnished gold
The images of those who died
Or were shut in the penal cell.
Here's to you Pearse, your dream not mine.
But yet the thought for this you fell
Has turned life's waters into wine.[194]

Ballads were also used as a means to represent and intensify various views on the Rising itself and the commemoration. All the bands played out of a repertoire of Irish nationalist songs and a shared musical repertoire was assumed by all. Poetry too, some of it local and nostalgic, played a similar unifying role between different locations. An intriguing verse sent to a Newry based newspaper in April 1966 by the Nationalist MP for Armagh South , E.G. Richardson, put forward the accepted view that 1916 acted as a groundbreaking event for Nationalism in that period.

Jubilee songs we sing today,
Waft them o'er the hills away,
We raise the cup of freedom ale
And bless our homeland Innisfail.

Nineteen–Sixteen lit a flame.
Marching men came out to claim
Freedom that was free from blame
For all our people to proclaim.

From Bantry Bay to Antrim glen
Was gathered there the valiant men;
In noon-day sun to weave a crown
For all of us in Dublin Town.

All honour to that gallant band,
That came at noon to free our land.
In truth and justice we acclaim
Their title to immortal flame.

For Christian value was their call,
Our cherished hope, a home for all;
Free from strife and every strain,
Where peace and love will ever reign.[195]

NORTHERN NATIONALISM IN 1966—ABANDONED BY THE
IRISH STATE AND DIVIDED WITHIN

MP Joseph Connellan expressed a hope that unity could be established
within nationalism. The 1966 Westminster election demonstrated the
extent to which this unity was absent in most of Northern Ireland.
While a single nationalist candidate—T.J. Mitchell, a republican from
Dublin—ran against the unionist candidate in the mid-Ulster
constituency, in Fermanagh–South Tyrone such an agreed nationalist
candidate did not emerge. In that constituency, the Republican
candidate, Ruairí Ó Brádaigh,[196] attacked what he labelled a 'Unity-
Liberal plot', whereby a liberal candidate would contest the election in
the event that the National Unity convention failed to nominate a
candidate for the election.[197] Attempting to decide on a nationalist
candidate in this constituency caused further divisions, epitomised in
a walkout by some 300 republicans from a convention in Tyrone. A
Mr Donnelly was chosen as the 'National Unity' nominee and he urged
Sinn Féin to see that their intervention would only aid the unionist
candidate.[198] Ó Brádaigh nevertheless stood as the Republican
candidate in the Fermanagh–South Tyrone constituency. In criticising
the decision by Donnelly to stand he appealed to the electorate to vote
for him in this jubilee year.

> This is the golden jubilee of 1916. I ask you to come out on
> polling day and do something you will not be ashamed of
> before your children and your children's children. I ask you
> to vote for the Republic of Pearse and Connolly and that
> will be the right and proper thing and will hasten the
> freedom of Ireland.[199]

This is an obvious use of the ideals and traditions associated with 1916
in attempting to appeal to the nationalist community and in repudiating
a rival nationalist candidate. Ó Brádaigh firmly connected himself and his
party with the republicanism of 1916 and claimed that nationalist
support for him would bring about the full realisation of 1916.

Debates relating to 1916 and the ideals of that period featured in the Westminster election in 1966. In fact, it was in nationalist electoral confrontations that such debates mainly took place. This was most obvious in the Mid-Derry constituency, where nationalist and republican candidates went head to head in the battle for the nationalist vote. Neil Gillespie, the republican candidate in Mid-Derry, referred to the decision of the Nationalist Party to contest the constituency in the general election and forecast a good republican poll, since he was sure that in the golden jubilee year the people of the Derry area would respond to the call of unadulterated Irish nationalism.[200]

Hugh McAteer, Eddie McAteer's brother, also spoke at republican meetings in support of Gillespie and against the nationalist candidate. The speakers called on the people to re-affirm their allegiance to the Irish Republic and claimed that national independence was not going to be won by drinking cups of tea at Stormont and shaking hands with unionist politicians, but by the people of Ireland standing on their feet and saying as in the past: 'Damn your concessions. We want a Republic'. Mr Gillespie called on the electorate 'to use the election to show your determination to own you own country and reject England's claim to rule any part of it'.[201] He stressed the republican links with the past in urging people to vote for him.

> Republicans drew inspiration from the past, they keep faith with the past but they keep their eyes fixed on the future. The Republican movement which symbolises the National tradition of opposition to the rule of the foreigner is the only organisation in Ireland that has formulated a social and economic programme for the whole nation. The Nationalists seek to restore the conditions of the past, conditions that the people of Ireland smashed—as they fondly hoped for ever—back in 1918…In this the 1916 Golden Jubilee year show that you remain true to the ideals of those who in the battered GPO, on the bullet swept streets of Dublin and at the hands of execution squads died for you and me that we might live in peace and harmony in the pride of full untrammelled Irish nationhood.[202]

At another republican election meeting, the president of Sinn Féin, Tomás MacGiolla encouraged voters to vote for Gillespie; he was the appropriate choice because of his commitment to the ideals for which the men of 1916 had fought. He asserted his belief that the objective of establishing a Republic by breaking the link with Britain was more pressing than ever. MacGiolla outlined what in his view were the implications of voting for the Nationalist Party and not for the Republican candidate. There was clearly a message which he wished to promote in 1966, and voting for the Nationalist Party would only give the wrong impression about nationalism at that time.

> It is unfortunate that there has been intervention by the Nationalist candidate. This is the first time since 1918 that an anti-Unionist candidate in the Derry Constituency has proposed attending Westminster. Ever since Eoin MacNeill contested this constituency the opponent of the Unionist has called for rejection of Britain's claim to rule this country by abstaining from Westminster. It would be most regretful and a backward step nationally if Derry was to give much support to this watered down Nationalism in this Jubilee year of 1916. It would also give heart to the Stormont regime who would think that Derry had come to heel at last.[203]

In contrast, the Nationalist Party leader, Eddie McAteer, claimed that the nationalist community ought to continue the fight for freedom by electing a direct voice to Westminster.

> We may have to change our methods of fighting through the years. It is essential to carry the fight for freedom and against second-class citizenship in to the citadel itself. We do not particularly wish to send people to Westminster but it is essential to send Paddy Gormley at this moment.[204]

Neil Gillespie denied the accusation that because republicans were concerned with breaking with Britain they were not adequately involved with socio-economic issues. He assured the nationalist community of this.

> It might be that because Republicans strove first to break that connection with England some people regarded them as being unconcerned with the everyday problems of life. Day to day, Republicans, within the limits that the denial of full sovereignty and the partitioning of their county permitted them, were becoming more involved in the daily struggle of the people against economic and other evils.[205]

In the same address, Gillespie reiterated his hope that, in the year that they had commemorated the fiftieth anniversary of the Easter Rising, the people of Derry would demonstrate once more that they were a republican people. This would be done by making a protest by electing an abstentionist candidate rather than sending a representative to Westminster. Seán Keenan, who presided at the meeting, presented the republican position on whether national unity or socio-economic issues should be prioritised when he said that republicans wanted a university, houses and employment, but that if the electorate supported them in solving the one great problem of the division of their country then the other problems would disappear overnight.[206]

Thus, there was an obvious clash between the Nationalist Party and republican candidates on what was the best way forward for the nationalist community in the circumstances of 1966. Clearly, republicans felt that the most appropriate way to honour and commemorate the Easter Rising of 1916 was through continued abstentionism, while the Nationalist Party now claimed that it wanted to provide nationalists with a useful voice at Westminster and also to engage in bridge-building exercises with unionists. The republican response to this was explicitly stated by Hugh McAteer when he addressed a 1916 Commemoration concert in Letterkenny, Co. Donegal:

> Hands across the Border, Stormont tea parties and shaking the hands of the Unionist Quislings may all be very liberal and broadminded, but has it brought unity one step closer; has is brought the slightest amelioration to the conditions of the second-class citizens of the North? However else it may come, one thing seems certain, and that is that independence will not be won in the drawing rooms of the intellectuals.[207]

He attacked those who were willing to be involved with the commemorations but were not, in his view, willing to continue the traditions of 1916 and who were merely paying tribute to men 'who apparently may be admired, but must not be emulated'.[208]

CONCLUSION

The commemoration of the fiftieth anniversary of the 1916 Rising at Easter time in 1966 in Northern Ireland was engaged in by a diverse

number of national organisations, which ranged from the Ancient
Order of Hibernians to the GAA, the Gaelic League, the Nationalist
Party and republicans. They were all in agreement in their high praise
for the leaders of 1916 and in endorsing the ideals that informed the
1916 Easter Rising. The Rising was viewed as part of a wider nationalist, literary and language movement that was also separatist. Because the
Rising was seen in these terms, and because of the participation of a
large range of organisations in the commemoration, all were able to
have ownership of the commemoration; and thus conflict within
nationalism, which was deeply divided, was largely avoided. The importance of the roles played by a number of northerners in the 1916 Rising
was highlighted; the role of Thomas Clarke was therefore given prominence in the commemorations, as was that of Bulmer Hobson and Dr
McCartan in Tyrone.

A number of speakers at Easter commemorative events talked of the
tasks that still remained unfulfilled; national unity was an obvious one
and was referred to by speakers from the GAA, Ancient Order of
Hibernians and republicans. While the quest for unity was held as the
greatest ambition of all, it was placed within the wider objective of a
Gaelic, cultural and language-based revival. The GAA especially sought
to reassert its role and to revitalise its contribution to Gaelic traditions
in the commemorative year. The emphasis that was placed on the idea
of 'Ireland one, Ireland Gaelic' reflects the large contribution made by
the GAA in the Easter commemorations.

The Nationalist Party was also asking questions of itself at this time,
but this questioning was not directly connected with the Easter
commemorations. The party articulated the need for an improved
dynamism, organisation and party unity. It offered a more realistic
interpretation as to the appropriate response in the current political
circumstances. It encouraged a pragmatic acknowledgement of
Stormont and partition, but this had to be offset by improvements for
the nationalist community.

The Ancient Order of Hibernians stressed its repudiation of violence
but supported the ideals of freedom and unity. It was the Nationalist
Party that remained least vocal on partition. In fact, the presence of the
Nationalist Party was less than evident at the commemorative events in
Northern Ireland. It seems clear that, through conversations with politicians in Dublin and conversations with O'Neill's cabinet at Stormont,
the party was anxious to minimise the capacity for tension potentially
inherent in the commemoration. Most of the public addresses at the

1916 commemoration ceremonies were conducted by members of the GAA, the Ancient Order of Hibernians and republican speakers.

As expected, republicans referred to the need to follow the teaching of 1916 and were clear in their assertion that the men of 1916 did not die for two Irelands. An explicit message was sent to the Irish government that republicans in the north were not satisfied with remaining under the rule of Stormont and that all republicans remained committed to seizing the opportunity to renew the physical struggle against Britain. The scale of the jubilee commemorations was held up as evidence of a revival in nationalism in Northern Ireland and was thus perceived as giving hope to the cause of national unity.

In addition, republican candidates in the general election of 1966 appealed to the nationalist community to send a clear message of support for republicanism to the British government in the commemorative year. Voting for republican candidates was presented as the proper way to honour the men of 1916. The lineage between the then republican candidates and the men of 1916 was thus maintained. The electoral campaigns by both republicans and nationalists where republicans claimed that lineage provided the background for conflict on the issue of 1916. That conflict could perhaps have been avoided had it not been for the March 1966 general election. However, while there was debate over what political direction would best befit the men and ideals of 1916, shared ownership of the commemoration and of 1916 was achieved through their portrayal as part of a wider nationalist, language-based, Gaelic and separatist tradition. The commemoration, therefore, belonged to all those who shared the dream of a free, independent, united and Gaelic Ireland.

Nevertheless, the nature of the northern commemorations in 1966, and their partitionist actuality, underlined the fact that however deep the divisions within northern nationalism went, they were as nothing to the divide between northern nationalists and an Irish state that seemed capable of conceiving of itself as a nation without them.

NOTES

[1] *Irish News and Belfast Morning News*, editorial, 11 April 1966.

[2] Seamus Heaney, 'Requiem for the Croppies', from *Door into the dark* (London, 1969). Seamus Heaney, in a recent interview (*Guardian*, Review Section, Saturday, 27 May 2006), says that he composed this poem on 'the fiftieth anniversary of the 1916 Rising in 1966'. He later omitted it from collections, partly because it 'sounds uneasy in the Unionist zones...I think the young nationalist in me was trying to give voice to things that the culture in Northern Ireland did not admit. There was no official space for anything of that kind'.

[3] For studies of this process, see Gillian McIntosh, *The force of culture: Unionist identities in twentieth century Ulster* (Cork, 1999); Brian Walker, *Dancing to history's tune; history, myth and politics in Ireland* (Belfast, 1996) and Ian McBride (ed.), *History and memory in modern Ireland* (Cambridge, 2001).

[4] For an obvious example of such exclusion, see Gerry Fitt as quoted in Chris Ryder, *Fighting Fitt* (Belfast, 2006), 56. Christopher Manson, in his PhD on the Somme commemorations, notes that there were shared commemorations until the 1930s, and that in certain places they continued to be shared. See Christopher Manson, 'The commemoration of the Great War in Belfast, Ulster and Northern Ireland , 1918–39', unpublished PhD thesis, University of Ulster 2005. See also Catherine Switzer, *Unionists and Great War commemoration in the north of Ireland, 1914–1939* (Dublin, 2007). In 1938 in Newry, a town where there had been a high level of Catholic recruitment into the British army during the First World War, the Town Council agreed to provide funds to build both a First World War memorial and, in another part of the town, to erect a Celtic Cross in the Republican plot, bearing the key nationalist dates 1798, 1848, 1867 and 1916. Government minister Dawson Bates vetoed the erection of the Celtic Cross. I am indebted to Dominic O'Hanlon for this information.

[5] This issue is explored dramatically in Frank McGuinness, *Observe the sons of Ulster marching towards the Somme* (London, 1986). Similar dislocations of allegiance or exclusions from official memory both north and south are explored by Sebastian Barry in *The steward of Christendom* (London, 1996) and *A long, long way* (London, 2005), where southern participation in the British war effort is explored.

[6] See Rebecca Lynn Graff, 'Remembering and forgetting 1916; deconstructing discourses of commemoration and conflict in post-peace process Ireland', unpublished PhD thesis, School of Politics, International Studies and Philosophy, Queen's University Belfast, 2007, for a brilliant analysis of the political uses of commemorations in the past decade in Ireland.

[7] See Henry Patterson and Eric Kaufmann, *Unionism and Orangeism in Northern Ireland since 1945* (Manchester, 2007), for the controversy provoked by commemorative parades in Boveragh and Dungiven in 1953.

[8] Marianne Elliott, *The Catholics of Ulster* (London, 2001). Marianne Elliott's own verbal account of being at the Toomebridge commemoration in person in 1966 is one full of foreboding; see also Marrianne Elliott, *Robert Emmet, the making of a legend* (London, 2003), for mention of the Robert Emmet commemorations in Belfast in 1953 and her accounts of her father's production of nationalist pageants as part of the northern nationalist culture of memorialising. See also representation of such remembering in the plays of Seamus Finnegan. Toomebridge was historically significant for its association with the legendary hero of 1798 Roddy McCorley, who 'goes to die on the bridge of Toome today'. He was immortalised in song for modern northern political memory by the writer 'Ethna Carbery' in the key journal of the northern nationalist revival of the late-nineteenth and early-twentieth century, *The Shan Van Vocht*.

[9] In recent years, the Somme has been appropriated by paramilitary organisations 'to legitimate their own activities but also to distance the loyalist working class from the former hegemonic Britishness of official unionism and the sectarianism of the Orange Order'. See P. Graham and P. Shirlow, 'The Battle of the Somme in Ulster memory and identity', *Political Geography* 21 (2002), 881–904. For the Northern Ireland government's plans to commemorate the Battle of the Somme at Thiepval and Balmoral in 1966, see Public Records Office of Northern Ireland (hereafter cited as PRONI) FIN/18/45/20. In this instance the northern government tried to include all churches in its plans.

[10] See Mary E. Daly, Chapter 1, this publication.

[11] See R.W. White, *Ruairí Ó Brádaigh: the life and politics of an Irish revolutionary* (Indiana, 2006), for an insight into the role of anti-Fianna Fáil republicans in commemorating the Rising from the 1920s onwards. Among such political formations, the commemoration—whether of 1916 or 1798 or the deaths of Republicans on hunger strikes in the Curragh in the early 1940s—was almost as significant a genre as the funeral. See also Diarmaid Ferriter, Chapter 5, this publication.

[12] Instituted by Ernest Blythe after the death of Michael Collins and consolidated after the Boundary Commission outcome of 1925. See Ronan Fanning, *Independent Ireland* (Dublin, 1983).

[13] National Archives of Ireland, Department of the Taoiseach (hereafter cited as NAI DT), 98/6/495, 'IRA Organisation', hand-written minute by Nicholas Ó Nualláin, 16 April 1966.

[14] See Gillian Deenihan, 'Seán Lemass and Northern Ireland,1959–66', unpublished MPhil thesis, University College Cork (1999), quoted by D.G. Boyce, 'No lack of ghosts', in Ian McBride (ed.), *History and memory in modern Ireland* (Cambridge, 2001), 254–71.

[15] Northern nationalist leaders were, however, invited to official events in Dublin. The *Derry Journal*, 8 April 1966, reported that Eddie McAteer together with Nationalist MPs and senators were invited to two functions in Dublin by the government—to a special showing of the documentary film 'An Tine Bheo' at the invitation of the Minister for External Affairs, Frank

Aiken, 'next Sunday'; and to the reception to be hosted by the taoiseach, Seán Lemass, on the following Sunday.

[16] In West Belfast in 1964 Rev. Ian Paisley demanded that the RUC remove a tricolour flying from the electoral office of Billy (Liam) McMillan off the Falls Road in Belfast. Technically, under the Flags and Emblems Act of 1954, such a symbol could be deemed to be provocative and thus require police removal should complaints be made. In this instance, the arrival of the RUC provoked the worst trouble on the streets of Belfast since the 1930s. For Bovevagh and Dungiven and the row within unionism that led to the passing of the Act, see Patterson and Kaufmann, *Unionism and Orangeism*. See also PRONI FIN/18/8/52 Civil Authorities (Special Powers) Act N.I. (1922), memo to Cabinet by Minister of Home Affairs.

[17] See Margaret O'Callaghan and Catherine O'Donnell, 'The Northern Ireland government, the 'Paisleyite Movement' and Ulster Unionism in 1966', *Irish Political Studies* 21 (2) June 2006, 203–22.

[18] Cumann Luthcleas Gael, Coiste Chontae Aontroma 1953–99, 'Official re-opening souvenir programme, 5 September 1999', (Belfast, 1999). See also St Agnes Gaelic Athletic Club, fiftieth anniversary programme, 'Naomdh Una 1951–2001', (Belfast 2001). On Roger Casement see Mary E. Daly (ed.), *Roger Casement in Irish and world history* (Dublin, 2005); and Margaret O'Callaghan, '"With the eyes of another race, of a people once hunted themselves" Casement, colonialism and a remembered past', in George Boyce and Alan O'Day (eds) *Ireland in Transition, 1867–1918* (London–New York, 2004) 259–75.

[19] Russell was a key figure in the United Irishmen movement in the north. He staged a rebellion in support of Robert Emmet's and was hanged by the state.

[20] For the concept of *lieux de memoire* or sites of memory, see the hugely influential work of Pierre Nora, translated from the French as *Realms of memory*, English language translation with a foreword by Lawrence D. Kritzman (New York, 1996).

[21] *Derry Journal*, 11 February 1966.

[22] *Derry Journal*, 11 February 1966.

[23] *Derry Journal*, 18 February 1966.

[24] *Derry Journal*, 18 February 1966.

[25] *Derry Journal*, 25 March 1966.

[26] *Derry Journal*, 29 March 1966.

[27] See Austin Currie, *All hell will break loose* (Dublin, 2004).

[28] Ó Brádaigh polled 10,370 votes, or 19% of the vote. The other nationalist candidate standing as a Unity candidate polled 14,645, or 26% of the vote. F.W.S. Craig, *British parliamentary elections 1950–70* (Chichester, 1971).

[29] White, *Ruairí Ó Brádaigh*.

[30] The best brief account of this process is still to be found in Henry Patterson, *The politics of illusion: a political history of the IRA* (London, 1989 and 1997), 96–139; see also R.H.W. Johnston, *Century of endeavour: a biographical and autobiographical view of the twentieth century in Ireland* (Dublin, 2005):163–260; Lorenzo Bossi, 'Truly days of hope and anger: the Northern Ireland Civil

Rights movement as a case study in the development, outcome and legacies of social movements', unpublished PhD thesis, School of Politics and International Studies, Queen's University Belfast 2005; Desmond Greaves, *The Irish question and the British people* (London, 1963), *Reminiscences of the Connolly Association* (London, 1978).

[31] Denise Kleinrichert, *Republican internment and the prison ship Argenta 1922* (Dublin, 2001).

[32] Interview with Eamon O'Cianáin, 17 May 2005, Cultúrlann, Falls Road, Belfast. See too Uinseann MacEoin, *The IRA in its twilight years 1923–1948*, (Dublin, 1997), 689–704, where O'Cianáin is also referred to as Eddie Keenan.

[33] See Catherine O'Donnell, Chapter 7, this publication.

[34] See Roy Garland, *Gusty Spence* (Belfast, 2001) and O'Callaghan and O'Donnell, 'The Northern Ireland Government'. See also BBC Ulster's *Sunday Sequence* programme, 28 May 2006, featuring Roy Garland discussing the circle around Paisley in 1966, plus long clips of O'Neill's public statements at the time.

[35] PRONI CAB/9F/224/3, Report to Terence O'Neill from the Rt Hon. E.W. Jones, QC, MP, Royal Courts of Justice, Belfast, 22 March 1966, re. conference in Londonderry on the future of the city, meeting attended by Erskine Childers, Neil Blaney and Senator FitzGerald of UCD. Blaney proposed a free-trade area between Donegal and Northern Ireland. See also the report of the conference, 'The development of an area—West Ulster—first report, one-day school on development', 19 March 1966, Derry.

[36] Gillian Deenihan, 'Seán Lemass and Northern Ireland, 1959–66', unpublished MPhil thesis, University College Cork 1999, 255–6, as quoted by D. George Boyce, '"No lack of ghosts": Memory, commemoration and the state in Ireland', in Ian McBride (ed.) *History and Memory in Modern Ireland* (Cambridge, 2001) 254–71.

[37] See F.X. Martin (ed.), *Leaders and men of the Easter Rising: Dublin 1916* (London, 1967).

[38] See note 2 above.

[39] Edna Longley, 'The Rising, the Somme and Irish memory', in Edna Longley (ed.), *The living stream: literature and revisionism in Ireland* (Newcastle upon Tyne, 1994), 69–85.

[40] Margaret O'Callaghan, 'Old parchment and water; the Boundary Commission of 1925 and the copperfastening of the Irish Border', *Bullan, An Irish Studies Journal* 4 (2) (2000), 27–55.

[41] For studies of the nationalist north, see Eamonn Phoenix, *Northern nationalism, nationalist politics, partition and the Catholic minority in Northern Ireland, 1890–1914* (Belfast, 1994); Enda Staunton, *The nationalists of Northern Ireland, 1918–1973* (Dublin, 2001); and Lorenzo Bossi, 'Truly days of hope and anger'.

[42] Devlin was the undisputed leader of northern nationalism from the pre-First World War era to his death. See the section on Devlin in Richard Kirkland, *Cathal O'Byrne and Northern revival* (Dublin, 2006).

[43] Interview, Eamon O'Cianáin, 17 May 2005.
[44] For nationalist or Catholic Belfast see A.C. Hepburn, *A past apart—studies in the history of Catholic Belfast, 1850–1950* (Belfast, 1996); Alan Parkinson, *Belfast's unholy war; the Troubles of the 1920s* (Dublin, 2004); J. McDermott *Northern divisions: the old IRA and the Belfast pograms, 1920–22* (Belfast, 2001). See also the 'Belfast' chapter in Robert Lynch, *The Northern IRA and the early years of partition* (Dublin, 2006).
[45] See Catherine Hirst, *Religion, politics and violence in nineteenth century Belfast—the Pound and the Sandy Row* (Dublin, 2002); on the Pound Loney, a poor Catholic area at the bottom of the Falls Road at the city side. It demonstrates the power of the sectarian geography of Belfast.
[46] This territory is explored in Brian Moore, *The emperor of ice cream* (London, 1966).
[47] Maurice Hayes, *Black puddings with Slim: a Downpatrick boyhood* (London, 1996).
[48] Denis Donoghue, *Warrenpoint* (London, 1991).
[49] Patrick Shea, *Voices and the sound of drums* (Belfast, 1981).
[50] See Frank Ormsby (ed.), *A rage for order: poetry of the Northern Ireland Troubles* (Belfast, 1992).
[51] For an outline of Sinn Féin's plans, see NAI DT, 98/6/495, 'IRA organisation', *aide mémoire* December 1966; draft plan in the possession of Seán Garland, IRA chief of staff, when arrested in September 1966. See also NAI DT 97/6/161 on Coiste Cuimhneacháin Seachtain na Cásca, the 1916 Golden Jubilee Commemoration Committee, which had as its address the Sinn Féin offices in Gardiner Street, Dublin.
[52] See O'Callaghan and O'Donnell, 'The Northern Ireland government'.
[53] Geoffrey Warner, 'Putting pressure on O'Neill', *Irish Studies Review*, 13 (1) (2005), 13–31. See also Margaret O'Callaghan, 'Genealogies of partition. History, history-writing and "the Troubles" in Ireland', *Critical Review of International Social and Political Philosophy* 9 (4) (December 2006), 619–34.
[54] See Ian McAllister 'Political opposition in Northern Ireland: the National Democracy Party, 1965–1970', *Economic and Social Review* 6 (3) (April 1975), 353–66, for details on the Garron Towers meeting.
[55] See PRONI CAB 9B/205/3 for earlier (1964) ineffective letters to Labour representatives at Westminster from individual members of the Campaign for Social Justice in Northern Ireland (CSJNI) in relation to housing, particularly in Dungannon. A letter to Harold Wilson from Mrs Patricia McCloskey of the CSJNI, dated 14 December 1964, was, like all of the others, simply forwarded by the Home Office to C.J. Bateman of the Cabinet Office at Stormont.
[56] Interview, Eamon O'Cianáin, 17 May 2005; see also, for his earlier career, Uinseann MacEoin, *The IRA in the twilight years, 1923–48* (Dublin, 1997), 698–704.
[57] The Felon's Club on the Falls Road was originally set up as a West Belfast ex-prisoners' club for those who had been in A-wing of the Crumlin Road prison together in the 1940s.

[58] *Irish News and Belfast Morning News*, 30 August 1965.

[59] McMillan had polled just 3,256 votes, or 6% of the West Belfast vote, as Sinn Féin candidate. Harry Diamond of Republican Labour had polled 28% of the vote, with William Boyd of Labour taking 24%. James Kilfedder for the Unionist Party was elected on that occasion.

[60] Frank was married to Rebecca McGlade, and they were the parents of the political activist Brid Roddy. Information from Michael Farrell.

[61] Frank McGlade had stood as a Sinn Féin candidate in Belfast North in the 1955 and 1959 Westminster elections and as a Republican candidate in 1964.

[62] *Dungannon Observer*, February 1966.

[63] *Irish News and Belfast Morning News*, 3 January 1966.

[64] *Irish News and Belfast Morning News* 17 January 1966.

[65] *Irish News and Belfast Morning News*, 24 January 1966.

[66] Brian Walker has pointed out that a similar refusal to the 1798 commemoration committee in 1948 had been successfully challenged by a High Court action.

[67] *Irish News and Belfast Morning News*, 4 March 1966.

[68] Alf Murray (Ó Muirí) (Antrim), Seán Harte (Armagh), Pat Mullan (Derry) and T.P. Murphy (Down).

[69] *Belfast Telegraph*, 25 March 1966.

[70] MacMahon was a distinguished teacher and writer from Listowel, Co. Kerry. He was commissioned by the GAA to write a commemorative piece. He wrote the impressive but lurid tableau *Seachtar Fear, Seacht La*.

[71] *Irish News and Belfast Morning News*, 25 March 1966.

[72] *Irish News and Belfast Morning News*, 21 March 1966. See also O'Callaghan's "'With the eyes of another race'".

[73] *Irish News and Belfast Morning News*, 11 April 1966.

[74] *Irish News and Belfast Morning News*, 11 April 1966.

[75] *Irish News and Belfast Morning News*, 11 April 1966.

[76] *Irish News and Belfast Morning News*, 14 April 1966.

[77] *Irish News and Belfast Morning News*, 14 April 1966.

[78] Interview, Eamon O'Cianáin, 17 May 2005.

[79] Joe Clarke, quoted in *Irish News and Belfast Morning News*, 18 April 1966. Clarke was president of the Sinn Féin Gardiner Street commemoration committee; see NAI DT, 96/7/1490.

[80] *Irish News and Belfast Morning News*, 18 April 1966.

[81] *Irish News and Belfast Morning News*, 18 April 1966.

[82] This information was provided by Ann Hope, who took part in the parade.

[83] *Irish News* and *Belfast Morning News*, 18 April 1966.

[84] MacThomáis was born in Dublin, 1927. He joined Sinn Féin and the IRA in 1950s; was treasurer of Sinn Féin; manager of and contributor to *United Irishman*; and was interned in the Curragh, 1957–9.

[85] *Irish News and Belfast Morning News*, 18 April 1966.

[86] For details on Costelloe, see Jack Holland and Henry McDonald, *INLA: deadly divisions* (Dublin, 1994).

[87] *Irish News and Belfast Morning News*, 18 April 1966.

[88] *Irish News and Belfast Morning News*, 18 April 1966.

[89] Johnston, *Century of Endeavour*. See also Bossi, 'Truly days of hope and anger'.

[90] Garland, *Gusty Spence*, 56–59.

[91] *Belfast Telegraph*, 23 June 1966.

[92] Garland, *Gusty Spence*, 57–59.

[93] Interview, Sir Kenneth Bloomfield, September 2005.

[94] *Irish News and Belfast Morning News*, 4 July 1966.

[95] *Irish News and Belfast Morning News*, 4 August 1966.

[96] *Irish News and Belfast Morning News*, 4 August 1966.

[97] *Irish News and Belfast Morning News*, 4 August 1966.

[98] *Irish News and Belfast Morning News*, 4 August 1966.

[99] Frank was married to Rebecca, a sister of Eamon O'Cianáin's wife. There was also a family connection to Liam (Billy) McMillan.

[100] Conversation with Michael Farrell.

[101] See Tom Hennessy, *Northern Ireland: the origins of the troubles* (Dublin, 2005), citing Department of Justice document 'Stormont estimates to London'.

[102] MacEoin, *The IRA in the twilight years*, 689–704.

[103] *Dungannon Observer*, 1 January 1966.

[104] *Dungannon Observer*, 29 January 1966.

[105] *Belfast Telegraph*, 3 January 1966.

[106] *Dungannon Observer*, 5 February 1966.

[107] *Dungannon Observer*, 5 February 1966.

[108] *Dungannon Observer*, 29 January 1966.

[109] *Dungannon Observer*, 19 January 1966.

[110] *Dungannon Observer*, 16 April 1966.

[111] *Dungannon Observer*, 16 April 1966.

[112] *Dungannon Observer*, 16 April 1966.

[113] *Dungannon Observer*, 2 April 1966.

[114] *Dungannon Observer*, 16 April 1966.

[115] *Frontier Sentinel and Down, Armagh and Louth Advertiser*, 16 April 1966.

[116] *Derry Journal*, 8 April 1966.

[117] *Frontier Sentinel and Down, Armagh and Louth Advertiser*, 1 January 1966.

[118] *Frontier Sentinel and Down, Armagh and Louth Advertiser*, 26 March 1966.

[119] *Dungannon Observer*, 8 January 1966.

[120] *Frontier Sentinel and Down, Armagh and Louth Advertiser*, 26 February 1966.

[121] *Frontier Sentinel and Down, Armagh and Louth Advertiser*, 5, 12 March 1966.

[122] *Frontier Sentinel and Down, Armagh and Louth Advertiser*, 9 April 1966.

[123] *Dungannon Observer*, 23 April 1966; see also *Frontier Sentinel and Down, Armagh and Louth Advertiser*, 9 April 1966.

[124] *Frontier Sentinel and Down, Armagh and Louth Advertiser*, 16 April 1966.

[125] *Dungannon Observer*, 23 April 1966.

[126] *Frontier Sentinel and Down, Armagh and Louth Advertiser*, 16 April 1966.

[127] *Frontier Sentinel and Down, Armagh and Louth Advertiser*, 16 April 1966.

[128] *Frontier Sentinel and Down, Armagh and Louth Advertiser*, 16 April 1966.

[129] *Frontier Sentinel and Down, Armagh and Louth Advertiser*, 16 April 1966.

[130] *Frontier Sentinel and Down, Armagh and Louth Advertiser*, 16 April 1966.

[131] *Frontier Sentinel and Down, Armagh and Louth Advertiser*, 16 April 1966.

[132] *Frontier Sentinel and Down, Armagh and Louth Advertiser*, 12 April 1966.

[133] *Frontier Sentinel and Down, Armagh and Louth Advertiser*, 2 April 1966.

[134] *Frontier Sentinel and Down, Armagh and Louth Advertiser*, 9 April 1966.

[135] *Frontier Sentinel and Down, Armagh and Louth Advertiser*, 16 April 1966.

[136] *Frontier Sentinel and Down, Armagh and Louth Advertiser*, 16 April 1966.

[137] *Frontier Sentinel and Down, Armagh and Louth Advertiser*, 16 April 1966.

[138] *Frontier Sentinel and Down, Armagh and Louth Advertiser*, 23 April 1966.

[139] *Frontier Sentinel and Down, Armagh and Louth Advertiser*, 16 April 1966.

[140] *Frontier Sentinel and Down, Armagh and Louth Advertiser*, 16 April 1966.

[141] *Impartial Reporter*, 24 March 1966; *Derry Journal*, 18 March 1966.

[142] *Frontier Sentinel and Down, Armagh and Louth Advertiser*, 16 April 1966.

[143] Indeed, both Cardinal Conway and the Stormont government made separate appeals for 'utmost restraint', see *Derry Journal*, 22 February 1966.

[144] *Derry Journal*, 18 February 1966.

[145] *Derry Journal*, 8 April 1966.

[146] *Derry Journal*, 18 February 1966.

[147] *Derry Journal*, 22 February 1966. The local City of Derry rugby club in fact declined the offer to participate, *Derry Journal*, 8 April 1966.

[148] *Derry Journal*, 8 March 1966.

[149] *Derry Journal*, 8 April 1966.

[150] *Derry Journal*, 8 April 1966.

[151] *Derry Journal*, 8 April 1966.

[152] *Derry Journal*, 12 April 1966.

[153] *Derry Journal*, 12 April 1966.

[154] *Derry Journal*, 12 April 1966.

[155] *Derry Journal*, 21 June 1966.

[156] *Derry Journal*, 28 June 1966.

[157] *Derry Journal*, 26 July 1966.

[158] *Derry Journal*, 12 April 1966.

[159] *Dungannon Observer*, 5 February 1966.

[160] George Tinnelly, County Down GAA chairman, *Frontier Sentinel and Down, Armagh and Louth Advertiser*, 16 April 1966.

[161] *Frontier Sentinel and Down, Armagh and Louth Advertiser*, 16 April 1966.

[162] *Dungannon Observer*, 16 April 1966.

[163] *Dungannon Observer*, 9 April 1966.

[164] *Dungannon Observer*, 16 April 1966.

[165] *Dungannon Observer*, 16 April 1966.

[166] *Dungannon Observer*, 5 March 1966.

[167] *Dungannon Observer*, 5 March 1966.

[168] *Frontier Sentinel and Down, Armagh and Louth Advertiser*, 26 February 1966.

[169] *Dungannon Observer*, 16 April 1966.
[170] *Dungannon Observer*, 16 April 1966.
[171] *Dungannon Observer*, 16 April 1966.
[172] *Impartial Reporter*, 24 March 1966.
[173] *Frontier Sentinel and Down, Armagh and Louth Advertiser*, 19 March 1966.
[174] *Frontier Sentinel and Down, Armagh and Louth Advertiser*, 19 March 1966.
[175] Mr McAteer had been rather more emollient in private discussions about a year earlier with Terence O' Neill and three other senior Northern Ireland government ministers. See PRONI CAB 9B/305/3, meeting of 4 May 1965.
[176] *Frontier Sentinel and Down, Armagh and Louth Advertiser*, 19 March 1966.
[177] Connellan was Nationalist MP for South Armagh from 1929 to 1933 and was MP for South Down from 1949 to 1967.
[178] *Frontier Sentinel and Down, Armagh and Louth Advertiser*, 26 March 1966.
[179] *Dungannon Observer*, 16 April 1966.
[180] *Frontier Sentinel and Down, Armagh and Louth Advertiser*, 16 April 1966.
[181] *Frontier Sentinel and Down, Armagh and Louth Advertiser*, 16 April 1966.
[182] *Derry Journal*, 12 April 1966.
[183] *Derry Journal*, 12 April 1966.
[184] *Derry Journal*, 12 April 1966.
[185] *Derry Journal*, 12 April 1966.
[186] *Frontier Sentinel and Down, Armagh and Louth Advertiser*, 29 January 1966.
[187] *Frontier Sentinel and Down, Armagh and Louth Advertiser*, 16 April 1966.
[188] *Frontier Sentinel and Down, Armagh and Louth Advertiser*, 29 January 1966.
[189] *Dungannon Observer*, 5 March 1966.
[190] *Dungannon Observer*, 5 March 1966.
[191] *Dungannon Observer*, 26 March 1966.
[192] *Dungannon Observer*, 26 March 1966.
[193] *Dungannon Observer*, 29 January 1966.
[194] *Dungannon Observer*, 5 March 1966.
[195] *Frontier Sentinel and Down, Armagh and Louth Advertiser*, 16 April 1966.
[196] White, *Ruairí Ó Brádaigh*.
[197] *Frontier Sentinel and Down, Armagh and Louth Advertiser*, 26 March 1966.
[198] *Impartial Reporter*, 17 March 1966.
[199] *Impartial Reporter*, 24 March 1966.
[200] *Derry Journal*, 8 March 1966.
[201] *Derry Journal*, 15 March 1966.
[202] *Derry Journal*, 18 March 1966.
[203] *Derry Journal*, 22 March 1966.
[204] *Derry Journal*, 25 March 1966.
[205] *Derry Journal*, 25 March 1966.
[206] *Derry Journal*, 25 March 1966.
[207] *Derry Journal*, 29 March 1966.
[208] *Derry Journal*, 29 March 1966.

3. 'I AM THE NARRATOR OVER-AND-ABOVE...THE CALLER UP OF THE DEAD'[1]: PAGEANT AND DRAMA IN 1966

By Roisín Higgins

INTRODUCTION

Ferdia MacAnna, writing of his part in the 1916 commemorative pageant at Croke Park in 1966, which was scripted and directed by his father Tomás, recalled the issue of payment for boys who played extras for the crowd scenes, '...we made representations to the management...At one stage there was talk of a strike: there would be no new nation at the end of the show, we warned, unless financial terms were agreed'. Payment for the nation's youth came in the form of a limited-edition souvenir ten-shilling piece, which bore the image of P.H. Pearse. Mac Anna held onto his coin for longer that most others, who traded them for treats. One day, however, he walked into a shop and swapped his coin for ten 64-page comics, that week's editions of the *Victor* and the *Valiant*, a box of aero chocolate bars and a plastic German paratrooper's helmet. 'For years afterwards,' he wrote, 'I felt like a traitor'.[2]

The school boys of the Croke Park pageant were not the only ones who were trading in the image of Pearse for material advantage. The idealism of the 1916 leaders was being repackaged in the service of the economic development of 'modern' Ireland. Like the event it commemorated, the 1966 jubilee of Easter Week concealed the advent of change behind the rhetoric of continuity. The commemoration provided an opportunity to assure the Irish population that the legacy of the patriot dead would be fulfilled through economic achievement rather than in the isolated dignity of frugal comfort. It offered confirmation that Irishness would not be diminished by free-trade agreements or membership of the European Economic Community. The victory of new over old would have its own monument in the towers of Ballymun, named for the signatories of the Proclamation. These tower blocks demonstrated crude, concrete confidence in the modern and were the only memorials to the signatories of the Rising built by the government in Dublin in 1966.

In April that year, the *Tablet* reported that some 20 people had been injured on the night Nelson had been blown off his pillar in the heart of Dublin. The injuries had come at the airport, where 'a mob of youngsters had gathered…to welcome home the hero of the hour, Dickie Rock', who had just been placed fourth in the Eurovision Song Context in Luxembourg. The *Tablet*'s correspondent speculated that the 'pop-song hysteria' had been motivated either by the desire for escape from 'an over-rich dosage of heritage and national identity, from a native language which the natives did not speak and an idealism that bore no evident relation to the search for a job or the lure of the building sites of Britain'.[3] Alternatively, the young fans were framed as cosmopolitans groping to become part of a world that was bigger than the little island on which they lived.

Both explanations offered by the *Tablet* suggested that heightened interest in the Eurovision song contest represented a rejection of the little island. This newspaper positioned the theme of the Rising as having been set by the poets and dreamers of its number, which had created a maelstrom at the heart of Irish society in which the 'death-wish had lived on long after it had served its purpose'. The dilemma for the Republic therefore, 50 years on, was 'a hankering to keep the dream as long as it [did] not impinge on the reality'. The *Tablet*'s Dublin correspondent concluded:

> [w]hether we are perilously perched between two stools or crossing the hump between one era and another remains to be seen. Explosions in the night remind us of our past and make us apprehensive. Pressing needs in education, industrial relations and living costs deter us from philosophising about the future.[4]

THE COMMEMORATION AND 'MODERN IRELAND'

The golden jubilee of the Rising was, in fact, part of the process through which the Republic crossed over the hump. The memory of the dead was being used to navigate the country through the uncertainty of accelerated modernisation. Throughout the commemoration, the government's favoured emphasis on the needs and achievements of 'modern' Ireland was, to some extent, understood in its literal sense: from the Latin root *modo* 'just now'. However, the term is also clearly imbued with a comparative aspect through which that which precedes the modern suffers from its apparent backwardness. Within colonial conditions, the modern was more often associated with foreignness and, therefore, was not easily naturalised in the process of social and economic development.[5] In Ireland, modernisation had been associated with Anglicanisation, and nationalists had fashioned Irishness as traditional, ancient and therefore, theoretically at least, culturally resistant to the forces of modernity. The difficulty in the 1950s and 1960s was in creating a new rhetorical position in which 'modern' connoted progress and was fully naturalised within the national imagination, so that modernisation and patriotism became inseparable.

Conceptions of modernity, however, typically suggest an 'epochal rupture'—a point at which the pre-modern ends and the modern begins. This dislocation creates a conflicted relationship with the immediate past, which must be ejected or negated due to the necessity to signal the new order.[6] This rupture is often negotiated with reference to a more distant past—thus the popularity of appeals to mediaeval chivalry in Britain at the end of the nineteenth century to ease the functionalism behind industrio-capitalist relationships. The Irish trajectory of progress, however, had been bound to the story of the national struggle for independence. It had gained its momentum from a cyclical as well as a linear narrative, which could absorb failure and re-invent it as part of a greater success. The generational cycle had been clearly articulated by Pearse in the Proclamation and also shaped Seán Lemass's thinking. At a press conference to announce his retirement as taoiseach in November 1966, Lemass said:

> I believe,...that it is right that the representatives of the newer generation should now take over ...The 1916 celebrations marked the ending of a chapter in our history and

150

a new chapter has now to begin. As one of the 1916 generation, this marked the end of the road for me also.[7]

The handing over of power was an implicit but underlying aspect of
the jubilee. However, power would be handed over on the condition
that young Ireland understood the wherefore of its birth. If modernity
requires a rejection of the immediate past, then what constitutes the
past becomes critical. For those who had not been born in 1916, the
past was the Easter Rising. For those who had been born, the Rising was
part of the living present. The guarantee of the living link was Eamon
de Valera and, despite his own plans to retire, Lemass spent the summer
campaigning for de Valera's continued presidency.

Central to the official commemoration was an elaborate military
parade, which followed an essentially traditional format. It was Bord
Fáilte that offered the suggestion that there should be more audience
participation in the event.[8] The result of this was a people's parade that
followed the army contingent down O'Connell Street for the opening
ceremony. The Commemoration Committee's initial idea, therefore,
was to provide a spectacle upon which the public could look and
applaud. It was clear, however, that ownership of the event would not
be the government's alone.[9] Pageantry—literally empty spectacle—
would not be the whole of the jubilee. Rather, there would be *pageants*,
held up and down the country, including two in Croke Park in March
and April 1966. Such pageants had the specific advantage of involving
large, local casts.

REPRESENTATIONS OF YOUTH

Pageants had been popular in Europe at the turn of the nineteenth and
twentieth centuries. Stephen McKenna—sometime editor of *An
Claidheamh Soluis*—had noted the revival of the medieval dramatic
form in an article in the *Freeman's Journal* in 1909, which Pearse
republished in the Christmas edition of *An Macaomh*. McKenna
praised the pageant for its ability to combine great intensity of emotion
with 'lyric poetry' and 'the ornate prose of solemn discourses'. He
argued that the pageant as a cultural form could 'gather together the
broken threads of our own national history'.[10]

Pearse had overseen many pageants at St Enda's and in 1913 an
account of the slaying of Ferdia by Cúchulainn had been performed in

the public grounds at Jones's Road, now Croke Park. Pageants of this period across Europe had generally celebrated various forms of heroic masculinity.[11]

The central heroic figure in the pageants performed at St Enda's was of course Cúchulainn, and Elaine Sisson has explored in her work the way in which Christian themes were mapped onto bardic heroic deeds so that, as Stephen McKenna suggested, Pearse's ideal Irishman would have been 'Cúchulainn baptised'.[12] Sisson has also argued that while the St Enda's boys looked to the vibrant youth of Cúchulainn before 1916, in the aftermath of the Rising it was the hero's sacrificial death that defined his legend in the popular imagination. This aspect of the Cúchulainn saga in turn became inextricably linked to the death of Pearse.[13] True heroism, therefore, was cast retrospectively onto life only once it had ended in martyrdom. This was certainly not a new convention for Irish nationalism, but Pearse's own writing had given the link a poignant articulation and, across Europe during the First World War, heroism rested with young men who were dead.

This forced a reconfiguration of the existing image of youth, which had imbued childhood with nostalgia for a more innocent past. Declan Kiberd has noted, in the short stories of Pearse, the 'redemptive strangeness' of the child, who bore to 'fallen adults messages from another world'.[14] After the Rising and War of Independence, it was those who had fallen in battle who bore the messages from that other world and in whose actions the potential for redemption lay. The young were seen as increasingly detached from knowing the nation. Pearse had offered his death for the sake of future generations, but by 1966 his sacrifice was their burden. Walter Benjamin wrote about that secret agreement between past generations and the present one: 'Our coming was expected on this earth. Like every generation that preceded us, we have been endowed with a *weak* Messianic power, a power to which the past has a claim. That claim cannot be settled cheaply'.[15] A reluctance to recognise the expectations of the past meant that in 1966 the young represented destabilising presences who threatened the redemptive acts that were now the preserve of old veterans and the dead. A major gap to be bridged during the jubilee, therefore, was between the old and the young. The major challenge was to turn an event that had death at its centre into a living example.

Bryan MacMahon, author of the GAA pageant in Croke Park, had been commissioned to write four plays for Telefís Éireann in the weeks leading up to the jubilee. One, 'The Boy at the Train', drew from MacMahon's own experience. He told the *RTV Guide*, 'I was only a scrap of a lad at the time, yet I clearly recall going to the local railway station every evening of Easter Week in 1916 to ask the passengers how the fighting was faring in Dublin'. His more recent memory was of standing in O'Connell Street at the end of the previous February (for the filming of a reunion) and watching a cluster of elderly men gathered at the pillars of the GPO who wore their medals proudly and chatted like children. He recalled:

> [a]s I watched them from mid-road my mind went back over the years. I closed my eyes: again I was a boy waiting for the train to enter the station. And these men, too, were young, eager, vital and filled with the great adventure of serving a people whose devotion to freedom has scarcely been surpassed in the human story.[16]

For those who were alive during the Rising, its memory suspended them in the vitality of youth. Their difficulty was not only in conveying this to the young in 1966 but in conceding youth to them. This cross-generational relationship is pivotal in the transference of personal or family stories into a more general social memory that can then be expressed in history, fiction, exhibitions, museums and pilgrimages.[17]

Memories are enhanced by retelling or re-enactment—either privately or publicly—facilitating the transmission from the embodied or living memory into cultural memory. The latter is used to describe the type of memory that survives through stories and practices once eyewitnesses and participants have died.[18] The fiftieth anniversary of an event is particularly charged as it occurs at the point at which the living memory is visibly dying, making it imperative that younger generations accept their responsibility to remember.

Seachtar Fear, Seacht Lá

MacMahon addressed this tension between young and old in his pageant, which had been commissioned by the GAA, in which he allowed the young to question the dead. Resolution was only achieved once the seven signatories had given an account of themselves and their actions. *Seachtar Fear, Seacht Lá*—'Seven Men, Seven Days' was performed in Croke Park on the 17, 18 and 19 March, with a further performance by the full Dublin cast in Casement Park, Belfast. The cast of almost 400 included the Artane Boys Band, two pipe bands, 150 boys from the Dublin County Board of the GAA and 100 girls from the Dublin Camogie Board.[19] The pageant used the imagery available from the Easter resurrection of a nation, and it wove the words of the signatories into the unfolding spectacle.

In a simple design, an ornamental dais, with a public address system, stood in the centre of the field in Croke Park. It was flanked by members of Fianna Éireann and Cuman na mBan. Into this scene marched the narrator, dressed in a white shirt and trousers accompanied by four attendants in similar dress, but with shirts the colours of the four provinces. They were followed by a young man and a young woman. Stage directions indicated that both of these would be 'attired in dress that suggests the Ireland of to-day (Aran ganseys perhaps) but which does not conflict with the ceremonial occasion'.[20] The narrator opened with the lines:

> I am the narrator Over and Above…
> I am the caller-up of the dead
> The Challenger of the living
> The Inspirer of the Unborn
> And if to-day I seek to call and challenge and inspire
> I do so with this over-riding purpose in my mind
> That when we have adequately honoured those I call
> We honour them in all the long to-morrows of our land
> In every action of the passing day
> By justice, labour and a deep integrity.[21]

Despite the echoes of the morning offering, the doubts of youth were then addressed. The Young Man and Young Woman took alternate lines:

> YW: It was so long and long ago—ere we were born.
> Y.M. Ere we were born. And yet, 'tis said that they were
>   young like us.
> YW: They say it was for us they died. I do not know.
> YM: I know them by the poetry they wrote
>   And yet I am not certain that I know.[22]

This is reminiscent of William Morris's *The water of the wondrous isles*: 'Coming to the Isle of the Young and the Old / Birdalone findeth it / Peopled with children'. In this fantasy tale, the mythical traveller, Birdalone, asks a young man of fifteen, 'Wilt thy now take me to…the place where dwelleth the old man?', to which the young man replied, 'I neither know of an old man, nor rightly know what it means, the word'.[23] Morris had both a dislike of the modern industrial age and an interest in medieval epic stories. The sense of dislocation between the young and what had gone before is well evoked. Yet, it also alerts us to a curiosity in the depiction of the executed leaders of 1916 in MacMahon's pageant: in reality these men were not young; Pearse was 36, Connolly 48, and Tom Clarke 59. They had, in fact, been absorbed into the more general European memory of the First World War dead.

The narrator filled the possible gap between the young audience and their past with a short, ten line history of Ireland from Cúchulainn through the Normans, ending with the lines:

> I was the shaft of sunlight in the cell of Tone
> I saw the Fenians stumble in the snow
> And I was a bystander in O'Connell Street
> When, fifty years ago to-day,
> Seven men in seven days.[24]

The voice of Pearse then read from the Proclamation. And the young man and woman replied:

> YM: There is renewal in the air.
>   The drums are good: their rhythm bites into the blood.
> YM: Even my woman's body answers the drums.
> YM: And yet, I am resolved to question those who died.
> YW: To find the why and wherefore of their dying
> YM: To see them as men of flesh and blood, not effigies of history.
> YW: They must be seen and questioned.[25]

MacMahon linked the young figures to the signatories through a primitive, tribal beat but this did not deny the need for the past to live in order to be questioned. To the soft tapping of drums the narrator intoned:

> Truths that are clear to age, to adolescence seem unclear.
> The young know not the night of slavery when only the
> pulse-beat of the heart
> Vouched that the dream of centuries still lived.[26]

Here, we see the reversal of the idea that truth lies with the innocence of youth. In fact, what we see is that Irishness, rather than resting in its purest form in the child, is much more securely tied to those who had to struggle for its survival. The narrator called each signatory in turn to 'speak to Ireland's youth on this, your jubilee of blood...'

On the arrival of Pearse on the podium, young men and women appeared from all parts of the field, some of them in traditional costume and others dressed in 'bright modern dress (slacks, etc.)'. They danced forward so that, as the stage directions indicate, 'the whole effect is that of a ballet with undertones of traditional dancing which is light-hearted and impromptu'.[27]

As the pageant progressed, each signatory appeared, accompanied by an attendant group or witnesses: Pearse with young men and women; Tom Clarke with the Fenians; Joseph Plunkett with monks; Eamon Ceannt with pipers; Seán MacDermott with transport groups (air, sea and sky); Thomas MacDonagh with singers and James Connolly with workers. Rather than being represented by their participation in a single event, the signatories were used to express different aspects of Irish life. Therefore, MacDermott said:

> I was a Transport man and so from men and women too
> who man the Transport of our Irish earth and sea and sky
> I call my witnesses...Let them come forth
> And vouch for Irish accuracy and zeal
> And, in this fashion, honour Easter week and me.

He was then joined by Irish sailors, airmen, air hostesses and transport workers in uniform. Therefore, the leaders were brought forward, not just to give an account of themselves, but to pay tribute to modern Ireland. The figure of James Connolly decried:

> Call up the workers once again to testify
> How much of dignity they've gained in fifty years
> The slums no more!
> Health not the sole province of the privileged
> And those who grovelled on their knees are erect.[28]

In conveying the vitality of the signatories, *Seachtar Fear, Seacht Lá* attempted to demonstrate that they were a vital part of contemporary Ireland. Ian Hamilton noted in the *Sunday Telegraph* that, 'When youth remains a relative condition rather than a virtue and human beings are not consigned to the scrapheap, old men keep their youthfulness'.[29] In April 1966 old men in Dublin had never seemed younger, to everyone but the young. John Jordan had complained in *Hibernia* in January 1966 of how the young generation would forget the lessons of the Rising because 'they are asked to admire abstractions' not acquaint themselves with real personalities.[30]

An attempt to resuscitate the participants of the Rising as individuals was a central device used in the two dramatisations that were most popular with young people during the commemoration: *Seachtar Fear, Seacht Lá* and Telefís Éireann's production of *Insurrection*. This series of eight, half-hour programmes was written by Hugh Leonard, whose script was an adaptation of Max Caulfield's *The Easter Rebellion*. Caulfield's book had been dedicated to his father Malachy, 'who remembers it all', and it had drawn on the testimonies of 125 eye-witnesses.[31] Caulfield had created a tribute to the lived experience of his father, which, through the technology of television, became a significant shared event in 1966.

COMMEMORATION AND THE NATIONAL BROADCASTER

Insurrection, which the national broadcaster RTÉ described as, 'undoubtedly the most difficult and ambitious project ever attempted by Irish television', was the story of Easter week as it might have been seen by an Irish news crew at the time.[32]

The format borrowed from the example of *Culloden*, a successful British drama, which had been broadcast in 1964. The central device used on-the-spot reporters, camera crews at a variety of locations and a studio news anchor, providing a depiction of the events of the Rising of such technological sophistication that was not only impossible in 1916 but was also well beyond the means of Telefís Éireann in 1966. Louis Lentin produced *Insurrection* and Michael Garvey directed the film sequences. Dr Kevin B. Nowlan of UCD had been employed by RTÉ as the historical advisor on all commemorative television and radio programmes. His brief included, 'consultation with survivors of 1916 and responsibility for sifting and evaluating the advice and information thus gathered into terms of programming reference', and *Insurrection* represented one of his chief projects.[33] The production involved 93 speaking roles, the services of 300 members of the Defence Forces and over 200 extras.[34]

Insurrection was part of a comprehensive schedule by RTÉ, which included 30 hours of radio programmes and television coverage of 4 programme series, 6 individual programmes and outside broadcasting coverage for 13 public events.[35] An estimated cost of £116,000 for the television programmes was approved by the Radio Éireann Authority in October 1965, some of which would be funded by the cancellation of existing dramas.[36] The eventual cost came in £6,000 under budget.[37] Nevertheless, the pressure on Telefís Éireann's resources was considerable. The *Monthly Report* for March 1966 noted that it was the busiest period since the opening of the station. The completion of *Insurrection* and *On Behalf of the Provisional Government* had, 'involved a considerable amount of editing and presented many operational problems never before encountered, and necessitated a considerable amount of work overnight'.[38] Editing rooms had to be hired in London to cope with the overflow and the Radio Éireann Authority anticipated hiring 40 additional staff on a temporary basis to cope with the commemorative schedule, at a cost of £22,000.[39]

The commemoration naturally raised political questions for RTÉ and, as a member of the Radio Éireann Authority, T.W. Moody expressed his concern that in presenting the programmes, 'all aspects of the Rising should be taken into account, and it was agreed [by the Authority] that in presenting the clash of idealism and emotions, the programmes should be as balanced as possible'.[40] Taoiseach Seán Lemass had written to Minister for Posts and Telegraphs Joseph Brennan in July 1965, expressing the anxiety of the Commemoration Committee that no radio and television schedule for the jubilee should be finalised without the committee's approval. Lemass concluded: 'I should like you to take this matter up with the [Radio Éireann] Authority both for the purpose of getting their ideas formulated and submitted soon, and to ensure that these programmes will be suitable. ('This means in particular no O'Casey)'.[41]

The Authority minutes recorded that, while it agreed that close communication should be maintained, 'it could not submit its programmes to the committee for prior approval'. Rather, the Director General undertook to impress upon the committee the importance of making *their* plans known well in advance, in order that appropriate broadcasting coverage was mounted.[42] The Abbey theatre had also been advised that 'an O'Casey play during the period of the celebrations would not be in keeping with the spirit of the occasion'.[43] Both institutions responded by including the *Plough and the Stars* in their schedules later in the year.

Reaching the audience(s)

In designing an 'appropriate' schedule, broadcasters had to take into account both how best to honour the event and how best to serve their audiences. Jack White, the assistant controller of programmes on Telefís Éireann explained:

> [i]n devising our own programmes for the week we have had to bear in mind that we are dealing with two generations. We are fortunate enough to have among us still a good many of the men and women who asserted Ireland's right to independence on that Easter Monday, fifty years ago. They are the first-hand witnesses: it is natural that we should want to hear them, and that they should want to be heard.
>
> On the other hand, as programme planners we are aware that the great bulk of our audience consists of men and women who were not even born or were in their infancy in 1916. Many of them have no clear idea of the events of Easter Week, and no deep understanding of the men who created the Rising. Our problem was to bring home to them some sense of the heroic drama of that week.[44]

Roibéard Ó Faracháin, controller of programmes on Radio Éireann, was also attuned to the dual audience. 'Radio, as it happens, has been commemorating the Rising for most of its forty years of existence', he wrote, but during the fiftieth anniversary, 'those of us who saw the clashing of arms and uniforms as men or as children looking through the keyhole, pay our Golden Jubilee tribute in common with the generations who had not yet been born'.[45] Ó Faracháin's assertion illuminates the complex position of 1916 in the Republic. There was a sense in which modern Ireland itself was a perpetual tribute to the Easter Rising. Moreover, the existence of a national broadcaster—through which a separate Irish culture could be described and defined—might also be seen to represent a continual memorial to the aspirations of the leaders of Easter week. Therefore, in one sense, the Easter Rising was part of the very fabric of the independent state, and in another sense its significance continually receded in the decreasing circles of experience: from that of the soldier, to the child at the keyhole, to the generation that had not yet been born.

On radio, Ó Faracháin anticipated that the 'most evocative' programme would be *The Voice of the Rising*, for which Bryan MacMahon had written a script compiled of songs, ballads, poems and the words of nationalist leaders.[46] The Features Department of Radio Éireann (which had responsibility for production) described this programme as 'the ghost at the feast...a stealthy intrusion on the note of celebration which we sound for 1916'. It continued:

> [i]t is hot and cold, as history is hot and cold; hot with the memory and taste of idealism; cold with remembered suffering and death. It transcends time and place. 1916 blends with '98 with '47 and with '67. The sense of national personality and continuity is overwhelming. Is anything worse than war? The old question is answered in the old way. Slavery is worse than war...Dishonour is worse than war...[47]

The Voice of the Rising offered a version of Irish history in which 1916 represented all time, and the experiences of the individual were subsumed into the greater personality of the nation. However, the resilience of narrative lies in its ability to function at the levels of both the abstract and the specific, and the story of 'the struggle for Irish freedom' was populated with heroic individuals—both allegorical and real—who personified the cause. *The Voice of the Rising* ended with the words of Thomas MacDonagh, from what was believed to be his address to the Court Martial in May 1916.

> The forms of heroes flit before my vision, and there is one, the star whose destiny sways my own;...The seed he sowed fructifies to this day in God's Church. Take me away, and let my blood bedew the sacred soil of Ireland. I die in the certainty that once more the seed will fructify.

MacMahon had himself said of the programme that much of his inspiration had come from listening to men like Liam O'Briain and Eamonn de hÓir of Limerick: 'One still finds in these men the granitic core that inspired them of old', he wrote.[48] Both MacDonagh and MacMahon looked to heroic shapes that were more solid than flickering, and this attention to individual characters continued as a central feature of the most successful dramatisations of the jubilee.

The flickering images of indigenous television in the Republic had been launched on New Year's Eve, 1961. By the end of April 1966, the network provided coverage for 98% of the country. The Irish TAM (Television Audience Measurement) survey for the end of that year estimated that 55% of homes in the country had television (77% in urban areas and 37% in rural areas). The increase in the number of television sets by 24,000 sets during the 1966 calendar year marked a decrease compared to the 50,000 extra purchased in 1965. Therefore, the jubilee itself was not a significant catalyst for the acquisition of televisions in Ireland.[49] A critical element in determining the possession of sets was the presence of children in the household. A sample survey carried out for RTÉ in March 1966 recorded that 69% of homes that did not have a television were also childless. Surveys taken throughout successive years confirmed that households with children accounted for the fastest growth in the spread of television ownership.[50] This demographic information was collected for advertisers but clearly had influence over the design of television schedules.

Insurrection

Insurrection was the most popular programme on Telefís Éireann during the 1916 fiftieth anniversary commemoration. Viewing figures for the week ending 17 April 1966 showed that the drama appeared five times in the top ten programmes. It was a lavish production, accompanied by widespread pre-publicity. The *Times* of London reported in January that 'The British soldier of today may think himself lucky that he serves in the army of a nation less historically minded than the Irish. The gallant troops of the Republic are reported to be up in arms, metaphorically speaking, because they have been conscripted as film actors and are not getting the overtime, subsistence, and travel allowances to which they think they are entitled'. Their role, according to the Army, included patrolling the streets of Dublin into the small hours in an attempt to capture the drama of the Easter Rising.[51] Closer to home, John Healy quipped in the *Western People* in February that programmes on Telefís Éireann were 'dying like British soldiers, gobbled up by the demands on studio facilities by 1916…and before it is all over I'll swear that there'll be more people involved in re-creating 1916 than there was in the original affair'.[52]

The *RTV Guide* for the week carried high-quality colour photographs from the *Insurrection* set and descriptive pieces from the major figures involved in the production. Hugh Leonard described it as 'a near-as-dammit, full scale reconstruction of the Rising, involving months of filming and weeks of studio work;...At the beginning', he said, 'the entire project seemed as gallant and as doomed as the Rising itself'. Leonard's favourite character was James Connolly: 'Bow-legged, fiery, an unquenchable optimist; cheering his men on with "Courage, boys, we are winning!" while the G.P.O. roof blazed overhead', while figures like Pearse and Plunkett remained aloof and unknowable. To remedy this, Leonard argued that, 'one dare not *invent*—merely select'; and to this end he used incidents that showed the insurgent leaders, 'not as haloed demigods, but as clerks, teachers, weavers, trade unionists and poets, who overnight turned into revolutionaries fighting a doomed war'. 'It was their ordinariness', he said, 'which made them and the Rising something to be commemorated after fifty years'.[53]

Pre-publicity set the scene for the viewer before a moment of *Insurrection* had been aired. The audience could anticipate that what they were about to see was 'as near-as-dammit' real. Leonard's claim that his role had been to select rather than invent over-looked the fact that the entire enterprise was an invention masquerading as hard news. Indeed, Louis Lentin recalled that while they were filming, a large number of the gathered onlookers 'were certain that it didn't happen like that at all, and said so!'[54] *Insurrection* opened with footage of the 64th day of the Battle of Verdun. The voice-over noted that casualty figures had not been released, but were believed to be high on both sides, adding that the 'French High Command continues to be optimistic about the chances of an offensive on the Somme no later than late June'. Archival footage has often been employed in cinema; used in part to explore the boundaries of both the imaginary and the real.[55] In *Insurrection*, there was a blurring of these boundaries as the viewer navigated actual footage, reportage and re-enactment. Genres were also crossed and cross-referenced, so that what unfolded was part documentary, part drama, part tragedy and part thriller.

However, the genre most associated with *Insurrection* was the Western. The 1916 drama had shared its place in the top ten most-watched programmes of the week with, among others, *The Riordans, Tolka Row* and *The Virginian*.[56] Leonard's drama was broadcast nightly at 9.15pm through the commemorative week. The most watched episode was that broadcast on Friday, 15 April, titled 'Do you think we'll win?', which dealt with the arrival of General Maxwell and the

eventual evacuation of the GPO. It had been preceded at 7.45pm by
The Virginian. The programmes in the schedule bled into each other, so
that *Insurrection* would live on in the popular imagination as an Irish
equivalent of 'Cowboys and Indians'. Fintan O'Toole would write later
that for quite a while he confused the Seven Leaders of 1916 with the
Magnificent Seven—having seen the film in the commemorative year—
so that 'Yul Pearse and Patrick Brynner became one'.[57] Peter Taylor
opens his book *Provos* with reference to the television drama and the
recollection of a member of the IRA who was eight in 1966:

> Each evening we would be sitting riveted to granny's
> television watching what was going on. Then we were
> straight out the following morning and, instead of playing
> Cowboys and Indians or Cops and Robbers, we would
> immediately engage in our own version of Easter Week.[58]

The imagery is also juxtaposed in the most recent work on
dramatisations of the Rising, which asserts that Leonard and Nowlan,
'were alarmed that their programme inspired children to play "Rebels
and Brits" where once they had played "Cowboys and Indians"'.[59]

Insurrection has passed into the popular memory as a programme
which, in dramatising the Rising, glamorised its violence. Telefís
Éireann showed its very expensive drama twice in 1966, and it has
never been shown again. For many of those who were young during
the jubilee, *Insurrection* is remembered as the most vivid representation
of the events being commemorated. It has therefore developed its own
mythology: too explosive to be seen again, a recruitment programme
for the IRA and un-transmittable after the outbreak of the conflict in
Northern Ireland. The more mundane reason for its burial in the RTÉ
archives is the effort involved in tracing and paying the actors, who had
not waived their right to repeat fees. More recent academic work by
James Moran and Harvey O'Brien has attempted to move beyond the
myths of *Insurrection*—by placing it in the context of theatrical
depictions of the Rising and documentary film in Ireland—and have
revealed the series to be more nuanced and challenging than is
popularly imagined.[60] However, the radical message of *Insurrection*
should not be overstated.

Television dramas provide an artificial thrill that is enjoyed by the
viewer who, understanding the convention, in fact always knows how
things will end. This was true twice over in the case of *Insurrection*. The

viewers were both literate in the conventions of cinema and television drama and they knew the events of the Rising: the 'false ending' of the executions leading to the happier conclusion of the independent Irish state. So, even within the innovative framework of *Insurrection*, the audience essentially felt protected by its prior knowledge.

Insurrection utilised the possibilities of a medium that was new to the Republic. The viewer watched as events unfolded as if in real time. Disbelief and knowledge were both suspended so that, despite the programme's title, the narrator and audience conspired in their apparent innocence of outcomes. The opening archival footage of the Western Front was followed by the fictional news programme. News anchorman Ray McAnally held up Eoin MacNeill's countermanding order and said into camera:

> [w]hat is the connection between this newspaper item and certain startling events off the Kerry coast? This evening we take a close look at Sinn Féin and we ask ourselves what is this organisation? Who are its leaders? And why have the Government not taken action against them for treasonable activities? Parades, marches and so-called manoeuvres are one thing but consorting and planning with the Germans is quite another. Strong words? Well, we shall see.[61]

This false naïveté (McAnally referred throughout to the 'Sinn Féin Rising') not only created a dramatic opening, it immediately introduced certain elements to the story that disrupted a straightforward heroic narrative. The Somme was mentioned within the first minutes of the series, which itself opened with images of the First World War. The 'startling events in Kerry' were the discovery of guns and ammunition on Banna Strand and the arrest of a man, claiming to be Richard Morton, who was in possession of five sovereigns, 11 shillings and correspondence in a foreign language (which local police instinctively surmised was suspicious). The capture of Roger Casement—because of course it was he—was accompanied by the discovery of three revolvers on the strand by the young daughter of a man who had been visiting a Holy Well to mark the fact that it was Good Friday. The juxtaposition of the innocent child with the guns clearly signalled that the rebels were a disruptive, potentially dangerous intrusion into the domestic lives of Ireland.[62] Moreover, as the realisation dawned on the newsroom that there would be a Rising,

McAnally asked, 'What sort of man will knowingly strike a blow at his lawful rulers undeterred by the knowledge that he cannot, and that his life is almost certain to be forfeited in exchange for a futile gesture?'.[63] This may be ironic innocence, but the point is still made that the actions of the rebels were not easily comprehensible to many of their compatriots.

The use of reporters 'on-the-spot' was often awkward and sometimes comedic. St Enda's school was door-stepped (Pearse would not be drawn into an interview), and it was an RTÉ reporter who first drew Tom Clarke's attention to MacNeill's countermanding order (to which Clarke responded, 'I don't believe it. I knew that MacNeill was...but why would he do a thing like that. The blaggard. The dirty blaggard').[64] However, the device also provided a way of introducing multiple voices. James Moran has pointed to the influence of the *Plough and the Stars* on Leonard's script, which reprises Bessie Burgess as 'the citizen of Dublin' whose husband is 'out in the trenches fighting for King and country' and breaks into 'God Save the King' and a Fluther figure, the 'comic drunk' who tries to articulate support for the rebels.[65] McAnally's commentary also drew attention to the suffering of the Dublin poor caused by the Rising, again in tune with the politics of O'Casey.

> In central areas [of Dublin] the plight of the civilian population grows more acute by the hour...In many back streets the dead have been lying for days unburied. Food is virtually unobtainable in the poorer districts where hundreds of families are believed to be starving. The threat of a typhoid epidemic looms over the entire city. And yet on the outskirts, the holiday atmosphere of Spring Show Week still prevails. Workers whose offices and factories have been closed by the Rising are crowding onto the beaches.[66]

Moreover, the European context of the Rising was not lost, even in the very local Battle of Northumberland Road. The on-the-scene reporter declared it an incredible sight, British troops taking cover in front gardens, in doorways and behind trees: 'Most of these men are raw recruits and it seems strange they should be getting their first taste of action, not in Flanders mud but in Dublin on a spring day'.[67] An interview with General Lowe, commander of the British forces in Dublin (who had taken time out of the fighting to join Ray McAnally in the studio), was a reminder that foot soldiers in the British Army were themselves victims of the insatiable demands of the First World War and could be mobilised as canon fodder on whichever front they were required. With the battle underway, the general described the position as 'highly satisfactory' and the exchange unfolded:

> R. McA.: But the battle has been raging for hours in Northumberland Road.
> Gen.L.: I shouldn't call it a battle exactly. More of an extended incident.
> R. McA.: The latest reports say that at least one hundred of the Sherwood Foresters have already been killed.
> Gen.L.: There are plenty more where they came from. The rebels will soon find that out.[68]

The heroic focus was not Pearse, whom Leonard had admitted finding a difficult character to realise. The Commander-in-Chief appeared out of touch—assuring the Rebels in the GPO that assistance was on its way from the country—and self-involved: 'If we loose it will mean the end of everything. People will blame us and condemn us. Perhaps in a few years they'll see what we were trying to do'. 'Oh God did anyone ever suffer like this for his country', was James Connolly's response as he lay wounded, in agony, and clearly beloved of the men and women who tended him.[69] The choice of heroic emphasis was questioned by Ruairí Brugha, as a member of the Radio Éireann Authority. He anticipated criticism of the programme for its failure to feature President de Valera and for featuring Michael Collins in six episodes.[70] He also objected to 'an uncomplimentary reference' to Eoin MacNeill and asked if the veracity of this reference could be checked.[71] (In fact, Caulfield records Tom Clarke's response to MacNeill, which the former confided to his bodyguard, 'MacNeill has ruined every-thing—all our plans. I feel like going away to cry'.)[72] Brugha could not, however, have objected to the depiction of his father.

Cathal Brugha emerged as the most dramatic hero of the South Dublin Union. In the re-enactment of the legendary story, RTÉ's corre-spondent reported that Eamon Ceannt's men were 'defeated, demoralised, waiting for capture or worse'. As the camera panned their broken faces the strains of someone singing 'God Save Ireland' could be heard in the near distance. A young man asked Ceannt, 'What happens when the military gets here?' To which he replied: 'We won't surrender now. We'll fight all the way. To the last man. We'll say a decade of the Rosary lads and then anyone who wants to smoke can do so'. The men recited an Our Father and Hail Mary in Irish before being interrupted by a young Rebel who burst in with the news that Brugha was still alive and was in fact the singer. The men, transformed by the news immediately wanted to fight on, only to discover that the British had left the building, worn down by the single-handed heroism of Cathal Brugha.[73]

The effect of Insurrection

The story of the Easter Rising clearly lent itself well to dramatic reconstruction. The impact of *Insurrection*, however, was threefold: it exploited the potential of a new medium in Ireland; it placed the Irish themselves at the centre of a heroic narrative; and it appeared to reinvent the national story. Central to conceptions of Irish nationalism was the idea that independence fulfilled the nation's destiny. The longer-term difficulty with this was that the achievement of freedom might come to be seen as rather unexciting in its inevitability. *Insurrection* used the artificial suspense of television drama to underline the historical reality that the events and outcomes of Easter 1916 were not necessarily pre-destined. In depicting the unpredictable, sometimes chaotic nature of events, Leonard underlined the heroic intervention necessary to bring the Irish state into existence. It was in this way that the national story was reanimated rather than reinvented.

Insurrection did attempt to complicate the politics of the Rising and might, in some sense, be seen as Telefís Éireann slipping O'Casey in through the back door. However, both the medium and the form determined the way in which the message was transmitted. The decision to re-enact the Rising in a television drama allowed the audience to indulge in the temporary illusion of surprise, while simultaneously confirming its belief in the destiny of the Irish nation. Hindsight was the key to much of the drama in *Insurrection*. The opening episode ended with Eoin MacNeill saying into camera, 'There will be no Rising'. This only worked as a cliff-hanger because the audience knew he was wrong. Moreover, the internal chaos of the drama was enfolded within the context of the subsequent independent Irish state. The fictional drama ended after the surrender of the Rebels; the external reality in April 1966, displayed in multiple public spaces, was the ultimate victory of their insurrection. The version of history in which the continuous struggle for freedom had moved inexorably towards the triumph of modern Ireland (however it stumbled) was played out in pageants and concerts throughout the country and was confirmed in the radio and television schedules.

Insurrection received critical and popular acclaim in Ireland and abroad. By 12 May 1966, RTÉ could confirm that the full eight-hour series had been shown by BBC2 in the UK and by ABC in Australia. A shorter, one-hour special edition had also been shown in Canada, Finland, Norway, Denmark, Belgium and Sweden.[74] Foreign sales provided a net income for the station of £8,500, and congratulations were extended to the Director General of RTÉ from the Radio Éireann Authority and from the director of BBC Television.[75]

CONCLUSION

The performances marking the 1916 anniversary commemoration that are remembered most vividly—the GAA pageant and *Insurrection* —were acts of translation through which the meaning of the Rising was made contemporary. Both attempted to convey the story in a way in which a generation brought up on the *Victor* and the *Valiant* and German paratroopers could understand. Cultural memory exists in acts of reconstruction so that,

> it is fixed in immovable figures of memory and stores of knowledge, but every contemporary context relates to these differently, sometimes by appropriation, sometimes by criticism, sometimes by preservation or transformation.[76]

Group identity develops through the perception of shared axioms and experiences, and nations also exist through the assumption of shared values, which (though not clearly defined) are groped towards through acts of repetition or commemoration: looking to the past for their co-ordinates and anticipating the future in a constellation of anniversaries. Thus, commemorative events become part of the shared memory of a nation, and each re-enactment alters the way in which the original event is experienced and understood.

Both *Seachtar Fear, Seacht Lá* and *Insurrection* attempted to remind the audience that those who participated in the Easter Rising had once been mortal, flawed heroes, in order that they might flash vividly in the imaginations of those who had not been alive at the time of the

1916 Rising. This emphasis also allowed for a degree of implicit criticism of the leaders, which might serve to inoculate the viewer from a more emphatic dissent in the belief of their heroism. 'To their memory [the Rebels]', Leonard wrote, 'had been fashioned a memorial by people who could not paint or sculpt'.[77] The memorial was a dual tribute to the Easter leaders and to 1960s Ireland. In making the immortal mortal, the living become taller.

NOTES

[1] Bryan MacMahon, *Seachtar Fear, Seacht Lá*, unpublished script, 1966, 3.

[2] Dermot Bolger (ed.), *Letters from the new island: 16 on 16: Irish writers on the Easter Rising* (Dublin, 1988), 37–8. Tomás MacAnna's pageant, *Aiséirí*, was funded by the Commemoration Committee and was part of the official programme of events.

[3] *Tablet*, 9 April 1966.

[4] *Tablet*, 9 April 1966.

[5] Emer Nolan, 'Modernism and the Irish revival', in Joe Cleary and Claire Connolly (eds), *The Cambridge companion to modern Irish culture* (Cambridge, 2005), 157–72: 159–60.

[6] Joe Cleary, 'Introduction: Ireland and Modernity', in Cleary and Connolly (eds), *Companion to modern Irish culture*, 1–21: 2.

[7] Government Information Service (hereafter cited as GIS), 1/222, Preliminary statement by the taoiseach for a press conference, Leinster House, 8 November 1966.

[8] National Archives of Ireland, Department of External Affairs (hereafter cited as NAI DEA), 610/20/5, From External Affairs to All Missions, 22 November 1965.

[9] On 2 February 1965 the government had decided to set up a committee to oversee the fiftieth anniversary celebrations of the Easter Rising. The committee was chaired by the taoiseach, and the inaugural meeting was held on 19 February 1965. NAI, Department of the Taoiseach (hereafter cited as NAI DT), 97/6/157, Cabinet minutes, 2 February 1965; Minutes of the Commemoration Committee, 19 February 1965.

[10] Elaine Sisson, *Pearse's patriots: St Enda's and the cult of boyhood* (Cork, 2005), 91

[11] Sisson, *Pearse's patriots*, 83.

[12] Sisson, *Pearse's patriots*, 80.

[13] Sisson, *Pearse's patriots*, 98.

[14] Declan Kiberd, *Inventing Ireland: the literature of a modern nation* (London, 1995), 103.

[15] Walter Benjamin, *Illuminations* (London, 1999), 245–6.

[16] *RTV Guide*, April 1966.

[17] Jay Winter and Emmanuel Sivan, *War and remembrance in the Twentieth Century* (Cambridge, 2000), 3.

[18] Ann Rigney, 'Plenitude, scarcity and the circulation of cultural memory', *Journal of European Studies* 35 (March 2005), 11–28: 14.

[19] GAA Ard Comhairle, 4 February 1966.

[20] MacMahon, *Seachtar Fear*, 2.

[21] MacMahon, *Seachtar Fear*, 3–4.

[22] MacMahon, *Seachtar Fear*, 6.

[23] William Morris, *The water of the wondrous isle* (London, 1972), 291.

[24] MacMahon, *Seachtar Fear*, 6.

[25] MacMahon, *Seachtar Fear*, 7.

[26] MacMahon, *Seachtar Fear*, 9.

[27] MacMahon, *Seachtar Fear*, 15.

[28] MacMahon, *Seachtar Fear*, 31.

[29] *Weekend Telegraph*, 6 April 1966.

[30] *Hibernia*, January 1966.

[31] Max Caulfield, *The Easter Rebellion* (London, 1965).

[32] *RTV Guide*, 8 April 1966.

[33] Radio Telefís Éireann Archives (hereafter cited as RTÉ Archives), 'Radio Éireann Authority, agenda and documentation', 22 September 1965. Nowlan had been brought on board by Francis McManus. I am indebted to Professor Kevin B. Nowlan for giving generously of his time to discuss the 1966 commemoration.

[34] RTÉ *Annual Report*, 1967, 7.

[35] RTÉ *Annual Report*, 1967, 4.

[36] RTÉ Archives, 'Radio Éireann Authority minutes', 20 October 1965. The combined radio and television output was known as Radio Telefís Éireann after 1961, however the broadcasting Authority continued under the name Radio Éireann Authority until March 1966. See R.J. Savage, *Irish television: the political and social origins* (Cork, 1996), 92.

[37] RTÉ Archives, 'Authority Minutes', 11 May 1966. The budget for commemorative radio programmes was £3,400 and was exceeded by £1,100.

[38] RTÉ Archives, 'RTÉ Monthly Report', March 1966. *On Behalf of the Provisional Government* was a series of half hour programmes on the seven signatories of the Proclamation, which included interviews with relatives and friends. I am indebted to Andreas Ó Gallachóir for giving generously of his time to discuss the making of these programmes.

39 RTÉ Archives, 'RTÉ Monthly Report', March 1966; Authority minutes, 20 October 1965.
40 RTÉ Archives, 'Authority minutes', 30 July 1965.
41 NAI DT, 97/6/158, Lemass to Joseph Brennan, 24 July 1965.
42 RTÉ Archives, 'Authority minutes', 30 July 1965.
43 NAI DT, 97/6/160, 'Report from the Commemoration Committee', [undated].
44 *RTV Guide*, 8 April 1966.
45 *RTV Guide*, 8 April 1966.
46 *The Voice of the Rising* was broadcast at 6.45pm on Easter Sunday, 10 April 1966.
47 *RTV Guide*, 8 April 1966.
48 *RTV Guide*, 8 April 1966.
49 RTÉ *Annual Report*, 1967.
50 RTÉ Archive, TAM Surveys.
51 *The Times*, 17 January 1966.
52 *Western People*, 5 February 1966.
53 *RTV Guide*, 8 April 1966.
54 *RTV Guide*, 8 April 1966.
55 Luke Gibbons, 'Narratives of the nation: Fact, fiction and Irish cinema', in Luke Dodd (ed.), *Nationalisms: visions and revision* (Dublin, 1999), 66–73: 66.
56 *RTV Guide*, 13 May 1966. The TAM Ratings for the week ending April 17 1966 showed the top ten television shows to be: (1) *Insurrection*; (2) *The Riordans*; (3) *The Virginian*; (4) *Tolka Row*; (5) *Insurrection*; (6) *The Late, Late Show*; (7) *Insurrection*, *Insurrection* and *On Behalf of the Provisional Government*; (10) *Quicksilver*, *Insurrection* and *School Around the Corner*.
57 Bolger, *Letters from the new island*, 41.
58 Peter Taylor, *Provos: the IRA and Sinn Féin* (London, 1997), 6.
59 James Moran, *Staging the Easter Rising: 1916 as theatre* (Cork, 2005), 115.
60 Harvey O'Brien, *The real Ireland: the evolution of Ireland in documentary film* (Manchester, 2004); Moran, *Staging the Easter Rising*.
61 *Insurrection*, 1966: Episode One.
62 *Insurrection*, 1966: Episode One.
63 *Insurrection*, 1966: Episode Two.
64 *Insurrection*, 1966: Episode One.
65 Moran, *Staging the Easter Rising*, 115.
66 *Insurrection*, 1966: Episode Five.
67 *Insurrection*, 1966: Episode Four.
68 *Insurrection*, 1966: Episode Four.
69 *Insurrection*, 1966: Episode Five.
70 RTÉ Archive, 'Authority minutes', 30 March 1966. The presence of Collins is certainly exaggerated.
71 RTÉ Archive, 'Authority minutes', 20 April 1966.
72 Caulfield, *Easter Rebellion*, 63.

[73] *Insurrection*, 1966: Episode Five.

[74] NAI DEA, 2000/14/106, RTÉ to External Affairs, 12 May 1966.

[75] RTÉ Archive, 'Authority minutes', 11 May 1966.

[76] Jan Assmann, 'Collective memory and cultural identity', *New German Critique* 65 (1995), 125–33: 130.

[77] *RTV Guide*, 8 April 1966.

4. More than a Revival of Memories? 1960s Youth and the 1916 Rising

By Carole Holohan

We'll acquire mellowness which is not there yet.
I think that's what's wrong with us really.
We're at the beginning of a new age really, a
new wonderful age in the world, but at the
beginning of it, and therefore it hasn't
any...tradition or character about it yet.
But it's acquiring it every moment every day.
And I wish it well.
I won't see it.
Liam Ó Briain, *Rocky Road to Dublin* (1968)[1]

Introduction

The fiftieth anniversary of the 1916 Rising provided a moment for national stocktaking, for the tallying of the successes, and more often failures, of the nation. The rapid economic development experienced by the Republic during the1960s, and its accompanying social and cultural changes, resulted in an identity crisis, as citizens and government grappled with traditional and 'modern' notions of themselves. While a new sense of confidence was evident in many circles from the time of the publication of T.K. Whitaker's *Economic Development* and its resultant economic programmes, this confidence was tempered by the anxiety generated by those who feared the consequential changes. Confidence was further undermined by growing industrial unrest, which peaked in 1966. During February and March of the commemorative year, the Institute of Public Administration conducted a series of lectures to commemorate the Rising. T.D. Williams wrote a lecture on the 'Political Scene', and his conclusions reflected this widespread unease.

> It would be wise not to rely merely on material achievement or economic performance: so fragile are the foundations of economic wealth and so provisional are the judgements of our economic angels. Traditions of any kind require a sense of confidence, morality and mission if they are to survive. We cannot, I think, survive without the rediscovery of our tradition and its adaptation to a world in which it is difficult to detect progress or retreat but which certainly is always in change. Ad hoc complaining, opportunism and technical skill are just not enough.[2]

As the Republic sought a more prominent role in the international community, a place always 'in change', change proved most evident in youth, the social grouping most receptive to it. The 1960s represented a time when the status and role of this grouping altered significantly. While in 1916 Pearse had gift-wrapped the future in the packaging of the past,[3] in the 1960s, with the country having ended its self-imposed isolation, hopes for the future of the Republic, like that of other economically advanced nations, were placed in the newly invested in and more dynamic younger generation.

Bearing this in mind, in what way would 1916 be presented to youth in 1966? At a time when the nation's future was being viewed in economic and international terms, how was the nation's past patriotism to be translated for a youth who would operate in this new context? In his analysis of the relationship between myth, memory and the construction of society, Hayden Whyte asserts that the construction of something new presupposes a destruction of something else, the remains of which can be used in the new edifice. Thus the construction of society implies the notion of reconstruction, and it is less an innovation than a recycling of fragments of prior structures.[4] If this theory is taken in terms of a new national project, in what way were the fragments of the Republic's foundation myth to be reconstructed? How, in the context of a rapidly changing society, were the 1916 Rising and its leaders to be portrayed?

This paper will identify the type of commemoration activities provided for the youth of the Republic in 1966. It will illustrate the messages promoted whilst demonstrating how for much of Irish youth, new messages were either obscured or irrelevant, delivered as they were in traditional forms. It will assess generational difference at this time of change, explaining why this difference did not produce open confrontation. It will end with an assessment of how, despite the older generations' wariness of many of the characteristics of the younger, the future was perceived as residing in the hands of the youth, and a sense of optimism prevailed in regard to that future.

COMMEMORATING THE SPIRIT OF THE PAST

Cultural nationalism saw resurgence during the commemorative year. The personal cultural achievements of the men of 1916 were highlighted, with the hope that such accomplishments would inspire the young. Ciarán Benson has argued that by paying special attention to ideals of cultural authenticity, citizens are able to identify with the nation as an ideal, which can then be emulated.[5] The state-sponsored competitions in literature, music and art, 'to help the writers and artists of [1966] to participate in the commemoration of a Rising, the leaders of which were themselves gifted in learning and art'.[6] Children under the age of fourteen were invited to write essays in both Irish and English, entitled 'An Easter Week veteran tells his story', while those under eighteen years of age were given the title '1916–2016'. Prizes were presented by George Colley, the Minister for Education, at Iveagh House, where he announced: 'if we and posterity were to understand better our own feelings, 50 years after, about the most extraordinary week in our near two thousand years of history, our attitude could best be caught not through the intellect alone, but through the intellect and senses combined'.[7] Similarly, the GAA organised essay competitions and, with the aid of Comhaltas Ceoltóirí Éireann, a ballad competition. The GAA also commissioned a pageant, *Seachtar Fear, Seacht Lá*, which, like the government's pageant *Aiséirí— Glóir réim na Cásca* was firmly directed at the youth.

Low Sunday, 17 April, was named 'Lá na nÓg', and 20,000 students from 200 Dublin schools marched to Croke Park for a special performance of *Aiséirí*. At official provincial centres and local commemoration ceremonies, secondary school students were generally selected to read the

Proclamation after the Easter parades.[8] On 22 April the Proclamation, copies of which had been issued by the Department of Education, was read in schools throughout the country. A commemorative booklet entitled *Oidhreacht* was issued to every schoolchild. Schools commemo- rated the Rising by attending special masses, which were preceded by a parade to the local church. Upon the return of the parade to the school, a pupil or, where possible, a veteran or relative of one of the men of 1916, unveiled the new copy of the Proclamation. This was accompanied by the raising of the tricolour on the school grounds and the remainder of the day was then free. Around the country, events for teenagers and older youth ranged from ceilís and ballad sessions to debates on topics such as 'Has Pearse turned in his grave?', organised by bodies such as Muintir na Tíre and Conradh na Gaelige.[9]

The focus on Gaelic cultural traditions when it came to youth-based or cultural activities hardly marked a new departure for an Irish govern- ment, and in particular for a Fianna Fáil government. The 1916 generation had long been promoted as an ideal by the state, with the result that this generation came to act as what Karl Mannheim has described as a 'crystallizing agent', as later generations attached them- selves, or were encouraged to attach themselves, to a generation that was seen as having achieved a 'satisfactory form'. In this way, the impulses and trends peculiar to a generation can remain concealed because of the existence of the clear-cut form of another.[10] While commemorative activity in 1966 did not represent a clear departure from previous policy, as Gaelic culture and identity continued to be promoted as ideals to be emulated, there was a change of emphasis. In the 1960s, the men of 1916 were not simply heroes to be revered. Instead, they represented examples of personal achievement, excellence, co-operation and initiative, and it was these qualities that were considered appropriate examples for contem- porary youth. It was hoped that if 1960s youth could emulate such positive traits, then perhaps economic successes could be achieved without negative social and cultural repercussions.

When speaking to fellow party members in 1965 about the forthcoming commemorations, Taoiseach Seán Lemass acknowledged these repercussions when he observed how the present time was one that placed great emphasis on economic achievement, which encouraged a more materialistic attitude to national affairs than the leaders of 1916 could ever have understood This, he continued, had resulted in people's pursuit of sectional aims, and he hoped that the occasion of the commemoration of 1916 would 'urge all people to learn, to think, to act again as Irishmen and Irish women first', before an attitude of indifference to national consequences became too firmly established.[11] In an attempt to correct what was seen as the development of selfish individualism, the golden jubilee of the 1916 Rising was to be used as a mechanism by which the spirit of the men of 1916 was to be revived and instilled in the nation, particularly in young people. Speaking to a packed cathedral at a jubilee mass in Kilkenny, Rev. Daniel Collier asserted that, 'The most important thing in 1916 was not the fighting but the spirit which inspired it', while an editorial in the *Cork Examiner* contended that the men of 1916 were to be remembered for their 'individual qualities' as well as their 'unity of purpose'.[12] Alf Ó Muirí, president of the GAA, declared that the fiftieth anniversary of the Rising presented a chance that must not be missed if the patriotic spirit of 50 years earlier was to be revived. 'Very few of our young people now ask', he continued,

> 'What can I do for my country?' Very few of them are seeking to find ways in which they may help to keep 'Ireland a Nation' alive. If the Jubilee of 1916 is to mean anything it must be more than a revival of memories. It must be a reawakening of the spirit that inspired the men who were prepared to fight and suffer, who were prepared even to die, that the Nation might live on.[13]

Practical patriotism

Writing in 1962 in *The Irish and the new Europe*, Dr W.D. Philbin, Bishop of Down and Connor, contended:

> the reason why [Irish] patriotic instincts are not positively engaged is because we do not feel that patriotism belongs with business and everyday work. We have read and sung about it in relation to military conflict and political struggles and we cannot visualise it in any other settings. Our emotions are not worked on by economic difficulties. There is no glamour in fighting an adverse balance of trade.[14]

Similarly, when discussing the problem of modern youth in 1967, Walter Forde asserted that Irish patriotism had been synonymous with fighting and dying for so long that Irish people had not been convinced of the need to live for the country, nor had they been convinced that they had a part to play in the destiny or enterprises of the country that would make a difference.[15] The fiftieth anniversary of the Rising witnessed the promotion of practical or constructive patriotism, as the spirit of 1916 was to inspire citizens, and the youth in particular, to attend to their civic duties. It provided an opportunity to remould the meaning of patriotism, to switch the emphasis from pride in noble sacrifice to pride in practical accomplishments.

Thus, the boys and girls of Holy Faith Convent, Celbridge, were informed that the Proclamation was a call to each one of them to love their country, and while this could be done by speaking the Irish language, or by fostering a love of Irish music, dancing and culture, it could also be done by buying Irish goods. It was further suggested to them that they could best honour the men who died by showing a greater pride in their own town and to refrain from littering the streets with sweet papers and to see that others did likewise.[16] Fr Larkin, of Peterswell in Galway, exhorted people, and particularly those of the younger generation, to study closely the character of the 1916 men. 'Good patriots of today were those', he said, 'who did their work well for Ireland; those who spoke Irish; and those who bought Irish'.[17] In Easter parades around the country, historical floats paraded along with those relating to the industrial concerns of the town and district.[18]

During Easter week Minister for Agriculture Charles Haughey, when speaking at the opening of Mellowes Agricultural College in Athenry, asserted that, to have the land used as Pearse would have wished, individual farmers would have to acquire the necessary education and training in order to meet the ever growing challenges presented to them by Ireland's inevitable involvement in the affairs of an international community. 'A country cannot be built up in 50 years, nor even in a hundred years', declared the minister. 'Every generation must make its share in the improvement.' He noted how the present and each future generation owed it to the men of 1916 to make well-organised and intelligent efforts to improve the land of Ireland and exploit its resources.[19] The improvement of educational opportunities was a prevalent issue in the 1960s, and in line with the promotion of the positive characteristics of the 1916 leaders, Dublin County Council added four scholarships to its existent scheme in 1966. Similarly, the Educational Building Society made memorial scholarships available to post-primary schools, demonstrating, in the words of George Colley, that it 'really understood what the men of 1916 were about'.[20]

The historic task of a new generation

So many of the characteristics of the men of 1916, from simple initiative to their educational pursuits, seemed in scarce supply in the Ireland of 1966. Writing for the *Boston Globe*, Lemass asserted that

> the slave spirit, born of centuries of foreign rule, which was once the main curse of the Irish, has now virtually disap peared, and the degradation, moral as well as material, which was its fruit has disappeared for ever.[21]

The key word here, however, is 'virtually', and the aim of the promotion of practical patriotism was the total eradication of the slave spirit from the younger generation. That there was something inherently wrong, but fixable, in the Irish personality was a message often presented to the youth. In 1966 the Christian Brothers' monthly magazine *Our Boys*, a publication for primary school boys, featured seven articles entitled 'Civics'. The first of these, with the heading 'The modern challenge', quotes Pearse: 'Wise men, riddle me this, what if the dream comes true?' The fact that the Republic had its voice heard at the council tables of Europe was deemed evidence that most of that dream had come true, and therefore the 'modern challenge' for current generations, 'one as vital and as dangerous to Ireland's survival as any she had had to cope with in her history', was to compete effectively in the European Common Market as protectionist tariffs were soon to be done away with. In this context, Ireland's national image was of huge importance in the 1960s, and the article in *Our Boys* identifies how that image could be improved. Those of other nations, the authors explained, viewed Irishmen 'as often lacking in common sense, emotional rather than logical, good planners with plenty of ideas rather than good executors who will carry out a boring task with perseverance and constancy'. The point at which Irish men got bored and quit was considered well below the average. The authors of the piece asserted that

> perhaps, the coming of the Common market is the best thing that could happen to make us pull ourselves together, and be more worthy of our long tradition of unselfish devotion to the cause of our native land.[22]

Lemass described the historic task of a generation of Irish youth in 1966 in the following way:

> Pearse said 'every generation has its task', and I think that they [the 1916 leaders] would accept that the historic task of this generation is to consolidate the economic found-ations which support our political institutions, recognising that unless this is accomplished now the nation's future will always be in danger.[23]

Thus ordinary citizens, rather than heroes, had a primary role in the nation's future. This was reflected in the Christian Brothers' treatment of 1916. In May 1966 a feature in *Tír na nÓg*, the Irish language supplement to *Our Boys*, contended that although information on the Rising was readily available in the newspapers, television broadcasts and newly published books, there was a danger in focusing too much on the leaders of the Rising. Rather, the Christian Brothers promoted remembrance of the men who fought on Northumberland Road, or those Volunteers who fought outside Dublin.

Fintan O'Toole, a school-child himself in 1966, has described the depiction of 1916 in commemoration activities as an image that would convince people that their losses and defeats would be rewarded in the heaven of economic expansion.[24] But this seems far from what was envisaged. The message to the youth was one that denoted the essential nature of their participation to the nation's future success—the heaven of economic expansion was only a possi-bility if they were active participants in its attainment; losses and defeats would no longer be glorified. However, the switch of emphasis on the 1916 leaders from heroic soldiers to focused over-achievers may well have been lost for many, as commemoration activities for youth, focused as they were on cultural nationalism, and taking the traditional form of pageants and parades, often provided an oversim-plified picture of the leaders. Dermot Bolger recalls the golden jubilee in the following way:

> [m]emorials were unveiled, speeches made beseeching God that in her hour of need Ireland would find such brave young sons again. I doubt if the dignitaries making those speeches believed a word of it, I'm sure the businessmen paying for the monuments certainly didn't; but we, in short trousers and cropped hair, did.[25]

That the message was delivered in a familiar form, one usually simplistic, meant that a change in emphasis was perhaps imperceptible; a new message compromised by its traditional form.

COMMUNAL MEMORY

Whyte's aforementioned supposition that new forms are built out of elements already present on the scene of construction is accompanied by his assertion that this idea only applies to mythical perceptions, which derive from traditionalised memory. He distinguishes between two types of communal memory—traditionalised and rational. In traditional societies, or those parts of modern societies not yet modernised, 'experience is conceived to belong to the present, while meaning, or the moral significance of experience, is conceived as residing in the past'. He asserts that this part of the communal memory presents itself as tradition and as such stands at odds with memory that has been rationalised, that is, organised, catalogued and stored in institutions created to serve as depositories of information; a feature of so-called modern societies.[26] The delay of the arrival of the post-World War II boom to the Republic meant that in 1966 both types of memory—traditionalised and rational—contested the same space. This resulted in messages of a conflicting nature prevailing in 1960s Ireland. One need only compare the spirit of the Lemass–O'Neill talks in 1965 and de Valera's speech at the closing ceremony of the commemorations, when the president asserted that he, for one, was never going to believe that the land of the O'Neills and the O'Donnells would remain permanently severed from the rest of the country.[27] In 1966, deference predominantly went to the past, however, and commemoration practices, by their very nature traditional, would lend themselves more easily to traditional perceptions.

That the past would not hinder an economically successful and more cosmopolitan future was, however, the aim of the new national project, as defined by Lemass; and this was reflected in the work of the Study Group on the Teaching of History in Irish Schools, commissioned by the government in 1966. This group asserted that

> while history should give us greater knowledge of the indi-
> viduals who share our environment and of those who have
> contributed to the independence and freedom we now

enjoy, it should do more than illustrate this by examples of sublime patriotism, self-sacrifice and unswerving commitment to noble ideals.[28]

Teaching the past

The abandonment of protectionism and plans to pursue foreign capital for investment in employment-intensive manufacturing industries drew attention to educational policy, as it was recognised that such policy played an essential role in economic development. In 1965 a four-man team that had been appointed three years previously submitted a report from the Organisation for Economic Co-Operation and Development (OECD) entitled 'Investment in Education'. This report assessed the inadequacy of existing educational arrangements for achieving the state's new economic objectives. With this in mind, one can perhaps identify the impetus for forming a study group on Irish history, as a new operating version was needed for a changing Ireland.

The committee on the teaching of history consisted of two historians, Dr Margaret Mac Curtain and Professor T.D. Williams; a psychologist, Professor S. McKenna; an economist, Mr M. O'Donoghue; a teacher, Mr T. McGillicuddy; a headmaster, Dr R. Cathcart; and a parent, Mrs R. Brugha. They suggested that the factual content of the history curriculum could be more profitably weighted in terms of the recent past of the country, 'since this would appear to be the period of most relevance in forming an appreciation of the contemporary position in the minds of our future citizens'.[29] It was the task of history teachers to

> bring home to our young people that the ordinary people of Ireland who have worked well and honestly at their allotted tasks, have also contributed to the common good, and that they too have served Ireland in a patriotic way.[30]

Overall, the recommendations from the study group on the teaching of history reflect the inter-related themes of economic development and 'modernisation'. The group rejected the existing history curriculum being taught to primary and post-primary schools, which it described as teaching an 'Ireland versus England' theme up to 1916 and stopping there. In the primary school, the study group proposed a focus first on legends and folklore from the Irish oral tradition, followed by an examination of local history in a context of social history, whereby changes in dress, transport and communications since the time of the students' parents or grandparents could be discussed. In fifth class, the students could consider 'the succession of social changes commencing with the emergence of the urban settlements, stemming from Norse influence culminating in the consolidation of the landowning ascendancy in the middle of the eighteenth century'.[31] Any bias in favour of political or military history was to be minimised. Thus, a past focusing on Gaelic Ireland followed by a non-political history was suggested, and similarly proposals regarding the post-primary course included a shift of emphasis to 'social and economic movements'.[32]

However, despite these new emphases, it was contended that no child was to leave school in ignorance of the formation of the Irish state. How were such events to be portrayed? The report contended that the history teacher was in a better position than most to hand on memories of the past without any loss of integrity, and perhaps this explains why it fails to advise them on how to teach the events of 1916–22.[33] Instead, it simply admits that the formation of the state is a delicate and tendentious issue. The report recognised that teaching the period in question could create problems, while ignoring it was suppressing knowledge of a very important period in Irish history. It finally recommended that well-trained teachers should be given the responsibility of dealing with this challenge.[34]

John Coakley has described how Pearse's views on Irish nationalism had acquired 'an unquestioned orthodoxy not only through the efforts of informal socialisation agencies but also through a deliberate policy of political education promoted by the Department of Education'.[35] The Christian Brothers had endeavoured to uphold the moral goodness of Ireland by promoting the martyrs of 1916, giving Pádraig Pearse particular primacy.[36] *Our Boys* fixated on Pearse's desire for an Ireland not merely free, but Gaelic, placing particular emphasis on the Irish language and the moral character of Pearse. While on the one hand, Pearse was seen as continuing the struggle begun with the insurrections of the sixteenth-century O'Neills, nothing could exceed 'the affection he bore to his mother' from whom he inherited the 'Catholic idealism of Gaelic Ireland'.[37] Anthony Cronin, a self-described victim of the educational process in the 1920s and 1930s, maintained that the events leading to the foundation of the new state were so sentimentalised as to make them seem to belong to a different world. 'Pearse in particular had been turned into an utterly unreal and boring figure, a mother-lover', he recalled, 'who was without human frailties and, consequently, without human virtues'.[38] Rather than re-evaluate him in history textbooks, however, the study group preferred to switch the emphasis for the younger generation.

An example of a series of texts, which represented this change in approach, was that published in 1973 for primary schools, entitled *The Living Past*, written by pseudonymous Tim McGillicuddy, a member of the aforementioned study group. The final book of the series informed children that whereas the author had written some of the story of Irish history for them, other parts they would have to find out for themselves. When doing this, they were to pay special attention to their own parish or district; for example, if finding out about electricity the suggestion was that they should investigate when electricity was first brought to their area.[39] The message of constructive patriotism, often expressed during the commemorative year, embodied McGillicuddy's explanation regarding the position in which the country found itself in the aftermath of the Civil War.

> This new country with all its problems had to be put in order again by a government of men who had little or no experience of the work. The progress made since is due to the efforts of Irish people and their governments. Nobody is fully pleased with the country as it is. Much remains to be done. Perhaps there are things that you feel need to be improved. There will always be work to be done if Ireland is to be a good country to live in. Each generation will have problems to face, but the story of the achievements of our ancestors is there to give us encouragement.[40]

This echoed the message at the end of the perfunctory account of the Rising and its failure given in *The Living Past*. These ancestors had taken part in a rebellion that they knew had little chance of success, but they 'believed that their struggle might revive the spirit of Irish patriotism'.[41]

While many recommendations of the study group are embodied in the series *The Living Past*, little was done to correct the problem of weighting the history course more towards the recent past of the country. After dealing with the Civil War, the text spends two pages dealing with Northern Ireland, and it then provides a few large photographic images of organisations that had helped improve the standard of living since 1921. There are five in all: the Electricity Supply Board, Bórd na Móna,

Bórd Iascaigh Mhara, Radio Telefís Éireann and Aer Lingus. It is suggested to students that they write to these organisations, as some might have leaflets or brochures available.[42] While the Bishop of Down and Connor had seen that there was no glamour in fighting an adverse balance of trade, it is likely that twelve-year-olds-of the early 1970s, saw little glamour in Bórd na Móna.

APING THE FOREIGNER: IRISH YOUTH IN 1966

A study of the 1966 commemoration reveals the Republic to have been an extremely self-conscious state. Presiding at an ecumenical gathering in Kilkenny city, the Right Rev. Dr H.R. McAdoo noted that 1966, as a juncture in history, had all the appearance of being a time of transition, a time of ferment.[43] That Ireland was undergoing a rapid and self-conscious transition was apparent, and the nation's own period of adolescence was mirrored by the arrival of the teenager in Ireland. While the term 'adolescent' has its origins in nineteenth-century psychology, 'teenager' came to prominence in the post-World War II period and was generally used to describe young consumers. Irish youth could broadly be defined as having four categories: primary-school youth, secondary-school youth, student youth and working youth. The disposable income of the latter provided for the emergence of Irish teenagers comparable to those in other industrialised nations.

The history of youth in Europe has everywhere moved along the broad lines laid down by economic development. Generational tensions tend to characterise societies experiencing economic change; indeed such change in eighteenth-century Europe, which led to younger members of society becoming waged, led to an almost universal lament about youthful extravagance and what was considered to be 'precocious consumption'.[44] Similarly, in the late 1950s and early1960s, changes in the Irish economy meant the arrival of a new source of wealth: the industrial wage. Vincent Power, in *Send 'em home sweatin'—the Showband story*, describes how young people developed a lifestyle based on spending what they earned each week.[45] The disposable income of young people in 1960s Ireland was spent on outlets that far from represented distinctive Irish cultural activities or those readily acceptable to older generations. Instead, popular culture reflected trends of British and American forms of entertainment.

De Valera saw the language as the mechanism by which sinking into 'an amorphous cosmopolitanism' could be avoided, and during his message to the nation at the closing ceremony of the 1916 commemorations asked if the revival of the Irish language would not be the resolve of the young men and women of 1966.[46] In 1949 he addressed the youth of a William Bulter Yeats Cumann, observing that,

> what we call western civilisation is at the crossroads...This nation will be what its individual citizens make it...You young people can in no small measure help to make the dream come true. That is your privilege and your task.[47]

Attempts to protect and fortify distinctive cultural forms had meant that deValera's Ireland had become increasingly isolated from international influences. While in the 1940s it had seemed under threat, it seemed it had never been under the direct attack that traditionalists felt they were witnessing in the 1960s. Static conditions had made for attitudes of piety, and in a static society the younger generation tends to adapt itself to the older, even to the point of making itself appear older. However, Mannheim describes how as the social dynamic strengthens, and at a time when there is a trend towards individualism, every individual then claims more than before the right to 'live his own life'.[48] He continues:

> ...any two generations following one another always fight different opponents, both within and without. While the older people may still be combating something in themselves or in the external world in such fashion that all their feelings and efforts and even their concept and categories of thought are determined by that adversary, for the younger people this adversary may be simply non existent: their primary orientation is an entirely different one.[49]

Anne Haverty's memories of what 1916 meant to her as a child reflect this theory. She recalls how she and her sister hated Irish dancing and would have much preferred it if a skating rink had appeared in the village or if they could have attended ballet classes, as these were the cultural activities they read about in their beloved English comic. Haverty was born in 1956, and she feels that during her childhood there was no longer any side to betray: while an earlier generation would have considered preferences such as ice skating or ballet a form of *shoneenism*, for her generation, the word *shoneen* no longer existed.[50]

Traditionalist forces in the nation, however, charged Ireland's youth with imitating other cultures and 1966 provided an opportunity to address what many saw as a cultural crisis. The cultural nature of so much of the commemoration activity and the fact that the Irish revolution had witnessed the pulling together of cultural traditions for the purpose of nation-building served to fuel this crisis. Pearse, after all, had hoped that the revolution would release the Irish people from the slavery of the intensely competitive, intensely individualistic modern world; they would be purified with the help of the language and the ideals of the peasant. Cultural nationalism of the late nineteenth and early twentieth century embodied a desire to return to a simpler past, to exchange *Gesellschaft* (society) for *Gemeinschaft* (community).[51]

The GAA, a body as much cultural as sporting and national, formed in 1884 with an ethos based on cultural nationalism, articulated the problem of 1960s Ireland as yet again being one of national identity, which endangered young people and, therefore, the future of the nation. At the GAA's annual congress in March 1966, one of the county delegates, P. Ó Braonáin, speaking on the issue of public relations, contended,

> [i]t is very important that we should get across to our youth the reason why we should play Gaelic games, dance Irish dances, and sing Irish songs. It is amazing that in 1966 we are more or less apologising to people because of our aims and ideals.[52]

In *Our Games*, the organisation's annual publication, Pádraig Ó Caoimh wrote of the necessity for members to recognise their individual duty 'during the present time of crisis when native ideals are being derided and the glamour of an alien meretricious civilisation is seen at every turn'.[53] In an article entitled, 'What does the GAA stand for', produced in the programme of the all-Ireland football semi-finals in the commemorative year, the association declared that it was not against internationalism or modernisation. However, it feared the development of a 'modern' nation that lacked distinction and asserted that it was nationalism and patriotism above anything else that could promote every aspect of economic and social development, as *Is beag a bhíonn buan i dtír gan anam* ('There is little that is permanent in a country without a soul').[54] Having been so involved in the cultural revival of the late nineteenth and early twentieth century, the GAA saw itself as facing a similar challenge in the 1960s. The chairman of the Connacht Board asserted that it was the duty of the association to try to infuse the spirit of the men of past generations into present day youth, by having them study more closely the ideals of the men of 1916. 'Let us not fool ourselves', he continued,

> the spiritual conquest of Ireland, which Britain for so long failed to achieve, would appear to be almost complete… How long more are we to stand idly by and allow ourselves to be carried away in this mad rush towards aping the foreigner?[55]

The Rising on television

While the term 'generation gap' is too extreme to be applied to the generational differences that characterised 1960s Ireland, there seemed to be many new differences that unsettled older generations. For them, it appeared that traditional values were being lost and this increased the importance of the fiftieth anniversary of the Rising. For many it was vital that the history of the 1916 Rising be passed on to the younger generation. It being 50 years after the event meant that the generation chiefly associated with the Rising was about to disappear. National memory would then be more reliant on the official writing of history, a highly contested issue at this time in itself. (See Michael Laffan, Chapter 10, this publication.) The commemorative year, therefore, sparked an interest in the particular version of history being supplied to the upcoming generation, and the medium used to present that version of history that would resonate most with this generation was television.

A plethora of historical programming was featured on Telefís Éireann, a new medium for such material. The importance of the serialised television show *Insurrection*, scripted by Hugh Leonard, which depicted the events of the Rising, cannot be underestimated. It appears to have resonated greatly with a generation who saw Irish men as gun-wielding heroes, rather than the heroes of the American Wild West, to whom they were familiarised. Unlike most of the 1966 commemorative events and activities for youth, *Insurrection*, with its use of a 1960s style newsroom and on-site interviewers, represented the portrayal of the old message in a modern guise. Brian Devenny writing in the *Irish*

Independent contended that if the buzz of comment, notably among the under 20s, meant as much as he thought it did, 'the scenes of animated history opened many minds, for which the Rebellion up to that had been a closed book, a date and a few names on monuments'.[56] Father P.J. Brophy, writing for the *Leinster Leader*, described Telefís Éireann's programmes as being a marked feature of the celebrations and he envied the young learner when he thought of 'the drab texts he had pored over at school'.[57]

However, concern was also expressed. Having watched the heroic endeavours of the men of 1916 acted out in dramatic fashion on television and on stage, and having listened to interviews with veterans of the Rising, some clearly feared that it could prove difficult for the young to reconcile the equation of dying for the nation and keeping it litter free as being two sides of the one coin of civic responsibility. Ruth Dudley Edwards wrote a letter to the *Irish Times* proposing the establishment of an expert consultative committee to advise the governing authority of Radio Telefís Éireann on historical questions, for fear that a one-sided interpretation of history would be imposed on the viewing public.[58] In an *Evening Herald* editorial it was contended that the national broadcaster's programming displayed 'a tendency to put television and its tricks first and history second'.[59] Such comments may reflect the contested nature of 1916 from 1965 on, particularly in academic circles, while the remarks of Father Brophy and Brian Devenny demonstrate how, for much of the public, that the youth's attention could be captured at all was a positive thing.

Developments in youth culture

That there was a difference between generations in 1960s Ireland was obvious; but this difference did not provoke direct confrontation. Acting as it does as a concealed metaphor for social change, the issue of 'youth' in industrialised nations like Britain and the USA, which emerged in the 1950s and peaked in the 1960s, was not self-contained, in that it was symbolic of the wider economic and social changes of society.[60] An American diplomat noted how in France in the late 1950s there was a much more clearly articulated family framework, backed by the still very relevant traditions of the Catholic church, which resulted in French teenagers having less opportunity to develop their own tastes and rituals.[61] While the notion of youth culture as being something distinct from mainstream culture was given credence in both Britain and the USA in the late 1950s, in France there was no mention of a separate culture until the early 1960s. Compared with the wealth of literature that emerged during that time about American teenagers and their subculture, in France there was only a trickle. When it came to youth affairs the focus was on who teenagers would become, i.e. adults, rather than on a separate teenage subculture.[62]

In Ireland, with its delayed economic boom and the dominant position of the Catholic church and traditional ways of life, the notion of a separate youth culture was rarely attested to, and throughout the 1960s the issue of youth was bound up in the more general problems of 'modern living', affluence, liberalism and materialism. This often led to a focus on the formation of adults rather than simply one on youth. Nevertheless, it was apparent in both Ireland and France that the problems associated with 'modern living' were most obvious in the social grouping where change is most conspicuous—youth.

Changes in the Irish economy resulted in the aforementioned arrival of a new source of wealth in the form of the industrial wage.[63] The increased disposable income available to youth was spent on outlets that leaned heavily in the direction of British and American forms of entertainment. A transitory phenomenon, showbands, dominated the cultural life of much of Ireland's youth, particularly in rural areas from about 1961 to 1967. While the fact that these bands were merely cover artists, imitating British and American music, rendered them unfavourable to some traditionalists, many viewed them as a source of national pride, because despite their imitative character, they represented a national phenomenon in themselves. The clean cut image of Irish showbands sat comfortably with the other forces of Irish social life. *Spotlight*, Ireland's first indigenous pop magazine, is described by Vincent Power as setting 'the right moral tone at a time when no self-respecting suitor ever left home on Sunday night without his Pioneer pin'.[64]

The showband phenomenon is representative of the results of the negotiated process that occurs when a country is in a time of transition. Power describes the showbands as being unique to Ireland, but this was only the case in terms of the form they took. While traditionalists and critics berated them for their imitative character, a similar discourse had occurred in England in the late 1950s. Critics then had complained about English music being a mere imitation of American music, as British pop stars of the late fifties like Cliff Richard and Tommy Steele neatly bridged the gap between the novelty of American rock and roll and the surviving British traditions of variety and show business.[65]

The negotiating process was one caused by economic development, which set in train a series of slower-moving social changes and resulted in Ireland experiencing a phase of what one could call adolescence. This, of course, was not a situation unique to the Republic and this was realised by many contemporaries. Ó Riain of the GAA stated in 1965 that

> this is a time of change. We are told that our attitude is outmoded and unrealistic. But we are not the only people who are encountering the impact of the times. Every nation is facing the same difficulties. Traditions are being shattered.[66]

In the late 1960s, a journalist by the name of Paul Neuburg travelled to Eastern Europe to research a book on the younger generation. He found that the modernising economic policies brought in by the Communist Party undermined the party's own ideals. However, while younger generations in Poland feared the censure of the Church and 'what people might say' much less than their parents did, the traditions handed down to the young by their parents ensured similar views on morality and faith survived. He described the effects of development as having gone far enough only to provide outlets for the more immediate drives of the young, but not for any real recklessness.[67]

A similar situation occurred in Ireland. The traditions and framework of the Catholic church and traditional society, along with the fact that the economy had not created an affluence that paralleled other industrialised nations, meant that by the 1970s, the issues surrounding a distinctive youth culture still had their roots in British and American debates. But while the traditions and influence of the church may have been more or less retained, its position as an authority that could restrain contemporary youth became less tenable. Irish society was becoming increasingly individualistic and therefore increasingly susceptible to secular influences.

In 1960s Ireland, comparisons between contemporary youth and previous generations were often unfavourable. Given the fact that the youth of its participants had been a feature of the 1916 Rising and the revolutionary period in general, it was natural that in 1966 a comparison would be made between contemporary youth and that of the heroic generation. Erskine Childers had called the Irish Volunteers 'the soul of the new Ireland, taken as a whole the finest young men in the country, possessed with an almost religious enthusiasm for their cause, sober, clean-living, self respecting'.[68] IRA members in their twenties were highly conscious of their youth and had been seen as acting out of a heightened sense of community, directing their violence towards outsiders and deviants, variously defined.[69] In direct contrast, the 1960s witnessed a rise in concern with the issues of delinquency, an activity anti- both society and community, and sexual permissiveness.

CONCLUSION

Despite the dichotomy between the generation of 1916 and that of 1966, Ireland's improved economic position meant that hopes were still high in most quarters for younger generations. Given the presence of never before experienced opportunity, there was a sense of optimism regarding the potential of the youth of 1966. Regardless of past achievements, the nation now, like other economically developed nations, looked to the future, placing its hope in the next generation. This is best expressed by Dr Peter Birch, Bishop of Ossory, writing in *Young Citizen*, a monthly bulletin on civics for secondary schools, first issued in 1967.

> Anyone who has fairly close contact with modern young people must be impressed by what they are capable of, and the influence they can have and use. If the person has a knowledge of history as well, he will realise that they are very like other young people who influenced many decisive periods in history, and it will not surprise him, therefore, if someone asserts that our young people are likely to force themselves very soon into a position where they can take over and set up a new vibrant social, political and religious scene...I am personally convinced that we are in such ferment at present, and that it is the time for new ideas and for youth. The political parties have recognised the signs, and so they are trying to attract young people. I do not think this will solve the problem. There may have been occasions in the past when it has worked. I cannot recall, though, any occasion where it has been anything more than a temporary solution. When society tires it needs, I think, total renewal of fervour, and only young people can give it...Their

methods and ideals will be questioned, or traduced and condemned, not for what they are, but for what they are not—simply for not being those of the old…It is hard on us older ones, but later on we hope history will be kind to us. It will level out and show that we tried, too, and perhaps, could not maintain the pace that our time needed. We had to move away from the marchers because we lost our first fervour, which is a sad, but natural failing that develops almost inevitably as people age.[70]

These 'modern young people', while not revolutionary and still respectful of their elders and the past, would find it more and more difficult to identify with not only the 1916 generation but with the ones that had followed. Ferdia MacAnna, whose father had written the pageant *Aiséirí—Glór réim na Cásca*, worked at the event. When he and his co-workers received their reward for their efforts on the final night, receptions to the form of payment were mixed. They each received a newly minted, limited edition souvenir ten-shilling piece. On one side was Pearse's profile, the other an image of *an claidheamh soluis* (the sword of light). While this wasn't exactly what they had hoped for, the real surprise was that they couldn't spend it. MacAnna recalls:

[t]he coin would be extremely important many years from now, people told us. We'd appreciate it when we were grown up. We would show it to our grandchildren. 'Bolix to my grandchildren', one boy said, 'I want to go and buy things'. None of the adults would listen. They way they looked at it, we had been paid for our labour with coins of inestimable historical and social significance. We were told that Pearse himself would have approved. That was the start of my disillusionment with Pearse.[71]

This story is symptomatic of its time. While generational differences reflected the atmosphere of change, deference would still be paid to the past even though, for the younger generation, it would no longer direct the future. In March 1966 the Literary and Historical Society (L and H) of University College Dublin put forward the motion 'That Easter 1966 should be quietly ignored'. While older and former auditors of the L and H such as Justice Farrell 'maintained that 1916 had given a sense of responsibility to our people', and Mr R.N. Cooke accused the university students of not understanding the 'men in the street, the men who actually fought in 1916', the attitude of the new generation can perhaps be gleaned from a weekly feature in the university's *Campus* newspaper, entitled 'The Definite Article':

> 1916 and all that: the gaunt old men march proudly, irregular columns of ye sainted IRA, grey heads and grey faces blanketed in impassiveness, daring the young men lining the route to jeer that they were fools to fight in that heroic gesture of defiance fifty years ago. The watching youths, as unimpressed as ever by ritual and ceremony do not see the silent tears that blind the grey eyes…they have seen the dream for which they fought brought to a certain reality, they have lived through decades of bitterness and blood feuds…they have struggled with compromise and failure, they have seen the young grow cynical and the inspiration of patriotism decay like an autumn leaf.[72]

The commemoration of 1916 in 1966 demonstrated many of the characteristics of national day celebrations in other European countries.[73] While the year's commemorative activities gave people the opportunity to berate the state for its failures, many citizens and the state saw an opportunity to gather and unite behind the national project, which had recently taken a new direction and in which citizens had a defined and active role. The fiftieth anniversary of the 1916 Rising provided the Republic with an opportunity to redefine itself and its aims as a nation geared towards a competitive future in the international community.

As witnessed in the 1990s with the development of Celtic Tiger Ireland and its Celtic cubs, fears that the nation would lose its distinctiveness and, hence, its soul, were rampant in the 1960s. Contemporary youth, the group in which societal change is most evident, became a source of concern as it was recognised that the youth represented the future of the nation. In order to instil in youth the qualities necessary for an economically successful future, the state in 1966 promoted a message of constructive patriotism, while traditionalists attempted to promote the patriotism they themselves had been taught. Both had limited success in getting their message across. The state would be able to use other means, such as a change in the school curriculum, to continue its campaign. Those who wanted to propagate the message of a more heroic type of patriotism would have less of an opportunity, however, especially after the outbreak of violence in Northern Ireland and the cancelling of Easter parades in 1972. For teenagers in the Republic in 1966, patriotism, whether it be heroic or constructive, held little appeal, as their culture became that of a wider, international community.

NOTES

[1] Liam Ó Briain, head of the censorship appeals board, quoted from the film *Rocky road to Dublin* (1968, directed by Peter Lennon; re-released 2005).

[2] T.D. Williams, 'Public affairs, 1916–1966: 1—The political scene', *Administration* 14 (1966), 191–8: 198.

[3] Declan Kiberd, *Inventing Ireland: the literature of a modern nation* (London, 1995), 207.

[4] Hayden Whyte, 'Catastrophe, communal memory and mythic discourse: the uses of myth in the reconstruction of society', in Bo Strath (ed.), *Myth and memory in the construction of community: historical patterns in Europe and beyond* (Brussels, 2000), 49–51.

[5] Ciaran Benson, *The cultural psychology of self: place, morality and art in human worlds* (London, 2001), 210.

[6] Department of External Affairs (DEA), *Cuimhneachán 1916–1966, Commemoration: A record of Ireland's commemoration of the 1916 Rising* (Dublin, 1966), 82.

[7] DEA, *Cuimhneachán*, 82.

[8] *Cork Examiner*, 11 April 1966; *Kilkenny People*, 8 April 1966; *Leinster Leader*, 19 April 1966.

[9] *Longford News*, 9 April 1966; *Leinster Leader*, 9 April 1966; *Tipperary Star*, 9 April 1966.

[10] Karl Mannheim, *Collected works of Karl Mannheim, vol. 5; Essays on the sociology of knowledge*, Paul Kecskemeti (ed.) (London, 1997), 309–10.

[11] National Archives of Ireland, Department of the Taoiseach (hereafter cited as NAI DT), Taoiseach papers 97/6/159, Speech made by Lemass at a dinner arranged by Dublin Comhairle Dáil Cheantair, Fianna Fáil, 9 October 1965.

[12] *Kilkenny People*, 15 April 1966: *Cork Examiner*, 11 April 1966.

[13] *Our Games*, no. 7, 1966, 18.

[14] Quoted in 'The teaching of history in Irish schools', *Administration*, 15 (1967), 268–85: 271.

[15] Walter Forde, 'The aimless rebellion', *Christus Rex* 21 (1967), 45–51: 49.

[16] *Leinster Leader*, 9 April 1966.

[17] *Galway Observer*, 23 April, 1966.

[18] *Offaly Independent*, 7 May 1966.

[19] *Irish Times*, 15 April 1966.

[20] *Irish Times*, 26 May 1966.

[21] NAI DT 97/6/160, 'The use made of freedom', by Lemass in the *Boston Globe*, January 1966.

[22] *Our Boys*, April 1966.

[23] NAI DT 98/6/476, Lemass's speech at the inaugural meeting of the Law Students Debating Society of Ireland, 18 February 1966.

[24] Dermot Bolger (ed.), *Letters from the new island: 16 on 16: Irish writers on the Easter Rising* (Dublin, 1988), 41.

[25] Bolger, *Letters from the new island*, 7.

[26] Whyte, 'Catastrophe, communal memory and mythic discourse', 54.

[27] University College Dublin Archives (UCDA), de Valera papers, P150/3381, RTÉ coverage of closing ceremony at the General Post Office, Dublin, 16 April 1966. De Valera had deviated from a written script, which was much shorter and made no mention of Northern Ireland.

[28] Study Group on the Teaching of History, 'The teaching of history in Irish schools', *Administration* 15 (1967), 268–85: 270–1.

[29] Study Group, 'The teaching of history', 271.

[30] Study Group, 'The teaching of history', 271.

[31] Study Group, 'The teaching of history', 275.

[32] Study Group, 'The teaching of history', 273–5.

[33] Study Group, 'The teaching of history', 271.

[34] Study Group, 'The teaching of history', 285.

[35] John Coakley, 'Patrick Pearse and the "Noble Lie" of Irish nationalism', *Studies* 71 (1983), 119–36: 120.

[36] Shauna Gilligan, 'Image of a patriot: the popular and scholarly portrayal of Patrick Pearse 1916–1991', unpublished MA thesis, University College Dublin, 1993, 24.

[37] *Tír na nÓg*, January 1966.

[38] Bolger, *Letters from the new island*, 16.

[39] Tim McGillicuddy, *The living past*, part 4 (Dublin, 1974), 1.

[40] McGillicuddy, *The living past*, part 4, 131.

[41] McGillicuddy, *The living past*, part 4, 124.

[42] McGillicuddy, *The living past*, part 4, 135.

[43] *Kilkenny People*, 15 April 1966.

[44] J.R. Gillis, *Youth and history: tradition and change in European age relations 1770–present* (London and New York, 1974), 47.

[45] Vincent Power, *Send 'em home sweatin': the showband story* (Cork, 2000), 16.

[46] *Cork Examiner*, 11 April 1966.

[47] Gilligan, 'Image of a patriot', 6.

[48] Mannheim, *Collected works, vol. 5*, 302.

[49] Mannheim, *Collected works, vol. 5*, 298–9.

[50] Bolger, *Letters from the new island*, 39.

[51] W.I. Thompson, *The imagination of an insurrection: Dublin 1916* (New York and London, 1967), 76, 237.

[52] Gaelic Athletic Association (GAA), 'Minutes of the Annual Congress', 20 March 1966.

[53] *Our Games*, 1966, 28.

[54] GAA, 'Programme for all-Ireland semi-finals, senior football', 21 August 1966.

[55] *Our Games*, 1966, 78.

[56] *Irish Independent*, 23 April 1966.

[57] *Leinster Leader*, 9 April 1966.

[58] *Irish Times*, 2 April 1966.

[59] *Evening Herald*, 20 April 1966.

[60] Dominic Sandbrook, *Never had it so good: a history of Britain from Suez to the Beatles* (London, 2005), 425.

[61] Arthur Marwick, *The Sixties: cultural revolution in Britain, France, Italy and the United States, c.1958–c.1974* (Oxford and New York, 1998), 95.

[62] Marwick, *The Sixties*, 95–6.

[63] Power, *Send 'em home sweatin'*, 16.

[64] Power, *Send 'em home sweatin'*, 200.

[65] Sandbrook, *Never had it so good*, 447.

[66] GAA, 'Minutes of the Annual Congress', 18 April 1965.

[67] Paul Neuburg, *The Hero's children: the post-war generation in Eastern Europe* (London, 1972), 238, 241.

[68] Peter Hart, 'Youth Culture and the Cork IRA', in David Fitzpatrick (ed.), *Revolution? Ireland 1917–23* (Dublin, 1990), 10.

[69] Hart, 'Youth Culture and the cork IRA', 22.

[70] *Young Citizen*, May/June 1969.

[71] Bolger, *Letters from the new island*, 37.

[72] *Campus*, 15 March 1966.

[73] Arve Thorsen, 'Foundation myths at work: national day celebration in France, Germany and Norway in a comparative perspective', in Bo Strath (ed.), *Myth and memory in the construction of community: historical patterns in Europe and beyond* (Brussels, 2000), 332.

5. COMMEMORATING THE RISING, 1922–65: 'A FIGURATIVE SCRAMBLE FOR THE BONES OF THE PATRIOT DEAD'?[1]

By Diarmaid Ferriter

INTRODUCTION

How to commemorate the 1916 Easter Rising in the aftermath of the establishment of the Irish Free State in 1922 was a question that confronted both government and opposition. It frequently led to political disagreement, cantankerous debate and uncertainty. For many, rather than being a question of solemn remembrance, the issue of commemorating the Rising provided an opportunity to seek to create political capital out of the contested republican legacy and to emphasise the divisions that existed within the Irish body politic.

Unsurprisingly, there were a variety of different views as to what should and should not be done and who should and should not be involved. More surprisingly, given the tendency to believe that commemoration only became difficult after the supposedly glorious, triumphant and retrospectively embarrassing fiftieth anniversary celebrations in 1966, it seems that well in advance of 1966 there was a growing resentment about commemoration of the Rising, which evolved into a general indifference.

The issue was often complicated by confusion as to whether the commemoration was a religious or political event, and the extent to which it could be 'a credible focus of reconciliation'.[2] There were also disagreements as to whether commemorative events and gestures should be focused on the capital city or should be nation-wide; the degree to which the government of the day or the former participants should spearhead such events; whose rhetoric should be used (and indeed rows over who was the *real* president of the Republic in 1916); and whether the graves of the executed 1916 leaders should be turned into a place of pilgrimage, and suitably adorned to attract large numbers, or left severe, plain and unobtrusive.

The words of Anne Dolan, in her book *Commemorating the Irish Civil War*, are partly applicable to the issue of 1916:

> There were years when it was useful, when it was embarrass-
> ing, when it suited best to say nothing at all. There were
> fashionable and fickle years, controversial and inconsequen-
> tial years. But there were always some who never noticed or
> cared about the difference.[3]

But to what extent would the words of Edna Longley, also quoted by Dolan, be true in relation to 1916?—'Commemorations are as selective as sympathies. They honour our dead, not your dead'.[4] How different was it for the 1916 commemorations than for the Civil War ceremonies? Dolan has suggested that with regard to commemorating 1916, 'there was never the same sense of regret; never the sense that death and ceremony were so plainly intended to divide. At Civil War graves it was a solemn return, a return to the death of 1916's type of hope'.[5]

THE DIVISIVENESS OF COMMEMORATION

There is a degree of truth in that assessment, but it underestimates the degree to which remembrance of 1916 encouraged political confronta-tion. Particularly in the 1930s and 1940s, the legacy of 1916 *was* divisive, a divisiveness that seems to have turned to tedium by the 1950s and 1960s. David Fitzpatrick suggests in his essay *A chronicle of embar-rassment*, that both Cumann na nGaedheal and Fianna Fáil were 'hesitant in exploiting the emotional capital' accumulated as a result of the national struggle, because such actions would be tainted by politics and potentially counter-productive'.[6] Nonetheless, this is only partly the case, and there has been a tendency to overlook some of the more interesting rows that commemorating the Rising caused.

The 1920s

The difficulties were obvious during the 1920s: a Sinn Féin movement so united on the surface in the aftermath of the Rising had been irrevocably split, and the country was red raw in the aftermath of the Civil War. Many who had fought side by side in 1916 were now fierce opponents. David Fitzpatrick records the suggestion in 1923 by Clement Shorter, widower of the poet and sculptor Dora, that William Cosgrave, President of the Executive Council of the Irish Free State, and leader of the Cumann na nGaedheal government, accept £1,000 from Dora Shorter's estate in order for her sculpture commemorating the executed rebels to be fashioned in marble, set on a pedestal of Irish limestone and erected in Glasnevin cemetery in Dublin, with an image of Pádraig Pearse as its centrepiece.[7]

Cosgrave doubted Mrs Margaret Pearse, mother of Pádraig, would want anything to do with a proposal that had his government's blessing. He wondered whether the sculpture would be better placed outside Leinster House, the location of Dáil Éireann, and was worried about the neglect of those killed other than by execution in 1916. He also feared the proposal would 'look as if we wanted to have one last slap at the British'. Eventually, the proposal was reluctantly agreed to, but for the next four years there were disagreements about where the sculpture would be located, recriminations about the danger of it overshadowing the grave of Arthur Griffith and disputes as to exactly whose names should be included. By 1927, when matters were settled, it was nonetheless decided that it would be politically wise to have no formal unveiling to avoid squabbling over the inheritance of 1916.[8]

Publicly, things had not been much easier for Cumann na nGaedheal. The state files held in the National Archives record that in 1924, the year in which Cumann na nGaedheal hosted the first formal military ceremony to commemorate the Rising, invitations were issued to relatives of the executed 1916 leaders, but only one, Mrs Mallin (widow of Michael Mallin), attended. It is no surprise Mrs Mallin was on her own, given the political affiliations of the other relatives, who were avowedly republican and hostile to the ruling government. In 1925, the government did not issue invitations to the ceremony at Arbour Hill to those TDs deemed 'Irregular'.[9] Rival republicans marched to Glasnevin cemetery for an alternative commemoration.

A year later, the tenth anniversary of the Rising, leading republicans including Eamon de Valera, Seán Lemass, Oscar Traynor, Mary

MacSwiney and Constance Markievicz, under the auspices of the Easter Week Commemoration Committee, attended Mass in the Carmelite church, Whitefriar Street, in Dublin City and then went on to the republican burial plot at Glasnevin, to continue the tradition of a rival republican commemoration. The *Irish Times* quoted de Valera as addressing them:

> The homage of our appreciation is not enough whilst the task to which they devoted themselves remains unfinished.[10]

Three years later, Frank Ryan and other republicans unveiled a modest memorial at one of these ceremonies, dedicated to some of the more obscure dead of 1916.[11]

Understandably, the Cumann na nGaedheal government was not going to go to great lengths concerning the commemorations; there was even a question as to whether flowers should be put on the graves of the executed leaders. Given the preoccupation with state security, and in the aftermath of the Boundary Commission dispute in 1925, which resulted in no alteration to the border separating northern and southern Ireland, anything in relation to 1916 was going to be relatively understated. As suggested by Adrian Keane in his thesis, 'Who fears to speak of Easter week?', 'history was moving and unfolding too rapidly for a settled, accepted view to emerge'.[12] As Shauna Gilligan in her thesis 'Image of a patriot' further amplified, governmental use of and reference to Pádraig Pearse was scarce until the late 1920s: in 1926 Cosgrave did authorise the renaming of Great Brunswick Street as Pearse Street, but the government largely ignored the fiftieth anniversary of Pearse's birth in 1929.[13] Cumann na nGaedheal opted to keep the ceremonies low-key, with Requiem Mass, a slow march with band, wreath-laying and a graveside rosary (later replaced by the playing of the Soldier's Song), the firing of a volley and the performance of the Last Post.

The 1930s

The question for the 1930s was how the new Fianna Fáil government would handle this issue. There was an unprecedented ceremony in 1932, which the *Irish Press* insisted was 'not for one party but for the people'.[14] Fianna Fáil also sought to gain political capital out of the death of Pearse's mother in 1932, despite the contention of the *Irish Press* in April that year, that 'whenever she appeared men felt the near presence of the inviolate tradition of nationhood. Party divisions dropped away'. This was, as Gilligan surmised, the era of the 'safe, homely, moral Pearse'; and in keeping with this, de Valera's speech at Arbour Hill in 1933 contrasted the military defeat in 1916 with the moral victory that followed.[15]

But in May 1933, Richard Mulcahy, a former Cumann na nGaedheal minister, asked Frank Aiken, Fianna Fáil's minister for defence, if invitations to the state's 1916 commemoration had been withheld 'from a number of persons who in previous years received such invitations'. Aiken's response indicated that Fianna Fáil was now going to attempt to take control of the legacy and strike off the list the perceived bogus pretenders.

> There was no good reason why some of those on the original list should have been included. 241 persons who were invited in former years were not included in this year's list; it is not known how many of them took part in the 1916 Rising. Neither is it known how many persons who took part in the 1916 Rising were excluded from the list in previous years.[16]

Fianna Fáil also made a point of allowing the public to gain access to the graves at Arbour Hill, which Cumann na nGaedheal had prohibited, and also initiated a further commemoration ceremony, which coincided with the actual date of the first executions of the leaders of the Rising.

As the 1930s progressed, and with the IRA declared an illegal organisation in 1936, the year of the twentieth anniversary of the Rising, it was even more important for Fianna Fáil to claim sole right to the 1916 inheritance. A year after Fianna Fáil's ascent to power, the first moves were initiated to get a 1916 memorial erected in the General Post Office, and it was with the commencement of this project that deep political divisions over the commemoration of the Rising came into the open. The idea of a memorial at the GPO was first mentioned publicly in the *Irish Press* in 1933, and a year later the idea of having sculptor Oliver Sheppard's work 'The Death of Cúchulainn' as the memorial was mooted.[17]

The provision of £1,000 for the project was voted for in the Dáil in August 1934, and the Minister for Finance, Seán MacEntee, indicated that the memorial was intended to be merely a feature of the building and not in any sense a national monument to commemorate 1916 in general and he indicated that the object of the memorial was to mark the special historical relationship of the GPO building to the events of 1916.[18]

A subcommittee of the government (the Easter Week Memorial Committee) was appointed to consider and submit a suitable inscription. A year later, it was decided that the third section of the Proclamation ('We declare the right of the people...exaltation among the nations') would be suitable.[19]

A row broke out soon afterwards about who should be at the unveiling ceremony. At a conference that included civil servants, ministers and Gardaí, 'it was felt that a distinction could not be drawn between TDs...with 1916 service and those without'; but for ex-TDs, only those with 1916 service would be invited.[20] A remarkable number of groups then lined up to announce that they would have nothing to do with this ceremony, as reported by the *Irish Press*: Clann na nGaedheal (the pre-Truce IRA), the 1916 Club, the Irish Republican Soldiers Federation and the Old Republican Rights Association, and eventually, and perhaps most significantly, Fine Gael, who issued a statement expressing the hope that

> [a]ll republicans will realise the necessity for the unity which will enable all organisations believing in the Proclamation of 1916 to take a fitting part in honouring the dead of the Nation without entering the sphere of internal differences of republican thought.[21]

In the Dáil, Richard Mulcahy, chief Fine Gael critic of Fianna Fáil's attempt to monopolise the 1916 Rising legacy, queried the composition of the Easter Week Memorial Committee and Fianna Fáil's partisan approach to the matter. An internal government memorandum acknowledged there was disquiet, noting

> [t]he suggestion has been made that the personnel of the Firing party has been taken exclusively from men who took part on one side in the Civil War. This has also been indicated as a possible source of bitterness which should be, if possible, absent from a function of this nature.[22]

The growing unease about the ceremony led to stormy debates in the Dáil, as well as to the resignations of the Clann na nGaedheal representatives from the memorial committee because, they maintained, they could not consistently identify themselves 'with any of the various ceremonies being held by different republican bodies'. Also in the Dáil, Fine Gael made much of the fact that Fianna Fáil was proposing to hold a flag day on Easter Sunday, accusing the government of using the army 'for the purpose of making a Fianna Fáil holiday to add to their Flag Day collection'.[23]

Fianna Fáil was also facing criticism from the other side—'true Irish Republicans'—who Maud Gonne MacBride (republican activist and former wife of Major John MacBride, executed for his role in 1916) hoped, 'would not go near the GPO'.[24] Clearly, the activities of this memorial committee were seen as politically controversial, and it was even wondered if civil servants should have to be specially authorised to associate themselves with the committee, although ministers insisted it was acceptable. On 17 April 1935 William Cosgrave turned up the political heat, and replaced Richard Mulcahy as the opposition's chief critic of the plans for the unveiling of the sculpture at the GPO by releasing a powerful statement. He was not attending the unveiling, he insisted, because

> the time is not yet ripe for an adequate commemoration of 1916 which would be accompanied by that generous national enthusiasm indispensable to success.

He went on, in this cleverly crafted contribution, to assert:

> [t]he anniversary of Easter week is an occasion which might be suitably employed by every party in sober reflection. Bitterness, suspicion, envy, we have in abundance—as well as parties. It was for a noble purpose that men fought in Easter week 1916, not for divisions in the homes of the people, in their associations, or in the national ranks. It is not possible to hide these national humiliations today or to cover them with a veil lifted from the bronze statue of Cúchulainn.[25]

The *United Ireland* newspaper, a publication that supported Fine Gael, echoed his comments a few days later. Insisting that the members of Fianna Fáil had nothing in their minds except a desire to make political capital for themselves and their party, the paper editorialised:

[i]t is always unseemly, if not indecent, for political parties
to engage in a figurative scramble for the bones of the patriot
dead.[26]

Furthermore, this editorial maintained that the Cúchulainn statue had
not even been specially made for this occasion but had been many years
ago [25 years previously], and 'lay ready to hand'. The ceremony in
1935 was also notable, as Fitzpatrick notes, for the arrival at the GPO
of a rival republican procession, en route to Glasnevin.[27]

From the late 1930s there were also frequent demands from Old
IRA associations to have 24 April, the date of the commencement of
the Rising, declared a public holiday; this idea was considered by the
government, but it was decided to adhere to commemorating the
Rising at Easter, whenever that fell. The following year de Valera
presented the National Museum with an ornamental role of honour,
listing, in Fitzpatrick's words 'thousands of supposed participants in
the Rising'.[28] It was a low-key affair with no speeches. More contentious, suggests Brian Walker, were the disturbances in the 1930s,
when members of the Communist Party, 'all 28 of them', would fall in
'uninvited behind the IRA ranks and display conspicuous red rosettes
in their buttonholes'.[29]

A SHIFT IN EMPHASIS IN MARKING THE ANNIVERSARY OF THE RISING

The 1940s

Some of the most interesting files in the archives of Department of the
Taoiseach deal with the plans to commemorate the twenty-fifth
anniversary of the Rising in 1941, consideration of which began in the
Autumn of 1939, with the Department of Defence taking a leading
role. But by early 1940 it was suggested, due to the ongoing World
War, that there might be something unseemly about neutral Ireland
having a glorious military celebration, or as a memorandum in
February 1940 put it, 'whether there should be any form of commemoration', and if there was, 'whether it should be of a purely religious
character or of a military character or whether it should be both'.[30]

Notwithstanding this sober reflection, in May 1940 some individuals in the Department of Defence were adamant that commemoration

on a grand scale was the order of the day because national resurgence had 'only been made possible by the sacrifice of Easter week'; though they acknowledged that they needed to look at the 'political implications' of working with the National Graves Association.[31] Some of the plans that emerged from the Department of Defence were exceptionally elaborate, including the idea of a pageant of history in the Phoenix Park, on an 'ambitious scale with searchlight effects', a 'mass victory parade past the GPO, a state ceilídhe [a communal Irish dance] to be organised on the most extensive possible scale', athletic functions and a ceremony involving the carrying of torches of freedom from the four provinces 'based on the Olympic games ceremonial'. The plans emerging from the Department of Defence also called for the co-operation of all theatre and picture houses 'in staging distinctively national programmes' (ironically including Seán O'Casey's *The Plough and the Stars*, a play that had sparked controversy in the 1920s due to its depiction of aspects of Dublin tenement life during Easter week 1916 and its thinly veiled assault on the militarism of the era).[32]

Eamon de Valera, as taoiseach, was quite adamant in his negative response to these ambitious plans for commemorating the twenty-fifth anniversary; clearly the officials in the Department of Defence had got carried away, and the words 'no question' were scribbled in the Department of the Taoiseach's response to the memorandum mentioned above; or as de Valera himself put it more officiously: 'in present circumstances the holding of a commemoration on elaborate lines would not be appropriate'.[33] In October 1940 he suggested the commemoration 'should be of a purely military nature and that it might be a single event...confined to one day only'. In December, in a memorandum from the Department of Defence headed 'victory parade past the GPO', the Department of the Taoiseach bracketed the word 'victory'.[34]

In January 1941 the word victory was dropped; now, it seemed, the ceremony would just be a parade. But despite this apparent preference for a scaling down of commemoration plans, on 14 April 1941, de Valera was reported in the *Irish Independent* as having reviewed 25,000 men in the 'largest and most spectacular military parade the city has seen'. Special 1916 medals had been minted; de Valera received the first one.[35] Interestingly, the *Irish Press* of the same day had warned against the practice of such commemoration, which had a tendency to 'fashion the Rising into a story heavy with sentiment and forget what it achieved'.[36] Adrian Keane has suggested that the events of 1941 were about de Valera 'revitalising the military parade' and the *Irish Times* claimed Fianna Fáil was once again monopolising the 1916 inheritance. Keane claims that this display in 1941 was aimed at Nazi Germany in order to emphasise Irish neutrality.[37]

This is also the view of Rosemary Ryan, who in a 1984 article on commemorating the Rising maintained the parade of 1941 was 'a direct response to the threats to Ireland's neutrality'.[38] Brian Walker has also developed this point and quotes a correspondent in the *Irish Independent* who assessed the 1941 commemoration:

> Ireland 1941—soldiers in field green, regiments of nurses in black stockings and white gloves—an entire nation prepared.[39]

De Valera, it should be pointed out, was conscious of the sensitivities of the government appearing to overdo the republican celebrations, not just because of World War II, but also because of the IRA bombing campaign in Britain during the war. On 24 March 1940 he had made a radio broadcast with these issues as a backdrop and, significantly, he spoke of Pearse's ideals, insisting that they could be realised only if the people of Ireland worked for them under the guidance of government.

> It is not the moral right of any individual or group of individuals to choose a means that is contrary to the public good or justice. The claim to choose such means can never be substantiated by an appeal to the facts or the conditions of Easter Week 1916—nor to the sentiments of the leaders. We can conceive of these men as wishing only the true good of their country and it cannot possibly make for the good of the nation to refuse due obedience to the freely elected Irish government which now controls the major position of our land.[40]

Another aspect of the commemoration in 1941 was an emerging critique of the failures of Irish independence and the failure to live up to the promises of 1916; or the idea of celebrating Irish neutrality on the basis of 'what we have got we shall hold'. In *The Bell* in April 1941, its editor, novelist Seán O'Faoláin, wrote an editorial article to co-incide with the twenty-fifth anniversary of the Rising, entitled 'Ireland 1916–1941; Tradition and Creation'. He posed many questions and wondered whether James Connolly, the labour leader executed for his part in the Rising, would be satisfied with the Ireland of 1941:

> Here, we know better than most how much a man's
> emotional bloodstream is made up of memories...If there
> is any distinct cleavage among us today it is between those
> who feel that tradition can explain everything and those who
> think that it can explain nothing...we are living in a period
> of conflict between the definite principles of past achieve-
> ment and the undefined principles of present ambition...
> contradiction is everywhere...of all our antique symbols
> there remain only two—the official harp, and a design on
> the half-penny stamp, which not one person out of a
> thousand understands.

He also took a swipe at the selective use of the language and legacy of
Pearse, quoting Pearse's criticisms of the writer J.M.Synge's realist
depiction of rural Ireland, about which Pearse concluded:

> Ireland in our day as in the past has excommunicated some
> of those who had served her best...when a man like Synge
> uses strange symbols which we do not understand we cry
> out that he has blasphemed and we proceed to crucify
> him...[41]

In 1946 the *Irish Times* radio critic criticised the intellectual laziness
of the state's radio service in its contribution to commemorating the
Rising, bemoaning the lack of imagination evident and the tendency to
use the same layout and material every year, including sections on
Charles Stewart Parnell, the nineteenth-century home rule leader, the
oration delivered at the funeral of veteran Fenian Jeremiah O'Donovan
Rossa by Pearse in 1915, the text of the 1916 Proclamation and quotations from Dorothy MacArdle's *Irish Republic*, a history book
sympathetic to Fianna Fáil and Irish republicanism.[42]

There were also complaints from the Dublin Brigade of the Old
IRA in the mid- and late-1940s that the commemoration momentum
was on the wane; in a letter to Minister for Posts and Telegraphs Patrick
J. Little, the members of the brigade informed him that 'the national
flag is not flown from any of the post offices in the South County
Dublin area on Easter Sunday'. The following year, the Old IRA Men's
Association wanted all buildings under government control to have the
flag flying on Easter Sunday and the week following, to which the
government's response was that the flags would only be flown on the
Sunday and Monday.[43]

In March 1945 Michael MacCárthaigh, a member of the Old IRA Men's Association, complained that there were several buildings in Cork city alone where the flag was not flying, including the GPO, Customs House, Model School, Board of Trade Office, Garda Station, Labour Exchange, University College Cork and the Munster Institute. This pressure seemed to be partly effective—up to now the flags were only flown in Dublin, on the GPO, Customs House and government buildings, but it was agreed that in future they would be flown on all state buildings 'equipped with permanent flag poles'.[44]

There were two reasons for a military parade in Dublin at Easter 1949: to celebrate the declaration of the Republic, and also to commemorate the Rising. Now that there was a coalition government in power, it was interesting that 1916 still seemed to cause suspicion in the party ranks, and that it was difficult to find unanimity. Seán MacBride, for example, the leader of Clann na Poblachta, one party of the coalition, was present at the annual IRA commemoration of 1916 at Glasnevin cemetery, while Fianna Fáil in fact boycotted the cere-monies at the GPO and went instead to Arbour Hill.[45]

Fianna Fáil certainly did not seem to have much enthusiasm for the idea of celebrating the new Republic. Taoiseach John A. Costello, in a magnanimous gesture, invited de Valera as leader of the opposition to join him in a broadcast to mark the occasion, an invitation de Valera rejected on the following grounds:

> We in Fianna Fáil are glad that henceforth there will be agreement amongst all parties in Dáil Éireann that the state shall be described as a Republic. We cannot convince ourselves however that the act merits that its coming into operation should be marked by national celebrations. Indeed, when the constitution came into operation in 1937, we decided that celebrations such as those now proposed ought to be reserved until the national task which we have set ourselves is accomplished. We still believe that public demonstrations and rejoicings are out of place and are likely to be misunderstood as long as that task remains uncom-pleted and our country partitioned.[46]

There was a glaring hypocrisy in these sour lines, as, to use de Valera's logic, Fianna Fáil should never have commemorated the Rising either. This Fianna Fáil stance was also articulated in other ways; Frank Aiken was quoted in the *Irish Examiner* as saying that his party rejoiced that the 'Republican' 1937 constitution was now recognised by all parties in the Dáil:

> not a single comma of our constitution had to be changed to enable the coalition groups belatedly to salute the Republic on Easter Monday. Never in the history of any national struggle for freedom was so much made by so many lawyers out of so little.[47]

The *Irish Press* went as far as to say that the coalition government was doing a huge disservice to nationalists in Northern Ireland, who 'have now seen the 1916 Rising linked with a Bill which changes nothing in their regard'.[48] Since the 1920s, northern Republicans had attempted to commemorate the Rising in such places as Milltown cemetery in Belfast and Derry City cemetery, but they were banned from doing so by the government and such a commemoration remained prohibited until 1948. In 1950 the commemoration at Milltown cemetery incorporated services held by the National Graves Association, the Irish Labour Party and the Old IRA, and during the 1960s marches continued to be held relatively unhindered, though there was some confrontation with police over the flying of the tricolour.[49]

The 1950s

Moving in to the 1950s, the question of commemoration in the Republic focused on the graves of the 1916 leaders at Arbour Hill and discussion about whether a proposed memorial should be located at Arbour Hill or elsewhere. In 1947 there had been tentative government approval for the establishment of a national memorial park (to commemorate lives lost in the 'fight for independence') on part of the St Anne's estate in Raheny in north Dublin, though this proposal was not followed through.[50] In March 1948 the Department of Defence had proposed a bronze plaque of simple design with the names of the leaders of the Rising on the wall over the graves at Arbour Hill. This proposal was based on the idea that 'the original austere appearance of the prison yard should, as far as possible, be preserved for future generations'.[51] The Commissioners of Public Works (CPW) considered these proposals inadequate and they

> suggested a scheme of their own which would involve a complete transformation of the environment of the graves—

this included the removal of the walls so the graves could be free standing, curved masonry on walls, paved terraces and broad flights of steps and rest of the area in lawns.[52]

Arbour Hill was also being subjected to official scrutiny because 'the burial plot, which is open daily to the public does not bear any sign of its significance and the names of those buried there are not indicated'.[53] In addition to the seven signatories of the Proclamation, Edward Daly, Micheal O'Hanrahan, William Pearse, John MacBride, Con Colbert, Seán Heuston and Michael Mallin were also buried in the plot at Arbour Hill.[54]

In August 1952 the government decided to pursue the scheme suggested by the CPW. There was also an attempt to establish the order in which the leaders of 1916 were interred in Arbour Hill; the CPW invoked the assistance of Jerome O'Connell who, prior to the Truce, had been in charge of the Irish Military Lands Records (Tom Clarke was interred first and Seán MacDiarmada last).[55]

The estimated cost of these plans was £12,500. There were concerns about the desirable standard of art and taste being reached; at the end of 1953 there was a suggestion that care should be taken to ensure that the use of three types of stone—marble, limestone and granite—would not result in an artistic clash, and the view was expressed that such a slab should be abandoned altogether as 'being too suggestive of a megalithic tomb'.[56] The Department of Defence was informed in April 1954 that the CPW could not guarantee the project's completion by Easter 1955. At the end of that year the *Evening Herald* reported a Limerick delegate at the Fianna Fáil *ard fheis* [annual conference] complaining that the graves at Arbour Hill were a sacred place 'that should not be disturbed' and that he had no confidence in the CPW.[57] While this work on the Arbour Hill graves was ongoing, other plans for commemorating the Rising were proposed, discussed and ultimately dismissed. In July 1954 the government decided to get the CPW to submit proposals for the erection of a memorial in St Stephen's Green 'on the lines of colonnaded structures which would also serve as a shelter with statues and plaques of persons prominently associated with the Rising'. The CPW thought this would be 'scarcely in keeping with the character of the Green'.[58]

Work on the Arbour Hill scheme dragged on into the late 1950s; according to a letter to the *Irish Independent* in 1958, it was 'fitting' that the plan had been conceived by a Fianna Fáil administration [1951–4] and executed by an inter-party government [1954–7].[59] In June of 1958, sculptor Michael Biggs implored the taoiseach to ensure he got the job of inscribing the words of the Proclamation at Arbour Hill [he eventually did], warning de Valera he would be professionally ruined if he did not get the commission. He had to write again in December of that year ('I believe that my work is an asset to the country where craftsmanship in general and this particular brand of it [i.e. calligraphy], are at a deplorably low level').[60] The carving of a cross on the ashlar wall was completed in 1959. Minister for Defence Oscar Traynor now wanted the text of the Proclamation carved into the ashlar wall of the memorial and a memorandum revealed his thoughts on this matter.

> The assistant principal architect [in the CPW] has also referred to the Gettysburg address in the Lincoln memorial at Washington which contains about 270 words as compared with about 500 in the Proclamation of 1916. This, he has stated, is incised directly on the wall of the memorial and is similar in scale and character to that which has already been proposed for the ashlar wall at Arbour Hill. The execution is perhaps not as good as would be expected to be got in the Arbour Hill memorial but nevertheless it is, in the architect's view, a thing of considerable distinction and dignity.

He concluded: 'It is difficult, if not impossible to achieve on anything like this scale a treatment of such a long inscription that is at all dignified or monumental'.[61] The taoiseach had also received a request to have the names of all the insurgents who died in 1916, not just those executed, inscribed on the walls at Arbour Hill, and he was supplied with 66 such names. What to do about this remained a problem right into the 1960s. The secretary of the Department of Defence wrote to the secretary of the Department of the Taoiseach in the autumn of 1962 on the subject.

> The Minister for Defence now feels that the Garden of Remembrance at Parnell Square might be a more appropriate place than Arbour Hill for a memorial of the nature contemplated. The significance of Arbour Hill in relation to 1916 is purely on account of the burial there of the executed 1916 leaders whose graves have become a place of pilgrimage. It has no particular significance in relation to any other patriots

who were executed in 1916 and buried elsewhere or who gave their lives at that time otherwise than by execution.[62]

The 1960s and the fiftieth anniversary commemorations

By the 1960s there were numerous complaints from members of old-IRA brigades as to the lack of centralisation evident in the commemoration of 1916 and the over-proliferation of parades. In June 1962 this prompted Frank Casey and Peter Nolan, of the Federation of IRA 1916–21, to write a letter to Taoiseach Seán Lemass:

> The Easter week commemoration parades held in Dublin this year occasioned a great deal of adverse comment among the old IRA and there is no doubt that every year these parades are becoming less impressive and have ceased to command the respect to which they are entitled from the public. The position is that an official state ceremony is held on Easter Sunday centering on the GPO. Another state ceremony is held at Arbour Hill early in May. The old Dublin Brigade also hold a parade on 24 April, with a ceremony at the GPO and the different battalions are accustomed to hold separate commemoration parades in the different battalion areas, usually in association with a memorial mass.
>
> This multiplication of parades has not been for the best. The citizens of Dublin have become so used to seeing handfuls of old men marching behind the national flag that they no longer turn their heads to look at them, while the drivers of buses and cars hoot them out of the way and break their ranks with indifference, if not contempt.[63]

It is true that by the early 1960s, many were turning their attention to the commemoration of the fiftieth anniversary of the Rising in 1966, but it is also the case that in light of these preparations, the government was conscious of two things—the general indifference of many people and the danger of reopening old wounds. With regard to the first, as the *Irish Times Annual Review* put it in 1965, in the general election of that year,

> partition, the Republic, the language and all the old constitutional questions were completely replaced by the social

and economic questions of the new era...It saw the resigna-
tion of many veteran leaders and the take over of a new
generation.[64]

The *Irish Times* went even further a month later, stating in January 1966:

> our young people want to forget. Boys in Dublin gravitate
> to coffee-skinned girls...the past is not only being forgotten
> by the young, it is being buried with great relish and even
> with disdain.[65]

Lemass was also aware of the failure of successive governments to
commemorate Irish soldiers who had died in the service of the British
Army during the First World War; during this era he acknowledged
their sacrifice, maintaining they had died 'as honourably as any of the
thousands of Irishmen who have given their blood'.[66] Lemass was also
undoubtedly frustrated by the correspondence he had to deal with in
1965 as another issue raised its head—the question of who should
figure most prominently in the commemorations of 1966. Kathleen
Clarke, widow of veteran Fenian Tom Clarke who had been executed
after the Rising, signed her correspondence as the 'only widow alive of
the signatories of the 1916 Proclamation', and insisted in a letter to
Lemass, 'I know more about the events both before and after the Rising
than anyone now alive'. She demanded that she be given a central role
in the plans to commemorate the fiftieth anniversary. She further
insisted that Tom Clarke had been president of the Republic in 1916:

> Seán MacDermot was always complaining to Tom that
> Pearse wanted everything. He was not satisfied with getting
> honours he may have earned but wanted to grab what was
> due to others.

Pearse, she alleged, had 'sat all the week writing in the GPO', and
was 'beneath contempt', as he had taken advantage of the confusion in
the GPO to sign himself 'President' on the documents of the week.
She continued:

> [s]urely Pearse should have been satisfied with the honour of
> Commander-in-Chief when he knew as much about
> commanding as my dog...I have remained silent in public
> for fifty years but the circumstances which first forced me to

remain silent no longer exist and the matter is now one of history. I had not intended raising the issue in public but I shall be forced to come out very strongly in public if the powers that be attempt to declare Pearse as President.[67]

CONCLUSION

Who wanted to be responsible for a wider opening of this can of worms? And where would it end? Were government ministers ready to be lectured on Irish history by the relatives of the 1916 leaders? Lemass replied to Clarke that there was nothing 'which I can usefully add' to this debate.[68] The tone of the correspondence emanating from the Department of the Taoiseach suggests Lemass was not keen on vigorous debate on the Rising or Pearse in the 1960s, particularly in the context of his determination to promote 'the building of Anglo-Irish good will'.[69] When pondering the suitability of Pearse's poem 'Invocation' as an inscription on the memorial wall in the Garden of Remembrance, he was 'disturbed by the fierce and vengeful tone of the poem, which was entirely appropriate to the circumstances of 1916, but will be less so to those years after 1966'.[70] This was not the observation of someone who was keen to get involved in a scramble for the bones of the patriot dead. In October 1965 the secretary of the Department of External Affairs reported on a discussion he had with the British ambassador to Ireland, who was worried about his presence in Dublin during the fiftieth anniversary commemorations.

> The Ambassador asked about the character of the commem-
> oration, and, in particular, whether it would be oriented
> towards the future or a re-enactment of the past. I referred
> to the Taoiseach's recent speech on the subject and told the
> Ambassador that I felt sure he could take it that the
> commemoration would be a forward-looking occasion
> without any attempt to re-open old wounds.[71]

Much has been made of the downplaying of the iconography of 1916 after the fiftieth anniversary. But as this paper has shown, there is evidence to suggest that prior to 1966, it was already becoming a sensitive and somewhat delicate subject.

NOTES

1 *United Ireland*, 20 April 1935.
2 David Fitzpatrick, 'Commemoration in the Irish Free State: a chronicle of embarrassment' in Ian McBride (ed.), *History and memory in modern Ireland* (Cambridge, 2001), 184–203: 195.
3 Anne Dolan, *Commemorating the Irish Civil War: history and memory, 1923–2000* (Cambridge, 2003), 1–6.
4 Dolan, *Commemorating the Irish Civil War*, 6.
5 Dolan, *Commemorating the Irish Civil War*, 1–6.
6 Fitzpatrick, 'Commemoration in the Irish Free State', 203.
7 Fitzpatrick, 'Commemoration in the Irish Free State', 195.
8 Fitzpatrick, 'Commemoration in the Irish Free State', 196.
9 National Archives of Ireland, Department of the Taoiseach (hereafter cited as NAI DT), S 9815 (A), 'Easter week commemorations', 25 April 1925.
10 *Irish Times*, 5 April 1926.
11 Fitzpatrick, 'Commemoration in the Irish Free State', 197.
12 A.T. Keane, 'Who fears to speak of Easter week?', unpublished MA thesis, University College Dublin, 1996, 1.
13 Shauna Gilligan, 'Image of a patriot: the popular and scholarly portrayal of Patrick Pearse 1916–1991', unpublished MA thesis, University College Dublin, 1995, 18.
14 *Irish Press*, 28 March 1932.
15 *Irish Press*, 23 April 1932.
16 NAI DT, S59815 A, 10 May 1933.
17 *Irish Press*, 8 March 1933.
18 NAI DT, S6405/A/1, 10 August 1934.
19 NAI DT, S 6405/A/1, 30 May 1934; *Dáil Debates*, 10 August 1934; *Irish Press*, 8 March 1933.
20 NAI DT, S 6405B, '1916 memorial GPO, unveiling ceremony, Easter 1935', 23 March 1935.
21 *Irish Press*, 1 April 1935.
22 NAI DT, S 6405B, 9 April 1935.
23 *Irish Press*, 10 April 1935; *Sunday Independent*, 14 April 1935; *Irish Times*, 15 April 1935.
24 *Irish Times*, 15 April 1935.
25 NAI DT, S6405B; *Irish Press*, 18 April 1935.
26 *United Ireland*, 20 April 1935.
27 Fitzpatrick, 'Commemoration in the Irish Free State', 188.
28 Fitzpatrick, 'Commemoration in the Irish Free State', 197.
29 Brian Walker, *Dancing to history's tune: history, myth and politics in Ireland* (Belfast, 1996), 87–91.

[30] NAI DT, S 11409, 1 February 1940.

[31] NAI DT, S 11409, May 1940.

[32] NAI DT, S 11409, Department of Defence memo, May 1940.

[33] NAI DT, S 11409, 25 October 1940.

[34] NAI DT, S 11409, Department of Defence memo, 25 October 1940.

[35] *Irish Independent*, 14 April 1941.

[36] *Irish Press*, 14 April 1941.

[37] Keane, 'Who fears to speak of Easter week?', 8ff.

[38] Rosemary Ryan, 'Commemorating 1916', *Retrospect 4* (1984), 59–62.

[39] Walker, *Dancing to history's tune*, 90.

[40] Gilligan, 'Image of a patriot', 44.

[41] Seán O'Faoláin, '1916–41: Tradition and creation', *The Bell*, 2 (1) (April 1941), 5–13.

[42] *Irish Times*, 25 April 1946.

[43] NAI DT, S 2818, 12 March 1945.

[44] NAI DT, S 2818, 20 March 1940.

[45] Keane, 'Who fears to speak of Easter Week?', 18.

[46] NAI DT, S 14440, De Valera to Costello, 7 April 1949.

[47] *Irish Examiner*, 23 April 1949.

[48] *Irish Press*, 18 April 1949.

[49] Walker, *Dancing to history's tune*, 90–1.

[50] NAI DT, S 9815 C, 19 August 1947.

[51] NAI DT, S 9815 B, Background explanatory memo, 19 August 1952.

[52] NAI DT, S 9815 C, 19 August 1947.

[53] NAI DT, S 9815 C, 19 August 1947.

[54] NAI DT, S 9851 B, 'Easter week commemorations at Arbour Hill', Department of Defence memo, 19 August 1952.

[55] NAI DT, S 9851 B, 'Easter week commemorations at Arbour Hill', 27 August 1952.

[56] NAI DT, S 9851 B, 'Easter week commemorations at Arbour Hill', Department of the Taoiseach memorandum, 16 December 1953.

[57] *Evening Herald*, 23 November 1955.

[58] NAI DT, S9851B 'Easter week commemorations at Arbour Hill', August 1953.

[59] *Irish Independent*, 30 May 1958.

[60] NAI DT, S9815 C, Michael Biggs to de Valera, 6 June 1958.

[61] NAI DT, S 9815 D/94, July 1959.

[62] NAI DT, S 9815 E/62, 'Easter week commemorations', 8 September 1962.

[63] NAI DT, S 9815 E/62, 'Easter week commemorations', Frank Casey and Peter Nolan to Lemass, 7 June 1962.

[64] *Irish Times Annual Review 1965* (Dublin, 1965), 5.

[65] *Irish Times*, 11 January 1966.

[66] NAI DT, S 8114 C 61, 19 February 1966.

[67] NAI DT, S 97/6/469, 'First president of the Republic 1916', Kathleen Clarke to Lemass, 11 May 1965 and 29 March 1965.
[68] NAI DT, S 97/6/469, 'First president of the Republic 1916', Lemass to Clarke, 15 June 1965.
[69] NAI DT, 97/6/532, '1916 GPO flag', Lemass to Harold Wilson (British prime minister), 31 March 1966.
[70] NAI DT, 96/6/193, February 1966.
[71] NAI DT, 98/6/495, 'Report of interview with British ambassador', 12 October 1965.

6. FORGET POLITICS! THEORISING THE POLITICAL DYNAMICS OF COMMEMORATION AND CONFLICT

By Rebecca Lynn Graff-McRae

INTRODUCTION

In this chapter, I aim to set out an introduction to a critical analysis of the politics of commemoration. Here I emphasise the way in which commemoration is intrinsically based on the construction and reproduction of oppositions—between public/private, inside/outside, us/them, past/present, memory/forgetting, unity/division. As such, it is intricately implicated in conflict, antagonism, violence and contestation. At the discursive level, commemoration involves the legitimation of one form of conflict over others, and re-inscribes axes of division within the social–political arena. At the same time, as illustrated by the conflicting interpretations of what 'the politics of memory' means and how it can/should be used, there is increasing conflict over the very ways in which commemoration is political and conflictual. Commemoration reproduces the ways in which all politics (and their relationship to the political) are antagonistic: the moment of the political, in which 'the undecidable nature of the alternatives and their resolution through power relations becomes fully visible', constitutes what Laclau calls 'the moment of antagonism'.[1]

The critical significance of this approach to commemoration is its call to

[c]onsider...the critical connections between the dead and the living, the past and the present, and most importantly

between acts of mourning and acts of political negotiation...
the difficult task of investigating the imbricated psychic and
political dimensions of a set of cultural customs which
would seem to represent the atavistic moment *par excellence*,
that is, commemoration.[2]

My primary objective, therefore, is to explicate this relationship
between commemoration, conflict and the political, and to take the
question to its most critical level: how is the very opposition between
'politics' and 'the political' implicated in the commemoration of conflict
and conflict over commemoration?

I. Commemorating Conflict, or Conflicting Commemorations

A nation reveals itself not only by the men it produces but also
by the men it honors, the men it remembers. (John F. Kennedy,
speech delivered at Amherst College, 26 October 1963.)

We are ready to die and shall die cheerfully and proudly...
You must not grieve for all of this. We have preserved
Ireland's honour and our own. Our deeds of last week
[Easter Week, 1916] are the most splendid in Ireland's
history. People will say hard things of us now, but we shall
be remembered by posterity and blessed by unborn generations. (Pádraig Pearse, in a letter to his mother on 1 May
1916, before his execution.)

The Irish, North and South, are as bound by their history as
they are divided by it...a fundamental aspect of the Irish
tragedy is that the past is continually and ritually sacrificed
to a caricature of the present. Threads are plucked from both
past and present, and woven into a smothering ideological
blanket of a uniform green, or orange.[3]

[W]e should build a monument to Amnesia and forget
where we put it.[4]

The comments cited above, taken together and independently, present
diverse attempts to define commemoration: as mourning or celebra-

tion, as a line of continuity traced between past and present; as a constitutive expression of identity; as a reflection of (unequal) power relations; or as a negotiated tension between remembrance and forgetting. The problem of commemoration is not the need to find a definition—it is all of these things and yet none. Commemoration is not merely an event, a parade, a statue, a graveside oration: parades can be disrupted or re-routed; statues defaced or bombed; speeches suppressed or re-written. Commemoration simultaneously inscribes, reinscribes and transgresses the borders between history and memory, between memory and politics and between politics and history. It is not an act or a word, nor is it inaction or silence. Commemoration is itself constantly under negotiation.

> Each instance of citation, incomplete in itself, fails to refer to a stable original model or context...[The key] emphasis is on the discontinuity between repetitions of these concepts [national identity, conflict resolution, etc.] and on the loss of legitimating foundations that comes from appealing simultaneously to the past and the future.[5]

Increasingly, cross-disciplinary work on cultural memory or memory studies has not only highlighted the differences and commonalities between approaches; crucially, it has also ignited a process of questioning and contesting conceptions of memory, history and politics that have to this point been taken for granted.

> Issues of memory are everywhere today. They raise—and are raised by—epistemological questions regarding history, experience, and truth. They raise—and are raised by—ontological questions of self-hood and identity.[6]

Moreover, such a process itself becomes 'political' in the widest sense of the term: debate, critique, problematisation, deconstruction, negotiation. Our objective in studying the past and its invocations, however, is not merely to debate about the whats and hows of a single event in a particular socio-historical context—in this instance the events commemorating the Rising that have centred on 1966—but to *negotiate* between our own disciplinary and personal positions; between a diversity of perspectives, interests and approaches; between the role of memory in politics and history, the role of politics and history in memory and, ultimately, the very meaning of those terms themselves.

It is with this in mind that I would like to pose a few questions about memory, history and politics—by no means the only or even the most pertinent questions, but a critical starting point. First of all:

- What is political about memory and commemoration?
- What is political about the role of memory in the construction (and reproduction) of history?
- How does history and its use of memory relate to the dynamics of power?

Each attempt to answer these questions provides one version of the politics of memory, and the discourses of commemoration that serve to express these dynamics. But while we must acknowledge the significance of its desire to emphasise resistance and subversion, each interpretation, like the epigraphs that begin this chapter, is highly problematic: it too leaves things unsaid; it too attempts to conceal its own discourses of power. In each of these cases, an obvious complex of binary oppositions is established—man against power, marginalised against hegemonic, memory against forgetting—in which one term is privileged and inequality is entrenched. Each version of commemoration seeks to establish its own relationship between truth, remembrance and liberation: if we can remember the truth, if we resist the forces that compel us to forget, we can triumph over hegemony and therefore over power.

Memory and commemoration

What remains unsaid, however, is that these formulations obscure the discursive negotiations by which 'truth' and 'memory' are defined, along with the relations of power that underpin them. This process involves two interconnected and mutually reinforcing elements.

First, the writing and re-writing of *the past*; that is, claims of legitimacy and ownership of a particular version of history that seeks to ascribe to that history a linear narrative[7]. In the words of Lewis Namier (written in 1942):

> [o]ne would expect people to remember the past and imagine the future. But in fact, when discoursing or writing about history, they imagine it in terms of their own experience, and when trying to engage the future they cite supposed analogies from the past: till, by a double process of repetition, they imagine the past and remember the future.[8]

From a postmodernist perspective, memory and commemoration assume a polysemic character, a near-infinite potential to be interpreted and reinterpreted within language.

> As in all communication, historical memorialization depends upon the interpretation of a signifier, a word or symbol that stands between the viewer and the event commemorated; once a powerful icon enters into circulation, its connotations are set in motion. Thus, historical revision inheres in the process of memorialization.[9]

It is this potential for re-writing and reinterpretation as well as the impossibility for history, memory, or the event to be objectively known, that contributes to the simultaneous necessity and uncertainty of writing 'the past'. Slavoj Žižek (as summarised by Jenny Edkins) formulates this paradoxical intersection in terms of the 'unfounded founding moment of politics' which has the potential to disrupt teleological writings of history:

> The political moment…is a turning point in history…It is a point at which the future is far from certain, a point at which anything can happen. Later, when a new social order has been established and the events that 'led up to' it incorporated into history, these events may appear as part of some general historical development. At the time, however,…[the] situation is one in which people are forced to make decisions, to 'act', in a manner for which they can find no guarantee in the social framework. That same framework is precisely missing, suspended, because it is in the process of reinvention. It is only by presuming the new social order…that the new order is brought into being, retrospectively.[10]

In this way, the past and the future are (re)invented simultaneously, in the 'present' of the political moment.

Second, memory engages in the (re)construction and contestation of *our past*: it is intricately bound to discourses of the nation, the state, identity and opposition, and thereby decrees who is to be included, excluded or marginalised from both the group and history itself.[11] That is, the way in which the intersection between memory, history and identity is drawn has significant implications for 'our' understanding of 'our own' past. In writing the history of the nation-state or ethnic group, this intersection seeks to *write the nation itself*.[12.]

> The making of a nation…lies not in codes or names but in its power to construct its unseen inner life from the minds and memories of those who live in it. To turn inhabitants into citizens and citizens into patriots.[13]

But this process is itself antagonistic, a tension between self-identity and national identity, between history as myth and memory as experience:

> If I could not remember a country, I could at least imagine a nation…Imagination. The word itself has the poignance of opposites. By imagining a nation, I was beginning the very process, awakening the very faculty which would bring me into conflict with it.[14]

This sense of conflict between the self and the nation is both produced by, and contested through, discourses of memory and commemoration: '…the past and its retrieval in memory hold a curious place in our identities, one that simultaneously stabilizes those identities in continuity and threatens to disrupt them'.[15] As such,

> [i]f the past is in one sense determinative [i.e. (re)productive] of who we are, it provides in another sense inversions of our present state. On the *positive side*, memory offers a certain scope for the kind of play or freedom that enables us to creatively refashion ourselves, remembering one thing and not another, changing the stories we tell ourselves (and others) about ourselves.[16]

Thus, 'memories are acts of commemoration…[which] do not merely describe the speaker's relation to the past but place her quite specifically in reference to it'.[17]

Commemoration thus (re)produces a relationship between memory, history and identity, past, present and future, that is itself inherently political. In this way, the politics of commemoration are crucially implicated in the (re)inscription of boundaries (inside/outside, now/then); the legitimation of 'acceptable' fora and axes of conflict (us/them); and the reproduction of discourses of memory, identity and politics, which themselves establish a hierarchical relation between conflict and consensus.

Commemoration as discourse

Commemoration, therefore, was never merely an event. Commemoration is a discourse in time and space—here and there, then and now, past, present and future. It is the (re)inscription of the event as such, achieved through the (partial and temporary) resolutions of oppositions—between us/them, peace/conflict, inside/outside, morality/injustice, democracy/tyranny, male/female, reconciliation/revenge—that are so thoroughly incorporated into our understandings of remembering (and, of course, forgetting) as to make themselves invisible. Within these oppositions, contradictions and paradoxes lies the key to the politics of commemoration. Commemoration is at the same time constructive and destructive, unifying and divisive, inciting reconciliation and warfare. Moreover, *the dynamics of commemoration itself are intrinsically predicated upon these oppositions, upon opposition as such.* Commemoration is therefore '[a] statement...[that] is something always about to be understood by discursive formations, and to be reiterated to political advantage within them'.[18] Acts of memory necessarily involve a failure to achieve full stability through commemoration, reappropriation or contestation.

> While [this]failure may not be acknowledged, it is indicated in the inability to fully account for the sacrifice that inhabits political decisions. It appears in the gaps, inconsistencies, and contradictions that prevent complete justification. ...it looks for possibilities within and beyond the desire to regain the seemingly lost ideals of unified nations, incorruptible documents, secure political institutions and historical foundations.[19]

The political dynamics of commemoration therefore present a paradox—a question rather than an answer. Above all, it is a *political* question: What is being commemorated, where and how? By whom is it commemorated, and by whom forgotten? Who is excluded or marginalised and whose interests does this serve? How is commemoration used in political conflicts—over sovereignty, territory, identity; equality amongst gender, class, ethnic, religious or ideological categories? How does this legitimate, (re)produce, or contest unequal power relations and particular understandings of political dynamics?

Commemoration and the political

What, then, is *political* about memory and commemoration? We can explore the politics of memory and commemoration on a number of levels, through a process of double-readings and problematisations.

In the most immediate sense commemoration is directly political, in that it takes place in/through official institutions and arenas (i.e. as a function of the state), or as opposition to, or outside of, the official arena. In this view, 'history' and 'memory studies' are concerned with uncovering the 'truth' about the past, and the ways in which it has been mobilised to particular motives. According to John Torpey, 'the scholarly pursuit of the past can be *political*, and hence contribute to revealing the subterranean aspects of the past, but it fails if it becomes *politicized*, subservient to narrowly political interests'.[20] Its concern is to ask, 'how does an entity such as the state, whose sole rational reason for existence is to ensure it continues to be, acquire the value-laden, inevitably selective ballast of cultural memory?'[21] Yet, while commemoration serves as a function of the state, performed within the state in order to (re)affirm state and national identity, at the same time,

> ...commemoration exposes the ephemerality of a state whose foundations are an effect of performative utterances, which legitimate themselves by creating their own referents. Such a state depends, obsessively, on repetition: on annual commemoration of the 1916 Proclamation or national martyrs, for instance. In such performances, continuity is both established and breached.[22]

Secondly, the events or figures marked in commemoration are inextricably symbolically linked to the 'history' of the state/nation/ethnic group as a 'myth of origin'. Thus *the politics of memory* is intimately bound to *the politics of identity*. Likewise, Gillis outlines the politics of commemoration as primarily being concerned with the use of commemoration in the construction of identities—that is, political and cultural identities within the social space of the nation-state. For Gillis, this mobilisation of memory from the past allows a degree of homogeneity to be constructed in the identities of the present: '[i]f the conflicts of the present seemed intractable, the past offered a screen on which desires for unity and continuity, that is, identity, could be projected'.[23] However, it is precisely these (politicised and political) attempts at homogenisation that can promote conflict:

> [c]ommemorative activity is by definition social and political, for it involves the co-ordination of individual and group memories, whose results may appear consensual when they are in fact the product of processes of intense contest, struggle and, in some cases, annihilation.[24]

Because of this correlation, commemoration involves the potential for conflict within and between groups in society, to be used as a weapon or battleground, or as a vehicle for explicitly interest-based campaigns. On the surface level, this can be seen as conflict between competing identities, in which the political and symbolic capital embodied within the past is fought over in a zero-sum game. Devine-Wright highlights '[t]he potential role of historical commemoration…in legitimizing or delegitimizing the social structure, representing a form of collective action that actively attempts to influence the socio-political *status quo*'.[25] It is this 'link between legitimacy and memory [that] reflects the temporal nature of ethnic conflict and the manner in which group leaders can seek to manipulate and distort memories for group purposes'.[26] In this view, commemoration is constructed as a site in which opposed groups seek to legitimise their territorial, social and political aspirations through competing claims to the past.

This framework, however, offers a rather reductivist formulation of the relationship between commemoration and conflict: it claims that, if competing or contradictory mobilisations of memory(ies) are a key factor in perpetuating and legitimating conflict in a divided society, then by promoting the acknowledgement of 'shared history' these divisions can be overcome. This is the logic behind the concept of 'parity of esteem' espoused by the 1998 Belfast Agreement.[27] Aside from encouraging a version of history that favours reconciliation by privi-leging constructive forgetting over contentious remembrance, this version of commemoration reinforces the 'two communities' mentality and the continuation of 'victim'/'perpetrator' counterclaims. In this way it serves to depoliticise and neutralise remembrance without addressing the actual sources of division.

Power and memory: alternative theories of commemoration

The intersection of commemoration and power can, however, be ap-proached in a radically different way. Post-marxist or Gramscian perspectives see conflicts over memory and commemoration as the struggle between dominant/hegemonic and subordinate/marginalised discourses in society. From this view, commemorations are the product of unequal relations of socio-political power, in which one version of the past and its uses for the future is imposed by the political motivations of the present. Such an approach aims to

> explore…the relations of power that structure the ways in which wars can be remembered, across forms that range from public commemoration orchestrated by nation-states through to the personal testimonies of war survivors; and from the cultural memories of war represented in films, plays, and novels, through to juridical investigations of wartime atrocities…[28]

Here the work of Foucault is particularly salient, in its focus on discourse, power–knowledge relations and, crucially, contestation or resistance.[29] It is not the substantive *what* that is being commemorated that is the issue; what is of importance is the way in which what is commemorated or forgotten (re)produces power relations and claims to ascribe meaning to these actions.

> By the *politics* of war memory and commemoration, we signal the contestation of meaning that occurs within and between these various forms and practices, and the (unequal) struggle to install particular memories at the centre of the cultural world, at the expense of others which are marginalized or forgotten.[30]

Discourses of memory are thus seen as 'attempts at closure, at decisiveness and imposition, like the sharp report of a fired gun at a military commemoration and the ringing silence that follows it: *this* is the sound of commemoration, *this* the silence'.[31] However, while this approach seeks to reclaim and reappropriate the forgotten, it can do so only by privileging 'the silenced'—in other words, claiming that 'memory' is an ideology produced by the powerful that must be uncovered and recovered by the marginalised. Here, it must be emphasised that the personal, private, local and marginalised have power-political interests just as the state, institutional and dominant, does.

Commemoration is therefore *always already* conflictual: it is not merely a product of unequal power relations, but crucially it (re)produces these power relations and frames the ways in which they can be understood. These dynamics rely on a particular formulation of 'politics' that often serves to undermine the political[32]. 'Politics' is the struggle to influence the distribution of power—within the state or among states; 'the political', therefore, is about the way in which that struggle is negotiated, legitimated and contested.[33]

Each of the approaches discussed above engages with key political themes and attempts to define 'the politics of memory'. These discursive constructions of commemoration posit a particular relationship between 'commemoration' and 'politics' in ways that obscure their own political bases (and biases). These questions, while undeniably significant, seem to inevitably establish their own resolutions. The attempt to define the politics of memory and commemoration ultimately fails, precisely because—as with all crucial concepts in politics—both the value and downfall of 'commemoration' lie in its tendency to slippage, its ability to stretch meaning. It can be fitted into any number of boxes, to suit any strategic, theoretical or ideological purpose or perspective.

'The politics of commemoration': this highly charged term is often made to appear unproblematic; we are encouraged to overlook its contestable nature and accept its definition and the role it is made to play without protest. 'The politics of commemoration' can be defined, but in the process it is always already defined *politically*: it is temporarily categorised, contained, bounded. It is produced and reproduced within a discursive nexus in contingent, partial and antagonistic series of negotiations. It displaces the question of its own politics: that is, what is remembered or forgotten in the politics of commemoration itself? Commemoration—far from being unproblematic—demands to be problematised.

Problematising commemoration

In *Trauma and the memory of politics*, Jenny Edkins embarks on such a project with a view to International Relations theory. Here, she develops a postmodern(ist) framework to explore 'how, and with what effects, we memorialise the traumatic events of the twentieth century'.[34] Using a complex of post-structuralist and psychoanalytic theory (from Foucault to Lacan), she traces the discursive intersections between trauma, time and memory, and highlights their implications for our conceptions of the political. In her key premise, Edkins distinguishes between 'linear time' and 'trauma time', and extends this to a distinction between 'politics' and 'the political': 'politics' involves a process in which 'the political' becomes *depoliticised*.[35] In this conception, what we call 'politics' represents the status quo, the institutionalised arena and processes of 'governance'. 'Linear time' is the 'time of the standard political processes…the time associated with the continuance of the nation-state, [in which] events that happen are part of a well-known and widely accepted story'.[36] 'Trauma time', on the other hand, constitutes 'a disruption of this linearity…It doesn't fit the story we already have, but demands that we invent a new account, one that will produce a place for what has happened and make it meaningful'.[37] This conception of time relates to 'the political' as disruption or innovation, the 'point at which the status quo is challenged…such challenges and the changes they produce…[can] appear traumatic. They upset, or escape, the straight-forward linear temporality associated with the regularity of so-called "politics"'.[38] In this way, linear time enables continuity, unity and consensus, while trauma time is perceived as the source of disruption, division and conflict.

Crucially, these temporalities are not inevitably opposed; rather, they are mutually constitutive and undecidable (*pace* Derrida). The nation-state, however, relies on the sense of continuity, stability and security constructed through linear narratives.

> Trauma time—the disruptive, back-to-front time that occurs when the smooth time of the imagined or symbolic story is interrupted by the real of 'events'—is the time that must be forgotten if the sovereign power of the modern state is to remain unchallenged.[39]

Drawing on the Lacanian concept of 'the Real', Edkins argues that traumatic political events[40] expose or disrupt the fantasy that the social order is complete and secure. In this way, trauma serves to highlight the gap between 'social order' and 'the real'. Not only is our world far from the secure, continuous, consensual narrative outlined by the seemingly coherent discourses of nation, identity, modernity, etc. but, crucially, the nation-state itself is guilty of producing this fantasy and at the same time of transgressing it: 'Sovereign power produces and is itself produced by trauma: it provokes wars, genocides, and famines. But it works by concealing its involvement and claiming to be a provider not a destroyer of security'. Crucially, this process involves not merely obfuscation, but forgetting:

> [a]s both Derrida and Žižek point out, once the state is in place, the violence that is involved in its foundation as a

particular historical form is forgotten; the state retroactively constitutes the basis for its own authority.[41]

While this can be achieved through direct violence, 'the state does this in no small part through the way in which it commemorates wars, genocides, and famines'.[42] A sense of trauma is produced when political events expose the violence concealed at the very foundation of the state.[43]

> By rewriting these traumas into a linear narrative of national heroism,…the state conceals the trauma that it has, necessarily, produced. Resistance to this rescripting—resistance to state narratives of commemoration—constitutes resistance to sovereign power.[44]

The nation-state, in this way, conceals its violence through the writing and rewriting of linear narratives of political trauma; through processes of co-option, appropriation, repression or forgetting, therefore, it is able to 'fit' political trauma into a coherent discourse of security. Thus, political trauma, and the processes by which it is remembered or forgotten, plays a pivotal role in the (re)production of power relations (*pace* Foucault); it is also, I propose, intricately bound up in the negotiation of conflict.

In this way, Edkins draws a theoretical 'connection between trauma, violence, and political community' to explicate the ways in which 'traumas such as wars or persecutions are inscribed and re-inscribed into everyday narrative' and, crucially, how '[t]his takes place in practices of remembrance, memorialization, and witnessing'.[45] It is in this sense that commemoration is ultimately political: it is the attempt to negotiate meaning between the past, present and future; between consensus and conflict; between 'politics' and the 'political'.

Within this theoretical framework, Edkins 'explores the connections between violence, the effects of trauma that it produces and forms of political community'.[46] In this way, she 'contribute[s] to understandings of the particular way in which power, the social order, and the person [i.e. the subject] are constituted in the contemporary West, through a study of practices of trauma, memory, and witness'.[47] Edkins re-emphasises and re-conceptualises the political construction of memory and commemoration in a way that challenges students of politics to deconstruct and problematise other configurations of power, politics and memory.

What I would emphasise here is the way in which commemoration is intrinsically based on the construction and reproduction of oppositions—between public/private, inside/outside, us/them, past/present, memory/forgetting, unity/division. As such, it is intricately implicated in conflict, antagonism, violence and contestation. At the discursive level, commemoration involves the legitimation of one form of conflict over others, and it reinscribes axes of division within the social-political arena. At the same time, as illustrated by the conflicting interpretations of what 'the politics of memory' means and how it can/should be used, there is increasing conflict over the very ways in which commemoration is political and conflictual. Commemoration reproduces the ways in which all politics (and their relationship to the political) are antagonistic: the moment of the political, in which 'the undecidable nature of the alternatives and their resolution through power relations becomes fully visible', constitutes what Laclau calls 'the moment of antagonism'.[48] A crucial aim in the study of commemoration, therefore, is to explicate this relationship between commemoration, conflict and the political, and to take the question to its most critical level: how is the very opposition between 'politics' and 'the political' implicated in the commemoration of conflict and conflict over commemoration?

I propose that commemoration functions as a fulcrum point in discursive construction of conflict and *the political*—in ways that serve to reproduce, rewrite and deconstruct its accepted/acceptable boundaries. This pivotal point enables us to excavate the ways in which the constructed opposition of conflict/consensus is negotiated and (partially, temporarily) resolved through and within discourses of commemoration; and it also allows us to emphasise the extent to which these negotiations have been obscured and depoliticised—that is, evacuated of their undecidable political potential through the 'closing-off', resolution and ordering of discursive possibilities. From this perspective, one can read commemoration(s) as political, precisely because commemoration demands a negotiation between 'politics' and 'history'.

II. COMMEMORATING CONFLICT IN IRISH HISTORY, OR COMMEMORATION, CONFLICT AND IRISH HISTORY

In the Irish case, history has conventionally been written as *history as conflict*: that is, 'the Irish story' is one of a series of invasions, battles, rebellions, struggles, defeats, risings—and Troubles. Conversely, Irish history itself has often become the focus of conflict, both ideological and physically violent conflict. The 1916 Easter Rising serves as the fulcrum point for the (re)production of these conflictual, oppositional discourses. From the Rising, and its reiteration through commemoration, one can trace the (commemorative and commemorated) narrative of Irish history from its 'founding event' through to the politics of the present day.

The construction of 1916 as the pivotal moment of Irish history, identity and memory has had lasting consequences for the Irish definition of political conflict. The commemoration (or lack thereof) of 1916 represents a locus of discourses surrounding the way in which Ireland understands and engages with conflict *per se*. It sets (or has been constructed as setting) the parameters for how 'other' conflicts within society past and present (e.g. feminist, ethnic, post-colonial, economic, academic) can or should be represented. My focus here is not, therefore, 'how was the event commemorated?', but rather 'what is *political* about the way(s) in which conflict has been commemorated or commemoration made conflictual in Ireland?'; and, crucially, 'in what ways have these intersections been *de-politicized*?'

1916, state formation and commemoration

For Ireland, the fundamental instability/uncertainty of nation, state, identity served to reinforce a much more ambiguous discursive complex of consensus and conflict. Ireland in 1916 faced a markedly different complex of contexts in framing both its experience of the Great War and its recollection (reproduction) of it. The Home Rule crisis meant that, while war waged in Europe for 'the rights of small nations', on the home front another struggle was being fought: the negotiation of Ireland's relationship to Britain, and the place of constitutional nationalists, republicans and unionists within Ireland. The crucial events of 1916—the Easter Rising and the Battle of the Somme—simultaneously reflected these discursive divisions and reproduced them, reshaped and re-appropriated, through the process of commemoration.

What was to be remembered and what forgotten of those events became entrenched in discursive negotiations between past, present and future; between competing versions of 'Ireland' north and south of a constructed border. Commemoration unifies and divides in ways that reflect and intersect with those questions of history and national/cultural identity—and, crucially, dictates the terms on which those questions can be engaged. The needs of 'the present', from partition and the establishment of the Irish Free State and of Northern

Ireland through to this current moment in time, have demanded different forms of engagement with, and reinscription of, these past events in ways that have served to reinforce solidarities and diversities.

The majority of 'understandings' of recent Irish history, north and south, implicitly or explicitly centre around the violent beginnings of the two states; and 1916 is invariably allocated a crucial role in the analysis of state formation and legitimation. Given its perceived centrality in the 'origin myths' of the dominant traditions on the island, the way in which 1916 is commemorated—officially celebrated or privately acknowledged, quietly forgotten or dragged kicking and screaming from the realms of amnesia—has gained an overtly political significance. The key events of 1916—the Rising of Easter Week and the Battle of the Somme on 1 July—are therefore firmly entrenched in the discursive negotiation between north and south, nationalist and unionist, past, present and future.

By juxtaposing events and their re-interpretations as snap-shots in time/place, from 1916 to now, in Ireland north and south, one can illustrate the play of commemorations across spatial and temporal borders. At the same time, this allows analyses to be implicitly inter-disciplinary: far from confined within the strict conventions of 'history' or 'memory studies', the problematisation of commemoration involves insights and tools from a wide range of disciplines—from cultural studies, social anthropology, geography and international relations theory. This highlights the need to explore the intersections and contradictions between these areas of understanding, and to underscore the political negotiations inherent in them.

CONCLUSION

Edna Longley, in 'The Rising, the Somme and Irish memory', declared that 'commemorations are as selective as sympathies. They honour *our* dead, not *your* dead'.[49] While this oft-cited quote has become the 'slogan' for remembrance in Northern Ireland (or, rather, a good excuse to encourage forgetting), in its original context it referred to the politics of commemoration south of the border: 'Charles Haughey cannot visit Béal na mBláth to honour Michael Collins, let alone wear a poppy. And even when the same person or event is being commemorated, splits occur'.[50] The reasons for these splits are not immediately explained; indeed Longley assumes that the problematic nature of these two prohibited commemorative practices is known and understood. This invocation of the (controversial) symbols of the Easter Rising and Irish Civil War alongside that of World War I allows Longley to construct and explore a juxtaposition of the ways in which the Rising and the Somme can be remembered.

The passage from Longley cited above initially posits commemoration as being divisive—as a process that creates, entrenches and reproduces 'Us'/'Them' oppositions related not only to exclusive identities, but to the expression of such identities in political conflict. At the same time, it raises questions as to who can commemorate what/whom/when/where—and, crucially—why. Furthermore, the reference to Haughey links these processes of commemoration, or their political impossibility, to narratives of the state and the nation, lines of legitimacy and practices of legitimation. These questions remind us that the quote, like the events it evokes, can be (indeed, must be) approached from diverse perspectives and interpretations. In so doing, Longley highlights the malleability of meaning to be taken from, or inscribed onto, an event, its remembrances and its forgettings.

Yet, for Longley, commemoration is more than a source of division —it is simultaneously a force for internal cohesion: 'Commemoration is a means whereby communities renew their own *religio*: literally, what ties them together, the rope around the individual sticks'.[51] Commemoration serves to unite, to unify groups by providing a basis for a shared identity and a practice to re-inscribe a common history. It is the process by which communities are bound together; but crucially, '"bound" hovers between bond and bind, between solidarity and suffocation...[and] commemoration, communal *religio*, does not merely remember. It reinvents and reconstitutes according to present needs'.[52]

There is, then, a constant negotiation, an undecidability, between consensus and conflict, unity and division—commemoration as a source of constructive unity but also a constricting limit on identity. This negotiation is played out through the contested processes of commemoration: whereas 'remember' suggests a *re*-collection (unchanged) from actual real-time events (as if such things could possibly exist), 'reconstitute' implies re-imagining, re-writing and re-producing as political processes for political purposes. In this sense, the remembrance of 1916 can be seen to represent '...moments of commemorative foundation in which presence is sought by recalling past figures and events which in turn were never present to themselves'.[53]

Irish history, then, is neither doomed to fatalistic repetition nor teleologically transcended; rather, the commemoration reiterates and rewrites history, invoking the past and the future in the construction of the present. Politically, these dynamics are crucial to the negotiation of unity and division, conflict and consensus. They exemplify the need to problematise and deconstruct the pivotal axes of conflict in twentieth-century Irish history as they have been constructed and reproduced through commemorative engagement. In this way these themes are drawn together and pulled apart, and questions for the past and the present, conflict and reconciliation, are laid bare. Ultimately, it is hoped that this project can encourage a degree of *repoliticisation* of commemoration and, on the other side of the mirror, that the deconstruction of commemoration can repoliticise the study of politics.

NOTES

[1] Ernesto Laclau, cited in Jenny Edkins, *Post-Structuralism and international relations: bringing the political back in* (Cambridge, 1999), 5.

[2] Laura Lyons, preface to Duncan Greenlaw, *Borders of mourning: remembrance, commitment, and the contexts of Irish identity* (Bethesda, 2004), ix.

[3] Alvin Jackson, 'Irish unionism', in D.G. Boyce and A. O'Day (eds), *The making of modern Irish history* (London, 1996), 120–21.

[4] Edna Longley, during a debate in Derry on the 26th anniversary of Bloody Sunday; cited in Longley, 'Northern Ireland: commemoration, elegy, and forgetting', in Ian McBride (ed.), *History and memory in modern Ireland* (Cambridge, 2001), 230–31; also cited original source: *Belfast Telegraph*, 17 February 1998.

[5] Greenlaw, *Borders of mourning*, 10.

[6] Paul Antze and Michael Lambek (eds), *Tense past: cultural essays in trauma and memory* (London, 1996), xxi.

[7] This intersection between history, memory and commemoration has been explored by several authors, utilising approaches from within diverse academic disciplines. See, for example, John R. Gillis (ed.), *Commemorations: the politics of national identity* (Princeton, 1994); Ian McBride (ed.) *History and memory in modern Ireland* (Cambridge, 2001); Maurice Halbwachs 'The social frame-

works of memory', L.A. Coser (ed. and trans.), *On collective memory* (London and Chicago, 1992); Pierre Nora and similar.

[8] Cited in Roy Foster, *The Irish story: telling tales and making it up in Ireland* (London, 2001), 33, n. 14.

[9] Claudia Koonz, 'Between memory and oblivion: concentration camps in German memory', in John R. Gillis (ed.), *Commemorations: the politics of national identity* (Princeton, 1994), 260.

[10] Edkins, *Post-Structuralism and international relations*, 7.

[11] Maurice Halbwachs is usually credited with making the crucial link between memory as a specifically social practice with implications for collective identity. See Halbwachs, *On collective memory*.

[12] See Homi Bhabha, 'DissemiNation: time, narrative, and the nation', in Homi K. Bhabha (ed.), *Nation and narration* (London,1990); see also Ray Ryan (ed.), *Writing in the Irish Republic* (Houndsmills, 2000).

[13] Eavan Boland, *Object lessons: the life of the woman and the poet in our time* (London, 1996), 71.

[14] Boland, *Object lessons*, 55–6. This echoes Lefebvre's view of the nation-state 'as the space that flattens or crushes conflicts and contradictions in the social or cultural spheres...' (cited in Ray Ryan, *Writing in the Irish Republic* (Houdsmills, 2000), 94), even as it provokes conflict between versions of the self.

[15] Antze and Lambek, *Tense past*, xvi.

[16] Antze and Lambek, *Tense past*, xvi; emphasis in original.

[17] Antze and Lambek, *Tense past*, xxv.

[18] Greenlaw, *Borders of mourning*, 79.

[19] Greenlaw, *Borders of mourning*, 7.

[20] John Torpey, *The politics of the past: on repairing historical injustices* (Oxford, 2003), 26; emphasis in original.

[21] Ray Ryan, *Writing in the Irish Republic*, 83.

[22] Greenlaw, *Borders of mourning*, 12.

[23] John R.Gillis (ed.), *Commemorations: the politics of national identity* (Princeton, 1994), 9.

[24] Gillis, *Commemorations*, 5.

[25] Patrick Devine-Wright, 'Theoretical overview of memory and conflict', in Ed Cairns and Micheál Roe (eds), *The role of memory in ethnic conflict* (Houndsmills, 2003), 9–34: 31.

[26] Devine-Wright, 31–2.

[27] See Lloyd and Bell's critique as interpreted by Greenlaw, *Borders of mourning*, 85, 97, 98.

[28] T.G. Ashplant, Graham Dawson and Michael Roper (eds), *The politics of war memory and commemoration* (London, 2000), xi.

[29] See Greenlaw on the adaption/utilisation of Foucauldian theory in this context: Foucault's framework: '"opposes itself to the search for origins"

(Foucault, 1977, 140), uncovering discontinuities and heterogeneity in previously assumed histories of continuous development', (Greenlaw, *Borders of mourning*, 63). 'Foucault focuses on revaluation as a place of "emergence" where new possibilities of conceptualization rupture previously dominant or homogeneous discourses, forcing these discourses to be recontextualized', (Greenlaw, *Borders of mourning*, 60).

[30] Greenlaw, *Borders of mourning*, 60; emphasis in original.

[31] Gerald Sider and Gavin Smith, *Between history and histories: the making of silences and commemorations* (Toronto, 1997), 7; emphasis in original.

[32] See Žižek's framework of arche politics, meta politics, para politics and ultra politics. (For a useful introduction, see Edkins, *Trauma and the memory of politics* (Cambridge, 2003), 16).

[33] See Edkins, *Post-Structuralism and international relations*, 4.

[34] Edkins, *Trauma and the memory of politics*, xiii.

[35] Edkins, *Post-Structuralism and international relations*, 4. Or, potentially, the reverse: the distinction between '"politics" as a separate social complex, a positively determined sub-system of social relations in interaction with other sub-systems (economy, forms of culture…) and "the political" as the moment of openness, of undecidability, when the very structuring principle of society, the fundamental form of social pact, is called into question' (Žižek, *For they know not what they do*, 1991, 193–5, cited in Edkins, *Post-Structuralism and international relations*, 3).

[36] Edkins, *Trauma and the memory of politics*, xiv.

[37] Edkins, *Trauma and the memory of politics*, xiv.

[38] Edkins, *Trauma and the memory of politics*, xiv.

[39] Edkins, *Trauma and the memory of politics*, 229–30.

[40] All trauma is political and all politics are traumatic—see Slavoj Žižek, *The sublime object of ideology* (*Phronesis*) (London, 1989); *For they know not what they do* (London, 1991); and *The ticklish subject: the absent centre of political ontology* (*Wo Es War*) (London,1999).

[41] Edkins, *Post-Structuralism and international relations*, 5.

[42] Edkins, *Trauma and the memory of politics*, xv.

[43] Edkins, *Trauma and the memory of politics*, 8.

[44] Edkins, *Trauma and the memory of politics*, xv; see also pp 5–6.

[45] Edkins, *Trauma and the memory of politics*, 15.

[46] Edkins, *Trauma and the memory of politics*, 9.

[47] Edkins, *Trauma and the memory of politics*, 9.

[48] Laclau, cited in Edkins, *Post-Structuralism and international relations*, 5.

[49] Longley, 'The Rising, the Somme, and Irish memory', in *The living stream* (Newcastle-upon-Tyne, 1994), 69.

[50] Longley, 'The Rising', 69.

[51] Longley, 'The Rising', 70.

[52] Longley, 'The Rising', 70.

[53] Greenlaw, *Borders of mourning*, 13.

7. PRAGMATISM VERSUS UNITY: THE STORMONT GOVERNMENT AND THE 1966 EASTER COMMEMORATION

By Catherine O'Donnell

INTRODUCTION

The commemoration of the fiftieth anniversary of the 1916 Rising in Northern Ireland provided a fresh challenge for Ulster unionism. For Ulster unionism, the 1960s were to a large extent defined by division,[1] and it is within this context of division that the response of the Stormont government to the commemoration is to be understood. In a speech delivered at a Twelfth of July demonstration in Ballymena in 1965, the Northern Ireland prime minister, Terence O'Neill, called on the Orange Order to give its support to what he termed 'positive Protestantism'.[2] He argued that 'negative Protestantism' continued to succeed in gaining attention and maintained that Northern Ireland must strive to 'demonstrate in the wider world those virtues which we ought to practice here in Ulster'. He made reference to the need to support the social and economic betterment of Northern Ireland through improved housing and employment.[3] A month later, at a Royal Black Preceptory Institution demonstration, the Grand Registrar of Antrim and later leader of the Ulster Unionist Party, James Molyneaux, questioned O'Neill's attitude towards fundamental Protestantism, as espoused by Ian Paisley of the Free Presbyterian Church:

> Recent months have seen determined efforts to convince us
> that adherence to a religious belief is bigotry: that loyalty to
> a political ideal is intolerance and that a firm stand on moral

issues is narrow-mindedness...I am astonished by the number of people who accept this nonsense.[4]

These speeches provide some sense of the challenges facing O'Neill. His reputation as a reforming leader had created suspicion and had made O'Neill many enemies within unionist circles and, in particular, among hard-line unionists.[5] O'Neill's statement reflected the fact that the image that Northern Ireland presented to Britain in this period was a continuing concern for him. The real threat that the growth of extremism within unionism posed, in the prime minister's view, was the damage this caused to his reputation and that of Northern Ireland at Westminster. O'Neill's attempts to harbour improved relations with Dublin as well as the signing of the Anglo-Irish Trade Agreement in late 1965, which met with some opposition in Northern Ireland, de-stabilised his position as leader, despite the vote of confidence he received in the November 1965 Stormont election.[6]

The pressure that was placed on O'Neill, not just as unionist leader but also as a respectable leader within the United Kingdom, served to dominate the political arena in Northern Ireland through-out 1965 and 1966. O'Neill's stance on the fiftieth anniversary commemoration of the 1916 Easter Rising in 1966 was very much dictated by his belief that an IRA campaign was imminent and that this would irreparably damage opinion in Britain, rather than by unionist opposition to the commemoration. He did, however, bow to pressure from Reverend Ian Paisley, who was strongly opposed to the Easter commemorations, by restricting north–south rail at one point during the Easter celebrations. The 1966 commemoration of the Rising later became one issue around which unionist divisions were formed, and it is as such that the significance of the commemoration for unionism is understood.

In addition to assessing the significance that the 1966 Easter commemoration of the Rising had for unionism, this chapter will also examine unionist perceptions of the commemoration and the position adopted by the Stormont government in relation to that event. The debates that took place as to whether the commemoration should be allowed to proceed were in fact informed to a large extent by the political exigencies of 1965 and 1966. As will become evident, a number of political trends, such as changing Stormont–Westminster relations and the prominence of an extremist element within unionism, determined the significance the commemoration ultimately posed.

THE COMMEMORATION AND THE POTENTIAL FOR VIOLENCE

The early discourse surrounding the 1966 Easter commemoration in Northern Ireland was characterised by the Stormont government's repeated references to the potential for IRA violence, IRA denials and nationalist allegations that the government was deliberately raising tensions. In November 1965 it was announced that any literature on 1916 would be monitored by the RUC. The *Belfast Telegraph* intimated that there was a fear that such literature might revive republican sympathies and lead to an increase in IRA membership.[7] In the course of the November 1965 Stormont election, the government admitted that cabinet ministers had been advised to take extra security measures because of police reports that the IRA was planning to disrupt the upcoming election. According to newspaper reports, the government had connected this reported IRA activity to a possible campaign to mark the fiftieth anniversary of 1916 the following year.[8] Home Affairs Minister Brian McConnell referred to an undercurrent of violent activity that the government had been made aware of.[9] There were also some reports of renewed recruitment campaigns being initiated by the IRA, in the form of 'Join IRA' leaflets distributed outside Catholic churches in parts of Armagh calling on the population not to abandon the ideals of 1916.[10] The *Belfast Telegraph* also claimed that the Irish government believed the IRA's campaign had taken a new direction. According to this newspaper, Dublin sources believed that:

> [t]hey [the IRA] are now apparently prepared to draw guns against the lawfully established forces in the South as well as those in the North, which is a complete reversal of policy from recent years.[11]

Reports of IRA activity in the Republic, and references to Taoiseach Seán Lemass's problem as to whether or not he should intern known IRA members, also reinforced the view of an IRA threat in Northern Ireland.[12]

The most obvious expression of the Northern Ireland government's belief that a renewed IRA campaign was possible is seen in its correspondence with the Home Office in London, in which the government requested that representations be made to the Ministry of Defence that ten Ferret Scout Cars, self-loading rifles and Browning Machine guns would be provided for the RUC and army in Northern Ireland. The correspondence with London stressed that these would be 'immensely valuable in dealing with the situation which may arise here during the celebration of the 50th anniversary of the Easter Rebellion especially if the occasion is used by the IRA to create civil commotion and strife'.[13] The requested 350 self-loading rifles and 12 Browning guns were made available for the beginning of March 1966.[14]

O'Neill also made a number of public statements of his fear of a renewed IRA campaign. For example, in November 1965 he called for restraint around the upcoming jubilee and confirmed that he had called the Stormont general election at this stage to avoid having it too close to the commemoration. He appealed to all to avoid the passions that might be aroused.[15] The government's reaction to the suggestion that the anniversary of the IRA's 1956 campaign on 12 December 1965 would provide the impetus for a renewed campaign also highlights the obsession with the possibility of violence. Despite the fact that McConnell declared that the government was not 'anticipating that anything may happen tomorrow [12 December] more than any other day', he continued 'we are ready to deal with trouble'; and it was reported that the RUC and the army were both reviewing their security measures in light of this anniversary.[16] McConnell was also quoted as saying that his government was 'more worried' about the build-up of IRA activity in the period around the fiftieth anniversary of 1916 than the 12 December anniversary.[17]

In the week before Easter 1966 the government issued a statement that included a warning to the IRA. The statement confirmed that, under the guidance of the prime minister, a Ministerial Security Committee had been established. Its duty was to investigate the extent to which an actual threat from the IRA existed. The statement went on to say that the government was in a state of 'instant readiness' if such a threat were to materialise.[18] The army was kept on full strength in Northern Ireland, with a view to dealing with any IRA activity.[19] The Security Committee had been, according to this government statement, monitoring this threat since the New Year. It had met some 12 times since its establishment.[20] Members of the committee included Brian McConnell, Minister of Commerce Brian Faulkner and Minister of Development William Craig. The mobilisation of the Special Constabulary and the purchasing of new equipment were among the measures taken by the committee.[21] The committee was also in touch with the British Home Office, which was kept apprised of information relating to a possible IRA threat.[22] A somewhat surprising development came in the form of reported North–South co-operation on security, with the Gardaí assisting the RUC through a 'hot-line' of communication.[23] Similarly, the capture of IRA papers in the Republic in May 1966 led to speculation that talks between officials from the Republic and Northern Ireland might be held in an effort to continue co-operation in combating IRA activity. The captured papers referred to plans by the organisation to take control of the entire island.[24]

Denials of a threat of violence

Allegations of IRA violence were countered at an early stage by the 1916 Golden Jubilee Commemoration Committee, which claimed that the Northern Ireland government was going out of its way to present the commemoration as 'an IRA plot'.[25] The Sinn Féin president, Tomás MacGiolla, denied that there was a potential IRA threat and the government's concentration on IRA violence was condemned as a 'ruse' by the Nationalist Party leader, Eddie McAteer.[26] A statement by the IRA, signed by Seán Caughey, referred to Stormont reports of imminent IRA activity as a 'fabrication' and aimed at creating an atmosphere that would justify the government's plan to introduce internment in the New Year.[27] While the Nationalist Party leader acknowledged the regrettable level of 'discord' surrounding the up-coming 1916 commemoration, many members of the opposition believed that the government was deliberately raising tensions.[28] Gerry Fitt, a Republican Labour MP at Stormont, argued that there was no need for O'Neill to start an IRA scare since there had been no such activity since 1962.[29] He dismissed the government's claim that a new IRA campaign was imminent:

> I for one do not believe that there is any serious threat of a recurrence of violence from the Irish Republican Army. It would appear to me that these statements are being issued by the Government with the intention of provoking violence. We all know that the year 1966 is going to be a contentious one with the 50th anniversary of the Irish Rising. We know that tempers on all sides are going to be high. The Government and the Minister should be doing all they can to placate rising tempers instead of trying to provoke violence. I do not believe that there is a strong threat of violence and I strongly deprecate this continued attitude of the Minister to do everything he possibly can to provoke violence in this community.[30]

Henry Diamond, Republican Labour Stormont MP for Falls, made a similar point about O'Neill's intimation of an IRA threat:

> Hon. Members will recall that last autumn before anyone this side of the House or any Nationalist source had mentioned commemoration services which are to be held this year in connection with the Easter Rising, the Prime Minister motioned this. Apparently it was uppermost in his mind. After a considerable time, when still no one mentioned it on the Opposition side of the House, the Prime Minister again referred to it. Steadily a fear has been built up in the community.[31]

Diamond went on to accuse the government of deliberately 'creating artificial tensions' in the community and called on the government to guarantee that 'any lawful and peaceful commemoration service [at Easter] will be permitted and not interfered with'.[32] Diamond argued that the government's suggestion that extra security measures were needed in the face of an IRA threat was informed by people who hoped to benefit from such a claim.[33] Brian Faulkner responded that incidents that had occurred recently were 'certainly not contrived', and he declared that the government viewed such incidents with concern.[34] Faulkner was referring to a number of disturbances that had taken place across Belfast in February 1966, involving the petrol-bombing of the Unionist Party headquarters on Glengall Street and in turn 'reprisals' against Catholic churches and a school.[35] All of this had followed an attack on an RUC patrol in Andersonstown.[36]

Despite IRA denials of involvement, the government initiated anti-terrorist measures.[37] The Belfast Corporation Estates and Markets Committee announced its decision to ban a Republican Party booking of the Ulster Hall for an Easter commemorative concert scheduled for 13 April, due to the possibility that it may lead to a breach of the peace. The National Democratic Party councillor, Seán McGivern, claimed that this

> denial of the civil rights of one section of the community… will only increase the tension which already exists as a result mainly of the provocative and inflammatory speeches that have been made recently by a fanatical group to whom permission to use the Ulster Hall was granted.[38]

The IRA issued a statement denying responsibility for recent incidents and blamed the Unionist Party for spreading rumours of IRA activity, which, it claimed, were 'designed to create a situation in which the observance of the 1916 jubilee by Irishmen in the Six Counties will become impossible'.[39]

Despite the Minister of Home Affairs's admission that 'the conduct of the people of Northern Ireland during the various Republican celebrations at Easter weekend' was 'exemplary', it was nevertheless followed by the announcement of north–south travel restrictions to be put in place the following weekend. McConnell and the government justified this decision as a desire

> not to permit the peace of Northern Ireland to be disturbed by provocative incursions of hostile elements from the south…to ensure that any persons arriving by road in Northern Ireland should be subject to intensive scrutiny by the police to ensure that they do not propose to engage in subversive activities or otherwise endanger the peace.[40]

This announcement was met with disdain from opposition members. Gerry Fitt accused O'Neill and his government of surrendering to the extremists within unionism and claimed that this decision represented an attempt to placate that section. He referred to

> the abhorrence with which this decision by the Minister of Home Affairs will be received [in his West Belfast constituency]. It seems to me that this statement is calculated to lead to a breach of the peace and should any untoward incidents occur the Government must bear the full responsibility for them.[41]

Austin Currie, Nationalist MP for East Tyrone, made a similar point. He claimed the government ought to concentrate on controlling extremist Protestants organisations. He referred both to Ian Paisley's Ulster Constitution Defence Committee and to reports of the reformation of the Ulster Volunteer Force (UVF) in various part of Northern Ireland. Currie condemned Paisley's attempts to spread sectarian bitterness and religious bigotry throughout Northern Ireland.[42] He revealed that he had received a threatening letter claiming to be from the UVF and which outlined that 'the UVF branch was formed "to save Protestants their heritage and to prevent rebel celebrations of the murders of 1916"'. Currie looked to the government to provide information as to whether these organisations existed and to outline any action it intended to take.[43]

GENERAL UNIONIST ATTITUDES TO THE COMMEMORATION

The Stormont government and unionist community were predominantly opposed to the celebration of the fiftieth anniversary of the Easter Rising in Northern Ireland. Attitudes ranged from total contempt for the celebrations to disapproval, but with a practical realisation that imposing a total ban on the commemorations would be unworkable. The latter represented the government's view, as will be seen below in O'Neill's statement on the issue. The debates in the Northern Ireland House of Commons provide interesting insights into the issues surrounding the commemoration. A Unionist MP, Joseph Burns, objected to the celebrations taking place in Northern Ireland and drew a distinction between the Easter parade and other Catholic parades, such as those held by the Ancient Order of Hibernians (AOH).

> We know enough about the 1916 Rebellion to make sure that there are no celebrations here…We have been accused of intolerance and bigotry. It has been said that because we ban parades we are intolerant, bigoted and ungracious people. I should like to remind Hon. Members opposite that on 17th March and 15th August an organisation known as the AOH has celebrations all over Northern Ireland…But the 1916 celebrations are a very different thing altogether. This is a very different cup of tea from the ordinary celebrations that we have here year after year.[44]

Walter Scott, Unionist MP for Belfast Bloomfield, expressed a similar view, yet maintained that the minority nationalist community should be afforded the freedom of speech.

> Like many of the Hon. Members in this House I feel that the Easter Week Rebellion is something that should not be celebrated in Northern Ireland at all—a rebellion against the things we held very dear at that particular time and at a very inopportune moment in the history of the United Kingdom. For that reason and for many other reasons this is something

that should not be celebrated in Northern Ireland. But if there is a fraction of this province which feels it has a right to cheer about this incident in past history we as a responsible party should allow freedom of speech, so long as it does not conflict with law and order.[45]

Another Unionist Party MP, Nat Minford, stated his objection to the Easter celebrations: 'I object strongly to any celebrations of a Rising that is abhorrent to me', but he went on to say,

[n]evertheless I would still fight for the right of these people to hold their celebrations provided they do it peaceably and in a sensible manner. I should like the Minister to tell the House and the country today exactly what is going to be allowed at these Easter celebrations.[46]

What is interesting here is the acknowledgement of the idea that the minority should be afforded such rights as freedom of speech and the freedom to celebrate events of importance to its members. This echoed the position of Harry Diamond, Republican Labour, who referred to the Easter celebration and the community's right to hold parades in terms of liberty of the individual.[47] Another point made by participants in the Commons debates was the need to promote tolerance and good relations in Northern Ireland. Attitudes as to how this would be achieved in relation to the 1916 commemoration differed across the divide in the Commons. For example, Dr Robert Nixon (North Down, Unionist Party) argued that the Easter celebrations had the potential to intervene with the objectives of reconciliation:

I would suggest that those who have influence should persuade any large groups of possibly 2,000 or 3,000 people who might come to Northern Ireland as a body to celebrate a Rising that was in Dublin…What would it profit such a group to do such a thing? The Rising did not occur in the North of Ireland. Let us work together for peace by ceasing to propound occasions which could lead to a conflagration of thoughts and emotions.[48]

Others were simply suspicious of the need to celebrate the Rising in Northern Ireland and the intentions of those involved. Again, Joseph Burns is an example:

In 1962 in this county there were Ulster Covenant celebrations. These were held in Belfast and in certain other places in Northern Ireland. This event was not celebrated in Dublin, in Cork or in Galway. I cannot see any reason at all why the anniversary of the Easter Rebellion should be celebrated in Belfast unless, of course, some people want to create incidents and trouble. The position is that no one wants trouble.[49]

A common objection to the Easter Rising commemoration was the timing of the 1916 Rising itself, which had taken place when large numbers of Irishmen were dying while participating in Britain's World War I effort in Europe. The contrast between the Easter Rising and the Battle of the Somme was highlighted. O'Neill stated that he and the majority of Ulster people, as loyal British subjects, commemorated 1916 not for the Easter Rising but because of the part played by many Ulstermen in the fight against the Germans at the Battle of the Somme.[50] A statement by a spokesman for the Belfast Ratepayers' Association explaining the decision not to allow a 1916 Rising commemorative event to be held at the Ulster Hall in Belfast also referred to the Battle of the Somme.

> For the majority of Belfast people the Ulster Hall is sacred—
> and to let it for a rebellion celebration would in any view, be
> an insult to the gallant men of the 36th (Ulster) Division,
> who were stabbed in the back by the rebellion.[51]

Unsurprisingly, the most fervent opposition to the commemoration came from the Reverend Ian Paisley and his followers. The leader of the Free Presbyterian Church criticised the commemorations of the fiftieth anniversary of the Rising as

> an insult to our constitution that they should be allowed to
> flaunt the tricolour and celebrate what was a great act of
> treachery against the Crown right on our doorstep,

and the Rising, in his view, was 'a Papal plot to stab England in the back' in the time of war.[52]

Paisley's paper, the *Protestant Telegraph*, offered the most strenuous opposition to the planned Easter commemoration. The paper labelled the 1916 Rising as 'a Papist–German plot of treason and murder', based on the claim made by the paper that the Vatican had given its blessing to a planned Rising in 1916.[53] Paisley organised a counter-demonstration in Belfast as well as a 'thanksgiving' service in the Ulster Hall for the defeat of the 1916 rebels.[54] He declared that his planned demonstration from Carlisle Circus to the Ulster Hall was not intended to clash with the 1916 commemorative processions at Casement Park.

> Ours is a procession of Protestant Loyalists which will go to the Ulster Hall to express disgust that the Easter Week celebrations have been permitted to take place in Northern Ireland.[55]

In his message of defiance to Prime Minister O'Neill, Paisley declared that he had substantial support throughout Northern Ireland and attacked the 'weakness of the government for not stopping the stream before it became a current'; and he declared that 'Ulster people are definitely not going to bow to IRA thugs'.[56] Paisley's march was reported to be 5,000-people strong, while the 8,000-strong Easter commemoration parade on the Falls Road attracted some 20,000 spectators.[57] These two parades came close to meeting at one point, but few incidents arose due to the intervention of the RUC.[58] Real trouble was avoided as a result of the decision by Paisley and his followers to call off a number of anti-1916 demonstrations planned for Newry and Armagh.[59]

THE STORMONT GOVERNMENT'S OFFICIAL STANCE ON THE 1966 COMMEMORATIONS

In early March 1966, Minister for Home Affairs Brian McConnell made a plea for calm at Easter. He had already expressed the hope that the IRA would demonstrate 'good sense' and not engage in violent activities in marking the fiftieth anniversary of the 1916 Rising.[60] He issued a warning of his government's intention to be firm to extremists on both sides, and he stated that any procession likely to cause provocation or offence would not be allowed to go ahead.[61] At Stormont, he outlined the government's position regarding the Easter parades. The minister began by stating that only a minority of the population approved of what was being commemorated.

> The events which are being celebrated do not commend themselves to the people of Northern Ireland as a whole. It

is the duty of the Government to ensure that any celebrations taking place within Northern Ireland do not offend
our citizens, and that they should not be held in such places
and in such circumstances as are likely to lead to a breach of
the peace.

The government's position was thus that:

[a]ny procession or meeting likely to cause a breach of the
peace or to result in an infringement of the law as laid down
in the Public Order Act of 1952 and the Flags and Emblems
Act of 1954 in such a way as to cause provocation or to
engender feelings of hatred and resentment, will not be
countenanced by the Government. Such feelings might well
erupt in riot and civil strife and this Government, in the
interests of the whole Community, will not tolerate [this].[62]

Despite the government's distaste at the commemoration and worry
over the possibility of communal strife, McConnell was clear from early
on that 'lawful peaceful celebrations which are not provocative or likely
to lead to a breach of the peace' would not be prevented.[63] In a later
debate on the same issue in the Northern Ireland House of Commons,
the minister elaborated on conditions under which the processions
would be allowed to proceed.

The procedure under the Public Order Act is that people
wishing to hold a procession which is not customary gave
notice to the police, who have got the power, where they
consider it necessary for the preservation of the peace, to re-
route a procession...Meetings of this kind have been held
at Easter for many years. It has been the policy of my pred-
ecessors that any meeting proposed in an area where it is
likely to cause a breach of the peace is not allowed. I intend
to continue with that policy. If it appears that a meeting
proposed for a particular area is likely to give offence to the
people living in the area or to result in a breach of the peace
it will be suggested to those organising it that it should be
held in some other place. If that is not possible or not
agreeable it may well be that no meeting will be allowed.[64]

The government's decision to allow the Easter commemorative
parades to proceed was largely a pragmatic one, aimed at avoiding

clashes between the IRA and police and subsequent bad press in Britain. The above statement by the minister of Home Affairs stressed that the government's position in 1966 did not differ from that of previous years. It also made explicit the government's willingness to countenance commemorative Easter processions in nationalist areas only.

Gerry Fitt claimed that the government had capitulated to unionist extremists by placing restrictions on north–south travel during the second weekend of the commemorative period. There is indeed some evidence to suggest that, in fact, the government's decision to limit cross-border travel was dictated more by the potential of a Protestant backlash to the commemoration than by any sense that the commemorations would unleash IRA violence. CIÉ (the national transport service in the Republic) reported that there was no need for a special train to be put on to cater for those travelling from the south to the commemorations in the north. This appeared to be due to the perception that 'enthusiasm' for 1916 was lacking in the north.[65] Thus, the relatively small numbers travelling from the south to the northern parades did not appear to warrant the border patrols and travel restrictions that were put in place.

Fitt's claim that O'Neill had felt the need to take firm action in the face of opposition to the 1966 Easter commemoration is confirmed by the level of opposition mounted by Paisley and also by government files that detail the pressure to which the prime minister was subjected. The government's instinct was to permit the 1966 celebrations. By allowing the commemorations, O'Neill largely ignored unionist opposition to those celebrations as expressed both by Paisley and from within mainstream unionism. However, he could not be seen to be totally out of touch with grassroots unionist fears of IRA activity, and more generally with the community's feelings in relation to the 1916 anniversary commemorations. Neither could he completely ignore Paisley's demonstrations against the commemorations. As a result, he made a gesture to those objecting by restricting north–south rail travel over the second weekend of 1966 anniversary Easter celebrations.

Wider unionist objections to the commemorations

We have seen Paisley's criticism of the decision to permit the 1966 commemorations, but O'Neill was also subject to pressure on the issue from other sections within unionism. Letters of opposition to the commemorative parades came from a number of sources, ranging from Student Union representatives at Queen's University, Belfast to Orange

Order lodges.[66] An examination of a sample of the representations made to O'Neill on the issue highlights the significant concern within the community about the Easter commemoration. A letter dated 26 March 1966, from the County Fermanagh Grand Orange Lodge to the Grand Orange Lodge of Ireland, subsequently forwarded to the prime minister, stressed the level of opposition to the commemoration.

> A number of Resolutions have been received from District and Private Lodges in the County registering very strong opposition to any Republican Demonstrations in any part of Northern Ireland in celebration of the 1916 Rebellion, or the display of the Tricolour on any public highway in Northern Ireland...These Resolutions have the fullest support of the loyalists of this area, and we are of the decided opinion that to allow any such celebrations in any part of Northern Ireland will do immense harm to our position...We, on behalf of our County, very strongly recommend that no celebrations in connection with the 1916 Rebellion be allowed to take place in Northern Ireland and a firm declaration be made to this effect at any early date, in order that any reactions have time to fade out before the Easter period arrives.[67]

This letter highlights the level of opposition to the planned Easter commemorative parades. It also underlines the Orange Order's worries about the impact of the decision to permit events commemorating the 1916 Rebellion. O'Neill also came under pressure from other Unionist MPs who had been approached by their own constituents about the matter. Derry MP Robin Chichester-Clark received a letter from a unionist voter, W. Campbell, who pledged that he and his family would not vote unionist in the next election if the Easter commemorations were allowed to go ahead. Chichester-Clark brought the matter to the attention of both O'Neill and Minister of Home Affairs McConnell.[68]

O'Neill's position on the 1966 commemorations is revealed in his response to the letter from the Grand Orange Lodge of Ireland. The prime minister began by stressing that 'the sentiments behind the 1916 celebrations are repugnant to me and my colleagues in the Government' and offered a reassurance that 'the Government will deal firmly with any attempt to organise offensive or provocative displays likely to lead to disorder'. O'Neill went on to outline the practicalities informing the government's pragmatic stance to the parades. The first determinant for O'Neill was the reception that a total ban would receive in Britain.

> Ceremonies commemorating the Easter Rising have taken place in Northern Ireland for many years, subject to the observance of instructions given by the police. The policy being followed this year is consistent with what has been done in the past...This year the Government have had to take account of some others [factors]. These are first the effect on public opinion in Great Britain and indeed throughout the world if, as a result of the banning of all individual celebrations, outbreaks of disorder were to occur when the ban is enforced: such outbreaks would be attributed by Ulster's enemies to repressive police action and however much we might attempt to justify our actions our reputation and standing would, undoubtedly, suffer.[69]

The second issue for the government was the issue of local security and the fear that the IRA would see any disorder surrounding banned parades as an opportunity to attack the police or to renew its violent campaign.

> The government have also had to bear in mind the general security of the province and in the face of the danger of IRA attacks—a danger which still exists—have had to ensure that the police are not over-committed in enforcing a number of bans in different parts of the country at a time when their supreme task is to maintain the highest possible state of readiness against the IRA. There can be little doubt that the IRA would welcome an opportunity to involve the police in civil strife, and/or to draw off their forces, and then to exploit the position on the Border or elsewhere. All of us feel most strongly that the best interests of Northern Ireland will be served by ensuring that the peace is kept.[70]

O'Neill's references to opinion in Britain are to be understood in the context of the changing relationship between Stormont and Westminster in the mid-1960s, and the perception within both nationalist and unionist circles that the new Labour government in London was willing to intervene in the affairs in Northern Ireland.[71] This feeling existed despite the fact that the pre-election manifesto by the British prime minister, Harold Wilson, ignored Northern Ireland because of the feeling that 'Northern Ireland is perfectly capable of speaking up for itself'.[72] It is sufficient at this point to highlight this. It is addressed more fully in the discussion below on divisions within unionism. As we have seen, from late 1965 onwards O'Neill justified his government's decision to place restrictions on certain parades and to step-up security by referring to the possibility of an IRA threat. It was this point that was also highlighted in O'Neill's correspondence with the government in Westminster. In a letter to the British home secretary, Roy Jenkins, O'Neill took the opportunity to thank Jenkins's office 'for all that you have done in London to assist us in our security precautions and for the helpful and understanding attitude that was adopted throughout'. The Northern Ireland prime minister went on to explain his government's approach to the 1916 anniversary commemorations, once again in terms of an IRA threat.

> We for our part were conscious of the need to avoid any action likely to exacerbate a potentially explosive situation and I am glad that through a combination of tolerance and firm action we have managed to prevent that communal strife which could have been exploited by the IRA.[73]

Thus, the possibility of a renewed IRA campaign, the effect that this would have on British opinion and, in particular, the fear that it might cause an intervention by the British government were O'Neill's main worries in terms of the 1966 Easter commemoration. While he did make a gesture to unionist opposition towards the commemoration by placing a restriction on north–south travel over the second weekend of the commemorative week, he did not yield to pressure, mainly from Paisley, to place an outright ban on the commemoration. Having avoided that temptation, the commemoration assumed a new significance in the following months.

THE COMMEMORATION AND DIVISIONS WITHIN UNIONISM

In making his decision to permit the fiftieth anniversary Easter Rising commemoration in 1966, O'Neill took a number of factors into consideration. In referring to the commemoration, O'Neill concentrated on the potential for IRA violence as well as on the implications that such violence would have in terms of the opinion of the British government. The question posed is whether or how O'Neill's government factored in the threat posed by Paisley and the ability of the commemoration to further exacerbate divisions within unionism. The O'Neill government could not have been unaware of Paisley's actions, and indeed the fact that the Easter commemoration might be used as a tool by Paisley and might have an impact upon unionism was highlighted for O'Neill. The possibility of a clash between commemorative parades and counter-demonstrations organised by Paisley was a concern for nationalists. Harry Diamond alluded to his community's fear that the government would not be prepared to protect the right of the nationalist community to hold lawful processions in the face of organised opposition by Paisley and his followers. In a debate in the Northern Ireland House of Commons, Diamond stated:

> [t]here is of course, one main concern, the preservation of law and order. I pointed out repeatedly to the Minister of Home Affairs that while actions of the gentleman [Paisley] referred to by the Hon. Member for Antrim were in the main responsible for provoking that situation in Divis Street, it never could have developed if the Minister of Home Affairs had ignored those kind of directives and avoided being dictated to by a fanatical and intolerant minority to take actions which led to the horrible state of affairs which existed in Divis Street…We want to ensure that in any area where there is no provocation and where commemorations are carried out peaceably the Government will not be dictated to by fanatical minorities or by individuals of an intolerant kind who say that this or that should not be allowed.[74]

Speaking during a debate on the Easter commemoration in the Northern Ireland House of Commons, Unionist Party MP Nat Minford was also clear that one factor that should be taken into account by the government on this matter was the growing support within unionism for Paisley and his fundamentalist politics.

> We all know that we are faced here at present with an organisation headed by the Rev. Ian Paisley…we are approaching a period when in fact, unless the Government keep very

rigid control of our affairs, this person could inflame hatred in his own particular and peculiar way.[75]

In the same contribution, Minford referred to the threat of the UVF, which, it seemed, was willing to take action in opposition to republican-organised Easter commemorations.[76] The commemoration did indeed feature prominently in the language of O'Neill's opponents. Paisley's paper, the *Protestant Telegraph*, devoted a number of columns to attacking O'Neill for his decision to allow the commemorative processions to go ahead. The potency of anti-O'Neill sentiment in this period is exemplified in the pages of this paper: it published the exchange of letters between the Grand Orange Lodge of Ireland and O'Neill, as referred to above. It also highlighted O'Neill's refusal to ban the 1966 Easter commemorations and accused the prime minister of merely 'capitulating to the rebels'.[77] The paper referred to the efforts to 'protest against this planned insult to our Queen and Constitution' as being 'misrepresented and denounced as a troublesome extremist minority'.[78]

The most overt attack on O'Neill came in June 1966. When O'Neill pledged to take a tough stance against all provocation and to rule without intimidation from any corner, the response from Paisley was quite considerable. The *Protestant Telegraph* reported a demonstration of some 50,000 Protestants that stretched from the Shankill Road to the Ulster Hall. The demonstration was organised to protest against the government's plan to restrict future processions and what the paper described as O'Neill's 'treacherous policies which can only lead to the destruction of Ulster' through his support for the ecumenical movement.[79] In the aftermath of a protest march to the Presbyterian Church of Ireland meeting on 6 June, which had been confronted by Catholic residents when it passed Cromac Square, the same paper accused the government of being guided by the 'Romanisers' in the Presbyterian church. Thus, the government was taking action against Paisley while 'the Papist savages of the Markets are both excused and exonerated'.[80]

These claims in relation to ecumenism made by Paisley are essential to understanding his ability to mobilise dissatisfaction around the issue of the Easter commemoration. He argued that ecumenism posed a real threat to Protestantism as a whole. Paisley argued that O'Neill was guided by the values of ecumenism and was, therefore, also a threat to the future of Protestantism. In making this argument Paisley was aided by O'Neill's language of liberalist reform, his gestures at north–south conciliation and the presentation of the decision to permit the commemoration of the 1916 Rebellion in terms of freedom of speech and expression. At the anti-commemoration rally in Belfast, Paisley maintained that the O'Neill government was not a Protestant one because of its decision to allow the fiftieth anniversary commemorations to go ahead.[81] He later referred to O'Neill's supporters as being both Papists and supporters of ecumenism.[82]

Paisley's accusation that the Easter Rising was a 'Papist plot' placed the issue at the centre of the debate about ecumenism. In addition, the election of Gerry Fitt, Republican Labour, as Westminster MP for west Belfast, the increased activity by the Campaign for Social Justice and the Campaign for Democracy in Ulster (two movements that were raising issues relating to Northern Ireland at Westminster and on the international stage), together with the interest in Northern Ireland demonstrated by the British government, further accumulated pressure on O'Neill. At this point, Paisley appealed both to those who feared that O'Neill was not effective in defending against movements such as the Campaign for Social Justice and Campaign for Democracy in Ulster and to those who thought that he was in fact associated with or implicated in the ecumenical movement. O'Neill had calculated that allowing the 1916 commemorations to go ahead would avoid clashes between nationalists, the IRA and the RUC and army, and that this would in turn maintain a good image of Northern Ireland in Britain. He may also have hoped that the unionist community may have united behind his quest to avoid a renewed IRA campaign—a fear of which remained real for the majority of the community. O'Neill prioritised these issues, but in doing so he presented Paisley with an event around which to mobilise dissatisfaction.

O'Neill's handling of Paisley's opposition to the commemoration

Given the level of discussion about the possibility of a clash between Paisleyites and the participants in the 1966 Easter commemorative parades, it is reasonable to assume that O'Neill factored Paisley's reaction to the commemoration into his decision to allow those parades to proceed. It might be suggested that O'Neill, in emphasising the potential for IRA violence, was in fact feeding into the language of Paisleyism and the fears from which Paisley drew support. However, if O'Neill was not seen to refer to unionist fears relating to the commemoration of 1916 he would certainly have been open to fresh criticism from Paisley. Instead of ignoring the fears of IRA violence, O'Neill sought to assure the unionist community of his awareness of this and offered an alternative to Paisley's suggestions of a total ban. He appealed for tolerance in allowing the commemorative celebrations in nationalist areas. He no doubt hoped that this would unite the unionist community and improve or at least avoid damaging community relations. Unfortunately for O'Neill, this was not the subsequent outcome. O'Neill perhaps underestimated the level of dissatisfaction within the unionist community, a feeling to which his position in relation to the Easter commemoration added. It was this dissatisfaction with O'Neill that was exploited by Paisley.

Because of Paisley's subsequent ability to use the issue of the commemoration in his attacks on the government, the commemoration assumed a new importance to unionist politics in the months after Easter 1966. As a result, O'Neill later looked back on Easter, with the aid of hindsight, and pinpointed it as the start of the problems that were to trouble him throughout the rest of that year. Thus, having resisted pressure to ban the commemorative parades, O'Neill was subsequently forced to respond to party members who became angry that the government had presented Paisley with the opportunity to mount a serious challenge to the government. The issue of the commemoration of the 1916 Rising began to exacerbate already existing problems and divisions both within the Unionist Party and within unionism in general. Thus, the ultimate danger caused by the commemoration was not IRA violence, but rather the strengthened position of the extreme wing of unionism, led in 1966 by Ian Paisley. O'Neill's perceived failure to act decisively in dealing with Paisley caused problems for the prime minister later in the year. As a result of Paisley's agitation throughout the summer of 1966, many members of O'Neill's party looked back on the decision to allow the Easter commemorations to go ahead and viewed it as an error, because it had enabled Paisley to mobilise support around dissatisfaction at that decision.

A number of statements in the weeks and months prior to the Easter commemoration in 1966 saw O'Neill ask the unionist community to ignore the appeal of the more extremist section within the community. O'Neill hoped that his practical approach to the commemoration would minimise Paisley's ability to use the event to mobilise support. He addressed the question of a unionist response to the Easter commemorations in early March. He said that while the event to be commemorated was not one with which the unionist community had much sympathy, the response should be 'first and at all times dignity and restraint'.[83] The prime minister urged the unionist community not to be provoked into action. He admitted that 'some mischievous people would no doubt like to provoke people', but he maintained that 'if we yield to provocation, or allow others to exploit it, we will be giving them a cheap success. Let no one, therefore, take the law into his own hands'. Once again, O'Neill referred to Northern Ireland's image throughout Britain:

> At the beginning of July, throughout Ulster, we will be having a great national festival of remembrance for the men of the Ulster Division who fell at the Battle of Somme. Let those events characterise all that we know of Ulster at its best—in loyalty to the Throne, in willingness to make sacrifices for the nation, in steadfastness and dignity. Let our affirmation of loyalty be a positive thing, and not a negative response to other events.[84]

O'Neill also talked about ongoing investment in Northern Ireland, which was vital to its success. He warned that such investment would only continue if the community did not commit self-inflicted wounds by creating divisions within Northern Ireland. The economic success of Northern Ireland depended, in his view, on the community's ability to remain united.[85] Unfortunately for O'Neill, his pleas fell on deaf ears, as within a number of weeks a split within the Unionist Party over the north Belfast election was reported. Edward Carson planned to contest the upcoming Westminster election as a protest against the government's decision not to name a new Belfast bridge after his father, Lord Carson.[86] The issue forged divisions within the party, as Carson's decision to enter the contest came at the behest of and encouragement from Paisley.[87]

Carson pledged to 'cause as much trouble as possible. A serious injustice has been done to my father's name'. He pointed to the root cause of the problems that existed within unionism: 'I believe there is a rot in Ulster Unionism which began when Captain O'Neill got in touch with Mr Lemass. It was quite an unnecessary move'.[88] O'Neill was forced to cut short a visit to England and return to a Unionist Party meeting in which the matter of whether a seat should be found for Carson, as demanded by Paisley, was discussed. O'Neill won the support of his party to reject such demands. Some members in the party, sympathetic to Carson, had threatened to nominate independent candidates throughout Belfast in the election; but O'Neill defeated the challenge, seemingly due to a lack of public support for Carson.[89]

The Unionist Party at Stormont maintained a united front in favour of a firm stand in the face of Paisley-led demonstrations.[90] O'Neill maintained that while the Easter celebrations of the fiftieth anniversary of the Rising had passed off without any trouble, Paisley's actions on the night of 6 June at Cromac Square and at the Presbyterian Church of Ireland General Assembly had merely presented a fresh opportunity to the IRA.[91] The disturbances between the Paisleyites and Catholic residents at Cromac Square and the protest against the governor of Northern Ireland, Lord Erskine, outside the General Assembly meeting received media coverage across the United Kingdom. As a result, O'Neill lamented the negative image of Northern Ireland that was being presented by the recent disturbances.[92] During a House of Commons debate, Basil Kelly, the Unionist MP for Mid-Down, condemned Paisley as promoting 'intolerance, insults and abuse'; and Austin Ardill, the Unionist MP for Carrick, claimed Paisley was presenting himself in an unwelcome fashion as the saviour of Northern Ireland.[93] The prime minister concluded the Stormont debate by likening Paisleyism to the threat of fascism in the 1930s, and he confirmed his government's intention to

> keep the peace without intimidation from any quarter. I am confident that this is what the house and the country would wish us to do. We will deal sternly with those who either give provocation or who respond to it with violence.[94]

The minister of commerce, Brian Faulkner, appealed to the public to reject the violence associated with the extremist, Paisley-led faction. Speaking in July 1966 at the opening of a new Orange Hall in Co. Derry, Faulkner expressed a view similar to that of O'Neill: 'The people of Ulster must not allow a vociferous minority of misguided foolish men to destroy the hard won progress'.[95] The minister made a similar attack on Paisley a few days later at another gathering. He asked

> [w]hy, when Northern Ireland seemed to be settling down quietly to a period of peace and prosperity, such as we had never enjoyed before, should we be plunged back 40 years into hatred and suspicion?

Going on to discuss the recent Easter commemoration, Faulkner claimed that this should not have been a matter for too much concern.

> Our constitution is strong enough and we should have suffi-
> cient faith in it not to let such activities disturb us. Certainly
> the Ulster government will not tolerate any weakening of
> the constitutional position.[96]

The government's approach at this stage was to highlight the danger inherent in Paisleyism. O'Neill did so again at a 12 July meeting when he reminded his fellow Orangemen that the Northern Ireland Constitution would be damaged by 'violence, by abuse and by the gun'.[97] Again, O'Neill referred to the damage caused to the image of Northern Ireland and to the fact that headlines relating to Ulster were no longer dominated by economic development but by shootings and riots.[98] The prime minister went on to present Paisley not as a saviour, but as an enemy of Northern Ireland, and he vowed to continue the fight against Ulster's enemies.[99] The editorial of the Protestant *News Letter* paper said that it was now 'time to call a halt' to the breaches of peace brought about by Paisley's behaviour and claimed that the Protestant community had had enough.[100] The *News Letter* also claimed that O'Neill had the backing of the people for any restrictions placed on Paisley's demonstrations.[101] The Northern Ireland Labour Party also condemned Paisley and called on O'Neill to show courage on the issue.[102] Despite the level of opposition to Paisleyism within unionism, however, Paisley's movement, the Ulster Constitution Defence Committee, reportedly had some 100 branches throughout Northern Ireland. There was also movement towards the establishment of a branch at Queen's University, Belfast.[103]

Consequences for O'Neill of his handling of events

While O'Neill was subject to hecklers at a number of 12 July events in 1966, the level of support that he enjoyed within his party at this stage was high.[104] There is no doubt that once the Easter commemoration had passed off without incident, and given the number of disturbances with which Paisley was associated in June and July of 1966, condem-nation of unionist extremism increased.[105] In addition, the banning of the newly reformed UVF in the aftermath of murders in June 1966 also led to criticism of extremist Protestantism. The UVF had issued a statement in May 1966 through Captain William Johnston, who purported to be the assistant adjutant of the 1st Belfast Battalion of the UVF, declaring:

> [w]ar against the IRA and its splinter groups. Known IRA men will be executed mercilessly and without hesitation… Property will not be exempted in any action taken. We are heavily armed in this cause.[106]

The perceived link between Paisley and the UVF as referred to in O'Neill's speeches added to criticism of Paisleyism. Although Paisley denied any relationship between his movement and the newly formed UVF, O'Neill intimated that there was a very clear link.[107] The prime minister referred to a statement by Paisley in the Ulster Hall on 16 June 1966. In this speech Paisley had reportedly referred to resolutions from a number of divisions of the Ulster Volunteer Force, which pledged that they 'were solidly behind Mr Paisley'. The prime minister also referred at this point to a statement of thanks which Paisley extended to the UVF at a march on 17 April.[108] Minister of Commerce Brian Faulkner condemned the dangerous faction that was emerging under Paisley's leadership.[109] Stanley McMaster, MP for East Belfast at Westminster, addressed a 12 July gathering in Kilkeel. He said:

> Our peace, security and very existence are being threatened by militant, extremist elements in our midst who, if given their head, would destroy our cherished liberties and independence. Orangemen must now give a clear lead to the rest of the community. They must, by their example and by any other means they could summon, use the entire and united weight of their influential organisation to promote tolerance and understanding between all sections of the community.[110]

Support for O'Neill's stance against Paisley also came from the leader of the Conservative Party, Edward Heath. In a letter to Paisley's Ulster Constitution Defence Committee, the Conservative leader was clear in his condemnation of 'any words or actions which stir religious or racist antagonism', and he went on to describe Paisley as 'abhorrent'.[111] But, despite mounting criticism of Paisley from various quarters, Prime Minister O'Neill's position did not improve. In fact, O'Neill's worst fears had already begun to be realised in May 1966, when members of the opposition parties in Northern Ireland secured the interest of the British prime minister, Harold Wilson, in discussing the 'goings-on' in Northern Ireland. Both Gerry Fitt and Nationalist MP John McCarron expressed hope that an inquiry into the running of Northern Ireland might result.[112] In the course of the same Westminster debate, Fitt raised the question of the operation of the Government of Ireland Act (1920) and the fact that matters relating to Northern Ireland could not be aired in Westminster.[113] Wilson's response was to suggest that he and his home secretary, Roy Jenkins, meet for informal talks with Terence O'Neill.[114]

There was an air of optimism at this point within nationalist circles that some progress might have been made. Eddie McAteer believed that 'now there will be light in the darkness. I shall certainly ask for a place at the conference table to ensure a balanced view of the problem'.[115] This added pressure did not bode well for O'Neill at an already stressful time. The proposed meeting took place in early August. Prior to the meeting, Wilson explained that his government had become 'disturbed' by the recent events in Northern Ireland and that he had decided that the best course of action was to have 'informal talks' with O'Neill.[116]

The pressure from Westminster continued throughout the rest of 1966. In November of that year Home Secretary Roy Jenkins agreed to meet with a deputation of Labour MPs to discuss Northern Ireland and the constitutional rules governing its discussion at Westminster.[117] The issue of Northern Ireland and electoral reform was raised in the House of Commons at Westminster soon after this.[118] Fitt had successfully lobbied and won the support of a number of Labour MPs at Westminster for the Campaign for Democracy in Ulster, which had been highlighting events in Northern Ireland throughout 1966.[119] Attempts were also under way to enlist Conservative Party support for electoral reform and an end to discrimination in Northern Ireland.[120] This represented a key development within nationalism, and also a fresh source of pressure for O'Neill.

A significant outcome of the talks between O'Neill and Wilson, in the context of the commemoration of the 1916 Rising, related to O'Neill's admission on his return from London that 'it was suggested that the recent manifestations in Northern Ireland have been a backlash to something which took place in April and I would not be disposed to deny that'.[121] The Easter commemorations alone had not caused the demonstrations and riots that had marred the summer months; rather, it was that the decision to allow them to proceed provided O'Neill's opponents with an event around which to mobilise dissatisfaction. In turn, O'Neill's position in his own party came under attack; not because the party disagreed in principle with the decision to allow the commemoration of the Rising to take place, but because that decision had strengthened the extremist element within unionism. Austin Currie referred to O'Neill 'being hauled over the coals'; while Eddie McAteer referred to the meeting at Westminster as O'Neill's 'court-martial'.[122] McAteer also announced his own planned meeting with Home Secretary Roy Jenkins. Suggestions from nationalist corners that the meeting between O'Neill and Wilson had come about due to pressure from nationalists in Westminster, in addition to McAteer's successful attempts to establish contacts with the British government, pointed towards dangerous times for unionists at Westminster.

It is not surprising then that the challenge to O'Neill's leadership, which had threatened since July 1966, came in September of that year in the aftermath of his meeting with Wilson in August. A petition signed by a number of backbenchers in the Unionist Party was presented to O'Neill on 21 September. The petition was reportedly supported by a number of Cabinet members who were not sympathetic to the fundamentalism of Paisley. It criticised O'Neill's inability to garner widespread support for his policies.[123] Among the reasons mentioned to explain the growing level of dissatisfaction with O'Neill's administration was the recent outbreaks of violence with which Paisley was involved.[124] Once again, reference was made to resentment within the party that the government had allowed the commemorations of the 1916 Rising to go ahead in April.[125] At the meeting to discuss the leadership challenge against O'Neill, the prime minister did receive a vote of confidence from members of the Unionist Party both at constituency and parliamentary level, but he came under severe criticism from some twelve MPs for having given permission for the Easter commemorations to go ahead throughout Northern Ireland.[126]

After he survived the leadership challenge there was some other good news for O'Neill. The Official Unionist candidate, Harold Smith, easily defeated Ian Paisley's wife, Eileen Paisley, in the contest for the Duncairn seat on the Belfast City Council in October, and this must have seemed like a good omen. Reverend Paisley's ongoing incarceration in Crumlin Road Gaol, as a result of his refusal to agree to keep the peace in the aftermath of the protests outside the Presbyterian Church of Ireland General Assembly in Belfast in June, was not enough to swing support behind his wife's campaign.[127] In addition, the Belfast City Council voted to support O'Neill's attempts to promote good relations between the two communities in Northern Ireland. The council passed a resolution giving 'its full support for the economic policy of the Government of Northern Ireland and the efforts of the Prime Minister to promote tolerance and goodwill throughout the community'.[128] However, O'Neill's difficulties were not over. Not only were representatives of the nationalist community criticising his failure to introduce reforms, Paisley's release from prison on 19 October re-ignited tensions within unionism.[129] The new minister of home affairs, William Craig, immediately took a firm stance and warned Paisley that his disregard for the law would not be tolerated.[130] This warning came after Paisley's release had resulted in celebratory bonfires and a vocal attack once again by Paisley on O'Neill and the government.[131] Despite the warning, Paisley announced his plan to hold a rally at Dundonald, irrespective of any ban.[132] There were reports also that Paisley planned to form a new party with which to attempt to gain the support of the electorate for his policies.[133]

CONCLUSION

The Northern Ireland government's instinct in relation to the fiftieth anniversary commemoration of the 1916 Rising was to allow parades to proceed during Easter 1966 where they were not likely to cause a public disorder, despite the government's obvious disapproval of the object of celebration. The government took this pragmatic approach because of a fear that attempts to impose a blanket ban might result in civil disorder and possibly a renewed IRA campaign. The government was also particularly worried about the image of Northern Ireland in London, given an increased interest in Northern Ireland on the part of the British government. Indeed, maintaining a good image of Northern Ireland in Britain and abroad appeared more important to O'Neill at this stage than did domestic opinion. The debates in the Northern Ireland House of Commons illustrate that O'Neill had significant support for this pragmatic approach. The Grand Orange Lodge of Ireland actually also accepted this position despite opposition from various individual Lodges.[134] The government resisted the pressure from Reverend Ian Paisley and sections of the Unionist Party to ban the Easter events. Instead of placing a blanket ban on the commemorations, O'Neill made a gesture towards the growing level of opposition within unionism regarding the parades by restricting north–south rail travel. In O'Neill's calculations, it was best to avoid the possibility of clashes between commemoration organisers and police that could have unleashed a renewed IRA campaign.

In the months before the Easter commemoration, O'Neill prioritised avoiding IRA violence and maintaining the favour of British opinion. He no doubt hoped that if his pragmatic approach could be seen to have avoided the emergence of a dreaded IRA campaign and a British government intervention in Northern Ireland, this would then unite unionism behind him rather than Paisley. Unfortunately for O'Neill, this did not happen. Instead, Paisley continued to mobilise unionist dissatisfaction, and one issue that he utilised in doing so was the Easter 1966 commemoration of the 1916 Rising. As a result, O'Neill's party began to view him as having failed to deal sufficiently with the threat posed to the government by Paisley and extremist Protestantism in general. Ultimately, the commemoration of the 1916 Rising assumed a new importance to unionism in the summer months of 1966 because of the manner in which Paisley utilised the issue as part of a wider attack on O'Neill and his government.

The important point in appreciating Paisley's ability to use the issue of the commemoration in this way is understood by the fact that the commemoration was represented as further evidence of O'Neill's conversion to ecumenism, which was presented as a threat to Protestantism. This, the liberal language used by O'Neill in relation to the commemoration, reforms and north–south conciliation, together with the election of Gerry Fitt to Westminster and increased activity at Westminster by the Campaign for Social Justice and the Campaign for Democracy in Ulster, were cumulative factors in explaining the growing divisions within unionism and, in turn, the appeal of Paisleyism. It is very important to understand these points in appreciating the significance of the commemoration for unionist politics in the period.

The events of summer 1966 also had implications for O'Neill's position as leader of the Unionist Party. When violent demonstrations surrounded Paisley's protests that summer, attention was drawn to Northern Ireland. The negative attention this brought to O'Neill's administration was a worrying development for unionists given, as stated above, the perception that the British government was preparing to interfere in Northern Ireland's affairs. The suggestion that O'Neill's meeting with Wilson in August of 1966 had come about as a result of that attention and was a sign of the British government's intentions meant that O'Neill was subjected to internal party criticism.

The perception at the time that the Labour government at Westminster might intervene in Northern Ireland's affairs caused members of the Unionist Party to be critical of O'Neill's handling of Paisley. In this context, the retrospective belief growing in the party— that the decision to permit the Easter commemoration had been a mistake in terms of responding to Paisley—was one of the key factors that led to considerable dissatisfaction within the Unionist Party. So, whereas an IRA campaign did not occur as feared, the British government's interest in Northern Ireland was nonetheless sparked by Paisley's activities throughout the summer of 1966. In this sense, O'Neill's main worries were realised, despite his pragmatic stance in relation to the fiftieth anniversary Easter commemoration of the 1916 Rising. As a result, O'Neill agreed that the problems that he and Wilson discussed had originated at Easter 1966. The trouble witnessed in the summer of 1966 was not caused by the Easter commemoration itself, but rather by the ability of Paisley to utilise that event to undermine the government's position. Paisley's ability to do so left O'Neill open to a barrage of criticism from within his own party and subsequently vulnerable to a leadership battle.

NOTES

[1] For an analysis of Ulster unionism in the 1960s, see Marc Mulholland, *Northern Ireland at the crossroads: Ulster unionism in the O'Neill years, 1960–9* (Basingstoke, 2000).
[2] *Belfast Telegraph*, 12 July 1965.
[3] *Belfast Telegraph*, 12 July 1965.
[4] *Belfast Telegraph*, 28 August 1965.
[5] Clive Scoular, *James Chichester-Clark: prime minister of Northern Ireland* (Killyleagh, 2000), 51–2.
[6] For example see the reaction of the Ulster Farmers Union in the *Irish News and Belfast Morning News*, 21 December 1965; *Belfast Telegraph*, 26 November 1965.
[7] *Belfast Telegraph*, 20 November 1965.

[8] *Belfast Telegraph*, 11 November 1965.
[9] *Belfast Telegraph*, December 1965.
[10] *Belfast Telegraph*, 22 November 1965.
[11] *Belfast Telegraph*, 21 February 1966.
[12] *News Letter*, 10 March 1966.
[13] Public Record Office of Northern Ireland (hereafter cited as PRONI), Cabinet minutes, CAB 9G/73/14, Letter marked 'Secret', Harold Black to Robin. M. North, Home Office in London, 18 February 1966.
[14] PRONI, Cabinet minutes, CAB 9G/73/14, Robin North, Home Office, London to Harold Black, 28 February 1966.
[15] *Belfast Telegraph*, 27 November 1965. O'Neill later claimed that he had called a pre-Christmas election so as to avoid it coinciding with the Westminster elections, which were called in February 1966. See *News Letter*, 12 February 1966.
[16] *Belfast Telegraph*, 11 December 1965. In fact, in the Northern Ireland House of Commons on 16 February 1966, Minister of Home Affairs Brian McConnell referred to additional revenue that he had needed to fund extra security precautions, including the mobilisation of part-time members of the Special Constabulary, in response to the threat of renewed IRA activity. See Northern Ireland Commons Debates (hereafter cited as NICD), vol. 62, col. 1066, 16 February 1966.
[17] *Belfast Telegraph*, 8 December 1965.
[18] *News Letter*, 8 April 1966.
[19] *News Letter*, 7 April 1966.
[20] *News Letter*, 8 April 1966.
[21] *Belfast Telegraph*, 7 April 1966.
[22] *News Letter*, 8 April 1966
[23] *Belfast Telegraph*, 8 April 1966.
[24] *News Letter*, 19, 21 May 1966. For the original report on the capture of 'a blueprint for a revolution', see *Irish Independent*, 14 May 1966.
[25] *Belfast Telegraph*, 20 November 1965.
[26] *Belfast Telegraph*, 11 November 1965.
[27] *Irish News and Belfast Morning News*, 9 December 1965.
[28] See *Belfast Telegraph*, 18 February 1966.
[29] *Irish News and Belfast Morning News*, 17 December 1965.
[30] NICD, vol. 62, cols 1067–8, 16 February 1966.
[31] NICD, vol. 62, cols 1411–2, 24 February 1966.
[32] *Belfast Telegraph*, 24 February 1966.
[33] *News Letter*, 17 February 1966.
[34] *Belfast Telegraph*, 24 February 1966; *News Letter*, 25 February 1966.
[35] David Gordon, *The O'Neill years: Unionist politics 1963–1969* (Belfast, 1989), 64.
[36] *News Letter*, 11 February 1966.

[37] *News Letter*, 12 February 1966; *Belfast Telegraph*, 21 February 1966.
[38] *News Letter*, 4 March 1966. McGivern was referring to the fact that the Ulster Hall was to be used for a planned Paisley event at Easter.
[39] *News Letter*, 23 February 1966.
[40] *Belfast Telegraph*, April 15 1966.
[41] *Irish News and Belfast Morning News*, 15 April 1966.
[42] *News Letter*, 9 June 1966.
[43] *Irish News and Belfast Morning News*, 15 April 1966.
[44] NICD, vol. 62, col. 1550, 2 March 1966.
[45] NICD, vol. 62, col. 1559, 2 March 1966.
[46] NICD, vol. 63, cols.230–1, 24 March 1966
[47] NICD, vol. 63, col.232, 24 March 1966.
[48] NICD, vol. 63, col. 289, 24 March 1966
[49] NICD, vol. 63, col, 242, 24 March 1966.
[50] *News Letter*, 3 May 1966.
[51] *News Letter*, 23 February 1966.
[52] *News Letter*, 7 February 1966.
[53] *Protestant Telegraph*, April 1966; *Protestant Telegraph*, 28 May 1966.
[54] *Belfast Telegraph*, 16 April 1966.
[55] *News Letter*, 14 April 1966.
[56] *Belfast Telegraph*, 16 April 1966.
[57] *News Letter*, 18 April 1966.
[58] Gordon, *The O'Neill years*, 68; *Belfast Telegraph*, 18 April 1966; *News Letter*, 18 April 1966.
[59] *Belfast Telegraph*, 9 April 1966
[60] *News Letter*, 21 January 1966.
[61] *Belfast Telegraph*, 2 March 1966.
[62] NICD, vol. 62, cols 1539–40, 2 March 1966.
[63] *Belfast Telegraph*, 20 November 1965.
[64] NICD, vol. 63, cols 245–6, 24 March 1966.
[65] *Belfast Telegraph*, 5 March 1966.
[66] See PRONI, Cabinet minutes, CAB 9B/299/1, 'Commemoration of the 1916 Rebellion', Letter from Student's Union, Queen's University, Belfast to Terence O'Neill, 11 March 1966.
[67] PRONI, Cabinet minutes, CAB 9B/299/1.
[68] See PRONI, Cabinet minutes, CAB 9B/299/1.
[69] PRONI, Cabinet minutes, CAB 9B/299/1, 'Commemoration of the 1916 Rebellion', Letter of reply from Prime Minister O'Neill to Sir George Clarke, Grand Orange Lodge of Ireland, as agreed at meeting of the Security Committee (Minister of Agriculture present) 4 April 1966, dated 5 April 1966.
[70] PRONI, Cabinet minutes, CAB 9B/299/1, 'Commemoration of the 1916 Rebellion', Letter of reply from O'Neill to Clarke.
[71] See Paul Bew, Peter Gibbon and Henry Patterson, *The state in Northern Ireland*

1921–1972: political forces and social classes (Manchester, 1979), chaps 5–6.

[72] *News Letter*, 8 March 1966.

[73] PRONI, Cabinet minutes, CAB 9B/299/1, 'Commemoration of the 1916 Rebellion', Letter from Prime Minister O'Neill to the Right Honourable Roy Jenkins, MP, Secretary of State for the Home Department, Home Office, Whitehall, London, 6 May 1966.

[74] NICD, vol. 63, col. 233, 24 March 1966.

[75] NICD, vol. 62, col. 1543, 2 March 1966.

[76] NICD, vol. 62, col. 1543, 2 March 1966.

[77] *Protestant Telegraph*, 28 May 1966.

[78] *Protestant Telegraph*, 28 May 1966

[79] *Protestant Telegraph*, 2 July 1966.

[80] *Protestant Telegraph*, 18 June 1966.

[81] *Protestant Telegraph*, 28 May 1966.

[82] *Protestant Telegraph*, 2 July 1966.

[83] *Irish News and Belfast Morning News*, 5 March 1966.

[84] *Irish News and Belfast Morning News*, 5 March 1966.

[85] *Irish News and Belfast Morning News*, 5 March 1966.

[86] *News Letter*, 16 March 1966.

[87] *Irish News and Belfast Morning News*, 18 March 1966; Gordon, *The O'Neill years*, 64; Demonstrations attended by Carson were organised by Paisley's Ulster Constitution Defence Committee. See *News Letter*, 25 February 1966.

[88] *News Letter*, 1 March 1966. O'Neill's decision to welcome the taoiseach, Seán Lemass, to Stormont in 1965 was generally welcomed within unionist circles and the media in Northern Ireland. But O'Neill's secrecy around this event created suspicion within his party. Some unionists, like Paisley, objected to Lemass's visit given the refusal by the Irish state to formally recognise the existence of Northern Ireland, and also because of the territorial claim over Northern Ireland that was explicit in the Irish Constitution at that time.

[89] *Belfast Telegraph*, 22 March 1966.

[90] *Belfast Telegraph*, 14 June 1966.

[91] *Belfast Telegraph*, 16 June 1966.

[92] *Irish News and Belfast Morning News*, 16 June 1966.

[93] *Belfast Telegraph*, 16 June 1966; *Belfast Telegraph*, 16 June 1966.

[94] *Irish News and Belfast Morning News*, 16 June 1966.

[95] *Belfast Telegraph*, 2 July 1966.

[96] *Belfast Telegraph*, 9 July 1966.

[97] *Belfast Telegraph*, 12 July 1966.

[98] *Irish News and Belfast Morning News*, 13 July 1966.

[99] *Belfast Telegraph*, 12 July 1966.

[100] *News Letter*, 8 June 1966.

[101] *News Letter*, 9 June 1966.

[102] *News Letter*, 18 June 1966.

[103] *News Letter*, 23 April 1966.
[104] *Irish News and Belfast Morning News*, 13 July 1966.
[105] See *Belfast Telegraph*, 23 July 1966. Protests at Paisley's imprisonment in the Crumlin Road Gaol resulted in the road being blocked by his supporters, see *Irish News and Belfast Morning News*, 22 July 1966.
[106] Reprinted in the *News Letter*, 29 June 1966.
[107] Paisley denied that he had any such connections with the UVF. See *Belfast Telegraph*, 30 June 1966.
[108] See *Irish News and Belfast Morning News*, 30 June 1966.
[109] *Irish News and Belfast Morning News*, 29 August 1966.
[110] *Belfast Telegraph*, 12 July 1966.
[111] *Belfast Telegraph*, 10 October 1966.
[112] *Irish News and Belfast Morning News*, 27 May 1966. Fitt had been calling for such an inquiry by Westminster and had raised the issue in his maiden speech there in April, much to the consternation of unionist MPs. See *News Letter*, 26 April 1966.
[113] *Belfast Telegraph*, 27 May 1966.
[114] *News Letter*, 27 May 1966.
[115] *Derry Journal*, 27 May 1966.
[116] *Irish News and Belfast Morning News*, 3 August 1966.
[117] *Belfast Telegraph*, 10 November 1966.
[118] See Gerry Fitt's statement at Westminster, *Belfast Telegraph*, 16 November 1966.
[119] See *Derry Journal*, 28 June 1966.
[120] *Belfast Telegraph*, 10 December 1966.
[121] *Irish News and Belfast Morning News*, 6 August 1966.
[122] *Irish News and Belfast Morning News*, 13 August 1966; *Derry Journal*, 5 August 1966.
[123] *Belfast Telegraph*, 22 September 1966.
[124] *Irish News and Belfast Morning News*, 27 September 1966.
[125] *Belfast Telegraph*, 22 September 1966.
[126] *Irish News and Belfast Morning News*, 28 September 1966.
[127] *Irish News and Belfast Morning News*, 6 October 1966.
[128] *Belfast Telegraph*, 1 November 1966.
[129] See Republican Labour MP, Harry Diamond's critique of O'Neill in *Irish News and Belfast Morning News*, 9 November 1966.
[130] *Irish News and Belfast Morning News*, 20 October 1966.
[131] *Irish News and Belfast Morning News*, 20 October 1966.
[132] *Belfast Telegraph*, 20 October 1966.
[133] *Belfast Telegraph*, 21 October 1966.
[134] PRONI, Cabinet minutes, CAB 9B/299/1, 'Commemoration of the 1916 Rebellion', John Bryans, County Grand Master, and Robert J. McMullan, County Grand Secretary of the Grand Orange Lodge of Belfast, to Minister of Home Affairs, R.W.B. McConnell, 23 April 1966.

8. Sites Of Memory And Memorial

By Roisín Higgins

Introduction

In 1959 when submitting his design for the sculptural centrepiece of the Garden of Remembrance, Oisín Kelly was concerned about the 'general difficulty of expressing the heroic in our time'. He intended in his design to create a new nationalist iconography. 'There is no tradition on which to build', he wrote, 'except harps and shamrocks and Lady Lavery and that bloody stone volunteer shooting splendidly into Bearna Baogail'.[1] The final image evoked by Kelly encapsulated a sense in which nationalist imagery projected itself into a 'violent gap' or void, replete with an unknown or unspecified danger. In Irish symbolism, the absences often resonate more clearly than the physically present. During the official golden jubilee of the Rising of Easter 1916, no monuments to the event or its leaders were unveiled. Instead, Easter week was the implicit omnipresence in images borrowed from other aspects of the nationalist canon. During the commemorations of 1966, statues were unveiled to Thomas Davis and Robert Emmet, and the Garden of Remembrance and Kilmainham Jail were ceremoniously opened. None of these memorials, however, had been commissioned for the jubilee; delay rather than design involved them in the commemoration. The explicit act of revolution in 1916 was blurred in the events of 1966 into a more vague anniversary of independence. The renaming of streets and railway stations was designed to mark the maturation of the

Republic, and the appropriation of public spaces underlined the legitimacy of the state. The story of national freedom nudged out the presence of other histories on the Dublin landscape, which was overlaid with new meanings. However, the problematic triumph of that long struggle for freedom, which was referenced around the capital city, found its iconic moment not in monument but anti-monument. The most dramatic reconfiguring of the nation's capital—an actual violent gap—came not from the government's hands but from those of maverick Republicans.

NELSON'S PILLAR

In 1964 the *Irish Times* was advised that the Transport Workers' Union of America had offered 'cheerfully to finance the removal of Lord Nelson' from O'Connell Street. The union president, Michael J. Quill, originally from Kerry, argued that visitors to Dublin were left with the impression that Nelson's Pillar meant to the Irish people what the Statue of Liberty meant to Americans, and he suggested that it should be transported to Buckingham Palace where Nelson was 'respected and loved for his many and victorious battles on behalf of the British Crown'.[2] Quill was not alone in advocating the removal of Nelson; the Pillar had long seemed incongruous. The Patrician year of 1961 gave a boost to those who argued the case for the national apostle as a suitable replacement for the admiral, and assassination increased the lobby for John F. Kennedy. While the more general view that 'it is about time such a monstrosity was replaced by one of our great patriots', left only the question of which of those most popularly nominated patriots—Pearse, Connolly and Collins—would triumph.[3]

The foundation stone of Nelson's Pillar had been laid amid great ceremony in 1808, and whereas, for some, it had become a source of irritation, for many—detached from historical association—it had become a central landmark by which to map the capital city. When asked to comment on the Pillar in 1923, W.B. Yeats had responded that it represented the feeling of Protestant Ireland for a man who had helped to break the power of Napoleon. 'The life and work of the people who erected it is part of our tradition', he said. 'We should accept the past of this nation, and not pick and choose'.[4] However, monuments to individuals are particularly vulnerable to shifts in political power, after which the heroism they once personified can be reread as grandiloquent hubris. The textured memory that Yeats had advocated was exploded in March 1966 by a Republican bomb.

The explosion in O'Connell Street underlined certain difficulties faced by the government during the golden jubilee year of the 1916 Rising. The removal of Nelson had never easily been in its gift. The Pillar was maintained by trustees, and the over-writing of their responsibility would have required a special act of the Oireachtas. However, the dramatic toppling of Nelson was contrasted in popular song with the bureaucratic indecision of political power. The state's plans for the jubilee were under threat of usurpation, both by dissenting groups and by dissent within groups. The government, which had viewed Nelson more prosaically than his detractors, as a potential traffic hazard, was now faced with the problem of how to remove the severed Pillar's stump. A report from the Department of Defence warned that damage to adjoining property was likely to be greater than had been caused in the original explosion, as the charge required to demolish the remainder of the Pillar would need to be placed closer to the ground. The report concluded: 'It must also be considered that if we are directed to do this work, no matter what happens, the public will make invidious comparisons with our work and the previous effort'.[5] As it happened, the superior engineering skills of the IRA would indeed become part of the mythology of the Pillar's demise.[6]

Repercussions of the destruction of the Pillar for the official 1966 commemorations

Despite the government's efforts to create a choreography for the commemoration that would present Ireland as a modern and harmonious nation, it was unable to control the popular response. The image promoted to an international audience was one of a confident nation celebrating its independence, without drawing too clearly the British connection or disconnection. The carnival atmosphere that greeted the transportation of Nelson's head down O'Connell Street, however, gave a lie to this image. The promotion of Ireland as a tourist destination was also jeopardised by the whiff of impending trouble. In particular, the Irish ambassador to Canada was advised by Irish International Airlines that the 'incident of the Pillar' had 'dramatically altered' the plans of passengers who had intended to go to Dublin for the Easter period, particularly given the subsequent publicity, which suggested that '[t]he Pillar is only the first of many such incidents that are anticipated'.[7]

The state wanted a commemoration that remembered the actions of Easter week without celebrating the violence at their heart. It attempted to embrace the heroic ideal of the 1916 leaders while simultaneously transforming it. The blowing up of Nelson's Pillar represented the most literal commemorative act of 1966. Physically, it reproduced rubble on O'Connell Street; and symbolically, it re-enacted the toppling of empire. Nations do not need to re-create in order to remember; however, the blowing up of Nelson's Pillar threatened to upstage the government's plans to mark the fiftieth anniversary of the 1916 Rising: the state would find it difficult to offer a single event that would be so instant and iconic/iconoclastic. The hope of Taoiseach Seán Lemass that the memory of the Rising could be harnessed to the needs of practical patriotism was always in danger of unleashing a populist Republican moment in 1966. The banning of 'rebel songs' on sponsored programmes on Radio Éireann during the jubilee period was an attempt to set—but would not necessarily control—the tone of the commemoration.

The position of Northern Ireland added a more serious note to an outpouring of nationalist sentiment. United States Congressman Robert Sweeney of Ohio, speaking in the House of Representatives, noted that 'the program of urban renewal in Dublin City' should

> serve as a reminder to all of us that the problem of a divided Ireland still exists in a troubled world, and this once free and independent nation is still arbitrarily and unnaturally partitioned by the will of Great Britain.[8]

Irish diplomatic correspondence in the United States could present the Congressman as an 'amiable, if somewhat over-enthusiastic, well-wisher of ours', and the *Washington Post* might feel that he would be better employed concerning himself with problems in Ohio, but the link made by Congressman Sweeney was one that would resonate.[9]

The site of the Cyclops on O'Connell Street acted as a receptacle for the selectivity (one-eyedness) of Irish history. Those who cast a blow at the Pillar rejected the place of the Anglo-Irish in Ireland's past. However, it was not Nelson himself, but the tradition of those who had erected the Pillar that Yeats wanted to be remembered. G.B. Shaw, in attempting to unpick the complexities of the position of the Anglo-Irish, had ridiculed Nelson as an intensely English Englishman, drunk with glory and nerved by the vulgarest anti-foreign prejudice, 'and apparently unchastened by any reflections on the fact that he had never had to fight a technically capable and properly equipped enemy except on land, where he had never been successful'.[10] Nelson as hero and as representative of the authority of the Anglo-Irish had both been problematic. Further selectivity was present in the government's attempt to frame the Rising as an isolated act of military sacrifice that could have no contemporary echo. But, as Congressman Sweeney articulated, some would see the proxy toppling of empire on O'Connell Street as a reminder of the British presence in the north. Therefore the blowing up of Nelson's Pillar threatened to expose the partial nature of many competing views surrounding the commemoration, as well as to destabilise the event itself.

Monuments and symbolism

Lord Nelson had become a symbol of the past that held no mystical presence. The body of the hero is a site on which the aspirations of the nation can be placed. A.J. Lerner, in assessing nineteenth-century statuary in France, sees in monuments to Napoleon a continuation of the public circulation of the mystical body of Christ. The doctrinal shift of the twelfth century, in which the consecrated host became the *corpus Christi* rather than the *corpus mysticum*, transferred the latter status onto the Church so that the host became the sacrament of the collective.[11] The nation, as mystical body, has a relationship to the heroic body that is equally dependant. The individual provides the sacrifice and service through which he or she becomes an embodiment of the nation. Therefore, the procession of monuments throughout the city acts as a demonstration of faith in the nation, just as the *Corpus Christi* procession acted as a demonstration of faith in the Church. As Lerner also points out, in constructions of nationalism, heroes of the past must continue to live in the afterlife of the nation and it is through the monument that the living might commune with the dead.[12]

For Tom Hennigan, writing of the jubilee commemoration in the *Evening Herald*, the veterans of the 1916 Rising occupied a space somewhere between life and afterlife. While watching them he was reminded of the lines from Yeats's *Countess Cathleen*: 'The years like great black oxen tread the world…And I am broken by their passing feet'.[13] He animated the narrative of the parade of veterans through the city centre during the jubilee commemorations with reference to the inanimate, so that:

> [t]hey advanced on the GPO from many points, marching
> past stout Dan O'Connell confronting the centuries, secure

of his place in them...Through College Green came the old men...watched by the ghosts of Smith O'Brien, Gavan Duffy, Thomas Davis and poor wasted Clarence Mangan, babbling of his Dark Rosaleen.

Waiting for the marchers was the GPO...As it waited for them once before. Now, we seemed to be seeing the Ionic portico of Portland stone with the six fluted columns for the first time.

For the first time too, the grave, impassive figures of Hibernia, Mercury and Fidelity on the roof.[14]

In this version, the commemorative march breathes heroic life, not simply into old men and dead men, but also into the post office building that facilitated the Rising; even anticipated it. However, without the attendant commemorative reminders, monuments can slip out of view. Reverend Dom Bernard O'Dea, addressing Muintir na Tíre in February 1966 asked,

[c]an we find no other way to perpetuate greatness than with a dickied-up tombstone...There are few things that so glorify the people who set them up, and torment the people who come later, as monuments. They become the accepted wart in the local face; all see them but nobody notices.[15]

As an example, O'Dea cited the best view of the upcoming Easter Sunday national celebrations, which would be had 'by a chap who will look down with a one-eyed sailor's grin—the fellow who saw it all, and is still around—looking askance. Monuments my eye!'[16]

Although the procession of statues in the urban landscape can underwrite the historical journey of the nation, their presence can also be problematic. Monuments can be seen to stabilise time and narrative and, as James Young has pointed out, bring events into some cognitive order by placing them in a 'topographical matrix that orients the rememberer and creates meaning in both the land and our recollection'.[17] Nelson disrupted the national narrative demonstrated on O'Connell Street, which flowed from the Liberator and Parnell. The Pillar overshadowed the GPO, which was situated at the confluence of the nineteenth-century traditions. Katherine Verdery concurs with Lerner in seeing the transubstantive quality of monumental figures in which 'statues are dead people cast in bronze'. By arresting the process of the individual's bodily decay, she contends, a statue moves that person into the realm of the timeless or sacred. Within the statue, time is frozen at the moment of the individual's historical importance, suggesting the continuation of the values he or she personified. The destruction of a monument reveals the hero as mortal and symbolically destroys the temporal and spatial conceptions that the figure represented.[18] This is why the removal of statues is so common after a change to the ruling structure. But, as Verdery has also pointed out, the destruction of monuments may in fact be more important for regimes that differ little from that which has gone before. In which case legitimisation requires an even greater need to stress discontinuity through the decapitated monument.[19]

Nelson altered the landscape of O'Connell Street. A climb to the top of the Pillar had afforded a panoramic view of Dublin. The city could be seen from above as a totality—a 'real' and independent subject. The aerial viewpoint provided a certain detachment through which the capital city could be read in a way that diminished the individual activities of urban existence. Those who climbed to the top became voyeurs of Dublin life as well as participants in that life. This view from above, which has been associated with both the colonial and global gaze, casts those beneath in miniature and reduces the sense of local. Conceptually, it allows for a greater sense of order, or at least the ability to organise. Nelson on O'Connell Street was often depicted as all-seeing and all-hearing. Moreover, Nelson's removal was a reminder that the panoptical gaze is not simply an abstract construction but one that is spatially ordered, and locally situated.

In other words, imperial and global disciplines are not simply imposed from above but are operated and implicated at the local level. Setting Irish and English as simply oppositional identities does not offer a complete understanding of their relationship. One of the winning entries in the schools essay competition organised as part of the jubilee commemorations of the Rising told the recent history of Ireland through the eyes of the Admiral. 'I see everything that goes on in Dublin and I hear everything that goes on outside it,' the statue told the fictional narrator. 'And don't be misled by people telling you I am English. I may bear a resemblance to that British admiral...but inside I am only Leinster granite of fine old Dublin stock, and Irish to the core'.[20]

The Pillar's demise allowed the subsequent state commemorative parade to pass down O'Connell Street unencumbered by Nelson's physical or historical presence, and in his absence Dubliners would have to find different coordinates with which to map out their city; by which to orientate themselves. The debate over who should best tower over the capital was reconfigured, as was the gaze the Pillar afforded. For the *Church of Ireland Gazette*, there was little to be gained by arguments on the architectural, sentimental or utilitarian rights and wrongs of the affair: '[t]he Pillar has gone and nothing will bring it back'. The *Gazette* argued that a myth as well as a monument had disappeared. This was not the myth of an inclusive Republic, but rather the myth that the government was, 'through its law agents, in possession of the knowledge and ability to put restraint on the forces of disorder that have, from time to time, shown their contempt for the law by acts of violence'.[21] The presence of those who had the means to carry out a major act of sabotage in the capital had been swept, with Nelson's remains, 'under the carpet with a ruthless efficiency'. For the *Gazette*, 'No doubt the broken column would have been too rude a reminder to be allowed to remain'.[22] A half-Nelson, as the *Vancouver Washington Columbian* referred to it,[23] would indeed have held a different meaning.

THOMAS DAVIS

Successive governments had understood the importance of populating the landscape with memorials that underlined the history of the state and reflected party political positions. Monuments to Collins and Griffith, Cúchulainn and the First World War dead had all courted a certain controversy. Lemass was open to the idea of investing in the nation's past, and in 1962 he expressed his interest in a proposal by Donogh O'Malley for the creation of a National Monuments Board. He wrote to Minister for Finance Jim Ryan.

> Because I think we, as the first generation of Irishmen which has power to do something effective about it, have defaulted in our obligation to preserve and, if possible, to restore these relics of our national past, I am very interested in these proposals.
>
> There is a danger that they may be pushed aside in your Department because of pre-occupation with more urgent business, unless you take an interest in them which I urge you to do.[24]

Ryan did not disagree with the sentiment, but warned that 'colossal increases' in some of the Estimates for the coming year, made it difficult to see how they could be met.[25] Nevertheless, the approaching jubilee of the Rising gave an added sense of urgency for the completion of projects such as the Thomas Davis statue, the Garden of Remembrance and the Kilmainham Jail museum, which was being undertaken by voluntary effort.

The construction of the Thomas Davis statue in College Green had been beset with bureaucratic difficulties from the outset. A proposed statue had been approved by Dublin Corporation in 1945, to commemorate the centenary of Davis's death, and instructions had 'been issued for the removal of the air raid shelters from College Green in ample time for the event'.[26] The original plan had been to approach Albert Power to create a sculpture, but his death was followed by a competition that did not elicit suitable alternatives and it was not until 1962 that a maquette from Edward Delaney was approved by the Arts Council.[27] However, on seeing Delaney's plans, the Cabinet held the unanimous view that, while the general design of the memorial was suitable, the model of the statue of Davis himself was quite unsuitable.[28]

Minister for Finance Jim Ryan was charged with the task of informing the sculptor and asking him to produce one or more alternatives, 'showing a more acceptable representation of Davis in the traditional rather than the modernistic style'.[29] More specifically, the problems with the statue proposed by Delaney were that it bore no facial resemblance to Davis, the head was too small, the body and arms too long and the legs too squat.[30] An artistic compromise and political solution were found in the agreement that the sculptor's conception would be freely based on the Hogan statue of Davis in City Hall.[31]

For government ministers, the body of Thomas Davis was not an appropriate site for modernistic expression. And the statue, when it was unveiled, was not generally popular. The *Irish Times*'s 'Irishman's Diary' found it impossible, 'to reconcile oneself to the penguin effect of the lower part of the figure',[32] and the *Donegal People's Press* opined that:

> Davis was an intellectual. His statue does not give any suggestion of that intellectuality. Davis was a man who inspired thousands of Irishmen by his writings. The statue does not represent a man who had sensitivity in his nature.
>
> It is square and solid, heavy in its treatment and, all in all, greatly disappointing.[33]

Indeed, the structure of the Davis statue is visually elaborate while the figure itself lacks emphatic detail, is anonymous and, more significantly, static.

The Office of Public Works reported that the statue of Thomas Davis would be completed by the end of 1965, and it was decided that the erection and unveiling of the work should be held over to form part of the official jubilee commemoration ceremonies.[34] Davis the patriot had remained a less controversial Young Irelander than contemporaries who had lived to be old. His place in College Green opposite Trinity College and the series of lectures run by Radio Éireann under his name clearly linked Davis with the struggle for freedom through education. College Green was also a significant location, as de Valera noted at the statue's unveiling: 'home of the old Parliament for which Grattan, Flood and the Volunteers won independence from the British Parliament until Pitt, by bribery and corruption, got a majority to vote it away'.[35] The delay in building the Davis statue meant that its home was not entirely glorious. The Office of Public Works had expressed concern that altered traffic conditions left the original site less suitable than it had been and, when another site could not be agreed, that the taxi rank should be removed to facilitate the effectiveness of the design.[36] However, the site of the statue in front of Trinity College did allow de Valera to echo Davis's address to his fellow students, 'Gentlemen you have a country', and to hope that

> the statue of Davis would remind students that they were Irish students, that this country was their country,...that the nation was only too happy to have them without any consideration of any differences whatsoever.[37]

This nod to inclusivity was somewhat shaken by the late realisation that no Protestant schools had been asked to participate in the children's choir that sang 'A Nation Once Again' at the end of the unveiling ceremony.[38]

In the final design, the ten foot figure of Davis overlooks a fountain pool by which four bronze figures—Heralds of the four provinces—blow sprays of water through trumpets. Six granite tablets with bronze reliefs surround the pool. Five of these reliefs depict poems written by Thomas Davis. Here, set in stone and bronze is the traditional view of the position of the Young Irelander in Irish history. The series begins with a depiction of 'The Penal Days'. The ballad recalls a time, 'When Ireland hopelessly complained...When godless persecution reigned'. It concludes:

Let all unite
For Ireland's right,
And drown our griefs in freedom's song;
Time shall veil in twilight haze,
The memory of those penal days.[39]

The conflict within Davis's own position was well illustrated in the recasting of his ballad in bronze. Davis had attempted to create a nationhood that masked the socio-political reality in Ireland. In his construction, sectarianism was a division that could be overcome by an appeal to an inclusive Irish identity. The inclusiveness, however, depended on an exclusion of Englishness. It has therefore been suggested that Davis, 'was, in a sense, asking Irish society to stand still, perhaps even to go into reverse, and retreat from modernization and Anglicanism'.[40] However, Davis used the tools of that modern society— literacy, newspapers, industry—to argue for his alternative. The contradictions inherent in the state's position (and indeed in the concept of modernity itself) during the 1966 jubilee were also present in the statue's design. Irishness was presented in a traditional form while the government also attempted to reformulate the country's image as modern. As in the writing of Davis, an appeal to nationhood was used to obscure the structural inequalities in Irish society.

The sequence of bronze reliefs at the foot of the statue was also illustrative of that version of Irish history which underpinned the jubilee celebrations of the Rising. The reliefs move from 'The Penal Days' through 'Tone's Grave', to 'The Burial', which was written to mark the funeral of Rev. P.J. Tyrell who had been indicted with O'Connell in 1843 during the Repeal campaign. The tributes to Davis's balladry are completed with depictions of 'A Nation Once Again' and 'We Shall not Fail', both rallying cries for independence. The final relief imports into the series the history of the Famine, which Davis's death prevented him from committing to verse. Its inclusion reconfigures the others, so that within this context the penal days are referenced, not as a distant memory, but as part of a larger sequence of memories of oppression that explain the continuous struggle for independence ending in the validated state.

In his review of T.P. O'Neill's essay in *Cuimhneachán*—the official souvenir booklet of the commemoration of the Rising—the historian F.X. Martin had noted that although O'Neill criticised the Proclamation of the Republic as an 'over-simplification of Irish history', he was himself guilty of a similar fault. O'Neill 'identifies Thomas Davis's political aim with that of Wolfe Tone', Martin wrote, '[t]his makes flapdoodle of the historical facts. Davis was a high-minded patriot but he was no Republican'.[41] Martin used more academic language to interrogate the Pearse myth the following year and argued that in the Proclamation, Pearse had soronously yet clearly expressed:

> the declaration that the insurgents acting in the names of Tone, Emmet, Davis, Mitchell and O'Donovan Rossa represented the political aspirations of an oppressed Irish people. At the very outset of the Rising, therefore, the pitch was being queered for the historians. The proclamation of the republic was presenting them with an interpretation of the past in order to explain the present.[42]

In his memorial statue, Davis's balladry is also used as an interpretative tool for the past that is present-centred. The alternative use of his well known 'Orange and Green Will Carry the Day', sung to the air of 'The Protestant Boys' would also have been illustrative of Davis's writings. An extension of his work beyond the ballad would have facilitated a Round Tower motif or a shelf of books.

The choice of ballads rather than prose has further significance. Luke Gibbons has contrasted the official memory incorporated in public monuments with those memories of the vanquished, 'which attach themselves to fugitive and endangered cultural forms such as the street ballad'.[43] For Gibbons, the power of the ballad in Ireland suggests an alternative formation of national consciousness that eschews the centralising impulse of European nationalism, now understood in its relation to print culture and, more specifically (through Benedict Anderson[44]), the newspaper. In contrast, Ireland's national identity existed in unstable images and the fractured, fluid power of allegory and the oral tradition. However, in responding to the mechanisms of British imperialism, Irish nationalism was weakened by accepting a unified sense of national consciousness that mimicked (but could never mirror) the centralised European model.[45]

Thomas Davis was part of this process. Along with Charles Gavan Duffy, he recognised the power of street ballads to create significant moments of resistance. Through the *Nation* newspaper, the Young Irelanders sought to harness the street ballad to their aim of creating an Irish nationality. They attempted take the popular ballads and broadsides that have been described as 'a popular commentary from below' and turn them into commentaries of a different nature. In appropriating the ballad into the *Nation*, the Young Irelanders took a mobile form of communication that preceded the newspaper and formalised it as an adjunct to that medium.

This process takes another step in Davis's statue, in which the ballad is further solidified. Rather than being a form that is open and oppositional, it is incorporated into an official public monument. The meaning is conscribed within a teleological sequence that legitimises the new centralised Irish state. It denotes a shift in Irish nationalism from nationhood to statehood. Through this process the ballad is in some ways divested of its power—which rested in its informal status and encoded meaning—by being formalised. The difference in the ballad as song and ballad as official art was well reflected in Radio Éireann's 'exercising of editorial control' regarding the playing of rebel songs during sponsored programmes broadcast as part of the 1966 jubilee commemorations of the Rising.

ROBERT EMMET

All history is a queered pitch. Irish leaders well understood this and some were expert in defining their own legacy. The role of Robert Emmet as head of a 'two hour rebellion' had been given historical gravitas by his quite brilliant speech from the dock. Emmet's unwritten epitaph hung in the air as the great unanswered challenge of Irish history. From the grave, Emmet passed judgement on the partition of the island, an unknown concept during his life. Two statues to Emmet were unveiled as part of the official golden jubilee celebrations of the 1916 Rising: one at Iveagh House, with President Eamon de Valera in attendance, and one in Washington, D.C. (the 'Smithsonian' statue), as the centrepiece of the Irish embassy's commemoration. The latter, sculpted by Jerome Connor, had been presented to the National Gallery of Art in Washington in 1917. It was a replica of this statue that was presented in Dublin in 1966.

The original 'Smithsonian' statue was to be handed over to the National Park Service for public display on Dupont Circle, at Massachusetts Avenue and 24th Street. William Fay, the Irish ambassador in Washington, reported that (apart from a commemorative Mass organised by the Irish American Social Club) the 'only special event of importance connected with the Jubilee celebration which took place in the Washington area was the rededication of the statue of Robert Emmet'.[46] The accompanying ceremony, he wrote,

> was a worthy commemoration of this great event in our history. It would be impossible to think of a more appropriate means of commemorating 1916 than by dedicating a statue to the patriot who inspired the men of 1916—Robert Emmet.

The ambassador continued:

> The statue had, moreover, the great advantage of being aesthetically a fine one, indeed, quite outstanding among the statuary on public display in Washington, and the fact that it was sponsored by the Congress of the United States through the Speaker of the House of Representatives and by the attendance of members of the Cabinet and the Judiciary, showed that this was a truly national tribute to Ireland's independence by the Government and the people of the United States.[47]

A Marino band was present at the rededication ceremony to play 'those melodies of Thomas Moore which [had] particular relevance to Emmet'. In his remarks from the platform, the ambassador emphasised that relations with England were no longer those that had obtained either in Emmet's day or in 1916. This emphasis Fay had thought to be appropriate, due to the fact that misreporting in the American press had tended to exaggerate and over-dramatise the various 'minor incidents of a violent character' that had taken place in Ireland during the jubilee period. Moreover, the Emmet statue had been unveiled within a relatively short time after a statue to Winston Churchill had been erected outside the British embassy further up Massachusetts Avenue ('a gift from the English-speaking Union, but of poor artistic quality'[48]). Fay reported that this had been 'seized upon by journalists to found a completely baseless suggestion' that the Emmet ceremony was 'intended in some way as a counter-blast to Sir Winston'. Fay insisted that those involved with the Emmet statue had been ignorant of the plans for Churchill until a relatively short time before their own dedication.[49]

The statue in Iveagh House was presented to the people of Ireland by a group of US Congressmen on behalf of its owners, Mr and Mrs Francis Kane. A replica had originally been commissioned by the US government in 1922 for this purpose but had not been presented. The discovery, 40 years later, that the statue had indeed been cast prompted Seán Dowling to argue for its inclusion in the commemoration ceremonies in 1966 in a way that would give the American friends of Ireland an official part in the proceedings.[50]

The *Irish Times* reported that at the statue's unveiling de Valera made his first public reference to partition during the official golden jubilee commemoration. In what was described as a quietly spoken, spontaneous reference to Emmet's speech from the dock, the president said that while the patriot's motives had been vindicated in the hearts of the Irish people, and while Ireland's name was well known among the nations of the world, Emmet's epitaph could not be written

> because the Ireland he wished for, the Ireland that Tone wished for, that Lord Edward Fitzgerald wished for, the Ireland in which differences between sections of our people would have been forgotten—that day has not yet arrived.

He continued:

> And it is only when that day has arrived that anyone can truly write the epitaph of Emmet. We all hope that day will come soon. We know that in a democratically elected government the great majority of the Irish people hold safe in their hands the trustees of our nationhood and that with prudence and patience and time all those sections that Tone wished to unite in a united Ireland will come together and that it will achieve the august destiny which the men who wrote the Proclamation of 1916 predicted for it.[51]

The failure to end partition was much easier to concede than other failures within the Republic. Disappointment was cushioned in an optimism that the trustees of nationhood would in time, with patience and prudence, secure that which was Ireland's destiny. The nation might stumble but it would prevail. But the ghosts of dead martyrs could chastise as well as inspire. Reverend O'Dea's address to Muintir na Tíre (which was widely reported), argued that Pearse did not die so that Ireland could dispossess her own and force emigration on those rural communities that 'had weathered the Famine but not the Freedom'.[52] He indicted the nation with the view that Emmet's epitaph was closer to being written in 1916 than it was in 1966. O'Dea subverted the idea of the nation progressing through time, a notion that is central to nationalist thinking.

The epitaph was also part of that sense of movement towards a complete future that underpinned the psyche of the still-young and 'incomplete' state. Marianne Elliott has pointed out that the building of a memorial to Emmet had become firmly associated with the writing of his epitaph.[53] The fact that the martyr's burial place was unknown meant that, 'The island [was] his monument / Of him the hills [were] eloquent',[54] giving an even greater sense of connection between Emmet's uninscribed tomb and the history of the nation. The use of an existing statue that had been sculpted in a time innocent of the reality of partition navigated this problem. The work had not been commissioned by the state—which would have been tantamount to admitting the national struggle was at an end—but was a gift and gesture of brotherhood from the United States. The statue in Washington bore the following inscriptions:

> I wished to procure for my country the guarantee which
>   Washington procured for America…,
> I have parted from everything that was dear to me in this
>   life for my country's cause…
> When my country takes her place among the nations of the
>   earth, then, and not till then let my epitaph be written.

In this way, any suggestion that a final statement on the life and death of Robert Emmet had been written underneath his image was denied by his own injunction.

Ambassador Fay had not immediately arrived at the idea that Emmet represented the most fitting memorial to the 1916 dead. In the year before the jubilee he had suggested an exhibition of Early Irish Art in the National Gallery in Washington to mark the occasion, and that a more permanent commemoration for Ireland's 'national independence day' should take the form of the re-establishment of the Ministry for Arts.[55] However, Emmet was not unfitting, given his influence over Romantic nationalism and the template he set for the actions of Pádraig Pearse, and also because of that sense of forward motion that his legend lent to the national story. The appeal of Connor's statue was that it too appeared to be in motion. Fay had considered whether or not it would be in better taste to leave the plinth of the Emmet statue in Washington without an inscription beyond the patriot's name, but he concluded that as the speech from the dock had been the principal statement on the man's character and motives, some extracts from that speech would be appropriate. Along with the famous last sentence, Fay suggested including on the plinth 'My country was my idol', because, according to Fay, the 'youthful figure exemplified in the statue almost looks as if he were saying this'.[56]

Máirín Allen, in a series of articles on the work of Jerome Connor for the *Capuchin Annual*, spoke of the lightness and fluidity of the bronze Emmet. Noting that the statue was unique in Connor's *oeuvre*, Allen speculated that perhaps there was no moment in Irish history quite like that in which the work was brought forth, indeed that even as he prepared the full-size model for casting, the sculptor could have read of the Kilmainham executions. 'If it were not so simply sculptural in its inner architecture,' Allen wrote, 'this figure might recall the tension, the baroque elegance, of an el Greco saint. There is aristocracy in the nervous, refined head'.[57] Previously, the artist's best work had stressed stability, but with Emmet movement flowed out of the mind and body, 'spontaneously, as it seems, in the speaking gesture of the hands,…appealing beyond the judges to posterity.'[58]

Connor's Emmet had been cloned once before. De Valera had spoken at the unveiling of a replica in San Francisco in 1919. The likeness in the statue was inspired by a combination of Petrie's death mask of the patriot and the face of actor Brandon Tynan. In 1916 the *New York Morning Telegraph* had reported that a young actor would pose for Connor and that, thirteen years previously,

> at the age of 21, Brandon Tynan, who is now appearing in 'The Melody of Youth' at the Fulton Theatre, portrayed the title role of Robert Emmet, a play from his own pen. At the time, the young actor's resemblance to the great Irish patriot was so close as to cause widespread comment.[59]

This, despite the fact that Emmet's actual appearance was almost as unknowable as his final resting place. The statue that had been 'brought forth' at the time of the Rising and had been dedicated by de Valera before the Civil War, was to be unveiled anew in 1966, giving Emmet a dual presence in the Rising commemoration. The patriot whom Pearse said had died 'that his people might live, even as Christ died', was to be reborn in the commemorative act of Easter 1916 and in its commemoration 50 years later. The statue of Emmet the redeemer and prophet represented earlier memories of hope and redemption, and it was this hope that those involved in the official commemoration sought to re-gather in 1966.

THE GARDEN OF REMEMBRANCE

The remaining memorials unveiled during the official 1966 jubilee derived their importance from the way in which they reconfigured the spaces they occupied. The Garden of Remembrance excavated a place for itself in the capital city and the museum at Kilmainham Jail reordered the meaning of the prison. The idea of creating a public park by the Rotunda hospital was first suggested in 1935 by the Dublin Brigade Council of the Old IRA. It was on this site that the Irish Volunteers had been founded in 1913. The sculptor, Oisín Kelly, thought the site ill-advised. He wrote to the Office of Public Works' chief architect, Raymond McGrath, in 1959, 'Parnell Square has already been profaned by buildings which have no consonance whatsoever with the existing Square'.[60] Feeling that the garden would further break up the space, Kelly argued strongly,

> that if we are in earnest that such a Memorial should exist, we must have a site where it does not compete with so many discordant voices. I am not suggesting that we must think big but rather than we must think whole.[61]

McGrath also doubted the desirability of the site for a national monument due to its 'vulgarization' by signboards, mess, snack bars and dance halls.[62]

The space occupied by the Garden of Remembrance demonstrated Ferdinand Leon's description of how the montage of time in the modern city infiltrates the mind of even the most casual visitor,

> [i]f we step from an eighteenth century house into one from the sixteenth century, we tumble down the slope of time…Whosoever sets foot in a city feels caught up in a web of dreams, where the most remote past is linked to the events of today….[63]

Nelson's Pillar had shown that monuments alter landscapes but do not necessarily transcend altered political circumstances. The Thomas Davis statue, with its long gestation, situated a traditional view of Irish history among the taxi-ranks and urban traffic of modern Dublin. The Garden of Remembrance would attempt to place references to ancient Ireland among the snack bars and dance halls and organise the slope of time within and without as a tumbling resistance to the values of the Victorian and Georgian landscape.

At the opening of the Garden of Remembrance on 11 April 1966, as at the unveiling of the Davis statue, de Valera ignored the discordance of the surroundings. He said the site in Parnell Square was in every way suitable due to its proximity to the Rotunda, which had held meetings of the Gaelic League, the IRB and the Irish Parliamentary Party. On the north side of the garden, Coláiste Mhuire held the library in which Tom Clarke and leaders of the IRB had met in September 1914 and come to the 'far-reaching decision that whatever the fortunes of the war might be, there must be an Irish Uprising before it came to an end'.[64]

The architect of the garden, Dáithí Hanley, in his vision in the competition for the design of the garden proposed to create a certain intimacy between the memorial garden and passers-by and to provide a space in which those sitting in the garden should feel both secluded and inspired with respect for the patriot dead.[65] The juxtaposition of symbols from different points of history was an attempt to place them in a sequence that suggested a continued line of Irish heroism from ancient to modern.[66] At the official opening de Valera stated:

> …the whole design of the Garden is symbolic. It represents faith, hope, peace, resurgence and is a challenge to all the generations that come, to make Ireland of their day worthy of the Ireland of the past. All who enter here, or who pass this Garden by, will, I hope, as they murmur a prayer for the departed, pray also that God may preserve this old nation of ours, and have it always in his keeping.[67]

The garden takes the form of a cross—symbolic of the dead—and is surrounded by a raised lawn. It is laid out as a basilica but with a western-facing apse within which an elevated platform accommodates the symbols of state rather than church. The raised area was designed to facilitate the Army Guard of Honour during ceremonies and is flanked by the national flag and those of the four provinces. The garden's reflecting pool is also cruciform and contains a mosaic of six groups of weapons, taken from Ireland's heroic age, which are broken, symbolising peace. The peace motif is further explored in the protective railings of the garden, in the central panel of which the Irish State Harp is inset with an olive branch interlinked with the Balllinderry Sword, pointing downwards. A limestone column at the eastern entrance of the garden is decorated with a broken chain, symbolising release from bondage. As a memorial, the garden it is not appended onto the landscape in the form of a cenotaph or obelisk but has been sunk into it. The choice of symbols suggests an archeological integrity for the site, as it unearths beneath Georgian Dublin artefacts of a more ancient Ireland.

In designing the sculptural centrepiece of the garden, Oisín Kelly saw the architecture as the setting for a sculpture that would give the garden its meaning and enable it to function spiritually as well as physically: 'I cannot overemphasize that the sculpture is not an ornament...as something added to increase the beauty of an object...In this case the sculpture signifies the purpose, the serious and unique purpose of this garden...'.[68] Given the weight of the project and the pressure of other commitments, Kelly had taken some time to produce his report on the central feature, which, he admitted on submission, 'has been hanging over me so long I shall almost miss it'.[69] His anxiety came from the desire to create a new nationalist iconography, which, he felt, would require a poet, 'and I have not the grace for poetry'.[70] The lack of an indigenous cultural language was evidenced in existing memorials, which were 'a conglomeration of foreign elements, Irish in nomenclature and detail but alien in spirit'. For the sculptor, the only exception was Cúchulainn at the GPO, which was too small in scale for its position but in which the theme was 'universal, simple, and part of the popular imagination'.[71]

Kelly's research for the garden centrepiece had consisted of reading poetry and Irish mythology and resulted in his choice of the transformation of the Children of Lir into swans, illustrating the line from that fable: 'Once we were men, now we are epochs'. He suggested that the theme was of enough grandeur to illustrate the function of the park and that it was, 'both national and universal, and would be easily comprehensible while being of a nature to permit the use of modern idioms, as this sculpture must be contemporary as there is no alternative'.[72]

Kelly's idea for the sculpture had replaced the original plan of the architect for a representation of Éire and the four provinces. The more challenging design was disliked by Tánaiste Seán MacEntee for its pagan subject matter. Lemass had asked the tánaiste to interest himself in the design, 'with a view to getting more rapid progress' in the matter,[73] so that the memorial would be completed for the jubilee. In November 1963 the taoiseach considered that it was now better to leave the settlement of the design entirely to the Office of Public Works, with the understanding that the government would have the opportunity to approve any proposals.[74] The Children of Lir design was officially rejected in 1964 and it was not until Jim Gibbons, as the new parliamentary secretary to the minister for finance, suggested to Lemass that the Arts Council be consulted on the design that the life of the sculpture was revived the following year.[75]

The Arts Council unanimously endorsed Kelly's design, arguing that 'it promises to be one of the masterpieces of Irish sculpture in this century and that its non-acceptance would be a national catastrophe'.[76] The report from the Arts Council continued:

> No representational image, however much it might initially win facile acceptance, could hope to have such a lasting effect on our people's deepest and finest instincts. With sureness of vision Oisín Kelly has realised that the longest series of sacrifices that have gone to the making of a free Ireland, could only be adequately expressed sculpturally through some great 'myth'. History cannot be carved; the thousands of mouldering long-forgotten historical statues in every land give sad proof of the fact.
>
> For the Garden of Remembrance Oisín Kelly's theme of utter transformation is superbly appropriate. It makes use of a true not a bogus romanticism that befits the type of men and the quality of people who are being remembered. Superbly appropriate also is that this should be so brilliantly done through the use of one of the country's greatest stories which is at once unmistakably Irish and of course almost blatantly Christian.[77]

The government accepted the recommendation and issued a press statement, which acknowledged the advice of the Arts Council and the recommendation that the theme was at once national and universal and made use of a true Romanticism. Reference to bogus romanticism was quietly dropped. The statement also addressed the relevance of the sculptural figures, swans being the 'generally-accepted image of resurgence, triumph and perfection, with undertones of regal sadness and isolation'.[78]

The sculpture did in some sense both clarify and elaborate the meaning of its surroundings. Within the highly structured space it also offered a moment of movement and iconographic imagination. Kelly's design looked to an ancient legend from Ulster for its symbolic reference, in keeping with the gestures to history in the surrounding architecture. The garden and reflecting pool were designed in the shape of a cross: symbol not just of the dead, but of transformation from life to death to eternal life. This cycle of metamorphosis was central to the sculpture. Kelly's influence—'Once we were men, now we are epochs'—revealed those to whom the garden was dedicated as part of a great moment in history and also in that moment made great. The mythical nature of the subject matter of the sculpture underlined the grandeur of the heroic sacrifice. The fusion of the understanding of legend and myth underlined the timelessness of both the symbolic and actual Irish nation.

However, the sculpture of the Children of Lir also shifted the meaning of the garden, which had had a sense of resolution within its symbolism. The *Connaught Sentinel,* in assessing the plans for a shrine, 'apparently, in memory of all who died for Ireland from 1169 to 1921', recognised a general acceptance for the Children of Lir as the centrepiece, 'which would probably be the best and safest symbolism in the circumstances'.[79] Noting that the country had become quite sensitive about these matters, the *Sentinel* concluded, 'There appears to be no objection to memorials to those who died for Ireland provided they are not presented as representing finality or the consummation of the age-old ideal'.[80]

The Children of Lir, which McGrath had argued 'are a symbol of the long Irish struggle for freedom', were depicted in Kelly's statue at the point of transition from children to swans, not from swans to adults.[81] The swans stretch skyward reaching towards a utopian future; but there is a tension as the eye is pulled earthward towards the crouching human figures. Kelly does not depict the end of the legend but the middle. He sculpts the transitory moment between the 'childhood' of the nation made infantile by the imperial gaze and before the 'adulthood' of full independence. A recognition of this restraint was contained within the government press statement, which had juxtaposed the imagery of swans as resurgent, triumphant and perfect with undertones of regal sadness and isolation.

The *Kerryman,* commenting on the delay in approving the statue, remarked that official thinking appeared to be that, 'after three hundred years on the waters of the Moy, three hundred years on Lough Foyle, and three hundred years somewhere else, the swans won't mind waiting another three hundred years or so in the Office of the Board of Works'.[82] The span of the period during which the children were swans also suggested itself as a fitting analogy for the long years of Irish history that followed its 'golden age'. The statue was not unveiled until July

1971, on the fiftieth anniversary of the Anglo-Irish truce but against the background of the conflict in the North. The theme of Irish freedom as an ongoing project became, therefore, much more explicitly political. At the eventual unveiling of the sculpture, Jack Lynch, as taoiseach, made a call to the British government to declare its interest in the unity of Ireland. He returned to the theme three years later when in opposition. In a Dáil debate he had tabled on events in Northern Ireland following the breakdown of the Sunningdale Executive, Lynch accused Taoiseach Liam Cosgrave of having lost focus on Irish unity and concluded with the words of the poet John Hewitt:

> This is our fate: eight hundred years' disaster,
> Crazily tangled as the Book of Kells,
> The dream's distortion and the land's division,
> The midnight raiders and the prison cells.
> Yet like Lir's children banished to the waters
> Our hearts still listen for the landward bells.[83]

The statue of the Children of Lir in the Garden of Remembrance managed to convey an extreme sense of both hope and sorrow. Kelly produced a challenge to existing nationalist iconography but did not succeed in replacing it. The imagery of this statue, unlike Cúchulainn, did not have Pearse's imprimatur and lacked the instant gratification of a dead body cast in bronze. However, McGrath wrote, while arguing the case for the statue against MacEntee's objections:

> [w]hat the sculptor has done, and this particular sculptor is as much a poet as a sculptor, is simply to use the idea of metamorphosis as a theme for a feature with the universal significance—'once we were men, now we are epochs'. I think even a simple person is as likely to grasp this imagery as he is that of Heaven and Hell, unless he gets befogged in the details of the Lir legend'.[84]

Kilmainham Jail

The idea of restoring the jail at Kilmainham as a historical museum was the initiative of the engineer Lorcan Leonard. His interest in the site became urgent on learning that the Office of Public Works intended to invite tenders for the demolition of the prison. Leonard was also frustrated by the limits of Irish imagery and saw plans to level Kilmainham Jail as

> the last act of the philistines who had already provided a rash of 'Mother Eire's [sic] and celtic crosses from one end of the country to the other to prove, I suppose, the respectable and Catholic character of the 'four glorious' years.[85]

In 1958 Leonard decided, along with Paddy Stephenson,[86] to call a meeting of people who might be interested and, 'who by their "records" would add weight'[87] to the eventual petition to the government. There followed the circulation of information to men, known to the organisers as at one time or another having been closely identified with the Republican movement, in order to expand the base of volunteers.[88] The committee therefore comprised of representatives of the Old IRA Literary and Debating Society, the Old Dublin Society, the Old Citizen Army and the Old Fianna. In February 1960 the government approved a scheme which would lease the property to the Kilmainham Jail Restoration Committee for five years at a nominal rent of 1d a year. If the committee's restoration operation failed, the jail would revert to being the property of the Commissioners for Public Works.[89] It was at the inaugural meeting of the newly empowered committee that Brendan Behan proposed to put 'the split' at the top of the agenda.

It was Leonard's intention to 'elevate that weed-grown, debris-strewn yard...to the most holy spot in Ireland'.[90] The task was difficult as years of neglect had left the prison in a state of dangerous disrepair. The Restoration Committee cleared the idea of voluntary recruitment with the trades unions, and over 200 volunteers began the process of reclamation. Restoration sub-committees were set up in London, Cork and New York and industrialists and businessmen were asked to donate the price of restoring one cell each at 100 guineas.[91]

The money-raising efforts were more difficult than expected. The committee in London, which was made up of members of various Irish organisations in Britain, gained publicity from the donation of £2.2.0 to their fund from the Irish ambassador in London, Hugh McCann. They received £10 donations from the GAA, the Anti-Partition League of Ireland and the Irish Club London and £20 from the Gresham Ballroom, Highgate; but fundraising events were poorly attended. McCann reported that, '[a]lthough I set a headline by making a personal contribution to the fund—which was mentioned in the press…the appeal for the fund met with very limited success in London'.[92] Nevertheless, the extensive programme of volunteering and fundraising in Ireland progressed sufficiently to allow for the opening of the museum within the jail to be incorporated in the jubilee commemoration of the Rising in 1966.

In an editorial for the *Dublin Historical Record*, Paddy Stephenson had said of Kilmainham:

> Grey, gaunt, old and sadly battered it stands like a fortress on the south west approach to the City, symbolic of the power that erected it, as if still defending the usurpers in their wrongful possessions and resisting the attempts of the rightful owners outside to make violent incursion to regain their heritage…It still stands, but broken and showing the marks as of a defeated warrior with cloven head gaping to the sky. But these marks of defeat were not gained in heroic combat, to our shame, they are marks of indifference and neglect… Neglect of this generation to acknowledge the debt it owes to those who agonised within its grey walls for our sake.[93]

Kilmainham Jail, like the GPO, had come to be seen as an almost living participant in the history of Ireland. It had been built in 1796, as an extension of the existing jail, on the gallows hill and was finally closed to inmates in 1924. The opening of the new jail at the end of the eighteenth century had coincided with the emergence of the United Irishmnen, and throughout its history Kilmainham had been home to a majority of the leaders of the Irish nationalist cause. The jail had been dubbed the 'Irish Bastille' by Charles Teeling, a contemporary of the 1798 rebellion and a Kilmainham inmate. The term did more than link Irish Republicanism with the ideals of the French Revolution. It encapsulated an understanding of the building as representing both oppression and liberty. It was this combined meaning that gave the building such significance. In a historical booklet issued to raise funds for the restoration project it was noted that the 'fabric itself is a museum piece, a document in stone illustrating the social conscience of the eighteenth and nineteenth centuries'.[94]

Kilmainham Jail had come to represent the continued presence of its occupants. 'If ghosts can walk again the stones of Kilmainham must re-echo to the footsteps of the countless dead who suffered here for Ireland', the Restoration Society suggested.[95] These ghosts were not simply those of renown who were documented in official histories or who were present in the known nationalist narrative. The society noted the absence of historians to chronicle the struggle of Irish people in the first half of the nineteenth century, 'the silence of poets to sing their praise'. But the dungeons of Kilmainham had not been 'untenanted in those dark and evil days'.[96] Moreover the Invincibles, whose memory in particular Leonard had wanted to perpetuate and who, it was felt, had often been omitted from the nation's story, had been held in Kilmainham: Tim Kelly sang songs throughout the night before his execution, ending with 'The Memory of the Past' before he 'lay down to sleep for the last time'.[97] For those who restored it, the power of Kilmainham as a memorial lay in its relationship with the inmates. The building as witness, the Restoration Committee felt, would not be influenced by the ebb and flow of historical fashion.

However, the early meetings on restoration had been assured that 'in order to preserve unity of purpose nothing relating to the events after 1921 would be introduced into any activity, publicity or statements in connection with Kilmainham'.[98] The attempt to limit possible divisions by jettisoning the Civil War demarcated the jail as a less contested site in Irish history and underlined its place of importance in the struggle against British authority. The narrative arc incorporated in Kilmainham appeared to reach its end at the opening of the museum when the former prisoner, Eamon de Valera, returned as president of Ireland. 'I am not strange to this place', he told those assembled, 'I have been here before, but it was not as bright then as it is now...'.[99] But the story of Kilmainham was much more complicated than this. De Valera had indeed been there before; the last time in 1924, imprisoned by his former comrades.

Kilmainham Jail, like Nelson, was depicted as an all-seeing, all-hearing witness to Irish life. The East Wing of the prison had been built in 1861 and, although an imperfect panoptican, had been designed in the spirit of that disciplinary gaze. The restoration of the prison, therefore, reclaimed it from its imperial associations and reconstituted it as an integral part of the nationalist narrative. The privileging of this story meant that in fact the jail would be used as a selective witness. The stories of non-political prisoners would not be incorporated into the history of Kilmainham until several years into the life of the museum. Rather, the lives of those prisoners who had resisted the reforming mechanism of the prison, designed to control minds as well as bodies, conformed to an alternative order of things. The panoptical prison system operated differently from that older system of punishment in which public flogging or execution was intended to offer an example and deterrent to the rest of society. The nineteenth-century penal system was concerned with the impact of the punishment on the individual. The restoration of Kilmainham returned the suffering of the prisoners to the public's gaze and the prisoners' lives, displayed as spectacle, were intended as a moral reminder of the brutality of the British system and the virtue of the Irish struggle for independence.

CONCLUSION

The memorials unveiled during the official commemoration of 1966 did not encapsulate in a single figure the revolutionary action of the 1916 Easter Rising. However, through the ritual of their unveiling these memorials were interpreted as different parts of the same struggle: a struggle that was given legitimacy by subsequent events and which gave legitimacy to Pearse's understanding of his place in history as set out in the Proclamation. Through his speeches at the memorial sites, de Valera offered them as compasses by which the landscape of the city could be navigated in its relation to the journey towards freedom.

The commemoration in 1966 had two competing realities at its heart: the achievement of independence and the failures of freedom. The former was nominally celebrated in monuments around the capital city. Fifty years after the event, the Rising straddled the generations of those for whom it was a lived experience and those for whom it was part of the normative culture. Those who had been rebels in 1916 now had the power to formalise their memory in symbol and narrative, and ultimately to oversee the casting of the collected memory of the nation in monument. Pierre Nora's view of collective memory sheds light on the process at work: 'The less memory is experienced from inside the more it exists through its exterior scaffolding and outward signs'.[100] Or, as Young has clarified, 'once we assign monumental form to our memory, we have to some degree divested ourselves of the obligation to remember. In shouldering the memory work, monuments may relieve viewers of their memory burden'.[101] Thus, in requesting that the relics of the national past be restored, Lemass was in some sense delegating to the monuments the responsibility for remembering. In having achieved almost 50 years of unbroken statehood in the Republic, and having marked this moment with statues, the Irish nation in that jurisdiction was being released from the burden of having to remember its own history. Indeed, it is possible to argue that the commemorative moment of 1966 was part of a longer process of forgetting, leading to the silence which surrounded the 75th anniversary of the Rising in 1991.

However, there was a compelling pull from that other reality in 1966. The failures of freedom were in abundant evidence: partition, the status of the Irish language and emigration. A sense of the nation's lack of completion was present in the sculpture of the Children of Lir, in the inability of the Kilmainham museum to deal with the Civil War and in Emmet, who was memorialised but not epitaphed. So it was in the absences (of Pillar, epitaph and aged Children of Lir) that the commemoration was defined. And it was the anti-monument (which most clearly symbolised the hybrid state of free and unfree) that provided the iconic moment of the golden jubilee.

NOTES

[1] Office of Public Works, (hereafter cited as OPW), A/96/6/9/1, (17), (24), 'Garden of Remembrance', Oisín Kelly to Raymond McGrath, 13 March 1958 and 23 January 1959. *Bearna Baogail* translates as the 'violent gap' or 'gap of danger'.

[2] *Irish Times*, 22 January 1964.

[3] *Sunday Press*, 21 May 1961.

[4] Quoted in the *Evening Herald*, 17 January 1961.

[5] National Archives of Ireland, Department of the Taoiseach (hereafter cited as NAI DT), 97/6/18, 9 March 1966.

[6] In fact, a Dáil statement noted that claims for compensation for the first explosion amounted to £18,924 and claims after the second explosion reached a value of £4,180. *Irish Independent*, 8 March 1967.

[7] NAI, Department of External Affairs (hereafter cited as NAI DEA), 2000/14/72, Smith McGrath, District Sales Manager, Irish International Airlines, Toronto, to John Belton, 14 March 1966.

[8] *Congressional Record: proceedings of 89th Congress, second session*, 8 March 1966; NAI DEA, Embassy releases 2003, 2001/37/781, P 153 II.

[9] NAI DEA, Embassy releases 2003, 2001/37/781, P 153 II, P. de Paor, Irish Embassy, Washington, to B. Uas. O Ceallaigh, Irish Consul General, Chicago, 4 April 1966. However, Sweeney, in his speech, was advocating political action not violence.

[10] G.B. Shaw, *John Bull's Other Island* (London, 1964), 19.

[11] A.J. Lerner, 'The nineteenth-century monument and the embodiment of national time', in Marjorie Ringrose and A.J. Lerner (eds), *Reimagining the nation* (Buckingham, 1993), 176–96: 180.

[12] Lerner, 'The nineteenth-century monument', 177–81.

[13] Quoted in *Evening Herald*, 11 April 1966.

[14] *Evening Herald*, 11 April 1966.

[15] *Irish Catholic*, 10 February 1966.

[16] *Irish Catholic*, 10 February, 1966.

[17] J.E. Young, *The texture of memory: Holocaust memorials and meanings* (London and New Haven, 1993), 7.

[18] Katherine Verdery, *The political lives of dead bodies: reburial and postsocialist change* (New York, 1999), 5.

[19] Verdery, *Political lives of dead bodies*, 6.

[20] NAI, Office of the Secretary to the President, 97/7/81, [undated], essay by Clara Connelly, F.C.J. Convent, Bunclody, Co. Wexford, joint runner-up in the under-18 essay competition in English, '1916–2016'.

[21] *Church of Ireland Gazette*, 18 March 1966.

[22] *Church of Ireland Gazette*, 18 March 1966.

[23] *Vancouver Washington Columbian*, 7 April 1966.

[24] NAI DT, S5004E/62, Lemass to Ryan, 21 December 1962.

[25] NAI DT, S5004E/62, Ryan to Lemass, 31 December 1962.

[26] OPW, A99/3/5 (2), 'Thomas Davis statue', Corporation of Dublin to the Department of Defence, 26 July 1945.

[27] OPW, A99/3/5 (220), 'Davis', Arts Council to the Office of Public Works, 9 May 1962.

[28] NAI DT, S13610D/62, Cabinet Minute, 23 November 1962.

[29] NAI DT, S13610D/62, Cabinet Minute, 27 November 1962.

[30] NAI DT, S13610D/63, Cabinet Minute, 19 February 1963.

[31] NAI DT, S13610D/63, Cabinet Minute, 17 April, 1963.

[32] *Irish Times*, 10 December 1966.

[33] *Donegal People's Press*, 29 April 1966.

[34] NAI DT, 97/6/158, Minutes of the third meeting of the Commemoration Committee, 30 April 1965.

[35] Department of External Affairs (DEA), *Cuimhneachán 1916–1966, Commemoration: a record of Ireland's commemoration of the 1916 Rising* (Dublin, 1966), 62.

[36] OPW, A99/3/5 (153), 'Davis', Supplementary notes for Parliamentary Questions, 14 November 1960; OPW, A99/3/5, (220), From the Arts Council to the Office of Public Works, 9 May 1962.

[37] DEA, *Cuimhneachán*, 62.

[38] OPW, A99/3/33 (63), 'Davis', Memorandum for the chairman of the Office of Public Works, 16 April 1966.

[39] Thomas Davis, *National and historical ballads, songs, and poems* (Dublin, 1869), 147.

40 D.G. Boyce, *Nationalism in Ireland* (London, 1991), 164.
41 *RTV Guide*, 16 December 1966.
42 F.X. Martin, '1916—Myth, fact and mystery', *Studia Hibernia* 7 (1967), 7–124: 9.
43 Luke Gibbons, *Transformations in Irish culture* (Cork, 1996), 145.
44 Anderson's seminal work illustrated ways in which the newspaper incorporated senses of time, space and ritual, which were central to the imagined unity that underlies the nation. See Benedict Anderson, *Imagined communities: reflections on the origins and spread of nationalism* (London, 1983).
45 Gibbons, *Transformations*, 139.
46 NAI DEA, 2000/14/83, William Fay to Department of External Affairs, 23 June 1966.
47 NAI DEA, 2000/14/83, Fay to Department of External Affairs, 23 June 1966.
48 NAI DEA, 2000/14/83, Fay to Department of External Affairs, 23 June 1966.
49 NAI DEA, 2000/14/83, Fay to Department of External Affairs, 23 June 1966.
50 NAI DT, 96/9/96, Seán Dowling to Piaras MacLochlainn, 27 October 1965. Seán Dowling was an Old IRA man who became chairman of the Restoration Committee of Kilmainham Jail and was one of the original members of the government's Commemoration Committee for the fiftieth anniversary of the Easter Rising.
51 *Irish Times*, 14 April 1966.
52 *Irish Catholic*, 10 February, 1966.
53 Marianne Elliott, *Robert Emmet: the making of a legend* (London, 2004), 212.
54 Elliott, *Robert Emmet*, 168.
55 NAI DEA, 2000/14/97, Fay to Department of External Affairs, 9 November 1965; NAI DEA, 2000/14/98, Fay to Department of External Affairs, 19 January 1965.
56 NAI DT, 96/6/96, Fay to the Department of External Affairs, 20 January 1966.
57 Máirín Allen, 'Jerome Connor—Two', *Capuchin Annual* 1964, 353–69: 364.
58 Allen, 'Jerome Connor—Two', 364.
59 *New York Morning Telegraph*, 6 March 1916.
60 OPW, A/96/6/9/1 (29), 'Garden', Report of Oisín Kelly to the Office of Public Works,12 May 1959.
61 OPW, A/96/6/9/1 (29), 'Garden', Report of Oisín Kelly, 12 May 1959.
62 OPW, A/96/6/9/1 (34), 'Garden', Memo from McGrath regarding Kelly's report, 26 May 1959.
63 Luke Gibbons, 'Where Wolfe Tone's statue was not', in Ian McBride (ed.), *History and Memory in Modern Ireland* (Cambridge, 2001), 139–59: 141.
64 University College Dublin Archives (herafter cited as UCDA), de Valera Papers, P150/3376, Copy of de Valera's speech [undated].
65 OPW, A/96/6/9/1 (2), 'Garden', Report accompanying Hanley's original proposal for the architectural competition [undated].
66 Síghle Breathnach-Lynch, 'Commemorating the hero in newly independent Ireland: expressions of nationhood in bronze and stone', in L.W. McBride

(ed.), *Images, icons and the nationalist imagination* (Dublin, 1999), 148–205:158–63.

[67] UCDA, de Valera Papers, P150/3376, Copy of de Valera's speech, [undated].

[68] OPW, A/96/6/9/1 (29), 'Garden', Report from Kelly, 12 May 1959.

[69] OPW, A/96/6/9/1 (28), Kelly to McGrath, 12 May 1959.

[70] OPW, A/96/6/9/1 (24), 'Garden', Kelly to McGrath, 23 January 1959.

[71] OPW, A/96/6/9/1 (30), 'Garden', Report from Kelly, 12 May 1959.

[72] OPW, A/96/6/9/1 (30), 'Garden', Report from Kelly, 12 May 1959.

[73] OPW, A/96/6/9/1 (152), 'Garden', Lemass to MacEntee, 21 November 1963.

[74] OPW, A/96/6/9/1 (152), 'Garden', Lemass to MacEntee, 21 November 1963.

[75] OPW, A/96/6/9/1 (312), 'Garden', Gibbons to Lemass, 14 July 1965.

[76] NAI DT, 96/6/193, Report for the Office of Public Works, 1 November 1965

[77] NAI DT, 96/6/193, Report, 1 November 1965.

[78] NAI DT, 96/6/193, Statement issued by the Government Information Service on behalf of the parliamentary secretary to the minister for finance, 26 February 1966.

[79] *Connaught Sentinel,* 16 April 1962.

[80] *Connaught Sentinel,* 16 April 1962.

[81] OPW, A/96/6/9/1 (52), 'Garden', Memo by McGrath, 18 October 1960.

[82] *Kerryman,* 8 February 1964.

[83] *Dáil Debates,* vol. 273, 26 June 1974.

[84] OPW, A/96/6/9/1 (319), 'Garden', Memo from McGrath, 23 September 1965.

[85] Kilmainham Jail Archive (hereafter cited as KJA), L.C.G. Leonard, *The Kilmainham project as I dreamt and lived it,* unpublished manuscript, undated, 2.

[86] Paddy Stephenson was a veteran of the Easter Rising and founder of the Old Dublin Society.

[87] KJA, Leonard, *Kilmainham project,* 3.

[88] KJA, Leonard, *Kilmainham project,* 3.

[89] NAI DT, S6521D/63, Memorandum for the government from the minister for finance, 13 February 1960.

[90] KJA, Leonard to Seán Dowling, 9 June 1958.

[91] *Irish Times,* 30 November 1960.

[92] NAI DEA, London Embassy, F100/11/8, McCann to Department of External Affairs, 5 December 1961.

[93] *Dublin Historical Record,* July 1957.

[94] Kilmainham Jail Restoration Society, *Kilmainham* (Dublin, 1961), 19.

[95] Kilmainham Jail Restoration Society, *Kilmainham,* 3.

[96] Kilmainham Jail Restoration Society, *Kilmainham,* 8.

[97] Kilmainham Jail Restoration Society, *Kilmainham,* 12.

[98] KJA, Leonard, *Kilmainham project,* 4.

[99] *Irish Press,* 11 April 1966.

[100] Pierre Nora, 'Between memory and history: *les lieux de mémoire*', *Representations* 26 (Spring 1989), 7–25, 13.

[101] Young, *Texture of memory,* 5.

9. STAGING 1916 IN 1966: PASTICHE, PARODY AND PROBLEMS OF REPRESENTATION

By Anthony Roche

INTRODUCTION

The decision to commemorate the fiftieth anniversary of the 1916 Rising by staging a pageant in Croke Park in 1966 was fraught with representational problems, in both theatrical and political terms. Tomás MacAnna of the Abbey theatre approached the Department of Defence and the Fianna Fáil government to suggest the pageant and supplied both script and direction. The minutes of the time are concerned mainly with the logistics of the operation: how many costumes will be required, whether certain actors will be available, etc. The intent is clearly stated:

> The pageant would re-enact the events of Easter Week 1916, taking as its inspiration, and format, the actual Declaration of Independence.[1]

But every enactment of an historic event is a re-enactment, not only of the originary moment from the past, but of how that event has been represented since. In the case of Easter 1916, the key theatrical representation—ten years after the event—had been the staging of Seán O'Casey's *The Plough and the Stars* at the Abbey theatre. The controversy it occasioned, particularly with the widows of the executed Rising leaders and the formidable silent figure of Mrs Margaret Pearse, mother of Pádraig and Willy, has itself become a focus of representation. During its centenary year in 2004, for example, the Abbey staged (at the Peacock) Colm Tóibín's *Beauty in a Broken Place*, which dramatised the staging of O'Casey's play in 1926 and the rows it occasioned.[2] Any positive celebration of the 1916 Rising, as a commemorative pageant would be, had to take account of the negative portrayal of the same event in O'Casey. I intend to examine how the script for the 1966 commemorative pageant situates and references not only this key drama of O'Casey's, but also the poetry of W.B. Yeats, whose 'Easter 1916' was a much more immediate, but no less canonical, articulation of the event. I will also consider two other relevant theatrical texts, Denis Johnston's *The Old Lady Says 'No'!* of 1929, in which Micheál MacLiammóir as Robert Emmet was transported to a post-revolutionary modernising Dublin of the 1920s; and two plays of the 1960s by the then emerging playwright from Northern Ireland, Brian Friel: *The Loves of Cass McGuire* (1966) and *The Mundy Scheme* (1969).

USE OF PAGEANT FOR COMMEMORATION

The theatrical mode of the pageant was, at one level, a singularly appropriate form in which to commemorate 1916. For that event was itself constructed along theatrical lines, with great attention to costuming, staging, etc., and with Pearse's primary role in promoting the rebellion being that of scriptwriter rather than active participant. As Ben Levitas puts it, the Easter Rising was itself 'staged as [a] production' and could be read as 'part mystery play, part melodrama, part avant-garde provocation'.[3] This critical approach to analysing the Rising has given increasing attention to the staging of theatrical pageants to a political end at Pearse's school, St Enda's. Pageants have a much greater provenance in Ireland than they do in England, where the Lord Chamberlain had always kept a tight censorial role on theatre scripts and, in collusion with the managers of the big theatres, saw that they were restricted to metropolitan, seated, roofed venues. And there had been a proscription in England on the staging of scenes from the Bible since the early Reformation. As Joan Fitzpatrick Dean puts it in contrasting the theatrical cultures of the two countries,

> the dramatization of biblical episodes and the representation
> of Christ were taboo in England but commonplace in

Ireland in religious dramas, mystery plays and nativity pageants.[4]

In the section of his autobiography on the staging of the 1966 pageant, Tomás MacAnna relates that, in addition to teaching drama at Coláiste Mhuire in Dublin,

> éiríomar Dráma Páise chomh maith, agus níor staonamar ó chrocadh Chríost a thaispeáint go h-oscailte ar an stáitse, radharc a bhain preab as an lucht éisteachta. ('we produced a Passion Play as well, and we didn't hold back from showing the crucifixion of Christ openly on the stage, a sight that gave the audience a hop'.)[5]

In Easter Week 1911 the boys of St Enda's and the girls of St Ita's had appeared in a Passion Play, written by Pádraig Pearse with his brother Willie appearing as Pontius Pilate, and staged at the Abbey theatre. As Ruth Dudley Edwards notes in her biography, 'although there were some who found the whole idea improper, especially on a public stage, it was a resounding success'.[6] Although describing the play as a 'straightforward adaptation [by Pearse] of the dialogue of the Gospels to an Irish social ethos', Edwards fails sufficiently to note that the latter is achieved primarily through Pearse's decision to write the play in Irish while leaving the setting and characters unchanged.[7] The issue is one of translation: of an Irish audience receiving the message of Christ in their own idiom; but the implicit corollary is the translation of this Christian exemplar into their own lives and practices.

The pageants staged at St Enda's more frequently sought this end through the staging of narratives drawn from the Irish legendary past, from pagan sources rather than from the central Christian narrative. *The Coming of the Fionn* by Standish O'Grady and Douglas Hyde was presented in the school gymnasium at St Enda's in March 1909, making it, in Mary Trotter's words, 'its first production of nationalist dramas for the public'.[8] Later in the same year, St Enda's staged a pageant written by Pearse himself, *The Boy Deeds of Cúchulainn*. The boys appearing in this pageant were outfitted as young Fenian warriors and equipped with spears and shields; the aim, as Pearse himself proudly admitted, was one of emulation:

> to send our boys home with the knightly image of Cuchulainn in their hearts and his knightly words ringing in their ears.[9]

What Pearse was working towards was not only a heightened militarism in his pedagogic practice, which would eventuate in rifles being handed out as school prizes, but a paradoxical fusion of the pagan warrior Cúchulainn with the crucified Christ. Yeats could manage the first aim, presenting the heroic example of an ancient idealism for a degraded modern age. But he could not do so in a way that connected with the Catholicism of the majority of the population; his Protestantism got in the way. Yeats's Cúchulainn in the poems and plays is represented as a misunderstood figure, one who is progressively isolated from the surrounding political milieu.

I will return to Yeats a little later. I first wish to highlight one aspect of Pearse's staging of pageants in relation to the 1966 event, upon which I have already touched. This has to do with the relationship between the staged representation and the surrounding social context. Is the pageant to be received as pure aesthetic spectacle or is it to be seen as a provocation towards political engagement? Both Dudley Edwards and Trotter highlight the occasion on which St Enda's pupils returned to Dublin's Amiens Street station, having presented the Cúchulainn pageant at Castlebellingham. They emerged onto the street and, as one of the pupils remembers it,

> a crowd gathered round, wondering at our strange weapons and our dusty faces. They followed us, and soon they were singing 'Who Fears to Speak of '98?' as they tramped and surged around us. [Thomas] MacDonagh was delighted at the commotion we had raised. 'Egad!' he said, as the crowd swelled to the dimensions of a riot, 'they expect us to lead against the Castle!'[10]

This transfer of the drama from aesthetic spectacle to the larger political arena, a transfer that Pearse was developing dramaturgically, has led recent commentators like Trotter to make a strong connection between the St Enda's pageants, the self-conscious construction of a national identity through a performance of 'Irishness' and the staging of the real-life drama of Easter 1916.

AISÉIRÍ—THE 1966 COMMEMORATIVE PAGEANT

How does this relate to the re-enactment of the Rising in the very changed Ireland of 1966? That modernising Ireland of Seán Lemass and T.K. Whitaker is conspicuous by its omission from the script of *Aiséirí*, as the jubilee pageant came to be titled. The original aim had been to keep the focus tightly on the Rising itself; but as the idea of the pageant developed, MacAnna decided to widen the historic focus. It would begin with the 1798 rebellion as 'the dawn of the Republican idea', proceed through the famines of the nineteenth century, up to 1916.[11] And beyond? His letter to the Department of Defence proposes to end the piece as follows:

> In final tableau, then, we see the Volunteers of 1918–21, the Irish Army and the Republicans—here there would be a moment of tribute to the Civil War dead—the Army of the Emergency, and finally today's Army. The final tableau would be that of the tricolour, right across the arena: green, white and gold.[12]

The script provides for many moments of visual spectacle in which disparate colours come together to represent the tricolour. The colour symbolism in relation to orange is inherently problematic—not in the early 1798 scenes, when it introduces Henry Joy McCracken and the United Irishmen of the north. But in the scenes covering 1912 and 1913 the orange of the tricolour serves to bring on the Ulster Volunteers, Edward Carson and opposition to Home Rule: 'On to the right hand stage and that part of the field comes surging a body of armed men, orange sashed and carrying Orange flags'.[13] The tricolour effect is more often achieved through the substitution of the more politically neutral and aesthetically pleasing 'gold' for 'orange'. The 'final tableau' posits a difficulty by explicitly raising the key issue of whether the revolution has been fully and successfully achieved by the Easter Rising. The shaping of the material, with the representation of Irish independence coming to a successful climax and achievement in 1916, means that only two of the script's 83 pages are allotted to the subsequent 50 years.

Those last pages in the completed pageant script do not quite follow the MacAnna outline. There is no mention of the Civil War, not even a momentary one. There is still the politically incongruous mention of World War II, the 'Emergency' years of 1940–5, explained as a tribute to the Irish army. After all, the Department of Defence was the producer of the pageant, and had supplied the services of the army and the FCA for free. Finally, when the youth of Ireland are summoned, 'the flag bearers, green and white, of the very first scene come on, and take up positions'.[14] The last piece of text in the script, and the only one to reference the Ireland of the day '[*inniu*'], addresses the citizens of the north ['*saoránaigh an Tuaiscirt*'] as those who will teach freedom to us and take arms ['*is iad san a mhúin saoirse dúinn agus a ghaibh airm chucha*'] and who remain forever our own people ['*ár muintir fhéin feasta*'].[15] This speech accompanies the completion of the tableau as 'the Orange flag holders march on, and there again is the tri-colour across the arena, and the triumphal music is "A Nation Once Again"'. This final moment obviously assumes more importance in historical retrospect; or as Tomás MacAnna put it in a letter to me: 'it is a sobering thought that had we put on that same pageant some ten or so years after, I and the entire cast might well have landed ourselves in jail!'[16] In expressing the same sentiment in his autobiography, MacAnna specifically names 'priosún Phort Laoise' [Portlaoise prison in Co. Laois].[17]

These lines just quoted also foreground the bilingual status of the pageant's script. The main role is split between the Poet and the Soldier (another source of instability in the text). When the Poet first speaks, it is in Irish; the Soldier speaks in English. But no clear or consistent meaning can be assigned to those portions of the text that are in Irish and those that are in English. The more usual stylistic effect is that Irish soon gives way to English, regardless of who the individual speakers are; indeed, single speakers move without warning from one language to the other. In terms of the sheer quantity of lines, English easily wins out; and Irish could thus be seen as a kind of seasoning along the lines of *ag labhairt cúpla focail* ['speaking a few words']. But this would not be fair, given MacAnna's own commitment to Irish language theatre in his many years at the Abbey.

There is an acknowledgement that the majority of listeners on this large public occasion would have had difficulty following a predominantly Irish script. Many of the extracts name the names of the rebels, performing a similar function to the use of the Irish placenames in Brian Friel's 1980 play, *Translations*. These placenames acknowledge both the persistence of the language in such remnants, and the huge cultural loss that has been sustained in the past century and a half. These fragments of the old language serve to connect us with that time, to keep that cultural and political memory alive. The pageant's movement into one of its most sustained stretches of Irish at the close, longer than that with which it began, links up with the present-day address to 'our people in the north' as the dramatic fulfilment of long held nationalist ideals.

THE MIXED INFLUENCE OF W.B.YEATS ON *AISÉIRÍ*

The script of the pageant is mixed in more ways than in its language. MacAnna describes it in a letter as 'music, commentary, verse and ballad'.[18] He might more accurately be described as its compiler or editor rather than author, since the script is composed of extracts from existing literary and popular sources. The text of *Aiséirí* precisely accords with the definition of 'pastiche' given in the *Concise Oxford dictionary of literary terms*: 'a literary work composed from elements borrowed from...various other writers'.[19] The key text source in this respect is the 1916 Proclamation, words from which are repeated throughout the script in both Irish and English. The Proclamation's first line resounds as the premonitory echo towards which the narrative is teleologically directed: 'In the name of God and the dead generations...'. But the predominant textual presence in the assembly of quotations is the writing of W.B. Yeats, in particular his poetry. Whereas certain texts are quoted over and over—such as the Proclamation or Thomas Davis's 'A Nation Once Again'—the greatest authorial presence is that of Yeats.

This is understandable, given MacAnna's key role in the National Theatre that Yeats helped to found. But the siren call of Yeats's poetry frequently operates against, rather than in consonance with, many of the other texts cited. Yeats himself disdained any propagandist intent, and while he sought to insinuate himself into the nationalist tradition of poetry in a work like 'To Ireland in the Coming Times', he did so in a heterodox way, not least by placing Thomas Davis in the company not only of Mangan—who at least did publish in *The Nation*—but also of Sir Samuel Ferguson, who most decidedly did not, confining himself to the Unionist *Dublin University Magazine*: 'nor may I less be counted one / With Davis, Mangan, Ferguson'.[20] Yeats frequently criticised the poets of the Young Ireland movement for their crude versification and martial rhythms, claiming that he sought in his own early verse to create a more subtle verbal music.

Many of these poems of the *fin-de-siècle* Celtic Twilight, frequently addressed to a Rose of predominantly occulted symbolism, are quoted extensively in MacAnna's script. So, for example, a ballad quatrain from 'The Wearing of the Green' enjoining the listener to 'Charge for Erin and her flag of Green!' is rapidly followed by 'Had I the heavens' embroidered cloth / Enwrought with golden and silver light...I would spread the cloths under your feet'. The reader is well able to supply the missing lines with their Yeatsian injunction, not to join in a military march but rather to '[t]read softly because you tread on my dreams'.[21] The direct political thrust of canonical nationalist ballads like 'A Nation Once Again' is countered and assuaged by the lulling rhythms of early Yeats.

There are two Yeats texts central to a 1916 pageant, both of them overtly political and both cited extensively in the MacAnna script. The first is not a poem but a play, *Cathleen Ni Houlihan*, first staged in 1902. The play was itself the product of a political centenary—that of the 1798 rebellion—and of Yeats's involvement with Maud Gonne in the organisation of the centenary commemoration in 1898. Yeats would later ask, in 'The Man and the Echo', 'Did that play of mine send out / Certain men the English shot?' His question was consciously responding to Stephen Gwynn's review of the first production of *Cathleen Ni Houlihan*, which asked whether its outcome might not be to foment revolution.[22] Subsequent scholarship has argued that *Cathleen Ni Houlihan* is not as exclusively Yeats's as his emphatic claim might suggest, establishing that it was co-authored by Lady Gregory and that she deserves the lion's share of credit for the authorship.

This elision of the role of women in the cultural and political movement at the turn of the century is reproduced in MacAnna's pageant, where Countess Markiewicz is the only one of the women involved in the Rising to merit a few lines. The central, and virtually sole, female role is the allegorical personification of Ireland as 'Éire' or Cathleen Ni Houlihan. The script of the pageant is strewn with lines from the Yeats–Gregory play, especially those referencing her 'friends' from across the sea and the 'four green fields'. The famous last two lines of the play put in an appearance. After the Poor Old Woman has exited, drawing the young man of the household after her, the twelve-year-old son returns and is asked by his father: 'Did you see an old woman going down the path?' He replies that he did not; rather, he saw a 'young girl and she had the walk of a queen'.[23] This youthful metamorphosis is predicated on the same rhetoric of blood sacrifice so central to Pearse's politics, and is certain to have influenced it. The Poor Old Woman has urged the young man of the household, who is about to be married, to relinquish his worldly hopes and instead offer himself as a martyr in the forthcoming rebellion, knowing that he will be 'remembered forever' and that his apparent defeat will help to prepare a future triumph.

In the play, the woman onstage representing Ireland is always seen as old. Only the young boy, who is the most directed towards the future, can witness her rejuvenating transformation, which has not yet been accomplished. The script of the 1966 pageant calls for a young woman to play 'Éire' (the role was played by Siobhán McKenna, who at that stage was middle-aged); in the original 1902 production, Maud Gonne was made up to play the old Cathleen, knowing that through her aging makeup a younger woman could be discerned. Does the specification of a young actress to play Cathleen Ni Houlihan mean that the revolution has been accomplished? It would seem so. But the young woman is clad in a cloak described as worn and aged, which she is enjoined to shed. So the transformation is not yet complete.

As the pageant approaches the staging of the Rising itself, the lines of Yeats's 'Easter 1916' come to the fore: 'And what if excess of love / Bewildered them till they died?'.[24] But the script has to be careful to omit a triplet from only a few lines earlier in the poem: 'Was it needless death after all? / For England may keep faith / For all that is done and said'. Yeats's poem is equivocal on the score of the Easter Rising of 1916; it admits doubts only to suppress them. His more scathing 'September 1913' has its refrain frequently cited in the pageant ('Romantic Ireland's dead and gone / It's with O'Leary in the grave').[25] Drawing on a poem by Joyce Kilmer, MacAnna's text accuses the poet with the question: 'Then Yeats what made that Easter dawn / A hue so terrible and brave?'.[26] But it does so with the adjective 'terrible', which cannot help but bring to mind Yeats's own memorable refrain of the 'terrible beauty'. The poem 'Easter 1916' is itself an answer or response to the despondency about the loss of political idealism expressed in 'September 1913'. The script of the 1966 pageant is steeped in the Romanticism that informs Yeats's reading of Irish history, with the 1916 Rising read as high tragedy redeeming the low comedy of bourgeois Dublin life in the early twentieth century.

SEÁN O'CASEY AND THE DEBATE OVER 1916

Seán O'Casey is a different matter, and the inclusion of his re-enactment of the Rising from *The Plough and the Stars* proves much more disruptive a presence in the pageant than the texts of Yeats. It has long been recognised that the platform speeches in Act Two of the play, delivered by the silhouetted Speaker, are a pastiche of Pearse: 'It is a glorious thing to see arms in the hands of Irishmen…Bloodshed is a cleansing and sanctifying thing, and the nation that regards it as the final horror has lost its manhood'.[27] The debate with Pearse over the blood sacrifice of Easter 1916 that O'Casey is conducting in *The Plough and the Stars* is by no means confined to the utterances of the Speaker in Act Two. Rather, it is sustained and developed throughout the play. It particularly emerges in the debate between the visibly pregnant Nora Clitheroe, who has sought her husband Jack in the streets to bring him home, and the other women.

> They told me I shamed my husband an' th' women of Ireland be carryin' on as I was…They said th' women must learn to be brave an' cease to be cowardly….An' there's no woman gives a son or a husband to be killed—if they say it, they're lyin', lyin' against God, Nature, an' against themselves![28]

The mother who had said she would willingly give her son to be killed was the eponymous speaker in Pádraig Pearse's famous poem, 'The Mother':

> I do not grudge them: Lord, I do not grudge
> My two strong sons that I have seen go out
> To break their strength and die, they and a few,
> In bloody protest for a glorious thing'.[29]

The definition of 'pastiche' I gave above goes on to consider whether the citation of a previously published literary work is intended positively or negatively.

> The term can be used in a derogatory sense to indicate lack of originality, or more neutrally to refer to works that involve a deliberate and playfully imitative tribute to other writers. Pastiche differs from parody in using imitation as a form of flattery rather than mockery.[30]

In O'Casey's play we are certainly in the realm of parody. When Uncle Peter says something and the Young Covey repeats it, Peter is sure something 'derogatory' is intended. Fredric Jameson links parody and pastiche along a historical continuum. Parody he associates with 'the idiosyncracies of the moderns and their "inimitable" styles: the Faulknerian long sentence, for example, [or] Lawrentian nature imagery punctuated by testy colloqualism…'.[31] Jameson could well have added O'Casey's idiosyncratic style, rhetorically ramping up a recognisable Dublin idiom with a profusion of assonance and alliteration: 'It would take something more than a thing like you to flutther a feather o' Fluther'.[32] What Jameson claims of modernist writers holds true for O'Casey's ostentatiously self-reflexive and inherently self-parodying style: 'they ostentatiously deviate from a norm which then reasserts itself...by a systematic mimicry of their wilful eccentricities'.[33]

When swatches of O'Casey's text are stitched into the *Aiséirí* pageant script in the mid-1960s, 40 years after the original play's premiere, the predominant style has shifted from parody to pastiche. The stylistic and historic shift neutralises the satiric intent of the original:

> it is a neutral practice of such mimicry, without any of parody's ulterior motives, amputated of the satiric impulse, devoid of laughter.[34]

Jameson attributes the stylistic fragmentariness of pastiche to the 'linguistic fragmentation of social life itself'.[35] It arises from a crisis in historical representation in which 'there is no longer an original event to be imitated' but only a series of images, of ideas and stereotypes:

> the producers of culture have nowhere to turn but to the past: the imitation of dead styles, speech through all the masks and voices stored up in the culture's literary and dramatic repertoire.[36]

But what has been left out or textually amputated can speak as eloquently, arguably even more so, as what has been incorporated in the fragmented body of the pastiche.

The Plough and the Stars questions the positive representation of Easter 1916 by placing it in the dramatic background. O'Casey's dramatic interest is instead centred on the Dubliners who had not taken an active part in the Rising. The MacAnna pageant seeks to reverse that emphasis. Pearse, Connolly and the other signatories resume centre stage, and indeed dominate Croke Park with the huge and familiar visual icons of the signatories of the Proclamation. In such a context the invocation of O'Casey, while probably inevitable, is no less potentially hazardous to an unequivocally positive representation. In MacAnna's script, a question mark has been placed alongside the inclusion of Bessie Burgess's memorable line: 'Yous are all nicely shanghaied now'.[37] It reminds us of those Dubliners who were and remained dedicated to the Redmondite line, whose sons were serving in the Somme, and who were proud to have them do so.

Bessie Burgess the Protestant finally makes one with her Catholic neighbours in the tenement when it comes to the attractions of looting. The 1966 pageant scrupulously seeks to exclude any reference to the widespread looting by ordinary Dubliners during the week of the Rising. All three of Pearse's manifestoes, which he issued from the GPO, are extensively quoted throughout the script. The second of these manifestoes was designed to create a sense of shame in the looters:

> Ireland's honour has already been redeemed; it remains to vindicate her wisdom and her self-control...The Provisional Government hopes that its supporters—which means the vast bulk of the people of Dublin—will preserve order and self-restraint. Such looting as has already occurred has been done by hangers-on of the British Army. Ireland must keep her new honour unsmirched.[38]

These lines are excised from the pageant; the quotations that remain from Pearse's second manifesto are instead directed at 'the armed might of England' advancing across the field. But the frequent verbal citations from Fluther Good, Bessie Burgess and the other characters of O'Casey's *Plough and the Stars* cannot help but bring with them dramatic memories of the looting that all of the characters engage in during Act Three. More than this, they reactivate the contested status of the Easter Rising in the political development of the country. It should be no surprise, therefore, that the Fianna Fáil government specifically prohibited any staging of O'Casey's plays during the fiftieth anniversary commemoration of 1916: 'An O'Casey play during the period of the celebrations would not be in keeping with the spirit of the occasion'.[39] This action contained multiple ironies. In 1976, as James Moran points out,

> the Abbey staged a lavish golden-jubilee production of the play [*The Plough and the Stars*], and perhaps mischievously, the theatre managers appointed Tomás MacAnna to direct this performance even though he had previously organised the hagiographic fiftieth-anniversary pageant for the Rising, *Aiseiri*.[40]

SEÁN O'CASEY AND THE POLITICS OF STAGING A PAGEANT

The prohibition on O'Casey's plays during the period of the 1966 celebrations must also be read against other developments in the ongoing
relationship between the exiled Dublin playwright and the staging of
his new plays in his native city. As recently as 1958, a mere eight years
earlier, plans to premiere a new O'Casey play, *The Drums of Father Ned*,
at the nascent Dublin Theatre Festival had to be scuppered. The festival
had arisen out of the inauguration in 1953 of An Tóstal, an annual
pageant of singing, dancing, recitations and staged scenes from Irish
political history held at Easter in Croke Park (and clearly a direct
influence on MacAnna's staging of the 1966 pageant). O'Casey had
heard of An Tóstal, approved of it as an effort to regenerate Irish culture
and made it central to his new play.[41]

The Drums of Father Ned dramatises an Irish country town in the
1950s, still simmering from Civil War divisions, which is caught up in
the excitement of staging a pageant. Actors wander around wearing
redcoat uniforms or bearing pikes and practicing scenes from a
Boucicault-style melodrama. The chief inspiration for the carnivalesque
atmosphere is the ubiquitous yet elusive Father Ned, a Godot-type
character who is much discussed but never seen. If Father Ned is the
spirit of a church seeking to inspire political and cultural renewal, the
parish priest Father Fillifogue, who repeatedly bursts into people's
houses, is the embodiment of an institutional Catholic church, quick
to detect and oppose any perceived threat to its authority. As the parish
priest declares to those involved in the pageant:

> So your play babbles about the rights of man. [*He chuckles
> mockingly.*] What with your rights of women, rights of
> children, rights of trade unions, rights of th' laity, an' civil
> rights…I'll show your Father Ned that th' Church comes
> before th' Tosthal'.[42]

This exchange was to prove prophetic of the fate of O'Casey's play.
At the commencement of the first Dublin Theatre Festival in the 1957
Tóstal, the Archbishop of Dublin, John Charles McQuaid, had said a
Solemn Mass to inaugurate the event. The 1958 festival was to
commence in the same way. It was then pointed out to the archbishop
that the theatre festival promised a staging of Joyce's *Ulysses* and a new
play by O'Casey. McQuaid did not have to read the play to form a

judgement (though if he had, the portrait of Father Fillifogue would hardly have endeared it to him). As O'Casey's biographer Christopher Murray puts it: 'McQuaid sent a curt note in response, withdrawing permission for the celebration of Mass as requested'.[43]

In the standoff that followed, the producers of the play asked O'Casey not only for minor textual revisions, but for major structural alterations. O'Casey refused and withdrew his play from the festival, claiming it had been banned. As Murray's biography reveals, 'in the Archbishop's archives are notes based on meetings held by the Festival Committee and the Tóstal Council at this time;' one of them states that O'Casey '"was being approached to allow technical corrections [and] would probably refuse, it was thought, and thus his play would go out of the programme"'.[44] The outcome of the *Drums of Father Ned* debacle in 1958 was that O'Casey withdrew permission for any of his plays to be staged professionally in Ireland. Thus, at a stroke, the three plays of the 'Dublin trilogy' were removed from the repertoire; this situation persisted for a further six years. In 1964, a few months before his death at the age of 84, O'Casey yielded to pressure and removed the ban, so that the Abbey theatre might stage productions of *Juno and the Paycock* and *The Plough and the Stars* in London, as part of Peter Daubeny's World Theatre Season. *The Plough*, therefore, had only just been restored to the Abbey repertoire when in 1966 it was removed for the period of the jubilee commemoration of the Rising. But, as I have sought to demonstrate, its echoes proved impossible to silence in *Aiséirí*, with the added resonance of the recent controversy over O'Casey's play about the staging of a pageant.

THE PARTICIPATION OF MICHEÁL MACLIAMMÓIR

Probably the most famous Irish actor of the day to be cast in the pageant was Micheál MacLiammóir, who supplied the voice of the Speaker. He was more traditionally associated with the Gate theatre, a byword for European cosmopolitanism, rather than the Irish nationalist drama of the Abbey. MacLiammóir had begun his professional acting career playing the role of Robert Emmet some 37 years earlier in Denis Johnston's *The Old Lady Says No!* The play had become, by default, the inaugural production of the fledgling Gate theatre run by MacLiammóir and his partner, director Hilton Edwards, when it was rejected by the Abbey (in the same year as it also turned down O'Casey's *Silver Tassie*).

Lady Gregory had said of Johnston's play that the only act she liked in it was the first, in which a romantic Emmet is seized by British redcoats when wooing Sarah Curran. That section of the play was made up almost entirely of quoted extracts from familiar poems and ballads from the nineteenth-century tradition (i.e. in a style very similar to that of the MacAnna pageant). When Emmet answers Major Sirr's charges, he is clubbed to the ground by one of the redcoats and lies still. The actor playing Major Sirr is forced to address the audience and ask whether there is a doctor in the house. In the phantasmagoria that follows, the concussed Emmet is propelled into post-revolutionary Dublin of the late 1920s, to be met by the new poetry of urban modernism:

> the throb of petrol engines, the hoot of motor horns, the rattle and pounding of lorries and, above all, the cry of the newsboys: 'Hegler Press' [Herald or Press].[45]

He wanders through the streets of the modern metropolis and finds his romantic nationalism incomprehensible to those he encounters, including his beloved Sarah as a Moore Street flower-seller. If MacLiammóir, therefore, brings the presence of a historical figure like Robert Emmet to the 1966 pageant (and he had reprised the role in Johnston's play as recently as 1956), he also brings with it the confrontation with modernity that is at the heart of Johnston's play and that *Aiséirí* was so anxious to exclude.

As Moran's book makes clear, Fianna Fáil governments, whether under de Valera or Lemass, strove 'to prevent Easter Week from becoming trivialised by any association with homosexuality'.[46] Moran is here speaking specifically about Roger Casement and the ongoing dispute over his diaries. But what Elaine Sisson calls 'the treacherous scholarly terrain of Pearse's homoeroticism and sexuality' had always been a cause for concern when it came to nationalist celebration.[47] One text of Pearse's that was not going to feature in the heavily allusive script of the pageant was his poem 'Little Lad of the Tricks', outlining as it did the desire of its adult male speaker to kiss the 'soft red mouth' of the young boy, a kiss with a 'fragrance' 'That I have not found yet / In the kisses of women'.[48] Susan Cannon Harris has argued that, as a way of 'coping with the impasse between his homosexual desires and his homophobic culture', it was culturally more acceptable 'for Pearse to wax rhapsodic on the beauty of children than to express or act on sexual desire toward adult men'.[49] Nowadays, the implications of paedophilia attaching to the poem make it more disturbing than any suggestion of same-sex adult desire would be. Either way, the poem and its implications had to be kept well away from any nationalist celebration in 1966.

But MacLiammóir (and his partner Edwards) were the most famous gay couple in Ireland, and the former had devised a camp style of theatrical performance and vocal projection that bespoke gayness in all but name. It took MacLiammóir virtually his entire lifetime, and the developments charted over the century in relation to sexual politics, publicly to acknowledge and address his own homosexuality. A crucial stage in this development was his decision in 1962 to stage a one-man show on Oscar Wilde, *The importance of being Oscar* (directed by Edwards). The show is extremely coy about Wilde's sexuality, referring to the Marquis of Queensbury's charge as 'libellous' and excising all of the infamous trial of Oscar Wilde except for the judge's reference to 'the crime of which you have been convicted'.[50]

But everyone knew precisely what that crime was, and MacLiammóir's identification of his own theatrical persona with that of Oscar Wilde in the early 1960s increased the overt gayness of that identity. Thus, his casting in the 1966 pageant would have particularly brought with it his most recent and acclaimed performance, that of Oscar Wilde, thereby activating the same-sex associations from which the government strove to keep celebrations of Easter Week free. The final irony relating to MacLiammóir and the pageant's performance of Irishness was the biographical disclosure after his death in 1977 that he was not born in Cork, as he had always claimed, but in London in 1899 as Alfred Willmore.[51] Micheál MacLiammóir's lifelong performance of Irishness, offstage as well as on, was the greatest theatrical illusion of all.

CONCLUSION: A NORTHERN PLAYWRIGHT'S RESPONSE

And what was the response of contemporary Irish playwrights to not only the fiftieth anniversary of the 1916 Rising in 1966 but also the commemorative pageant in Croke Park? In 1964 Brian Friel had set the theatrical world alight with his breakthrough play, *Philadelphia, here I come!*, in which a young Irish man is shown on the eve of his emigration to the US. Friel followed this in 1966 with *The Loves of Cass McGuire,* which reverses the process by showing an old woman returning to Ireland after many years in North America. Apart from one fleeting (and ironic) cry of 'Up the Republic!', there is little to tie the events of the play to the contemporary political landscape, since the focus (as so often with Friel) is primarily on a family. But the dates are suggestive. Cass had left Ireland, we are told, precisely 50 years earlier, which would place her departure in 1916 and her return in 1966; and the part of Cass was played by the actress who in the same year portrayed 'Éire' in the *Aiséirí* pageant, Siobhán McKenna. Fintan O'Toole began a review of the play as follows:

> When in the third act of Friel's *Cass McGuire* one of the residents of an old folks' home asks who General Custer was, another, an Englishman, replies: 'Wasn't he one of the leaders of your Easter Rebellion?' Written at a time when the Republic was wallowing in the celebration of the 50th anniversary of the Easter Rising, the play is, among other things, an astringent antidote to the historical self-congratulation of the time.[52]

This was even truer of Friel's ferocious 1969 political farce, *The Mundy Scheme,* which was rejected by the Abbey theatre and staged at the Olympia as part of that year's Dublin Theatre Festival. The play centres on the political establishment of the Republic through its portrayal of Taoiseach F.X. Ryan and his Cabinet colleagues, who devise a scheme to sell unproductive acres of land in the scenic west of Ireland to wealthy foreigners as burial places. The play is framed by a prologue that asks a series of piercing political questions.

> What happens to an emerging country after it has emerged? Does the transition from dependence to independence induce a fatigue, a mediocrity, an ennui? Or does the clean spirit of idealism that fired the people to freedom augment itself, grow bolder, more revolutionary, more generous?[53]

The prologue concludes: 'May we write your epitaph now, Mr. Emmet?' The taoiseach, one of his ministers and his private secretary all seek to profit by buying up acres of land cheap, before the scheme is announced; and they rely on the Donegal Garda Commissioner and his men to take care of any troublemakers. The progress of the first dead immigrants to arrive is tracked across Dublin: 'When they reached the general post office in O'Connell Street, the procession halted and a minute's silence was observed'.[54]

After the televised arrival in Achill Island, the minister for commerce observes:

> Couldn't have been more tastefully done. I'll tell you boys: there's a proud group of 1916 fellows sitting up in heaven this night. God Almighty, they'll turn the place into Croke Park. And the aul' sticks'll be flashing and...[55]

The conjunction of the 1916 leaders and Croke Park indicates that the reference is at least as much to the 1966 pageant as to a hurling match. The judgement, in the fateful year of 1969, of this northern nationalist playwright on the Republic's celebration of the fiftieth anniversary of the Rising is as much political as aesthetic.

ACKNOWLEDGEMENT

I wish to thank Tomás MacAnna for supplying me with a copy of the script of *Aiséirí* and for his helpful correspondence.

NOTES

[1] Military Archives, Cathal Brugha Barracks, Department of Defence (hereafter cited as MA DDA), 47969 (3), Tomás MacAnna to Department of Defence [Undated]. For details of the discussion of Mac Anna's memorandum and of the agreement to proceed with the pageant in Croke Park, see National Archives of Ireland, Department of the Taoiseach (hereafter cited as NAI DT), 97/6/157, 'Minutes of the second meeting of the Commemoration Committee', 19 March 1965.

[2] Colm Tóibín, *Beauty in a broken place* (Dublin, 2004).

[3] Ben Levitas, *The theatre of nation: Irish drama and cultural nationalism 1890–1916* (Oxford, 2002), 224.

[4] Joan Fitzpatrick Dean, *Riot and great anger: stage censorship in twentieth-century Ireland* (Madison, 2004), 24–5.

5 Tomás MacAnna, *Fallaing Aonghusa: saol amharclainne* (Dublin, 2000), 174.
6 Ruth Dudley Edwards, *Patrick Pearse: the triumph of failure* (Dublin, 1990), 140.
7 Dudley Edwards, *Patrick Pearse*, 140.
8 Mary Trotter, *Ireland's national theaters: political performance and the origins of the Irish dramatic movement* (Syracuse, New York, 2001), 154.
9 Trotter, *Ireland's national theatres*, 152.
10 Dudley Edwards, *Patrick Pearse*, 133; Trotter, *Ireland's national theatres*, 153.
11 MA DDA, 47969 (3), Tomás MacAnna to Department of Defence [undated].
12 MA DDA, 47969 (3), Tomás MacAnna to Department of Defence [undated].
13 Tomás MacAnna, *Aiséirí* (unpublished script, 1966). I am grateful to Mr MacAnna for his generosity in supplying me with a copy of the script.
14 MacAnna, *Aiséirí*, 83.
15 MacAnna, *Aiséirí*, 83.
16 Personal correspondence with Tomás MacAnna, 2 November 2004.
17 MacAnna, *Fallaing Aonghusa*, 176.
18 MA DDA, 47969 (3), Tomás MacAnna to Department of Defence, [undated].
19 Chris Baldick, *The concise Oxford dictionary of literary terms* (Oxford and New York, 1990).
20 Peter Allt and R.K. Alspach (eds), *The variorum edition of the poems of W.B. Yeats* (New York, 1977), 138.
21 MacAnna, *Aiséirí*, 10; Allt and Alspach, *Variorum edition of the poems*, 176.
22 Allt and Alspach, *Variorum edition of the poems*, 632.
23 R.K Alspach and C.C. Alspach (eds), *The variorum edition of the plays of W.B. Yeats* (New York, 1969), 231.
24 Allt and Alspach , *Variorum edition of the poems*, 394.
25 Allt and Alspach , *Variorum edition of the poems*, 290.
26 MacAnna, *Aiséirí*, 65.
27 Seán O'Casey, *Three plays: Juno and the Paycock, The Shadow of a Gunman, The Plough and the Stars* (London, 1980), 162.
28 O'Casey, *Three plays*, 184.
29 Pádraig Pearse, *Collected works: plays, stories, poems* (Dublin and London, 1917), 333.
30 Baldick, *Concise Oxford dictionary of literary terms*, 162.
31 Fredric Jameson, *Postmodernism, or, the cultural logic of late capitalism* (London and New York, 1991), 16.
32 O'Casey, *Three plays*, 174.
33 Jameson, *Postmodernism*, 16.
34 Jameson, *Postmodernism*, 17.
35 Jameson, *Postmodernism*, 17.
36 Jameson, *Postmodernism*, 17–18.
37 O'Casey, *Three plays*, 184.

[38] Dudley Edwards, *Patrick Pearse*, 291.

[39] NAI DT, 97/6/160, Report from the Commemoration Committee, [undated].

[40] James Moran, *Staging the Easter Rising: 1916 as theatre* (Cork, 2005), 112.

[41] Christopher Murray, *Seán O'Casey, writer at work: a biography* (Dublin, 2004), 390.

[42] Seán O'Casey, *The drums of Father Ned* (London, 1960), 40.

[43] Murray, *Seán O'Casey*, 396.

[44] Murray, *Seán O'Casey*, 401.

[45] Denis Johnston, *Selected plays of Denis Johnston* (Chosen and introduced by Joseph Ronsley), (Washington, D.C, 1983), 33.

[46] Moran, *Staging the Easter Rising*, 84.

[47] Elaine Sisson, *Pearse's patriots: St Enda's and the cult of boyhood* (Cork, 2004), 137.

[48] Sisson, *Pearse's patriots*, 143.

[49] Susan Cannon Harris, *Gender and modern Irish drama* (Bloomington and Indianapolis, 2002), 147–8.

[50] Micheál MacLiammóir, *The importance of being Oscar* (Dublin, 1978), 44, 77. See Éibhear Walshe, 'Sodom and Begorrah, or game to the last: inventing Micheál MacLiammóir', in Éibhear Walshe, *Sex, nation and dissent in Irish writing* (Cork, 1997), 157–62.

[51] See Christopher Fitz-Simon, *The boys: a biography of Micheál MacLiammóir and Hilton Edwards* (London, 1994).

[52] Julia Furay and Redmond O'Hanlon (eds), *Critical moments: Fintan O'Toole on modern Irish theatre* (Dublin, 2003), 231–2.

[53] Brian Friel, *Crystal and Fox and The Mundy Scheme* (New York, 1970), 157–8.

[54] Friel, *Crystal and Fox*, 304.

[55] Friel, *Crystal and Fox*, 307–8.

10. EASTER WEEK AND THE HISTORIANS

By Michael Laffan

INTRODUCTION

It was a time for praise. In April 1966, shortly before the official fiftieth anniversary commemorations for the 1916 Rising, Owen Dudley Edwards applauded some recent writings by Irish historians. He declared that

> whatever may be the ultimate verdict on the good taste and appropriateness of the general proceedings for the Golden Jubilee of the Rising, it must be stated that the historical publications on the event which have so far appeared this year could hardly be bettered.[1]

By then, a sustained neglect of early-twentieth-century Irish history was coming to an end. Historians and others who wrote about the country's past had overcome most of their inhibitions about tackling 'sensitive' or divisive topics, and gradually new or closely-guarded evidence was being made available. Apart from newspapers and parliamentary debates, few primary sources were accessible until the 1960s, while secretive and authoritarian habits prevented Irish researchers from using recent collections of secondary material.

In 1947 a Bureau of Military History had been established, and for the next decade its members conducted interviews with surviving participants of the Irish Revolution—taking care to avoid the controversies associated with the Treaty and the Civil War. The project was designed to collect what were regarded as the 'facts'—contemporary documents and the retrospective testimonies of participants—and to make these available to future scholars. The enterprise had been supported by professional historians, despite their justified suspicion of the government's involvement. But they became disillusioned by what they saw as an unprofessional approach to the collection of material, and they were dismayed by the use made of the 'confidentiality clause'. Originally this clause had applied only to people who expressed a formal wish that any information they supplied should not be made available to researchers until after their deaths. Without consulting historians the bureau extended the restriction, retrospectively, to the whole collection of testimonies and documents.

Florence O'Donoghue complained that

> whatever case may be made for denying...use of the witnesses' statements, no case whatever can be made for impounding original, contemporary documents, which would be available if they had not been given to the Bureau.[2]

Such protests were ignored, and subsequent events more than vindicated the fear expressed by James Hogan in 1960:

> it would be rather a paradoxical result of all this gathering of historical material if it made the writing of the history of the period not only more difficult but postponed it for another generation.[3]

The reality was even worse than Hogan feared, and all the bureau's files remained closed for a further 43 years, until 2003. The Irish past would continue be protected from prying eyes.

Despite such official obstruction of scholarship, individual historians did write occasional articles about the Easter Rising and related topics in the *Leader*, the *Irish Times*, the *Irish Press* and elsewhere, while survivors of the Irish Revolution reminisced at length in the columns of various newspapers. But over the years only a modest quantity of original material became available and, in consequence, few reassessments were made of the Easter Rising or of the revolutionary period in general. Edgar Holt's *Protest in arms*, published in 1960, was a popular work on the events of 1916–23 and provided little background information or context. It represented the inadequate state of knowledge and interpretation at the beginning of the decade. (The book's forward was unusually tepid in its praise. Cathal O'Shannon wrote grudgingly that

> my satisfaction is not indeed unqualified, but I am happy to be able to say that it is sincere and, within limitations, deserved...making allowance for errors of detail that are hardly serious enough to mar the quality of the whole... [Holt] has been reasonably objective.[4])

A tantalising acknowledgment expressed the author's gratitude for permission to read, in advance of its publication, a typescript copy of T.D. Williams's history of the Civil War. This was a unique privilege, since no-one else is known to have had the opportunity to read the book.

The same year saw the publication of a series of Thomas Davis lectures edited by Conor Cruise O'Brien. The volume included several formidable chapters, such as Nicholas Mansergh's on John Redmond and Terence de Vere White's on Arthur Griffith. But Dorothy Macardle was able to write of Connolly and Pearse that 'by causing the Rising of 1916 they caused the verdict of the electors in 1918, and the creation of Dáil Éireann, and two and a half years of fighting against the British Forces in its defence'.[5] There was a neat and uncomplicated explanation for the Irish revolution.

Four years later, a 'general' work similar to Holt's, Max Caulfield's *Easter Rebellion*, provided a novelettish and breezy narrative account of the insurrection. Passages such as '"the blighter!" swore Oates softly, and ducked through the hole', or '"next time I'll make sure I'll get him", thought little John Reid', would have been reassuringly familiar to readers of comics and adventure stories.[6] Its heroic tone ensured that it could be incorporated neatly into aspects of the official 1966 golden jubilee celebrations; some bureaucrats and politicians may have wished that more historians wrote with such uncritical enthusiasm. Numerous survivors of the Rising were interviewed and extensive dialogue was remembered in suspicious detail nearly 50 years later. The author cherished his many clichés and caricatures. O'Rahilly was 'handsome and empirically gallant' (sic), MacNeill was an 'ostrich-minded professor', Markievicz was 'the embodiment of that "wild Irish girl" the Anglo-Irish aristocracy once bred with a proliferating regularity', and a misdirected British artillery shell 'immediately led to one of those mad contretemps which inevitably appear to attend the English when they find themselves breathing in the pure, crystal air of Ireland'.[7] But Caulfield also provided vivid descriptions of the fighting in Easter Week.

Another two years later, in 1966, a new survey was written for the general reader. Its misleading title, *Six days to shake an empire*, concealed the fact that much of the book consisted of an unimpressive history of Ireland. Chapters with titles such as 'A papal bull and its consequences' and 'Oliver Cromwell and the Irish' indicated that the author would move through Irish history at a leisurely pace, and little more than half of the contents was devoted to 'the terrible six days in Dublin'.[8]

Setting a pattern that would be followed in later decades, some of those who wrote about Easter Week seem to have been dilettantes or popularisers. Edgar Holt was a military historian and the author of studies of the Boer War, the Maori Wars and the Carlist Wars; Charles Duff's publications included *The truth about Columbus* and *How to learn a language*; and Hedley McCay (author of a short life of Pearse[9]) was 'interested in modern philosophy, *avant-garde* literature, continental cabaret music, politics, drama and sport'—although, according to the biographical note in his book, he appeared not to have had any particular interest in history.

A DELUGE OF WRITINGS

But shortly before the publication of works such as these, which were written by amateurs and designed for an undiscriminating audience, a historiographical revolution had already begun. From the early 1960s onwards, the background, events and consequences of the Easter Rising were examined by historians with a new rigour. The process commenced with F.X. Martin's publication and assessment in *Irish Historical Studies* of two memoranda written by Eoin MacNeill in 1916 and 1917.[10] These revealed for the first time the reasons for his efforts to prevent the Rising, and they presented an alternative version of Irish nationalism to that which had been represented by P.H. Pearse—and which had been propagated by Irish governments over several decades.

Martin's extensive scholarly apparatus, and his critical examination of evidence and motives, showed that the Easter Rising and its impact could henceforth be examined in the same detached and critical manner as earlier phases of Irish history. He soon followed his initiative in publishing the MacNeill memoranda by editing collections of documents and articles on the Irish Volunteers and the Howth gun-running. More importantly, in the course of the following decade he and other historians also consulted other recently-available sources, and these in turn allowed or forced them to develop new interpretations.

The fiftieth anniversary of the Rising in 1966 provided an occasion for the publication or republication of numerous books and articles. Some old works were reprinted—such as James Stephens's classic *Insurrection in Dublin* and Desmond Ryan's *The Rising* (described as a fourth edition, but identical to the original version of 1949). Most of the material was fresh, and its quality varied widely.

Collections of new articles were balanced by anthologies of earlier writings. A series of Thomas Davis lectures edited by Martin, *Leaders and men of the Easter Rising*, was broadcast on Radio Éireann and subsequently published in book form.[11] Its biographical approach provided both opportunities and problems. The authors' subjects ranged far beyond what might reasonably have been expected from the book's title, and many of the historical figures who were included (above all, Provost Mahaffy of Trinity College) would have been appalled by their posthumous association with a nationalist rebellion. Nonetheless, the format encouraged examination of the roles played by unionists, British officials, home rulers and clerics, as well as by more predictable Irish revolutionaries.

In theory, the chapters on Craig and Carson should have drawn attention to the links between the planned unionist and the actual republican insurrections, but in practice, their authors made little attempt to discuss the unionist leaders' impact on the events of Easter 1916. Apart from one or two sentences by A.T.Q. Stewart, they tended to avoid the (embarrassing?) inspiration and example that the Ulster Volunteers had given to nationalists inside and outside the IRB. Some segments of the book were unwieldy—in particular that section dealing with 'Ceannt, Devoy, O'Rahilly, and the military plan'. David Thornley provided a chapter on Pearse, while confessing that it was virtually impossible at that time to write an objective study of his subject—'a man whose death elevated him into the most sacred realms of national mythology…it is not merely difficult but almost blasphemous to discern a human being of flesh and blood'. He admitted that he could make no more than an interim attempt to do so.[12]

The *Irish Times* printed a 16-page supplement of especially commissioned articles commemorating the Rising, and this was subsequently published in book form.[13] Some of the original contributions were omitted in the later version (such as Desmond FitzGerald's reminiscences of life in the GPO during Easter Week, and an account of 'Happenings outside Dublin'), while new material was included and original documents were now mixed with the chapters assessing the Rising and its context. Like *Leaders and men*, the book's net was cast widely, and it covered topics such as the Gaelic ideological origins of the Rising, the Royal Irish Constabulary, and 'the other half-million' Irishmen who fought in the British army.

Perhaps the most insightful chapter in the collection was Nicholas Mansergh's short study of the Conservative Party and the Union from 1886 to 1916, in which he argued that the Easter Rising had convinced sceptics such as Arthur Balfour that Irish nationalism was a genuine force and deserved to be taken seriously. Mansergh concluded that only the 1921 settlement rescued the Conservatives from their dogmatic defence of Irish unionism, restoring to the party its customary pragmatism and its freedom of manoeuvre. Henceforth, Conservatives were determined that there should be no new 'Ireland's in India or elsewhere.

Conor Cruise O'Brien's chapter, 'The embers of Easter', ranged speculatively over what might have happened if the Rising had been delayed for another two years. The threat of conscription in 1918 might have facilitated what did not occur in 1916: a mass uprising. This would have resulted in a guerrilla campaign, which in turn would necessarily have tied down large numbers of British troops and would have involved the use of terrorist tactics by the crown forces. The natural consequence, he continued, would have been mutiny and desertion among Irish troops on the Western Front, which would probably have spread to the French army and possibly also to the Germans. He soon abandoned these flights of contrafactual fantasy and displayed his characteristic vigour in attacking the various failures of independent Ireland. He saw the fiftieth anniversary celebrations as the funeral ceremonies of the Republic proclaimed in Easter Week.[14]

The Spring 1966 issue of the Jesuit periodical *Studies* contained several articles on the Rising and its legacy. The editor nailed his colours to the mast in his declaration that MacNeill's 1916 memorandum was

> a profound and inspiring profession of Ireland's nationhood…In this year of commemoration it should be made available to every schoolboy. It is much nearer to the realities of Irish life and history than is the proclamation of Easter Week.[15]

Clearly a debate had begun, of the sort that would have been difficult or impossible to conduct in the 1950s.

In one of the *Studies* articles, 'The significance of 1916', Garret FitzGerald took a long-term view. He hypothesised not about what might have happened if the Rising had been delayed for two years, but about what might have happened if it had not taken place at all. He claimed that the rebels revived a national consciousness that was then at a low ebb. He accepted the strength of the case against the Rising and the tradition of political violence that it had launched; he conceded that by the mid-1960s there had been a reaction against the association of the Rising with later patterns of death, destruction and demoralisation. He was not surprised that public attitudes towards 1916 had become more critical; 'the spurious claims made by propagandists for extreme nationalism…have contributed to a growing cynicism about the national movement of 1916 and the years that followed'.[16] He believed that the case for the rebels had been allowed to go by default.

Nonetheless, he argued, it was far from clear that Home Rule would necessarily have advanced much further than the British had envisaged before the First World War, or that under Home Rule Ireland might eventually have achieved full independence. Without the stimulus that the Rising gave to nationalism, a 'devolved' southern Ireland might have shrunk into a dependent provincialism, comparable to Northern Ireland after 1921. This would have been facilitated by the continuation of British agricultural subsidies and social welfare benefits. The south, too, might have suffered from stifling one-party rule. He concluded that 'a Home Rule Ireland could not have been merely a peaceful and more cultured version of the Irish Free State', and that Northern Ireland provided the best clue as to what it would have become.[17]

Despite the fact that publication was delayed until after the Easter Week commemorations had been completed, one article written for this issue of *Studies*—Francis Shaw's 'Canon of Irish history'—was carefully excluded. In his own later words 'it was judged, very understandably, that a critical study of this kind might be thought to be untimely and even inappropriate in what was in effect a commemorative issue'. The article appeared only in 1972, by which time Shaw himself was dead, Irish public opinion had changed and criticism of Pearse's ideas and legacy was seen as being less heretical than would have been the case six years earlier. (As the government and the people combined in 1966 to honour the Easter rebels, an Irish writer would still have found it more difficult than did the English literary critic Cyril Connolly to enthuse about the drama of Easter Week and yet to conclude that 'a terrible shambles was born'.)

The 1966 volume of the *Capuchin Annual* devoted almost 150 pages to commemorating the jubilee. The editor's introduction belonged to a different world from that represented by *Studies*, and it began

> [f]ifty years have passed—half a century—since the pulses of young Irish men and women beat fast with secret hope and urgent preparation for a rendezvous with honour…Only one who lived when they lived, who heard them talk, who knew their thoughts, would believe that men and women such as they lived in this world.

This seemed ominous, but the articles that followed avoided such traditional pieties. For the most part they consisted of down-to-earth reminiscences by participants in the Rising, and the writers tried conscientiously to describe what they did or saw—sometimes correcting errors in earlier accounts.

Roger McHugh edited an anthology, *Dublin 1916*, whose 400 pages included passages of literary and historical interest. These were organised under three general headings, and they ranged from contemporary accounts of the Rising to works written in the course of the previous few years.[21] Several of the articles had long been out of print, so their republication extended the range of easily-accessible information and interpretation.

M. Ó Dubhghaill's *Insurrection fires at Eastertide* adopted a very different approach from that taken by McHugh. The book consisted largely of extended quotations from an eclectic range of primary and secondary sources, stitched together with thin lines of editorial comment.[22] These were often didactic and exhortatory. Original documents were interspersed among passages from memoirs, from scholarly works, and from superseded textbooks, such as Hayden and Moonan's *Short history of the Irish people*.[23] The result was a more-or-less continuous narrative in a variety of forms and registers—interrupted at times by textbook-style summaries and directives to the reader. It was clear that Ó Dubhghaill had hoped to write a balanced work, and he often succeeded in this aim, but at times he could not contain his loathing for some of the historical characters whom he encountered. His mask slipped in remarks such as the mad antics of Sir Edward Carson and Bonar Law…we have already arraigned John Redmond before the bar of history…there seemed to be no limits to the lengths he would go in his servility to the cause of England.[24]

Old-fashioned historiography still flourished.

Two general histories of Ireland differed in their coverage of the Irish Revolution. In 1966 the Irish television channel Telefís Éireann broadcast a series of 21 lectures covering Irish history from the earliest times to the present. The events of 1916 received little attention; radical republican nationalism from the beginning to the end of the First World War—including the preparations for the Rising, Easter Week itself, and its lengthy aftermath—were all allocated a total of less than 20 lines.[25] In the circumstances of the time, such restraint was remarkable. Another general history of modern Ireland, considerably longer and covering a much shorter period, was able to devote almost five pages to the insurrection and its origins. Its account was crisp and balanced, and its conclusion was less than reverential: 'Ireland was quickly passing under the most dangerous of all tyrannies—the tyranny of the dead'.[26]

Memoirs, biographies and autobiographies

In earlier decades some participants in the Rising had written their memoirs, and two outstanding autobiographical volumes were published in the context of the jubilee commemorations. They had much in common, in particular an eye for detail, a self-deprecating sense of humour and accounts of the authors' difficulties in hiring taxis that might take them to join in the fighting—on a day when Dubliners going to the races at Fairyhouse provided them with formidable competition. Seán MacEntee's *Episode at Easter* described his journeys backwards and forwards between Dublin and Louth, followed by their happy conclusion: his ultimate success in joining the GPO garrison half-way through the Rising.[27] Desmond FitzGerald's memoirs were published more than 20 years after his death. Like C.S. Andrews's *Dublin made me*,[28] FitzGerald's book provides a fascinating retrospective glimpse into the mentalities of young revolutionaries.

His account of the moods and conditions in the GPO are both revealing and entertaining, and our image of the Rising is enhanced by his stories: for example, two Swedish sailors joined the rebel garrison because they disliked the English—having given advance warning that

they could stay only until Thursday, when their ship was due to leave
Dublin; Pearse's basic humanity led him to countermand his own order
that captured looters should be shot; and signatories of the republican
Proclamation discussed which German prince might become king of an
independent Ireland.[29]

One surprising feature of '1916 in the 1960s' is how few biographies
were written. Among those published was a short life of P.H. Pearse, less
than 100 pages long, which appeared in 1966.[30] It devoted less
attention to the Rising than might have been expected, and it dabbled
in the psychobiographical analysis that was becoming fashionable at
the time. In the book, Pearse was revealed to be

> undoubtedly undersexed and his normal development
> psychologically was due to a 'mother' complex allied to a
> tendency to excessive religiosity. This can account for the
> unnatural treatment of women and religion in his literary
> works.[31]

Two biographies of Countess Markievicz appeared almost simultaneously. Anne Marreco's book contributed little that was new, but
Jacqueline van Voris's *Constance de Markievicz* was more solidly based
and made a serious attempt to place her subject in context.[32] Neither
book devoted much attention to Markievicz's role in the Rising; the
proportions were, respectively, 10 pages out of 300, and 23 pages out of
350. In similar fashion, a study of Thomas MacDonagh was understandably more concerned with his literary achievements than his role as a
rebel leader in 1916.[33] A relatively long account of Seán MacDermott's
life and his part in the events of 1916 was published in the pages of a
regional journal, the author declaring with pride and dignity that his
work was 'pedestrianly chronological and contains details of mere local
interest. It is purposely so, that the fragments may not be lost'.[34]

Some writings of these years were designed to preserve a record or a
memory, in the hope that the works in question could make a contribution to fuller accounts that might be published in the future. There
seemed to be a tacit assumption (vindicated, as subsequent developments would show) that the time to take full advantage of such material
had not yet arrived. Since then, the authors of monographs and
syntheses have made grateful use of articles—often published locally—
containing valuable documentation or opinion that might not otherwise
have been available to them. In 1968 Joseph Lee wrote of Irish historiography in general that 'for two centuries evidence lagged behind

interpretation. Today, for the first time, interpretation lags behind evidence'.[35] But in the case of the Easter Rising (and for the revolutionary years in general), evidence was still in short supply, and those who preserved it performed a service to a later and luckier generation.

Exploiting new sources

In the late 1960s and early 1970s there was a dramatic increase in the quantity of original sources accessible by historians. This can be measured in crude terms through the columns of the 'Hayes Catalogue', an invaluable tool for researchers. Originally published in 1965, the catalogue consisted of eleven massive volumes listing manuscripts relating to Irish history and culture that had been deposited in Irish and foreign archives and libraries.[36] In 1979 a three-volume supplement covered documents added or discovered during the decade 1965–75, and it also described some collections in greater detail.[37] Eleven columns were devoted to '1916' in the first set of volumes, while the supplement devoted no less than 21 columns (in the same font and format) to listing newly acquired or newly catalogued 1916 material.

This paucity of Irish sources available to historians in the early 1960s helps explain the fact that two of the most remarkable publications associated with the fiftieth anniversary of the Rising relied almost entirely on British private and official papers. Few Irish sources had yet been opened to researchers that could be compared to those bequeathed by British politicians and civil servants. The wealth of material currently exploited by historians of the early twentieth century still lay in the future.

Leon Ó Broin's *Dublin Castle and the 1916 Rising* was a pioneering work.[38] Unusually for studies on 1916 written at that time, it was based largely on manuscript material, in particular on the papers of Prime Minister H.H. Asquith, Under-Secretary Matthew Nathan, and Arthur Hamilton Norway, the head of the Post Office in Ireland.

Ó Broin displayed exceptional warmth in his treatment of the Dublin Castle officials. It was clear that he liked both Nathan and Augustine Birrell, the chief secretary, and that he regretted their fate as the principal British victims of the Easter Rising. Since he was a professional civil servant he may have identified with the problems faced by members of the Irish executive. His book revealed a complacent and indulgent administration, tolerant (from its own point of view, excessively tolerant) towards radical nationalists, over-dependent on the advice of the Home Rule party, and ultimately brought down by its own trusting benevolence and inefficiency.

He traced the Castle's responses to the series of threats and rumours of rebellion since the outbreak of war in August 1914. In particular, Ó Broin devoted more attention than other historians had done (or had been able to do until then) to the Royal Navy's advance knowledge of the plans for a rebellion at Easter. The book's merits transcended minor blemishes such as an occasionally eccentric structure and a tendency to follow Nathan into some of his less important or less interesting activities. Thanks to Ó Broin's research, it was possible for the first time to understand the attitudes and actions of both sides in the conflict.

Another, shorter work that also appeared in the golden jubilee year examined some of the naval aspects of the Rising. In this book, John de Courcy Ireland criticised Karl Spindler's account of his captainship of the arms ship, the *Aud*.[39] The author probably sailed close to conspiracy theory in his suggestion that it would have suited British propaganda if a comparatively insignificant quantity of arms had been landed in Kerry from a German ship. This would have provided welcome 'proof' that the Rising had been organised by the Germans, and the navy intervened only when the Irish rebels failed to collect the arms shipment.[40] Their incompetence may have been a blessing after all.

The second significant publication to make use of British (or 'loyal' Irish) primary sources was Breandán MacGiolla Choille's edition of *Intelligence notes, 1913–16*. This was a carefully-annotated set of reports by the police authorities, arranged by county, for each of the four years covered by the volume. It also contained numerous other reports and tables relating to the 1913 Dublin lock-out, the 1914 gun-runnings, the 1916 Rising, and various normal, annually recurring features of Irish life such as 'persons boycotted' and 'cattle-driving'. The book was described by its editor as supplying, in part, the background to Ó Broin's *Dublin Castle*.[41] Its various tables provided much revealing statistical information about the country before, during and after the Rising.

By the end of 1966 historians had access to more contemporaneous evidence concerning the British responses to the rebels' plans and actions than about the rebels themselves. This pattern was soon consolidated by the British '30-Year Rule', which facilitated the public inspection of large quantities of material relating to the Easter Rising and the events of the years that followed—including invaluable police reports, organised county-by-county and month-by-month, which underpinned the documents published in *Intelligence notes*.

Not long afterwards, Ó Broin wrote another book about Dublin Castle, this time centred on Birrell's career in Ireland. It was based on a wider range of papers than had been available to him a mere few years earlier, and in particular he was able to use the newly released British Cabinet and Colonial Office papers.[42] But Irish governments still seemed to be content that the history of the Irish Revolution should be written largely on the basis of material held by 'the enemy', and London's good example was not followed by Dublin until the end of the 1980s.

Attempts were also made during these years to understand the role of the Home Rule party during and after the Rising. David Savage examined the papers of prominent British politicians such as Asquith, Lord Lansdowne and Austen Chamberlain when he studied the failure of the Home Rule negotiations in its immediate aftermath—negotiations that damaged the reputation and shattered the morale of the Parliamentary Party.[43] But his work appeared just too soon to benefit from the 30-year Rule, which would have provided him with further valuable material. Soon afterwards, in his magisterial biography of John Dillon, F.S.L. Lyons used Dillon's and other politicians' private papers to reveal how the Rising affected the moderate nationalist leadership.[44]

Despite the poverty of Irish sources, historians continued to investigate the aims and actions of the rebels and their successors. In a work published in the Irish language, Pádraig Ó Snodaigh exploited the manuscript and newspaper resources of the National Library.[45] F.X. Martin wrote two powerful and influential review articles, summarising and commenting on various publications on the Rising from the earliest, contemporaneous accounts to the most recently published studies.[46] He tackled different interpretations (such as 'faith and fatherland' and 'the Rising as drama'), looked at famous and obscure literary figures as well as at the different rebel leaders, asked questions such as 'how competent was the military council?', discussed the morality of insurrection in 1916 and assessed historiographical developments (or their absence). His articles represented a significant contribution to the study of the period. His research has worn well, and in his history of the Rising published in 2005 Charles Townshend remarked of Martin's second article—published 37 years earlier—that on the whole his 'knowledgeable judgement' on the rebels' lack of a blueprint for an all-Ireland Rising still seemed sound.[47]

Kevin B. Nowlan edited a collection of articles on various aspects of the Rising, which included two long and searching chapters by Maureen Wall.[48] In these Wall examined not merely the I.R.B. conspiracy within the Irish Volunteers, but also the similar conspiracy by a faction within the I.R.B.[49] Her work, reinforcing that of Martin in 'Myth, fact, and mystery', helped to undermine further the officially approved version of events, whereby the Easter Rising was above all the achievement of P.H. Pearse—with honourable mention for James Connolly. Credit was given, belatedly, to the two key revolutionary figures, Tom Clarke and Seán MacDermott.[50] In the same volume, G.A. Hayes-McCoy provided a concise and balanced military history of the rebels' intentions and actions, discriminating carefully between the original plans (in so far as these could be inferred) and the modified, sometimes improvised, form actually taken by the conflict during Easter Week.[51]

LITERARY INTERPRETATIONS

In some respects the most stimulating of the works to appear in the years following the 1966 celebrations of the jubilee of the 1916 Rising was by an American literary scholar, William Irwin Thompson. His *Imagination of an insurrection* began with an investigation of the literary and intellectual background to the revolutionary generation, in particular of figures such as Douglas Hyde and Standish James O'Grady.[52] It then examined in detail the poets of the Rising and three literary figures who responded creatively to it: Yeats, AE and O'Casey. Thompson studied the role of imagination in history, declaring that because he approached his theme 'with literary eyes' he could not avoid seeing history in the terms and shapes of imaginative experience.

He linked Ireland's literary renaissance to its military and political revolution, and he discussed themes such as 'the romantic simplification of complexity…in which ideas were turned into slogans, and the slogans turned into occasions for action'.[53] He played with irony, he drew striking parallels and he used vivid images. For example, he referred to George Moore as a 'master of the technique in which the author makes light of himself so that he is free to ridicule the enthusiasm of others'; he pronounced that 'the man who helped the Irish nation catch up with the advanced thought of its revolutionaries was General Maxwell'; and he viewed the Rising as an event in literature whereby the rebels 'march into tragedy with all the slain Irish patriots of the past'.[54]

At times Thompson was carried away by his enthusiasms and—like some other theorists—he imposed on the varied, confused and inconsistent motives of real historical characters a series of neat and elegant patterns. Historians tend to be suspicious of generalisations such as 'suddenly an individual awakens to his own moment in the longer movement of history. In the excitement of that moment History is seen to announce itself to the individual'.[55] When researchers were able to examine the large body of evidence left by 'non-literary' rebels and observers they found predictable patterns of mixed motives, of prosaic calculations, of accident and muddle, of plans being rescued or wrecked by good or bad fortune. Some rebel leaders may indeed have 'lived as if they were in a work of art...[unable] to tell the difference between sober reality and the realm of imagination', as actors in a dramatic performance;[56] others, such as Clarke and MacDermott, did not.

Until the publication of Thompson's book, discussion or investigation of the Rising had involved mainly the surviving participants, journalists, historians and (of course) politicians. His theories and his style forced scholars and others to look beyond the details that had preoccupied most of them until then. Although sceptical readers might doubt some of his claims and conclusions, he provided the study of the Easter Rising with a stimulating shift of emphasis. Few of the literary critics who have followed his incursion into the history of the Irish Revolution have made such a positive and creative impact.

A literary interpretation of a very different kind was Iris Murdoch's 'Irish novel' *The red and the green*, which was set in Dublin and which climaxed with the Rising. It featured the complex family and sexual relationships that characterise most of her works, but it was also the result of considerable research. Its tone was deeply sympathetic to romantic Irish nationalism—an attitude that Murdoch would disown in the coming decade when events in Northern Ireland revealed some of its unwelcome features.[57] (Seán O'Faoláin, whose review of the novel in the *Irish Times* was titled 'Baroque Melodrama', was lured into admiration of 'the perfect and splendid gesture of the symbolical bloodletting of 1916, which woke the soul of Ireland, and was in its own way as noble an event in history as Guernica or Agincourt'.[58])

CONCLUSION

As a result of such many and varied publications, and of the beginning of a pattern whereby costive hoarders of documents gradually released their treasures, by the end of the 1960s the historiography of the Easter

Rising looked vastly different from the position ten years earlier, when Holt's *Protest in arms* had been published—and had revealed little that was new. The end of the decade also marked the commencement of a new and savage phase in Irish history—the re-emergence of conflict in Northern Ireland, the beginning of a quarter-century of violence that would claim 3,500 lives. It would also, incidentally, make it more difficult for historians to maintain the dispassionate and scholarly approach to their discipline that had characterised most of their work in the peaceful 1960s.

In response to this bloodshed and polarisation historians came under pressure from some quarters to conform to nationalist stereo-types, to roll back the advances of recent years. Their more nuanced interpretation of the past was seen as being 'unhelpful' by Republicans and others who demanded wartime solidarity against their traditional enemies. Once again, writers about the Irish past were expected to salute the flag. When almost all historians repudiated such professional treason they were accused of being anti-nationalist or even anti-national, of being hostile to the revolutionary movement that had led to the establishment of an independent Irish state and of being sympa-thetic to the British or to the Ulster unionists.

They were also accused of belittling and vilifying the Easter rebels and their insurrection as an indirect means of repudiating the Provisional IRA. One among many such critics argued that

> [b]ecause the Provos laid claim to the tradition of 1916, those who correctly condemned the often barbaric and indiscriminate slaughter of the 1970s and 80s set themselves to unpicking the myth of 1916 so as to demolish the Provos' claim to heroic status...Many of us were convinced by the need to pull the historical rug from under the Provos...The revisionist project [sic] succeeded because of the urgency of shutting down the Provos, and for no other reason.[59]

Those who described historians and their writings in such a manner chose to disregard chronology; they ignored the easily proved and frequently reiterated fact that historians had been busily at work 'unpicking' the Easter Rising a decade before the Provisional IRA began its bloody campaign.

Naturally, historians (like everyone else in Ireland) were affected by the violence that re-emerged at the end of the 1960s, and naturally it influenced the way in which some of them interpreted past events. One revealing example is provided by Oliver MacDonagh. In 1968 he wrote a short survey of modern Irish history, entitled simply *Ireland*. In it he viewed the Easter Rising not merely as a product of the early twentieth century, but also in a wider chronological context.

> The historical accident that doctrinaire Irish nationalism was born in the 1790s stamped Republicanism and Romanticism upon its face forever...the least misleading categorization of 1916 is as the final flower of the Romantic Nationalism of the nineteenth century...the Rising was, therefore, not the end, nor even the beginning of the end, but certainly the end of the beginning. A line had been drawn across the page, cancelling an interminable tale of compromises sought and lost.[60]

Nine years later MacDonagh produced a revised and re-titled edition of *Ireland* in which he referred ruefully to the circumstances of its first appearance:

> the book was written in calm days: the current tumult was about to break, but there was then no forewarning...It is not often that an historian has the fortune, at once good and ill, to compose on the very eve of unforeseeable but decisive change...[Recent events provoked] the reappraisal, at greater depth and with more refinement, of certain of the nineteenth- and early twentieth-century phenomena.[61]

Yet, instead of merely re-writing the original text, he added a new chapter at the end in which he chose 'not to write the history of the latest years in any sense whatever, but to speculate historically about their northern aspect'. He began this speculation by analysing traditions of alternative government, beginning with the Whiteboys.[62]

Other historians, like MacDonagh, and like those who began the process of investigating the Easter Rising in a scholarly manner once the sources became available, naturally saw the Irish Revolution in the light of a new or a changed present. The symbol of the Easter Rising had become one inspiration, among many other more immediate and powerful inspirations, for a new generation of Irish republicans who waged war on the British and on Ulster unionists. The 1921 settlement, which had long ago been undermined and transformed in the south, now collapsed in the north. These developments imposed on historians both a new context and a new angle of vision.

But the fundamental change in their writings on the Irish Revolution in general, and on the Easter Rising in particular, had already taken place; and it had taken place, in MacDonagh's words, in 'calm days' before the tumult broke. This change, in the scale of historians' investigations and in the detached, sometimes critical style of their comments and conclusions, was not the result of political violence. On the contrary, it was a product of the more relaxed political circumstances of the 1960s. Crucially, it also depended on the slow seepage of information as archives were opened and as private papers were released, a process that had begun in the years *before* the outbreak of the northern Troubles. The historians' publication of new material and new interpretations accumulated steadily throughout the decade. This pattern reached a peak long before Northern Ireland exploded and imploded; it peaked in the context of the jubilee commemorations of the Easter Rising—in the historiographical *annus mirabilis* of 1966.

NOTES

[1] *Irish Times*, 2 April 1966.
[2] Evi Gkotzaridis, 'Revisionist historians and the modern Irish state: the conflict between the Advisory Committee and the Bureau of Military History, 1947–66', *Irish Historical Studies* 35 (2006–7), 99–116: 106–7.
[3] Gkotzaridis, 'Revisionist historians', 107.
[4] Edgar Holt, *Protest in arms: the Irish troubles, 1916–1923* (London, 1960), 8, 9.
[5] Dorothy Macardle, 'James Connolly and Patrick Pearse', in Conor Cruise O'Brien (ed.), *The shaping of modern Ireland* (London, 1960), 185–95: 185–6.
[6] Max Caulfield, *The Easter rebellion* (London, 1964), 286, 321.
[7] Caulfield, *Easter rebellion*, 63, 64, 95, 281.
[8] Charles Duff, *Six days to shake an empire* (London, 1966).
[9] Hedley McCay, *Padraic Pearse: a new biography* (Cork, 1966), back cover.
[10] F.X. Martin (ed.), 'Eoin MacNeill on 1916', *Irish Historical Studies*, 12 (1960–1), 226–71. For Martin's influence, see Michael Laffan, 'The decade of the Rising: F.X. Martin on 1916', in Howard B. Clarke and J.R.S. Phillips (eds.), *Ireland, England and the Continent in the Middle Ages and beyond: essays in memory of a turbulent friar, F.X. Martin, O.S.A.* (Dublin, 2006), 325–32.

[11] F.X. Martin (ed.), *Leaders and men of the Easter Rising: Dublin 1916* (London, 1967).

[12] Martin, *Leaders and men*, 151.

[13] *Irish Times*, 7 April 1966; Owen Dudley Edwards and Fergus Pyle (eds), *1916: the Easter Rising* (London, 1968).

[14] Conor Cruise O'Brien, 'The embers of Easter', in Dudley Edwards and Pyle, *1916*, 225–40: 226–7, 235.

[15] 'Editorial', *Studies* 55 (Spring 1966), 6.

[13] Garret FitzGerald, 'The significance of 1916', *Studies* 55 (Spring 1966), 33–6: 34.

[17] FitzGerald, 'Significance of 1916', 33–6.

[18] Francis Shaw, 'The canon of Irish history—a challenge', *Studies* 61 (Summer 1972), 117–53: 113.

[19] *Sunday Times*, 24 April 1966.

[20] *Capuchin Annual*, 1966, 152.

[21] Roger McHugh (ed.), *Dublin 1916: an illustrated anthology* (London, 1966).

[22] M. Ó Dubhghaill (ed.), *Insurrection fires at Eastertide: a golden jubilee anthology of the Easter Rising* (Cork, 1966).

[23] Mary Hayden and George A. Moonan, *A short history of the Irish people from the earliest times to 1920* (Dublin, 1921).

[24] Ó Dubhghaill, *Insurrection fires at Eastertide*, 116, 89, 94.

[25] Donal McCartney, 'From Parnell to Pearse (1891–1921)', in T.W. Moody and F.X. Martin (eds), *The course of Irish history* (Cork, 1967), 294–312: 307–10.

[26] J.C. Beckett, *The making of modern Ireland, 1603–1923* (London, 1966), 441.

[27] Seán MacEntee, *Episode at Easter* (Dublin, 1966).

[28] C.S. Andrews, *Dublin made me: an autobiography* (Dublin and Cork, 1979).

[29] Fergus FitzGerald (ed.) *The memoirs of Desmond FitzGerald, 1913–1916* (London, 1968). 131, 137, 141.

[30] McCay, *Padraic Pearse*.

[31] McCay, *Padraic Pearse*, 67.

[32] Anne Marreco, *The rebel countess: the life and times of Constance Markievicz* (London, 1967); Jacqueline van Voris, *Constance de Markievicz: in the cause of Ireland* (Amherst, 1967).

[33] Edd Winfield Parks and Aileen Wells Parks, *Thomas MacDonagh: the man, the patriot, the writer* (Athens, Georgia, 1967).

[34] Charles J. Travers, 'Seán MacDiarmada (1883–1916)', *Bréifne* 3 (1966), 1–46: 44.

[35] Joseph Lee, 'Some aspects of modern Irish historiography', in Ernst Schulin (ed.), *Gedenkschrift Martin Göhring* (Wiesbaden, 1968), 431–43: 440.

[36] Richard J. Hayes (ed.), *Manuscript sources for the history of Irish civilisation* (Boston, 1965).

[37] Richard J. Hayes (ed.), *Manuscript sources for the history of Irish civilisation: first supplement, 1965–75* (Boston, 1979).

[38] Leon Ó Broin, *Dublin Castle and the 1916 Rising: the story of Sir Matthew Nathan* (Dublin, 1966).

[39] John de Courcy Ireland, *The sea and the Easter Rising* (Dublin, 1966).

[40] De Courcy Ireland, *The sea and the Easter Rising*, 18.

[41] Breandán MacGiolla Choille (ed.), *Intelligence notes, 1913–16* (Dublin, 1966).

[42] Leon Ó Broin, *The chief secretary: Augustine Birrell in Ireland* (London, 1969).

[43] David Savage, 'The attempted Home Rule settlement of 1916' in *Éire–Ireland* 2 (Autumn 1967), 132–45.

[44] F.S.L. Lyons, *John Dillon* (London, 1969).

[45] Pádraig Ó Snodaigh, *Comhghuaillithe na Réabhlóide, 1913–1916* (Dublin, 1966).

[46] F.X. Martin, '1916—myth, fact and mystery', *Studia Hibernica* 7 (1967), 7–126; 'The 1916 Rising—a *coup d'état* or a "Bloody Protest"?', *Studia Hibernica* 8 (1968), 106–37.

[47] Charles Townshend, *Easter 1916: the Irish Rebellion* (London, 2005), 111.

[48] Kevin. B. Nowlan (ed.), *The making of 1916: studies in the history of the Rising* (Dublin, 1969).

[49] Maureen Wall, 'The background of the Rising, from 1914 until the countermanding order on Easter Saturday 1916', and 'The plans and the countermand: the country and Dublin', in Nowlan, *The making of 1916*, 157–97 and 201–51.

[50] This had been a minority tradition among earlier writers; see for example Diarmuid Lynch, *The I.R.B. and the 1916 insurrection* (Cork, 1957), 111–3, 123, 129, 147, who accused Desmond Ryan of exaggerating the roles of Pearse and (in particular) Connolly.

[51] G.A. Hayes-McCoy, 'A military history of the 1916 Rising', in Nowlan, *The making of 1916*, 255–338.

[52] William Irwin Thompson, *The imagination of an insurrection: Dublin, Easter 1916* (New York, 1967).

[53] Thompson, *Imagination of an insurrection*, ix, 67.

[54] Thompson, *Imagination of an insurrection*, 61, 103, 158.

[55] Thompson, *Imagination of an insurrection*, x.

[56] Thompson, *Imagination of an insurrection*, ix.

[57] Peter J. Conradi, *Iris Murdoch; a life* (London, 2001), 465–6.

[58] *Irish Times*, 16 October 1965. (Did he mean Roncevaux, rather than Guernica?)

[59] John Waters, *Irish Times*, 10 April 2006.

[60] Oliver MacDonagh, *Ireland* (Englewood Cliffs, New Jersey, 1968), 75, 76, 79.

[61] Oliver MacDonagh, *Ireland: the Union and its aftermath* (London, 1977), 10–11.

[62] MacDonagh, *Ireland: the Union and its aftermath*, 143–4.

BIBLIOGRAPHY

Máirín Allen 1964 'Jerome Connor—Two', *Capuchin Annual*, 353–69.

Peter Allt and R.K. Alspach (eds) 1977 *The variorum edition of the poems of W.B. Yeats*. New York. Macmillan.

R.K. Alspach and C.C. Alspach (eds) 1969 *The variorum edition of the plays of W.B. Yeats*. New York. Macmillan.

Christian Amalvi 1998 'Bastille Day: from *Dies Irae* to holiday', in Pierre Nora (ed.), *Realms of memory*, vol. 3, 117–162. New York. Columbia University Press.

Benedict Anderson 1983 *Imagined communities: reflections on the origins and spread of nationalism*. London. Verso.

C.S. Andrews 1979 *Dublin made me: an autobiography*. Dublin and Cork. Mercier Press.

Paul Antze and Michael Lambek (eds) 1996 *Tense past: cultural essays in trauma and memory*. London. Routledge.

T.G. Ashplant 2000 'War commemoration in Western Europe: changing meanings, divisive loyalties, unheard voices', in T.G. Ashplant *et al.*, *The Politics of war memory and commemoration*, 263–272. London. Routledge.

T.G. Ashplant, Graham Dawson and Michael Roper 2000 'The politics of war memory and commemoration: contexts, structures, and dynamics', in T.G. Ashplant *et al.*, *The politics of war memory and commemoration*, 3–85. London. Routledge.

T.G. Ashplant, Graham Dawson and Michael Roper (eds) 2000 *The politics of war memory and commemoration*. London. Routledge.

Jan Assmann 1995 'Collective memory and cultural identity', *New German Critique* 65, 125–33.

Chris Baldick 1990 *The concise Oxford dictionary of literary terms*. Oxford and New York. Oxford University Press.

Sebastian Barry 1995 *The steward of Christendom*. London. Methuen Drama, in association with Royal Court Theatre.

Sebastian Barry 2005 *A long, long way*. London. Viking Books.

Zygmunt Bauman 1989 *Modernity and the Holocaust*. Cambridge. Polity Press.

J.C. Beckett 1966 *The making of modern Ireland, 1603–1923*. London. Faber.

Walter Benjamin 1999 *Illuminations*. London. Pimlico.

Ciarán Benson 2001 *The cultural psychology of self: place, morality and art in human worlds*. London. Routledge.

Paul Bew, Peter Gibbon and Henry Patterson 1979 *The State in Northern Ireland 1921–1972: political forces and social classes*. Manchester. Manchester University Press.

Homi K. Bhabha 1990 'DissemiNation: time, narrative, and the nation', in Homi K. Bhabha (ed.), *Nation and Narration*, 291–322. London. Routledge.

Síghle Bhreathnach-Lynch 1999 'Commemorating the hero in newly independent Ireland: expressions of nationhood in bronze and stone', in L.W. McBride (ed.) *Images, icons and the nationalist imagination*, 148–205. Dublin. Four Courts.

Eavan Boland 1996 *Object lessons: the life of the woman and the poet in our time*. London. Vintage.

Dermot Bolger (ed.) 1988 *Letters from the new island: 16 on 16: Irish writers on the Easter Rising*. Dublin. Raven Arts Press.

Eberhard Bort (ed.) 2004 *Commemorating Ireland: politics, culture, history*. Dublin. Irish Academic Press.

Lorenzo Bossi 2005 'Truly days of hope and anger: the Northern Ireland civil rights movement as a case study in the development, outcome, and legacies of social movements', unpublished PhD thesis, Queen's University Belfast.

D.G. Boyce 1991 *Nationalism in Ireland*. London. Routledge.

D.G. Boyce 2001 'No lack of ghosts', in Ian McBride (ed.), *History and memory in modern Ireland*, 254–71. Cambridge. Cambridge University Press.

D.G. Boyce and Alan O'Day (eds) 1996 *The making of modern Irish history: revisionism and the revisionist controversy*. London. Routledge.

Ciarán Brady (ed.) 1994 *Interpreting Irish history: the debate on historical revisionism*. Dublin. Irish Academic Press.

Ed Cairns and Micheál Roe (eds) 2003 *The role of memory in ethnic conflict*. Houndmills. Palgrave-Macmillan.

Susan Cannon Harris 2002 *Gender and modern Irish drama*. Bloomington and Indianapolis. Indiana University Press.

Max Caulfield 1964 *The Easter rebellion*. London. Four Square.

Joe Cleary 2005 'Introduction: Ireland and modernity', in Joe Cleary and Claire Connolly (eds) *The Cambridge companion to modern Irish culture*, 1–21. Cambridge. Cambridge University Press.

John Coakley 1983 'Patrick Pearse and the "Noble Lie" of Irish nationalism', *Studies* 71, 119–36.

Peter J. Conradi 2001 *Iris Murdoch; a life*. London. Macmillan.

T.P. Coogan 1966 *Ireland since the Rising*. London. Pall Mall.

Farrel Corcoran 2000 'Technologies of memory', in Eamonn Slater and Michel Peillon (eds), *Memories of the present*, 25–35. Dublin. Institute of Public Administration.

F.W.S. Craig 1971 *British parliamentary elections 1950–70*. Chichester. Political Reference Publications.

Conor Cruise O'Brien 1968 'The embers of Easter 1916–1966', in Owen Dudley Edwards and Fergus Pyle (eds) *1916: the Easter Rising*, 225–40. London. MacGibbon and Kee.

Conor Cruise O'Brien 1974 *States of Ireland*. London. Panther. (Originally published 1972.)

Austin Currie 2004 *All hell will break loose*. Dublin. O'Brien Press.

Mary E. Daly 2002 'Nationalism, sentiment and economics; relations between Ireland and Irish America in the postwar years', *Éire–Ireland* 37, Special issue: Irish America, I and II (Spring/Summer), 74–92.

Mary E. Daly (ed.) 2005 *Roger Casement in Irish and world history*. Dublin. Royal Irish Academy.

Thomas Davis 1869 *National poems and historical ballads, songs, and poems*. Dublin. James Duffy.

Gerald Dawe 2004 'A question of covenants: poetry as commemoration', in Eberhard Bort (ed.), *Commemorating Ireland*, 215–22. Dublin. Irish Academic Press.

John de Courcy Ireland 1966 *The sea and the Easter Rising*. Dublin. Maritime Institute of Ireland.

Seamus Deane 1991 'Wherever Green is Read', in Máirín Ní Dhonnchadha and Theo Dorgan (eds), *Revising the Rising*, 91–105. Derry. Field Day.

Gillian Deenihan 1999 'Seán Lemass and Northern Ireland 1959–66', unpublished MPhil thesis, University College Cork.

Department of External Affairs 1966 *Cuimhneachán: 1916–1966, Commemoration: a record of Ireland's commemoration of the 1916 Rising*. Dublin. Department of External Affairs.

Department of Finance 1958 *Economic Development*. Dublin. Department of Finance.

Patrick Devine-Wright, 'Theoretical overview of memory and conflict', in Ed Cairns and Micheál Roe (eds), *The role of memory in ethnic conflict*, 9–34. Houndsmills. Palgrave-Macmillan

Anne Dolan 2003 *Commemorating the Irish Civil War: history and memory, 1923–2000*. Cambridge. Cambridge University Press.

Denis Donoghue 1991 *Warrenpoint*. London. Jonathan Cape.

Owen Dudley Edwards and Fergus Pyle (eds) 1968 *1916: The Easter Rising*. London. MacGibbon and Kee.

Ruth Dudley Edwards 1990 *Patrick Pearse: the triumph of failure*. Dublin. Poolbeg Press.

Charles Duff 1966 *Six days to shake an empire*. London. J.M. Dent.

Jenny Edkins 1999 *Post-Structuralism and international relations: bringing the political back in*. Boulder, CO. and London. Lynne Reiner.

Jenny Edkins 2003 *Trauma and the memory of politics.* Cambridge. Cambridge University Press.

Marianne Elliott 2001 *The Catholics of Ulster.* London. Allen Lane, Penguin.

Marianne Elliott 2004 *Robert Emmet: the making of a legend.* London. Profile Books.

Tony Fahey 2001 'Housing and local government', in Mary E. Daly (ed.) *County and town: one hundred years of local government in Ireland,* 120–9. Dublin. Institute of Public Administration.

Ronan Fanning 1983 *Independent Ireland.* Dublin. Gill and Macmillan.

Fergus FitzGerald (ed.) 1968 *The memoirs of Desmond FitzGerald, 1913–1916.* London. Routledge and Kegan Paul.

Garret FitzGerald 1966 'The significance of 1916', *Studies* 55, 33–6.

David Fitzpatrick 2001 'Commemoration in the Irish Free State: a chronicle of embarrassment', in Ian McBride (ed.) *History and memory in modern Ireland,* 184–203. Cambridge. Cambridge University Press.

Joan Fitzpatrick Dean 2004 *Riot and great anger: stage censorship in twentieth-century Ireland.* Madison, WIS. University of Wisconsin Press.

Christopher Fitz-Simon 1994 *The Boys: a biography of Micheál MacLiammóir and Hilton Edwards.* London. Nick Hern Books.

Walter Forde 1967 'The aimless rebellion', *Christus Rex* 21, 45–51.

Roy Foster 1994 'History and the Irish question' (first published 1988), as reprinted in Ciarán Brady (ed.), *Interpreting Irish history: the debate on historical revisionism,* 122–45. Dublin. Irish Academic Press.

Roy Foster 2001. *The Irish story: telling tales and making it up in Ireland.* London. Penguin.

Michel Foucault 1984 'Nietzsche, genealogy, and history', in Paul Rabinow (ed.), *The Foucault reader,* 76–100. New York. Pantheon.

Brian Friel 1970 *Crystal and Fox and the Mundy scheme.* New York. Farrar, Straus and Giroux.

Julia Furay and Redmond O'Hanlon (eds) 2003 *Critical moments: Fintan O'Toole on modern Irish theatre.* Dublin. Carysfort Press.

Roy Garland 2001 *Gusty Spence.* Belfast. Blackstaff.

Luke Gibbons 1991 'Challenging the revisionist canon. Revisionism and cultural criticism', in Seamus Deane (ed.), *The Field Day anthology of Irish writing,* vol. III, 561–8. Derry. Field Day.

Luke Gibbons 1996 *Transformations in Irish culture.* Cork. Cork University Press in association with Field Day.

Luke Gibbons 1999 'Narratives of the nation: fact, fiction and Irish cinema', in Luke Dodd (ed.) *Nationalisms: visions and revision,* 66–73. Dublin. Film Institute of Ireland.

Luke Gibbons 2001 'Where Wolfe Tone's statue was not: Joyce, monuments and memory', in Ian McBride (ed.), *History and memory in modern Ireland,* 139–59. Cambridge. Cambridge University Press.

Shauna Gilligan 1993 'Image of a patriot: the popular and scholarly portrayal of Patrick Pearse 1916–1991', unpublished MA thesis, University College Dublin.

John R. Gillis 1974 *Youth and history; tradition and change in European age relations 1770–present*. London and New York. Academic Press.

John R. Gillis (ed.) 1994 *Commemorations: the politics of national identity.* Princeton, NJ. Princeton University Press.

Evi Gkotzaridis 2006–7 'Revisionist historians and the modern Irish state: the conflict between the Advisory Committee and the Bureau of Military History, 1947–66', *Irish Historical Studies* 35, 99–116.

David Gordon 1989 *The O'Neill years: Unionist politics 1963–1969*. Belfast. Athol Books.

Rebecca Lynn Graff 2006 'Remembering and forgetting 1916: deconstructing discourses of commemoration and conflict in post-peace process Ireland', unpublished PhD thesis, Queen's University Belfast.

P. Graham and P. Shirlow 2002 'The Battle of the Somme in Ulster memory and identity', *Political Geography* 21, 881–904

Peter Gray and Kendrick Oliver 2002 'The memory of catastrophe: views on commemoration of historical disasters', *History Today* (February), 8pp.

C. Desmond Greaves 1963 *The Irish question and the British people*. London. Lawrence and Wishart.

C. Desmond Greaves 1978 *Reminiscences of the Connolly Association*. London. Connolly Association.

Duncan Greenlaw 2004 *Borders of mourning: remembrance, commitment, and the contexts of Irish identity.* Bethesda, MD. Academica Press.

Maurice Halbwachs 1992 *On collective memory*, Lewis A. Croser (ed. and tr.), 2nd edn. London and Chicago. University of Chicago Press.

Peter Hart 1990 'Youth Culture and the Cork I.R.A.', in David Fitzpatrick (ed.) *Revolution? Ireland 1917–1923*, 10–24. Dublin. Trinity History Workshop.

Mary Hayden and George A. Moonan 1921 *A short history of the Irish people from the earliest times to 1920*. Dublin. Talbot Press.

Maurice Hayes 1996 *Black puddings with Slim: a Downpatrick boyhood*. Belfast. Blackstaff.

R.J. Hayes (ed.) 1965 *Manuscript sources for the history of Irish civilisation*. Boston. C.K. Hall.

R.J. Hayes (ed.) 1979 *Manuscript sources for the history of Irish civilisation: first supplement, 1965–1975*. Boston. C.K. Hall.

G.A. Hayes-McCoy 1969 'A military history of the 1916 Rising', in Kevin B. Nowlan (ed.), *The making of 1916: studies in the history of the Rising*, 255–338. Dublin. Stationery Office.

Seamus Heaney 1969 *Door into the dark*. London. Faber and Faber.

Chris Hedges 2002 *War is a force that gives us meaning*. Oxford. Public Affairs Ltd.

Tom Hennessey 2005 *Northern Ireland: the origins of the troubles*. Dublin. Gill and Macmillan.

A.C. Hepburn 1996 *A past apart—studies in the history of Catholic Belfast, 1850–1950*. Belfast. Ulster Historical Foundation.

Catherine Hirst 2002 *Religion, politics and violence in nineteenth century Belfast—the Pound and the Sandy Row*. Dublin. Four Courts.

Jack Holland and Henry McDonald 1994 *INLA: deadly divisions*. Dublin. Torc Books.

Edgar Holt 1960 *Protest in arms: the Irish troubles, 1916–1923*. London. Putnam.

John Horgan 1997 *Seán Lemass: the enigmatic patriot*. Dublin. Gill and Macmillan.

Alvin Jackson 1996 'Irish Unionism', in D.G. Boyce and Alan O'Day (eds) *The making of modern Irish history: revisionism and the revisionist controversy*, 120–40. London. Routledge.

Fredric Jameson 1991 *Postmodernism, or, the cultural logic of late capitalism*. London and New York. Verso.

Denis Johnston 1983 *Selected plays of Denis Johnston* (Chosen and introduced by Joseph Ronsley). Gerrards Cross, Bucks. and Washington, DC. Colin Smythe and Catholic University of America Press.

Roy H.W. Johnston 2006 *Century of endeavour: a biographical and autobiographical view of the twentieth century in Ireland*. Carlow and Dublin. Tyndall Press and Lilliput.

Alacoque Kealy 1981 *Irish radio data: 1926–80*. Dublin. RTÉ.

A.T. Keane 1996 'Who fears to speak of Easter week?', unpublished MA thesis, University College Dublin.

Michael Kennedy 2000 *Division and consensus: the politics of cross-border relations in Ireland, 1925–1969*. Dublin. Institute of Public Administration.

Declan Kiberd 1991 'The elephant of revolutionary forgetfulness', in Máirín Ní Dhonnchadha and Theo Dorgan, *Revising the Rising*, 1–20. Derry. Field Day.

Declan Kiberd 1995 *Inventing Ireland: the literature of a modern nation*. London. Jonathan Cape.

Kilmainham Jail Restoration Society 1961 *Kilmainham*. Dublin. Kilmainham Jail Restoration Society.

Richard Kirkland 2006 *Cathal O'Byrne and the cultural revival in the north of Ireland, 1890–1960*. Liverpool. Liverpool University Press.

Denise Kleinrichert 2001 *Republican internment and the prison ship Argenta 1922*. Dublin. Irish Academic Press.

Claudia Koonz 1994 'Between memory and oblivion: concentration camps in German memory', in John R. Gillis (ed.) *Commemorations: the politics of national identity*, 258–80. Princeton, NJ. Princeton University Press.

Michael Laffan 2006 'The decade of the Rising: F.X. Martin on 1916', in Howard B. Clarke and J.R.S. Phillips (eds) *Ireland, England and the Continent in the Middle Ages and beyond: essays in memory of a turbulent friar: F.X. Martin, O.S.A.* 325–32. Dublin. University College Dublin Press.

Joseph Lee 1968 'Some aspects of modern Irish historiography', in Ernst Schulin (ed.) *Gedenkschrift Martin Göhring*, 431–43. Wiesbaden. Franz Steiner.

L.C.G. Leonard Undated *The Kilmainham project as I dreamt and lived it.* Unpublished. Kilmainham Jail Archive.

A.J. Lerner 1993 'The nineteenth-century monument and the embodiment of national time', in Marjorie Ringrose and A.J. Lerner (eds) *Reimagining the nation*, 176–96. Buckingham. Open University Press.

Ben Levitas 2002 *The theatre of nation: Irish drama and cultural nationalism.* Oxford. Oxford University Press.

Edna Longley 1994 'The Rising, the Somme and Irish memory', in Edna Longley (ed.) *The living stream: literature and revisionism in Ireland*, 69–85. Newcastle-upon-Tyne. Bloodaxe Books.

Edna Longley 2001 'Northern Ireland: commemoration, elegy, and forgetting', in Ian McBride (ed.) *History and memory in modern Ireland*, 223–53. Cambridge. Cambridge University Press.

Diarmuid Lynch 1957 *The I.R.B. and the 1916 insurrection.* Cork. Mercier Press.

Robert Lynch 2006 *The Northern IRA and the early years of partition.* Dublin. Irish Academic Press.

F.S.L. Lyons 1969 *John Dillon.* London. Routledge and Kegan Paul.

Tomás MacAnna 1966 *Aiséirí.* Unpublished script.

Tomás MacAnna 2000 *Fallaing Aonghusa: saol amharclainne.* Dublin. An Clócomhar Teoranta.

Dorothy Macardle 1960 'James Connolly and Patrick Pearse' in Conor Cruise O'Brien (ed.) *The shaping of modern Ireland*, 185–95. London. Routledge and Kegan Paul.

Oliver MacDonagh 1968 *Ireland.* Englewood Cliffs, NJ. Prentice Hall.

Oliver MacDonagh 1977 *Ireland: the Union and its aftermath.* London. George Allen and Unwin.

Seán MacEntee 1966 *Episode at Easter.* Dublin. Gill and Macmillan.

Uinseann MacEoin 1997 *The IRA in the twilight years, 1923–48.* Dublin. Argenta Publications.

Breandán MacGiolla Choille (ed.) 1966 *Intelligence notes, 1913–16.* Dublin. Oifig an tSoláthair.

Micheál MacLiammóir 1978 *The importance of being Oscar.* Dublin. Dolmen Press.

Bryan MacMahon 1966 *Seachtar Fear, Seacht Lá*, unpublished script.

Ian McAllister 1975 'Political opposition in Northern Ireland: the National Democracy Party, 1965–1970', *Economic and Social Review* **6** (3), 353–66.

Ian McBride (ed.) 2001 *History and memory in modern Ireland.* Cambridge. Cambridge University Press.

Donal McCartney 1967 'From Parnell to Pearse (1891–1921)' in T.W. Moody and F.X. Martin (eds), *The course of Irish history*, 294–312. Cork. Mercier Press.

Hedley McCay 1966 *Padraic Pearse: a new biography.* Cork. Mercier Press.

K.C. McCourt 1967 'Broadcasting—a community service', *Administration* **15** (3, Autumn), 173–181.

Jim McDermott 2001 *Northern divisions: the old IRA and the Belfast pogroms, 1920–22.* Belfast. Beyond the Pale Publications.

Tim McGillicuddy 1974 *The living past*, part 4. (4 parts). Dublin. Educational Company of Ireland.

Frank McGuinness 1986 *Observe the sons of Ulster marching towards the Somme.* London. Faber and Faber.

Roger McHugh (ed.) 1966 *Dublin 1916: an illustrated anthology.* London. Arlington Books.

Gillian McIntosh 1999 *The force of culture: unionist identities in twentieth century Ulster.* Cork. Cork University Press.

Karl Mannheim 1997 *Essays on the sociology of knowledge: Karl Mannheim: collected English writings*, vol. 5 (edited by Paul Kecskemeti). (8 vols.) London. Routledge.

Christopher Manson 2005 'The commemoration of the Great War in Belfast, Ulster and Northern Ireland, 1918–39', unpublished PhD thesis, University of Ulster.

Jules Marchal 2005 'Roger Casement in the Congo: reactions in Belgium', in Mary E. Daly (ed.) *Roger Casement in Irish and world history*, 34–5. Dublin. Royal Irish Academy.

Anne Marreco 1967 *The rebel countess: the life and times of Constance Markievicz.* London. Weidenfeld and Nicolson.

F.X. Martin (ed.) 1960–61 'Eoin MacNeill on 1916', *Irish Historical Studies* **12**, 226–71.

F.X. Martin (ed.) 1967 *Leaders and men of the Easter Rising: Dublin 1916.* London. Methuen.

F.X. Martin 1967 '1916—Myth, fact and mystery', *Studia Hibernia* **7**, 7–124.

F.X. Martin 1968 'The 1916 Rising—a *coup d'état* or a "Bloody protest"?', *Studia Hibernica* **8**, 106–37.

Arthur Marwick 1998 *The Sixties: cultural revolution in Britain, France, Italy and the United States, c.1958–c.1974.* Oxford and New York. Oxford University Press.

Brian Moore 1966 *The emperor of ice cream.* London. Deutsch.

James Moran 2005 *Staging the Easter Rising: 1916 as theatre*. Cork. Cork University Press.

William Morris 1972 *The water of the wondrous isle*. London. Ballantine.

Marc Mulholland 2000 *Northern Ireland at the crossroads: Ulster unionism in the O'Neill years, 1960–9*. Basingstoke. Macmillan.

Christopher Murray 2004 *Seán O'Casey, writer at work: a biography*. Dublin. Gill and Macmillan.

Paul Neuburg 1972 *The hero's children: the post-war generation in Eastern Europe*. London. Constable.

Máirín Ní Dhonnachadha and Theo Dorgan (eds) 1991 *Revising the Rising*. Derry. Field Day.

Emer Nolan 2005 'Modernism and the Irish Revival', in Joe Cleary and Claire Connolly (eds) *The Cambridge companion to modern Irish culture*, 157–72. Cambridge. Cambridge University Press.

Pierre Nora 1989 'Between memory and history: *les lieux de mémoire*', *Representations* 26, 7–25.

Pierre Nora 1996 'From *lieux de mémoire* to realms of memory', preface to the English-language edition, in Pierre Nora (ed.), *Realms of memory: rethinking the French past*, vol. 1, Conflicts and divisions, xv–xxiv. New York. Columbia University Press.

Kevin B. Nowlan (ed.) 1969 *The making of 1916: studies in the history of the Rising*. Dublin. Stationery Office.

Harvey O'Brien 2004 *The real Ireland: the evolution of Ireland in documentary film*. Manchester. Manchester University Press.

Leon Ó Broin 1966 *Dublin Castle and the 1916 Rising: the story of Sir Matthew Nathan*. Dublin. Helicon.

Leon Ó Broin 1969 *The chief secretary: Augustine Birrell in Ireland*. London. Chatto and Windus.

Margaret O'Callaghan 2000 'Old parchment and water; the Boundary Commission of 1925 and the copperfastening of the Irish Border', *Bullan, An Irish Studies Journal* 4 (2), 27–55.

Margaret O'Callaghan 2004 '"With the eyes of another race, of a people once hunted themselves": Casement, colonialism and a remembered past', in D.G. Boyce and Alan O'Day (eds) *Ireland in Transition, 1867–1918*, 259–75. London and New York. Routledge.

Margaret O'Callaghan 2006 'Genealogies of partition. History, history-writing and "the Troubles" in Ireland', *Critical Review of International Social and Political Philosophy* 9 (4), 619–34.

Margaret O'Callaghan and Catherine O'Donnell 2006 'The Northern Ireland government, the 'Paisleyite movement' and Ulster unionism in 1966', *Irish Political Studies* 21 (2), 203–22.

Seán O'Casey 1960 *The drums of Father Ned*. London. Macmillan.

Seán O'Casey 1980 *Three plays: Juno and the Paycock, the Shadow of a Gunman, the Plough and the Stars*. London. Pan Books/Macmillan.

M. Ó Dubhghaill (ed.) 1966 *Insurrection fires at Eastertide: a golden jubilee anthology of the Easter Rising*. Cork. Mercier Press.

Seán O'Faoláin 1941 '1916–41: tradition and creation', *The Bell* 2 (1), 5–13.

Patrick O'Mahony and Gerard Delanty 2001 *Rethinking Irish history: nationalism, identity, and ideology*. Houndmills. Palgrave.

Pádraig Ó Snodaigh 1966 *Comhghuaillithe na Réabhlóide, 1913–1916*. Dublin. An Clócomhar Teoranta.

Frank Ormsby (ed.) 1992 *A rage for order: poetry of the Northern Ireland Troubles*. Belfast. Blackstaff Press.

Alan F. Parkinson 2004 *Belfast's unholy war: the troubles of the 1920s*. Dublin. Four Courts.

E.W. Parks and A.W. Parks 1967 *Thomas MacDonagh: the man, the patriot, the writer*. Athens, GA. University of Georgia Press.

Henry Patterson 1989 (reprinted 1997) *The politics of illusion: a political history of the IRA*. London. Hutchinson Radius

Henry Patterson and Eric Kaufmann 2007 *Unionism and Orangeism in Northern Ireland since 1945*. Manchester. Manchester University Press.

Pádraig Pearse 1917 *Collected works: plays, stories, poems*. Dublin and London. Maunsel and Co.

Eamonn Phoenix 1994 *Northern nationalism, nationalist politics, partition and the Catholic minority in Northern Ireland, 1890–1914*. Belfast. Ulster Historical Foundation.

Vincent Power 2000 *Send 'em home sweatin': the Showband story*. Cork. Mercier Press.

Michael Quigley 1945 *Pictorial record: centenary of Thomas Davis and Young Ireland 1845–1945*. Dublin. Stationery Office.

Ann Rigney 2005 'Plenitude, scarcity and the circulation of cultural memory', *Journal of European Studies* 35, 11–28.

Desmond Ryan 1949 *The Rising: the complete story of Easter week*. Dublin. Standard House.

Ray Ryan (ed.) 2000 *Writing in the Irish Republic*. Houndmills. Macmillan.

Rosemary Ryan 1984 'Commemorating 1916', *Retrospect* 4, 59–62.

Chris Ryder 2006 *Fighting Fitt*. Belfast. Brehon Press.

Dominic Sandbrook 2005 *Never had it so good: a history of Britain from Suez to the Beatles*. London. Little, Brown.

David Savage 1967 'The attempted Home Rule settlement of 1916', *Éire–Ireland* 2 (Autumn), 132–45.

R.J. Savage 1996 *Irish television: the political and social origins*. Cork. Cork University Press.

Clive Scoular 2000 *James Chichester-Clark: prime minister of Northern Ireland*. Killyleagh. Clive Scoular.

Francis Shaw 1972 'The canon of Irish history—a challenge', *Studies* **61**, 117–53.

G.B. Shaw 1964 *John Bull's other island; How he lied to her husband; Major Barbara*, 2nd edn. London. Constable and Co.

Patrick Shea 1981 *Voices and the sound of drums*. Belfast. Blackstaff.

Gerald Sider and Gavin Smith (eds.) 1997 *Between history and histories: the making of silences and commemorations*. Toronto. University of Toronto Press.

Elaine Sisson 2004 *Pearse's patriots: St Enda's and the cult of boyhood*. Cork. Cork University Press.

Eamonn Slater and Michel Peillon (eds.) 2000 *Memories of the present: a sociological chronicle of Ireland 1997–1998*, Irish Sociological Chronicles, vol. 2. Dublin. Institute of Public Administration.

Enda Staunton 2001 *The nationalists of Northern Ireland, 1918–1973*. Dublin. Columba Press.

Study Group on the Teaching of History 1967 'The teaching of history in Irish schools', *Administration* **15**, 268–85.

Catherine Switzer 2007 *Unionists and Great War commemoration in the north of Ireland, 1914–1939*. Dublin. Irish Academic Press.

Peter Taylor 1997 *Provos: the IRA and Sinn Féin*. London. Bloomsbury.

W.I. Thompson 1967 *The imagination of an insurrection: Dublin, Easter 1916*. New York and London. Oxford University Press.

Arve Thorsen 2000 'Foundation myths at work: national day celebration in France, Germany and Norway in a comparative perspective', in Bo Strath (ed.) *Myth and memory in the construction of community: historical patterns in Europe and beyond*, 331–50. Brussels. P.I.E.–Peter Lang.

Fergal Tobin 1996 *The best of decades: Ireland in the 1960s*. Dublin. Gill and Macmillan.

Colm Tóibín 1993 'New ways of killing your father', *London Review of Books*, 18 November.

Colm Tóibín 2004 *Beauty in a broken place*. Dublin. Lilliput Press.

John Torpey (ed.) 2003 *The politics of the past: on repairing historical injustices*. Oxford. Rowman and Littlefield.

Charles Townshend 2005 *Easter 1916: the Irish Rebellion*. London. Allen Lane.

Charles J. Travers 1966 'Seán MacDiarmada (1883–1916)', *Bréifne* **3**, 1–46.

Mary Trotter 2001 *Ireland's national theaters: political performance and the origins of the Irish dramatic movement*. Syracuse, NY. Syracuse University Press.

Jacqueline van Voris 1967 *Constance de Markievicz: in the cause of Ireland*. Amherst. University of Massachusetts Press.

Katherine Verdery 1999 *The political lives of dead bodies: reburial and postsocialist change*. New York. Columbia University Press.

Brian Walker 1996 *Dancing to History's tune: history, myth and politics in Ireland*. Belfast. Institute of Irish Studies, QUB.

Brian Walker 2000 *Past and Present: history, identity and politics in Ireland.* Belfast. Institute of Irish Studies, QUB.

Robert (R.B.J) Walker 1993 *Inside/Outside: international relations as political theory.* Cambridge. Cambridge University Press.

Maureen Wall 1969 'The background of the Rising, from 1914 until the countermanding order on Easter Saturday 1916', in Kevin B. Nowlan (ed.) *The making of 1916: studies in the history of the Rising,* 157–97. Dublin. Stationery Office.

Maureen Wall 1969 The plans and the countermand: the country and Dublin', in Kevin B. Nowlan (ed.) *The making of 1916: studies in the history of the Rising,* 201–51. Dublin. Stationery Office.

Éibhear Walshe 1997 'Sodom and Begorrah, or game to the last: inventing Micheál MacLiammóir', in Éibhear Walshe *Sex, nation and dissent in Irish writing,* 157–62. Cork. Cork University Press.

Geoffrey Warner 2005 'Putting pressure on O'Neill', *Irish Studies Review* 13 (1), 13–31.

Yvonne Whelan 2003 *Reinventing modern Dublin: streetscape, iconography and the politics of identity.* Dublin. University College Dublin Press.

Robert W. White 2006 *Ruairí Ó'Brádaigh: the life and politics of an Irish revolutionary.* Bloomington, IN. Indiana University Press.

Hayden Whyte 2000 'Catastrophe, communal memory and mythic discourse: the uses of myth in the reconstruction of society', in Bo Strath (ed.) *Myth and memory in the construction of community: historical patterns in Europe and beyond,* 49–74. Brussels. P.I.E.–Peter Lang.

T.D. Williams 1966 'Public affairs, 1916–1966: 1–The political scene', *Administration* 14, 191–8.

Jay Winter and Emmanuel Sivan 2000 *War and remembrance in the Twentieth Century.* Cambridge. Cambridge University Press.

J.E. Young 1993 *The texture of memory: Holocaust memorials and meanings.* London and New Haven, CT. Yale University Press.

Slavoj Žižek 1989 *The sublime object of ideology (Phronesis).* London. Verso.

Slavoj Žižek 1991 *For they know not what they do.* London. Verso.

Slavoj Žižek 1999 *The ticklish subject: the absent centre of political ontology (Wo Es War).* London. Verso.

ACKNOWLEDGEMENTS

This project on the commemoration of the Easter Rising in Ireland in 1966 was funded by the Irish Higher Education Authority (HEA) under the Programme for North–South Research, which was approved as part of the Good Friday Agreement of 1998. The original proposal by Mary E. Daly and Margaret O'Callaghan was to build on Mary Daly's pre-existing project on the commemoration and extend it to look at the commemoration on both sides of the border. The core team consisted of Mary E. Daly, Roisín Higgins and Carole Holohan in Dublin, and Margaret O'Callaghan, Catherine O'Donnell and Rebecca Graff-McRae in Belfast. Diarmaid Ferriter, Michael Laffan and Anthony Roche were also involved in the original proposal and in cross-border seminars and conferences that we ran.

We are extremely grateful to the Irish government and to the HEA for providing the funding that made it possible to recruit two excellent researchers—Roisín Higgins and Catherine O'Donnell—and for financing the doctoral training programmes for Carole Holohan and Rebecca Graff-McRae. The funding also enabled us to run workshops and to bring students from Queen's University Belfast and University College Dublin together to debate issues arising from the project.

The UCD wing of the project was based at the Humanities Institute of Ireland (HII). Our thanks to HII administrators Brid Reason (who helped with the initial research bid, assisted by Alice Daly) and Valerie Norton, who helped us monitor progress and organise conferences; and to HII director Marc Caball for his support. HII also funded earlier research by Catherine Cox, which provided us with a superb database from Irish newspapers relating to the commemoration. At UCD we would also like to acknowledge the assistance of Susan Hedigan and David O'Shea. Special thanks to Garret Finnegan, who worked with the project as a student intern.

At Queen's University the project was based in the School of Politics, International Studies and Philosophy. We would like to thank Shane O'Neill for supporting the project and Paul Bew, Richard English, Sydney Elliott, John Garry, Brian Walker and Graham Walker and Catherine Madden for crucial assistance at different times.

For assistance with archival material, we would like to thank Seamus Helferty of UCD Archives; Cathal Goan, Peter Feeney and Brian Lynch in RTÉ; Caitriona Crowe of the National Archives in Dublin; Michael Kennedy of the Royal Irish Academy's Documents on Irish Foreign Policy project for assistance in locating material in the Department of Foreign Affairs files; Deirdre Flood of the GAA museum and Paul Rouse and Mark Duncan for assistance with material relating to the GAA; Niamh O'Sullivan and Pat Cooke at Kilmainham Gaol; Commandant Victor Laing and the staff of the Military Archives at Cathal Brugha Barracks in Dublin; John Brown at Bord Fáilte and Jenny Lonergan in the Office of Public Works; the staff in the newspaper library section in the Central Library in Belfast and the National Library in Dublin; and David Sheehy at the Dublin Diocesan Archives. Our thanks also go to Hugh Leonard, Kevin B. Nowlan, Pat Cooke and Garret FitzGerald and to the National Graves Association. Special thanks are due to David Huddleston in the Public Records Office of Northern Ireland for his assistance in accessing relevant files.

Thomas Hachey, director of the Irish Studies Programme at Boston College, and Robert O'Neill at the Burns Library facilitated Mary Daly's researches in Boston; and Catherine Shannon shared with us her outstanding expertise on Irish-American societies. Maureen Murphy and Angela Burke supplied us with copies of the 1966 newspapers and of *Cuimhneachán*. We are especially grateful to Tomás MacAnna for providing us with a copy of the script for his pageant, *Aiséirí*, and to Maurice MacMahon, son of the late Bryan MacMahon and the executor of his estate, for supplying a copy of the script of *Seachtar Fear, Seacht Lá*.

The Belfast team wishes to express our greatest thanks to Eamon Ó Cianáin, Maire McNally and Colette McCann Dornan, who provided us with a wealth of information and a copy of the 1916 commemorative calendar; thanks also to Ambrose Macauley, Malachi O'Doherty, Gillian McIntosh, Kenneth Bloomfield, Deirdre McMahon, Frank Callanan, James McGeachie, Shay Courtney, Christopher Manson, Christopher Farrington, Mark McNally, Peter McLoughlin, Fiona Lynch, Jane Leonard, Lorenzo Bossi, Marianne Elliott, Sheila McClure, Jim Smyth, Mary Burgess, Ann Hope, Dominick Bradley and Jonathan Tonge.

Finally, it has been a pleasure to work with Ruth Hegarty, Helena King and Fidelma Slattery of the Publications Office in the Royal Irish Academy in bringing this book to press. In particular, we would like to thank Helena King for her brilliant editing, extraordinary attention to detail and consummate charm under pressure—all of which have greatly enhanced the quality of the book. Fidelma Slattery's design is, as ever with her work, in a class of its own.

Mary E. Daly and Margaret O'Callaghan.
October 2007.